Preparation and Fulfilment

STUDIEN ZUR INTERKULTURELLEN GESCHICHTE DES CHRISTENTUMS
ETUDES D'HISTOIRE INTERCULTURELLE DU CHRISTIANISME
STUDIES IN THE INTERCULTURAL HISTORY OF CHRISTIANITY

begründet von / fondé par / founded by
Walter J. Hollenweger und / et / and Hans Jochen Margull †

herausgegeben von / edité par / edited by
Richard Friedli, Université de Fribourg
Jan A. B. Jongeneel, Universiteit Utrecht
Klaus Koschorke, Universität München
Theo Sundermeier, Universität Heidelberg
Werner Ustorf, University of Birmingham

Volume 124

PETER LANG
Oxford • Bern • Berlin • Bruxelles • Frankfurt am Main • New York • Wien

Paul Hedges

Preparation and Fulfilment

A History and Study of Fulfilment Theology
in Modern British Thought in the Indian Context

PETER LANG

Oxford • Bern • Berlin • Bruxelles • Frankfurt am Main • New York • Wien

Die Deutsche Bibliothek – CIP-Einheitsaufnahme

Hedges, Paul:
Preparation and fulfilment : a history and study of fulfilment theology in
modern British thought in the Indian context / Paul Hedges. – Oxford ; Bern ;
Berlin ; Bruxelles ; Frankfurt am Main ; New York ; Wien : Lang, 2001
(Studies in the intercultural history of christianity ; Vol. 124)
ISBN 3-906765-88-1

British Library and Library of Congress Cataloguing-in-Publication Data:
A catalogue record for this book is available from *The British Library,*
Great Britain, and from *The Library of Congress,* USA

ISSN 0170-9240
ISBN 3-906765-88-1
US-ISBN 0-8204-5311-0

© Peter Lang AG, European Academic Publishers, Berne 2001
Jupiterstr. 15, Postfach, 3000 Bern 15, Switzerland; info@peterlang.com

Printed in Germany

Preface

This work owes its existence to my PhD supervisor at Lampeter, Professor Paul Badham, who led me to embark upon the course of research that led to this book. It is, however, very different from the original conception that was suggested to me back at the end of 1995, and one might almost say that it came to be written by accident. Having had little success in my search for a supervisor for a thesis on the life and thought of Father Bede Griffiths, Paul suggested that one area in the field of Interfaith Dialogue that was unexplored was the thought of the major ecumenical missionary conferences of the twentieth century, and he gave me a great pile of literature and papers. I thus began my research by looking at the Edinburgh Missionary Conference of 1910, and Paul suggested that I then turn my attention to Farquhar. Observing that the fulfilment theology found in Farquhar and at Edinburgh seemed to be widely accepted I was surprised that for most authorities this marked its genesis – it seemed to me that there must be some previous history to the idea. From the few works that mentioned any history to fulfilment theology, I was led to the works of Slater and Maurice but soon found that they were but the proverbial tip of the iceberg. Gradually some form of coherent pattern of development started to emerge, though I found myself constantly rethinking the paradigms I developed as more and more pieces of the puzzle were uncovered. I discovered, also, that others had produced studies which intersected with mine at various points, and from these and my own researches I began to see that fulfilment theology was far more dominant at an earlier stage than anyone had previously suggested. What was, then, at the beginning, just a curious exploration into the background of my research became the whole object of research itself.

I have outlined how this work came to be written because I have often been asked what led me to research this area, which might at first seem a rather obscure study into the distant past of the history of Interfaith studies, when there are many contemporary aspects of the subject which could be explored. I hope the above answers this question. However, having said this, I do not believe that this study is of only historical interest. While I do not believe that fulfilment theology is a viable option for today, there are, nevertheless, aspects of its history that are informative. Firstly, it demonstrates how much theology is not progressive but cyclical, as different schools of thought come in and out of fashion; thus fulfilment theology flourished in the liberal climate of late nineteenth and early twentieth-century British theology, but declined as Neo-Orthodoxy became ascendent, and now is being used again by the Church – a recent report from the Church of England, *The Mystery of Salvation*, advocates a return to fulfilment theology. Secondly, it can help to break down our prejudices, for example of the stereotyped iconoclastic missionary, by seeing that many missionaries were amongst those at the vanguard of advancing our knowledge and appreciation of other faith traditions. And, thirdly, in exploring early modern attitudes of the Christian West to the world's other faith traditions, it will, hopefully, also shed light upon the underlying beliefs and assumptions behind many of our contemporary ideas.

My thanks for assistance in completing this work must go to a number of people, most of them, I hope, named in the acknowledgements for my thesis. However, those who have been influential in this work and helpful in bringing it to this form must be mentioned. Therefore my thanks go to Professor Paul Badham, Dr Gavin Flood and Professor Frank Whaling for supporting the publication of this work. Thanks also go to my family and friends. In addition I must thank all the staff at Peter Lang who have assisted in any way, especially the series editor for accepting this work, Andrew Ivett and Dr Graham Speake. Special thanks also go to my 'editorial team', Kathy Miles and Michael Hedges, who gave invaluable assistance in preparing the final manuscript. My apologies to anyone who has been forgotten or overlooked in these acknowledgements: do not think that your contribution has been unappreciated.

Finally, I would like to say that I realize this study is by no means complete or comprehensive – I could only give a cursory mention to many involved in fulfilment theology's history, and no doubt there are some of whom I remain ignorant – much research could still be profitably undertaken in this area. Also, having given my thanks to those involved in bringing this work to its current state of completion I must take responsibility for any errors, factual or otherwise, to be found within its pages.

Paul Hedges
Lampeter
Maundy Thursday 2000

Contents

Part IV: Fruition

Part V: Conclusions

Abbreviations

Abbreviations used for books are generally given on the works first mention in the text; abbreviations for archive sources are noted in the relevant section of the bibliography. The following list of abbreviations, however, may be of use:

Crown:	Farquhar, *The Crown of Hinduism*
Fulfil:	Sharpe, *Not to Destroy, but to Fulfil*
Ed.:	*World Missionary Conference*, Edinburgh 1910, reports of
Boyle:	Maurice, *The Religions of the World*
WPOR:	Barrows, *The World Parliament of Religions*
EDMS:	Papers submitted to Commission Four of the World Missionary Conference, Edinburgh 1910
LPLBenson:	Papers on Benson in Lambeth Palace Library
USPGCMD:	Archive material on the Cambridge Mission to Delhi

Note on the use of Sanskrit, Indian and Foreign Terms

Sanskrit, and other Indian or foreign words and names, appear in quotations as they appear in the text cited; thus a number of different forms of the same word, many archaic, are to be found in the text. No attempt has been made to unify such references with their form as used in the text of this work. Here, where numerous readings exist, an attempt has been made to use the form of spelling most commonly used today in the most authoritative and contemporary scholarly works. An example might be taken in the name of the Indian reform movement, the Brahmō Samāj (the form as used in this study), which has many alternative spellings such as Brahmo Samaj, Brahma Samaj, Brahmö Samāj, Brahmō Sāmāj, etc. It is felt that no confusion should arise over this matter, as the majority of the uses are similar enough, or even familiar enough, for it to be self-evident as to what they refer.

Some of the more archaic usages, such as Muhammedanism for Islam, may be felt to be offensive in some quarters. That they have been kept reflects the author's intention to remain true to the original source along the lines of the general policy stated above, and they should be read as reflecting the spirit of the age in which they were written rather than bearing any other connotation.

Part I: Introduction

Introduction to Part I

Aims, Argument and Plan

This work sets out to consider the history and conception of the doctrine of fulfilment theology as found in British theological thought from, broadly speaking, the mid 1840s until about 1914. The Anglican and Non-Conformist traditions are to be considered most important in this. This period coincides with the growth and development (or, perhaps, 'rediscovery' would be a better word) of the idea in modern British thought up until the time it received its best known exposition at the hands of John Nicol Farquhar. The period being discussed is quite broad, but, due to the nature of the material, to cut any time off at either end would make an unnatural break in the study.

To place this study within the context of previous academic work in the area, it should be noted that no major study of fulfilment theology throughout this period has been undertaken. Farquhar's work, looked at from its historical context, has received a thorough treatment from Sharpe,[1] but has not been comprehensively studied from a theological angle. Significant mention should also be given to the work of Maw, who has looked at the fulfilment theology of Westcott and the Cambridge Mission to Delhi.[2] His work, however, fails to place this school of thought within the context of fulfilment theology as a whole, and again, is largely historical rather than theological. An MPhil thesis, looking at the changing attitudes to the non-Christian religions from a Christian perspective in largely the same period of time as this study has been undertaken,[3] but this work looks at all aspects of the changing attitudes, rather than considering fulfilment theology specifically. Perhaps the most significant work in this area is that of

---

1 Eric J. Sharpe, *Not to Destroy but to Fulfil* (1965) and *John Nicol Farquhar: A Memoir* (1963)

2 Martin Maw, *Visions of India* (1990), this work is essentially Maw's PhD thesis, *Fulfilment Theology, the Aryan Race Theory, and the Work of British Protestant Missionaries in Victorian India* (1986).

3 Paul Charles Supple, *Christians and Religious Pluralism c. 1830–1914* (1991).

Cracknell,[4] who looks at a number of the important figures in this area,[5] though not specifically from the angle of fulfilment theology. His concern is more to see how the figures whom he considers develop an attitude of 'justice, courtesy and love'. While he gives some attention to the idea of fulfilment, it is mainly a sideline to him, and the development of the idea is not something he considers.[6] It should also be noted that Cracknell's work, being broader in scope than this study – which deals purely with British thought, specifically in relation to Hinduism, and in missionary terms with respect to India – helps show that the ideas developed here are not without their parallels elsewhere, particularly in America,[7] while British missionaries were developing similar concepts both in China[8] and Japan.[9] There is thus a need to look at fulfilment theology through this period[10] both from a historical and theological point of view. With particular regard to the latter, while

---

4   Kenneth Cracknell, *Justice, Courtesy and Love: Theologians and Missionaries Encountering World Religions, 1846–1914* (1995).

5   F. D. Maurice, B. F. Westcott, T. E. Slater, B. Lucas, J. N. Farquhar, and C. F. Andrews; he also gives consideration to the Edinburgh Conference.

6   Although one recurring theme in his book is the continuing influence of Maurice, both as a theologian, and as someone influential in altering peoples attitudes towards the non-Christian religions.

7   Cracknell looks at the two American theologians Alexander V. G. Allen and Charles Cuthbert Hall, as well as the American missionaries Robert Allen Hume and John P. Jones (see Cracknell, 1995, pp. 81 ff, 95 ff, 132 ff, and 144 ff respectively). The latter three particularly are names that have appeared with some frequency in the research for this work, especially regarding the situation in India (Jones appears in this study with respect to 'the Indian Witness debate' which surrounded some of Farquhar's work).

8   Cracknell cites Timothy Richards as a case in point (ibid., pp. 120 ff). Richards was born but a few miles from Lampeter at Ffaldybrenin and, significantly, his father was a friend of Rowland Williams. With reference to his father's circle of liberal acquaintances, Cracknell says, 'This may be the first clue to his son's wide outlook' (ibid., p. 120). We should observe that, while Cracknell, in a footnote, says that Rowland Williams 'also wrote *Christianity and Hinduism*' (ibid., p. 341, fn 91), he makes no suggestion that Williams' attitudes to the non-Christian religions may have had any direct bearing upon the future slant of Richards' thought.

9   The fascinating example of Arthur Lloyd is used by Cracknell as an example who saw himself as a 'Ronin for Christ' (ibid., pp. 151 ff).

10   Indeed, the fact that two recent works (Supple and Cracknell, 1995), have considered the question of Christian attitudes towards the non-Christian religions within largely the same period is suggestive that this is an area which is in need of attention.

fulfilment theology is often discussed in relation to other forms of comparative religion, the definition and understanding of it is frequently left very vague, a matter to be discussed below. This study seeks to offer an original contribution both in terms of its historical study, and in the theological definition given to fulfilment theology. Further, as a part of the above aims, this book will attempt to give a new perspective on the popularly understood connection between fulfilment theology and the Edinburgh Missionary Conference, 1910, and the role of Farquhar in its history. While both the conference and Farquhar's contribution, in particular his work *The Crown of Hinduism*, have both been seen as seminal in the history of fulfilment theology, this study will argue that fulfilment theology not just had a history stretching back long before this time, but also that it had a significant popularity prior to either the Edinburgh Conference or the publication of Farquhar's book.

This work is divided into five main sections. The first and last may be seen as more theoretical in outlook, and the middle three as more historical. The first section seeks to introduce the reader to the reasoning behind fulfilment theology, and the world-view which gave birth to it. Having established this, the next three sections, in many ways the main thrust of the book, provide an historical account of the development of fulfilment theology in the 1840s through to the writing of Farquhar's *Crown of Hinduism*. The significant figures and their contributions to fulfilment theology, as well as some of the interconnections between them, are discussed. The main schools of thought are identified, and the different uses made of fulfilment theology by scholars of comparative religion, missionaries, and theologians are all given consideration. The final chapter looks at the various criticisms to which fulfilment theology was subjected, both in the period under discussion and subsequently, as well as looking at any other possible objections. While the main survey is limited to looking at British thought, this section has a wider scope to look at criticisms and other perspectives from a whole range of areas in order to gain a better perspective on the limitations and possibilities of the idea.

While British Anglican and Non-Conformist thought of the mid to late nineteenth and early twentieth-centuries is the main concern of the whole work, a broader outlook is taken, and so references will often be cited to later figures, or those of different traditions, where it is felt that the particular perspective given may be of use in elucidating the argument.

Finally, this study looks at the development of fulfilment theology within the period under consideration, and thus supporters of this paradigm will receive the most consideration. This is not to deny, of course, that other attitudes existed. In particular, throughout the period under discussion, it would always be possible to find examples of those who took a much more hostile and condemnatory attitude towards the non-Christian religions. In not mentioning this dimension, this study does not seek to suggest that no such attitudes existed, the focus of the study does, however, mean that on the whole only one side of the story will be given prominence. However, it should be noted that one argument of this study is that fulfilment theology was far more dominant, and at an earlier time, than is commonly believed, and by virtue of this, that the 'old' condemnatory attitude was far less prevalent in British thought at the end of the nineteenth and in the early twentieth-century than might be supposed.

Methodological Introduction

Before turning to the question of what is meant by the term fulfilment theology, and considering the limits of this study, it will be useful first to give a brief account of the methodology employed. The aim here is not to engage upon an exhaustive discussion of methodological theory, but to mention some significant elements of thought in this area, and place this study in some relationship to them.

The main part consists of an historical survey, looking at the development of fulfilment theology in terms of the contributions of certain major figures in its history. In so doing, the importance of what was then the comparatively new method of historical-critical analysis will be considered,[11] and throughout this part of the study my methodology will be essentially continuing in the same tradition of analysis, in attempting to gain an understanding of the thought of that period. However, epistemological theory has moved on in the intervening hundred or so years,[12] and I do not wish to claim that the attitude that I adopt towards my sources is the same as that of

---

11   See Sharpe, 1965 (hereafter Fulfil), pp. 41 f.

12   With theories and approaches such as structuralism, deconstructualism, feminism, etc.

a scholar of the latter part of the nineteenth-century.[13] Modern scholarship insists that we are more aware than ever of the preconceptions that colour our own thinking and inhibit our interpretations,[14] an attitude with which the term 'postmodernism' may be associated,[15] a contemporary phenomena which has, at the very least, fired a warning shot across the bow of the most self assured assertions.[16] In respect, then, to the varied intellectual landscape of today, I feel it necessary to place myself within some context in relation to other people's methodological theories. However, I should also observe that this study is not a work on methodology per se, and that what I say here is intended merely to outline my general approach, rather than being in any way a statement or exploration of any new or novel theories regarding this subject.

With regard to the aims stated above, I should provide a description of postmodernism. The basic assumptions of postmodernism may be stated, as far as it can be, as follows, 'Postmodernism would seem to be rather clearly in favour of relativism, in as far as it is capable of clarity, and hostile to the idea of unique, exclusive, objective, external or transcendant truth.'[17] Or, as Gellner says, 'Objective truth is to be replaced by hermeneutic truth. Hermeneutic truth respects the subjectivity both of the object of the inquiry and of the inquirer, and even of the reader and listener.'[18] These ideas stem from the idea that the interpreter is him/herself[19] constantly engaged in a

---

13   Indeed, in view of the illustrious names given mention in this study, it seems almost presumptuous to suggest that my methodology represents an advance on their own.

14   Whether in terms of gender, class, race, religion, or whatever.

15   I place the term in inverted commas in recognition of the fact that it is itself a somewhat nebulous term whose meaning cannot clearly be defined (see Gellner, pp. 22–3), though we may note as a close a definition as has been given Lyotard's phrase of postmodernism as 'incredulity toward metanarratives' (Lyotard, p. xxiv).

16   Thus, our own postmodern world may be sharply contrasted with the Victorian era covered by this study, which, 'viewed now in the lengthening perspective of time, seems to have combined progress with order, experimentation with moral certainty, in a measure unique in history' (Reardon, p. 1). Though it is to be questioned whether one can so neatly summarize the thought of the Victorian (or even our own) era in this way, (Newsome, 1997, pp. 5 f, and p. 12) the changing spirit of the nineteenth and early twentieth-centuries will be one theme of this study.

17   Gellner, p. 24.

18   Gellner, p. 35.

19   While many modern studies use this term, or her/himself, I will use the more traditional 'himself' throughout this study. This should, however, be read as being gender neutral.

reinterpretation of the available material that stems from his own preconceived ideas, and his own cultural and linguistic heritage. Some have taken this idea to its extremes, suggesting a radical form of deconstruction. That is to say, the assumptions that there are no definite standards of logic or dialectic, and that any theory is as valid as any other. Norris refers to such 'commonplace ideas about deconstruction as a species of latter-day Nietzschean irrationalism, one that rejects the whole legacy of post-Kantian enlightened thought.'[20] In as far as the theory of deconstruction exists with regard to its main proponent Derrida, such an interpretation is, he suggests, invalid. Rather, he says:

> Deconstruction in this, its most rigorous form acts as a constant reminder of the ways in which language deflects or complicates the philosopher's project. Above all, deconstruction works to undo the idea – according to Derrida, the ruling illusion of Western metaphysics – that reason can somehow dispense with language and arrive at a pure, self-authenticating truth or method.[21]

Seen in this light, deconstruction has a valid place in intellectual debate. With regard, however, to some proponents of the theory, Norris does allow Ellis' criticisms,[22] stating that he is correct in saying that deconstructionalists:

> be held accountable to the standards of logical rigour, argumentative consistency and truth. He is also perfectly right to maintain that such ideas need testing through a process of genuine and open intellectual debate; that deconstructionalists are failing this test if they resort to a notion of open-ended textual "freeplay" or all-purpose rhetorical "undecidability"; and furthermore, that one simply cannot make sense of arguments that claim allegiance to a different, alternative or uniquely "Derridean" kind of logic whose terms they are then unable to specify with any degree of exactitude.[23]

---

20   Norris, 1990, p. 49. He suggests that this is the way Habermas, to his mind, wrongly, reads Derrida (ibid., p. 160, see Jürgen Habermas (translated by F. Lawrence), *The Philosophic Discourse of Modernity*, Cambridge, Polity Press, 1987).
21   Norris, 1982, p. 19.
22   Advanced in John Ellis, *Against Deconstruction*, Princeton University Press, 1989.
23   Norris, 1990, p. 134. The desire of some postmodernists to stress the unknowable and deny any certainty makes me wonder if it is not some reaction to the growing knowledge and certainty of science, which can, far more so than even in the self-perceived age of advance that was Victorian Britain, can explain, to startling degrees, the functioning of our brains, and is even positing a grand theory of everything. With science now offering answers to questions that were felt to be

8

Such extreme ideas, to my mind, push postmodernism to the extremes of nihilism, being little different from some kind of sixth-form Cartesian scepticism, which delights in the discovery that there is virtually nothing that can be definitely proven; yet postmodernism, if not pushed to extreme, does offer certain important values.

In contrast to the extremes of postmodernism, another method of approaching our necessarily subjective understanding has been suggested. This involves a self-reflexive approach of contemplating the terms by which we seek to classify phenomena; looking at what Husserl called 'intentionality',[24] that is to say, seeking to step back from the very constructs by which we order our understanding. Flood has used the term 'dialogical reflexivity' for the method whereby we consider how our words reflect our own presuppositions, gender, power relationships, etc.[25] Thus, by seeking to understand where one stands, it is suggested that it is possible to stand back from the preconceptions which one holds, at least to a certain degree. This approach does not suggest that it is possible to become free of our own preconceptions, but at least to become aware of them. This approach bears similarities to what Bowie suggests about the feminist approach to the teaching of theology and religious studies:

> A feminist standpoint perspective demands that the teacher comes to terms with her own beliefs, personal agenda, implicit aims, and cultural baggage, and that she helps her students do the same. This is not the same thing as the deconstructionalist project of Derrida or Foucault, which abstracts both the subject and the object of the discourse in an attempt to 'talk from nowhere, to become ungraspable, unapproachable, irrecupable in every way.'[26]

---

mysteries, even beyond human comprehension, it is, I would suggest, not surprising that many, particularly philosophers and literary theorists, feel threatened in their world of the subjective and opinio. They have, therefore, retreated to positions of unknowability, where, 'Words like development, progression, advancement, meaning[...] are supplanted by[...] dissemination, indeterminacy, deferral[....] Meaning is local, community is tribal, society is pluralistic[....]' (G. Ward, in Ford, p. 585).

24   See Bowker, pp. 173 ff.
25   Flood, 1999, p. 35.
26   Bowie, p. 44, quotation from Bertraud Poirot-Delpech, 'Maitres à dépenser', Le Monde, 30/4/1976, in Jeanne Farret-Saada (translated by C. Cullen), *Deadly Words: Witchcraft in the Bocage*, Cambridge University Press, 1980, p. 14, Farret-

The two approaches, that suggested by Flood, and that suggested by Bowie, appear to share a common aim in response to the postmodernist challenge by not responding to the relativity it propounds, by engaging in some form of a 'rhetorical "undecidability",'[27] or to seek to step outside of the normal modes of our own language to 'talk from nowhere,' but by seeking to gain an awareness of the nature of our own perspective, whereby we can modify our interpretation in relation to this.[28] They both acknowledge our subjectivity, or inter-subjectivity, but do not see it as necessary to fall into absolute relativistic nihilism.

I would now like to justify my placing of myself in the tradition of nineteenth-century historical-critical scholarship, by relating it to the discussion on dialogical reflexivity above. In this regard, the opinions of Jowett on what qualities the scholar should have are pertinent, 'The would-be interpreter must set himself to discover the original meaning[....] This demands historical sympathy[....] He should especially be aware of invoking the assumptions and imposing the standards of a later age.'[29] According to Reardon, to the modern reader 'such stipulations are merely trite,'[30] meaning that such standards in interpretation are now taken for granted. The standards of dialogical reflexivity are, however, merely a refinement of the same historical-critical method, though not just taking into consideration the way in which interpretations have changed through time, but also having an awareness of the personal agenda of the interpreter himself. While this might be seen as a new idea, it is implicit in the standards of nineteenth-century

---

Saada's work originally published as *Le mots, la mort, les sorts*, Paris, Gallimard, 1977.

27   Norris, 1990, p. 160 – full quotation given above.

28   In quoting Bowie's feminist interpretation, I do not wish to suggest that I see my work as embodying a distinctively feminist perspective in itself, I merely quote her as another example of someone expounding the methodology that I am seeking to employ here. Indeed, in regard to the fact that all the major figures considered in this study are men it might be seen as distinctly non-feminist in its approach, however this limitation owes more to the area of study in terms of both period and subject matter involved.

29   Reardon, p. 337.

30   Ibid.

scholarship.[31] One difference, however, between the nineteenth-century approach and that of today would be that:

> Whereas the modernist project analysed the contents of the faiths in the details of their stories and structures, and gave the liberal theologian a chance to 'compare and contrast' the different religions on the cosmic menu, the postmodern reality is a collection of *petites histoires* of the tribal deities that tell us little of the deities themselves, rather more of the cultures that formed them.[32]

That is to say that the 'modernist' methodology (i.e. nineteenth-century liberal thought) may have uncritically assumed that the theology of the non-Christian religions gave direct access to knowledge of the divine revelation they had received, while the 'postmodernist' methodology (i.e. that of the scholar today) is aware that there is a great deal of ethnological interpretive data underlying the thought of the non-Christian (and even Christian) religions. We will, though, see in this study that many scholars of past generations were not as unreflexive in this matter as many people today would assume them to be, the intermingling of what they saw as religion with national cultures being often uppermost in their minds.[33] Throughout the rest of this study, I shall make no explicit reference to this method, as I have already stated this is not a work on methodology per se, but it should be assumed throughout that the author is aware of the problems raised by modern epistemological theory, and that, at least, an attempt has been made to engage in a dialogically reflexive manner with the sources in an attempt to provide an interpretation that is as free as possible of any agenda-based distortion.[34] Evidently, I am not

---

31 Certainly as regards Husserl, who was referred to above, he is very much a child of this age in regard to his dates (1859–1938).

32 Hart, p. 1.

33 With regard to this I might note that in the final chapter the postmodern method of cultural linguistic theory will be considered as one of the many challenges to fulfilment theology.

34 Having made the above points, I feel that a few words should be said concerning the danger inherent in becoming too caught up in the problem of subjective interpretations, in this regard I can do no better than quote Gellner again, 'In fact the practitioners of the method (for which we may read all "postmodernists") are so deeply, so longingly, imbued both by the difficulty and the undesirability of transcending the meanings – of their objects, of themselves, of their readers, of anyone – that in the end one tends to be given poems and homilies on the locked circles of meaning in which everyone is imprisoned, excruciatingly *and* pleasurably.' (Gellner, p. 35).

embarking upon a radically revisionist postmodern agenda in this study, utilizing concepts such as Lyotard's 'paralogy',[35] where, 'No (even relatively permanent) consensus can be reached.' However, as David Jasper has noted, to 'take postmodernism seriously does not require one to be in accord with thinkers like Jacques Derrida or Paul de Man [or, for that matter, Lyotard].'[36] That is to say, as regards this study at least, it should be possible to accept what can usefully be gained from a postmodern perspective for academic interpretation, without accepting the excesses of the movement wherein one falls into 'the paradoxical void that envelops speech and gesture,'[37] therefore left incapable of approaching any sort of conclusion.[38]

The method outlined above, in terms of being an aspect of historical-critical inquiry, relates primarily to the central chapters of this study. In the first and final chapter a different approach is adopted. In the first chapter the constituent elements of fulfilment theology will be described and analysed, in an attempt to consider what is meant by the term, and how it may be classified, the methodology being more descriptive than historical. In the final chapter, fulfilment theology will be considered as a theological and philosophical concept, looking at the criticisms levelled against the idea, and the defences given for it, in terms of their justification in its usage in a theological context. It might be said, to sketch roughly upon a broad canvas, that the first chapter is concerned with looking at fulfilment theology from a traditional Religious Studies perspective; the central chapters look at fulfilment theology from the perspective of the history of ideas; while the final chapter adopts a traditionally Theological approach to fulfilment theology. This is suggested only in passing, and I do not wish to develop it

---

35   '"Paralogy" can be understood to mean "a move played in the pragmatics of knowledge" in which overlapping identities and differences are juxtaposed in such a fashion that all comparative elements are illuminated. Paralogy, as an interpretative strategy, should not be understood as simply looking for the innovative deviations from a paradigm, but rather the finite, but open-ended, play of otherness. No (even relatively permanent) consensus can be reached in such an investigation. See Jean-François Lyotard, *The Postmodern Condition: A Report on Knowledge*, translator Geoff Bennington and Brian Massumi (Minneapolis, 1984) pp. 61, 79.' (Happel, in Jasper, p. 115 fn 3).

36   Jasper, in Jasper, p. vii.

37   Happel, in Jasper, p. 91 (see J-F Lyotard, op. cit., p. 81).

38   Though, that is not, of course, to say that one should believe that what conclusions are reached should be regarded as definitive.

here, for it raises far too many questions, and in terms of an analysis would require answers to be given to questions such as what is a 'Religious Studies' or a 'Theological' perspective which would require too much space to be considered here.[39]

---

39   While, the question cannot be entered into here, reference may be made to Sharpe's discussion of this, Sharpe, 1988, chapter 1; see also, Wiles, 1976, Whaling, 1984 and 1985, and Capps, 1995.

1 The Concept of Fulfilment and Fulfilment Theology

The Scope and Aims of this Study

As mentioned previously, this work may be divided into three main sections, of which the central one will be considered first,[1] as this helps give a shape and structure to the remainder.

With regard to the historical survey, a broad scope of time is covered, relating to the time from which the idea of fulfilment theology was first taken up in any significant form within British theology, to the time when it received its most widely known and popular expression. This period[2] naturally encompasses many different changes with regard to religious thought and belief, not all of which can be dealt with in the space of this study. However, there are a number of central themes which are important to the history of fulfilment theology, and the changes and continuities within these themes are one feature of the study. The four most important of these themes are: first, the growth of the science of comparative religion; second, the use of the historical-critical method in relation to religious thought; third, the changes that occurred within missionary thought and policy, and the attitudes of the evangelical and conservative wings of the Church towards the non-Christian religions; and fourth, the influence of Logos theology, and the spread of 'liberal' thought. It should be noted that these themes are all inter-related with one another. The study itself centres upon important figures in the history of fulfilment theology, considered in the context of the their own

---

1   That is to say, the historical section.

2   Broadly speaking from the 1840s till the outbreak of the First World War. As has been noted: 'As a matter of pure chronology the nineteenth-century should presumably extend exactly from 1800 to 1900 [surely 1801–1900], but in practice most working historians have found it convenient to treat it as having begun in 1789 with the outbreak of the French Revolution, and as having lasted till 1914, the beginning of the First World War' (Neill, 1971, p. 243). I will therefore, as a general policy, refer to the fulfilment theology covered in this study up until Farquhar's time as nineteenth-century fulfilment theology.

15

traditions, and in relation to the other figures involved in the development of fulfilment theology. Having stated the scope of the study, something should now be said concerning the aims and purpose. Firstly, the study presents a much fuller history of fulfilment theology than has previously been given, and so exposes certain common misconceptions, in particular regarding Farquhar's contribution, suggesting that rather than being a founding figure in fulfilment theology, Farquhar was but one person in the long chain of its development. Sharpe's excellent study of Farquhar, *Not to Destroy But to Fulfil*, gave only a brief mention to the development of fulfilment theology prior to his time.[3] While since the publication of this work very little attention has been given to the subject of the history of fulfilment theology,[4] a new insight into the history of fulfilment theology is therefore offered in the historical aspects of this work.

Turning now to consider the other aspects of this study, which can be seen as integral to the historical context, the rest of this first chapter will be devoted to seeking to give an answer to the question as to what fulfilment theology is.[5] To this end, I will consider first the way in which the doctrine was justified by reference to scripture and the Church Fathers within the period covered, then some historical factors needed to put the development of the idea in perspective will be briefly mentioned, after which the usage of the term will be analysed, and some definitions considered.

The final chapter will consider the criticisms raised against fulfilment theology, particularly those criticisms made against Farquhar, and an attempt will be made to consider how far they are valid. Further other possible criticisms of fulfilment theology as a whole will be suggested and considered.

---

3   See op. cit., chapters 1 and 3.
4   It has been given a brief mention in certain works, particularly in T. Thomas' works.
5   It should be remarked that neither Maw, nor Sharpe, sought to define this. Both gave a definition of what particular figures meant by the term 'fulfilment', but neither asked what is entailed, or meant, by the term in a more general sense.

The Justification of Fulfilment Theology

In looking at the way fulfilment theology developed through the period under consideration, the justifications given for it, both in terms of scriptural references, and in precedents from the Church Fathers, provide a useful starting point for determining how fulfilment theology was understood. It should be emphasized that not every proponent of fulfilment theology used, or appealed to all, or even any, of these justifications. For instance, it should come as no surprise that while Anglican theologians often cite the Church Fathers, the same propensity is not found amongst Non-Conformists. However, they still provide a fair indication of the general tone of thought for most fulfilment theologians. We begin with the Biblical justifications.

Naturally, one of the most important references for fulfilment theology is that from which it takes its name, a saying of Jesus' to be found in Matthew, 'Think that I am not come to destroy the law, or the prophets: I am come not to destroy, but to fulfil.'[6] Indeed, it could be said that followers of fulfilment theology are those who interpret this passage in a broad sense.[7] Strictly speaking, exegesis of the passage does indicate that Jesus intended the passage to be understood in its narrow sense.[8] If, however, the passage is

---

6   Mt. V: 17.

7   By a 'broad' sense is meant the extension of its principle to include religions apart from that of the Judaic tradition, while the restriction of it to this one tradition alone may be referred to as the 'narrow' interpretation.

8   See Beare, p. 138. The passage forms part of Jesus' Sermon on the Mount (Davies, pp. 48–9, the Sermon covers chapters 5–7 of Matthew's Gospel). Worth noting is the fact that the authenticity of this passage, and of those surrounding it (verses 17–19) has been challenged (Beare, p. 140). According to one recent commentator, even if the passage itself is not genuine, nevertheless, 'the saying is a faithful statement of his [Jesus'] fundamental attitude' (Ibid.,p.142). According to another interpreter Matthew's Gospel leads up to this point, so, 'In the first four chapters, the narrative had already indicated that Jesus' life was to be understood as a fulfilment of scriptural expectations, and the instances of Jesus' teaching which follow in 5. 21–48 will show how his teaching is a fulfilment too. Looking at the whole narrative, however, it seems to suppose that "fulfil" can include change' (Davies, p. 51). The purpose of the passage can therefore be seen as a safeguard, for, as another commentator observes, within 'the Hebrew Scriptures God declares that, "You shall not add to the word which I command you, nor take from it" (Deut. IV: 2)[....] Josephus boasts about the law, "For, although such long ages have now

contextualized in relation to Jesus' teachings as a whole, and to the experience of the early Church,[9] then the question entails a broadening of the closed hermeneutical circle, to consider not just what specifically does the passage mean in the context of its surroundings, but also what implications this passage has for the church's mission as a whole.[10]

As questions leading off from that asked above, it is an interesting point for students of the history of religion to ask whether, in a particular case, a specific passage of scripture leads to a specific belief, or whether outside factors upon a tradition formulate a belief, which will then find a scriptural

---

passed, no one has ventured either to add, or to remove, or to alter a syllable; and it is an instinct with every Jew, from the day of his birth, to regard them as the decrees of God, to abide by them, and, if need be, cheerfully to die for them. Time and again ere now the sight has been witnessed of prisoners enduring tortures and death in every form at the theatres, rather than utter a single word against the Laws and the allied documents." (Against Apian I: 42–43).

'Before any example of Jesus' interpretation of the law is given, the auditors are warned that they are not to conclude that he annuls or contradicts it' (Garland, p. 61). Further it may be noted that, 'Matthew himself brings a broadly different interpretation of how the "fulfilment" of the law is accomplished, when he sums up the basic teaching of Jesus in the words of the Golden rule. "Whatever you wish that men would do to you, do so to them; for this is the law and the prophets" (7:12)' (Beare, p. 142). There is no parallel to this saying in any other of the Gospels, it should be noted (ibid., p. 138). In the light of the above then, the use of Mt V: 17 in fulfilment theology, takes it a long way from its original context. While there is a linkage in that it was part of Matthew's attempt to portray Jesus as a fulfiller, the passage itself appears to have been inserted as a defence against charges that the scheme Matthew presented was violating the strong Jewish taboos about altering the law. The passage was, then, originally a response to the warning in Deuteronomy, where those within the early Church were aware of the antinomy situation engendered by the need to show that Jesus truly was, not just in accord with the Mosaic law, but holding fast to it and, on the other side, the need to present Jesus' vision of what the law really entailed. Upon Biblical usage of the terms promise and fulfilment in general (מלא in Hebrew, πληροῦν in Greek), a more detailed discussion is found in Moule.

9   In this regard, attention might be given to Peter's vision in Acts X, with its subsequent interpretation regarding the expansion of the Christian mission to include Gentiles as well as Jews. This passage was used as a justification of fulfilment theology, see below.

10   While the possibility of this question being asked can be noted, it does, of course, go beyond the limits of this study. All that can legitimately be said here is that fulfilment theology is one of the ways this question *was* (and, indeed, still is) answered.

18

passage to support it. Certainly, no case is ever likely to be so clear cut In the first instance, it would be very difficult to imagine a tradition independent of outside circumstance, such that the scriptures could be consulted without the weight of past judgements bearing upon the interpreter, and in the second instance, a tradition, it must surely be assumed, will be informed by its scriptures, so that an understanding of them will influence any doctrinal formulation. I will not attempt to answer this question one way or the other, for, as I have indicated, there is no clear cut distinction between the two answers. It is, however, useful to note, in considering the scriptural passages that lie behind fulfilment theology,[11] that there is a certain tension over this matter. In terms of the parties within this study, one might broadly categorize the evangelical group as being inclined to favour the first of the two approaches, giving priority to scripture, while the catholic, and liberal traditions, would be more at ease of the idea of interpreting scripture in relation to tradition.

Turning back to the passages behind fulfilment theology, another very important one is found in Paul's epistles, 'Wherefore the law was our schoolmaster *to bring us* unto Christ[....]'[12] Again, this passage is, in fulfilment theology, taken in a broad sense, in that it is not only the Jewish law which is a teacher, but all the non-Christian religions are held to have been 'schoolmasters' for the people to whom they have been given in accordance with Divine Providence.

These two passages may be said to be the most important scriptural references for fulfilment theology, and in themselves encapsulate the essentials of the doctrine. A number of other references were also used, which deserve a mention here. Of these, mention may first be made of another quotation from Paul's teachings, 'Ye men of Athens, I perceive that in all things ye are too superstitious. For as I passed by, and beheld your devotions, I found an altar with this inscription, TO THE UNKNOWN GOD. Whom therefore ye ignorantly worship, him declare I unto you.'[13] Here, the passage is interpreted to mean, that not just the men of Athens, but all non-Christians are actually worshipping God, whom for Paul is made known through Jesus, though without knowing it. Also significant in this respect are Paul's words

---

11   Either giving rise to it, or being subject to eisegesis to later legitimize it; to give the two extremes.
12   Gal. III: 24.
13   Acts XVII: 22–23.

recorded in Acts, 'In past generations he [God] allowed all the nations to walk in their own ways; yet he did not leave himself without witness[....]'[14] This passage was used in terms of fulfilment theology to suggest that God had everywhere made himself known through prophets, in men's hearts, or otherwise.

Again from the Acts of the Apostles, Peter's interpretation of his dream at Cæsarea is also used, 'Of a truth I perceive that God is no respecter of persons: But that in every nation he that feareth him, and worketh righteousness is accepted with him.'[15] This passage was seen as important in giving credence to the idea that, even if the doctrines of the non-Christian religions were not in accordance with Christianity in terms of metaphysics, then at least it could be claimed that in so far as they inculcated moral values, and the non-Christian peoples lived an ethical life, they were acceptable before God.

The final passage to be quoted here is from the fourth Gospel, where it is stated that, '*That* was the true Light, which lighteth every man that cometh into the world.'[16] From this symbolism of light, with Jesus as the Light of the World,[17] came the commonly used expression of 'broken lights' to refer to the non-Christian religions.[18] According to the proponents of fulfilment theology, if Jesus is the 'light' which 'lighteth *every* man,' then any good to be found outside of Christianity, however impaired, must be a reflection of this one light.

The passages above do not exhaust the scriptural references adduced to support fulfilment theology,[19] but are amongst the most commonly used and representative passages.

---

14   Acts XIV: 16–17.
15   Acts X: 34–35.
16   Jn. I: 9.
17   Arnold's little book *The Light of Asia* may be mentioned here, as the title may well have been inspired by this imagery. Certainly the usage was seen in Arnold's day as a form of challenge to Christian claims of Jesus as Lux Mundi (see Almond, p. 2, reference may also be made to Kellogg's book *Light of Asia and the Light of the World*). We may also note one interesting fact, often overlooked, and that is that Arnold later published a poem about Jesus, and this was entitled *The Light of the World*.
18   See, e.g. Gairdner, p. 138.
19   See Farquhar, 1930 (hereafter Crown), p. 27.

20

Next to be considered is the precedent found for this idea in the Church Fathers. Far and away the most significant figure in this regard is Justin Martyr, and so he is the only person who will be dealt with here.[20] Justin believed that Greek philosophy, like the Jewish law, was a schoolmaster pointing towards the person of Jesus, 'We have been taught that Christ is the first-born of God, and we have declared above that He is the Word of whom every race of men are partakers; and those who lived reasonably[21] are Christians[...]'[22] Further he stated:

> [...] for whatever law-givers or philosophers uttered well, they elaborated by finding and contemplating some part of the Word.
> For each man spoke well in proportion to the share he had of the spermatic word[...][23]

The connection of this to the scriptural passages quoted above is clear. As has been alluded to above, this appeal to the Church Fathers would be of more concern to those within the catholic wing of Anglicanism, or to Roman Catholics, than to either evangelical Anglicans, or Non-Conformists. For those concerned with maintaining the traditions of the Church, the support of one of the early Church Fathers would be seen as an important in legitimizing this doctrine.

---

20   Support was also looked for from the two great Christian philosophers of Alexandria, Clement and Origen. These figures were referred to by the Anglican liberal party at Cambridge, see Westcott, 1892, pp. 118–9, and 1891, p. 251. Leo the Great and Irenaeus were also called upon for support (See Müller, 1873, pp. 227 ff).

21   That is to say, 'with reason' or 'the Word'.

22   Justin Martyr, Apology I, XLVI.

23   Justin Martyr, Apology II, X and XIII. On Justin see also Goodenough and Osborn.

Historical Factors Contributing to the Growth of Fulfilment Theology in Nineteenth-Century Britain

Having considered the way in which fulfilment theology was held to have been justified by both the scriptures and the Church Fathers, it will now be asked, what factors led to the resurgence of fulfilment theology in the nineteenth-century? This section will consist only of a brief introduction to the major themes, as the intellectual background and development associated with the major figures and innovations in fulfilment theology will be dealt with in the course of the study, as it becomes relevant.

Firstly, there was a great growth and knowledge of the non-Christian religions at this time. Indicative of this was the development of the new science of comparative religion. This growing knowledge led many to come to a greater appreciation of the values of the non-Christian religions.[24] Of course, not all responses to the non-Christian religions were positive.[25] The distinction as to whether one adopted a 'positive' or 'negative' attitude, as may be expected, depended upon the tradition from which one came.[26] What is most notable about the then new discoveries in comparative religion, was the fact that many similarities were held to exist between Christianity and the non-Christian religions, and it would not seem unreasonable to suppose that fulfilment theology provided the best answer for many Christians to explain this finding. That this belief was held generally can, perhaps, be best

---

24   In particular the Romantic Movement held India in high regard (see Halbfass, chapters 5 and 6).

25   See, e.g., Duff on Hinduism, 'Of all systems of false religion it is that which seems to embody the largest amount of variety of semblances and counterfeits of divinely revealed facts and doctrines. In this respect, it appears to hold the same relation to the primitive patriarchal faith, that Roman Catholicism does to the primitive apostolic faith. It is, in fact, *the Popery of primitive patriarchal Christianity*. All the terms and names expressive of the sublimest truths, originally revealed from heaven, it still retains; and under these it contrives to inculcate diametrically opposite and contradictory errors' (Duff, 1839(a), p. 179). This passage is particularly rich in terms of themes and ideas which will be picked up later in the study, particularly worth noting are his beliefs that Hinduism embodies many 'semblances[...] of divinely revealed facts,' the belief in a primitive revelation, and the objection to Roman Catholicism – all these are mirrored in Monier-Williams' thought, though he does not follow Duff on all points of interpretation.

26   This idea is seen most explicitly in chapters 2–5.

illustrated in the works of men like Duff and Morris who, though opposed to finding these similarities indicative of divine workings outside of Christianity, nevertheless felt forced to concede the similarities.

Secondly, and, indeed, one of the main reasons for the growing knowledge of the non-Christian religions, was the growth of missionary activity in the nineteenth-century.[27] Most missionary thought was cast in the mould of nineteenth-century evangelicalism,[28] and, especially in the earlier part of the century, tended towards a very iconoclastic and hostile attitude to the non-Christian religions.[29] Not all missionaries, however, even in the early nineteenth-century, were so negative,[30] and, as will be seen, from the 1870s onwards, a gradual, but major change overtakes missionary thought, at least in India.[31]

The third consideration, related to the second, is the British Empire and its effect upon thought in this country. The connection to the point above is the fact that, 'imperialism was intrinsic to the British missionary movement's foreign ambitions;'[32] indeed, the Empire itself was considered to be divinely ordained.[33] Of particular importance in this study is the fact that India was seen as Britain's most important colony.[34] Linked to this, there is the

---

27 In Britain many new missionary societies came into being, and missionary work rapidly expanded across the globe (Neill, 1971, pp. 252 f). It is surely no accident that one of Duff's works was entitled, *Missions the Chief End of the Christian Church* (Duff, 1839(b)). By the time of Livingstone's death in May 1873 'the Missionary spirit had become the characteristic feature of religion' (Thorne, p. 2, quotation from a speech by Rev. Arthur Tidman, foreign secretary of the London Missionary Society, from Richard Lovett, *The History of the London Missionary Society, 1795–1895*, volume II, London, Oxford University Press, 1899, p. 675.

28 B. Stanley, p. 61.

29 Examples of such thought is legion, see, for instance, the references to Duff above, B. Stanley, 1990, pp. 64 ff, Fulfil, pp. 25 ff, etc.

30 Especially may be noted John Muir (Fulfil, pp. 36 f); see also Fulfil, pp. 35–39 as a whole.

31 See chapter 4.

32 Thorne, p. 14. This subject is expanded upon in chapter 6.

33 Newsome, 1997, pp. 138 ff. More will be said on this throughout – see also the quotation from Duff in the next note.

34 It has been noted that, 'India[...] had lain at the heart of the British imperial system – not only was it the largest overseas possession, but it provided a cornerstone for Britain's power and authority in both the Middle and the Far East' (Royle, p. 226). Duff noted that, 'India is the most noted of heathen realms[...] India has been given to Britain in a way that is peculiar – Britain has an opportunity of conferring

Romantic Movement's understanding of India, wherein, 'The very idea of India assumed almost mythical proportions; the turn towards India became the quest for the true depths of our own being, a search for the original, infant state of the human race, for the lost paradise of all religions and philosophies.'[35] The British fascination with India goes some way towards explaining why fulfilment theology was mainly developed in relation to Hinduism,[36] and Hinduism appears to have exercised a greater fascination than any other religion upon both academic and popular thought in Britain during this period.

While the reasons why Hinduism was the religion most commented on in this period are not strictly relevant to our discussion here, it is nevertheless worth making some comments on this topic. In the early part of the nineteenth-century Buddhism appears to have been the most favoured of all the non-Christian religions by British commentators,[37] while by the 1890s there appeared to be a decline in its popularity.[38] Hinduism, on the other hand, was in the ascendant throughout the nineteenth-century in terms of British attitudes. Duff's condemnations may be taken as typical of most views of the earlier to middle years of the century,[39] yet as will be seen in this study, as the century progresses the idolatry and other observances for which Hinduism was previously condemned come to be seen as positive aspects. The reasons for this are no doubt numerous. Müller's works treating India as the birth-

---

benefits which no other nation ever had[....]
'The extent and magnificence of the empire which Britain has there reared, and the wealth and influence thence accruing to her, have necessarily fixed on India the anxious gaze of the most enlightened statesmen of the old and New Worlds' (Duff, 1851, pp. 99–100 and 144).

35   Halbfass, p. 72.

36   Though it was certainly applied in other countries, and in relation to other religions. The Edinburgh Missionary Conference of 1910 testifies to this (see chapter 6). Works were also published suggesting that fulfilment theology could be applied to other religions, particularly Buddhism (see Almond, pp. 137–8 on this, amongst contemporary works we may note those of Scott (see pp. 40 ff), J. F. Clarke and Jersey). Also worth noting is a peculiar book, published some years later, in which it is argued that fulfilment theology can be applied to the Druidic religion that was, according to its author, to be found in Britain in the early centuries C.E. (Morgan, pp. 48 ff.).

37   See Müller, in Almond, p. 3.

38   Almond, ibid.

39   See, e.g., Duff, 1851, pp. 145 f.

place of religion, coupled with his translations of the Vedas and Upaniþads, presumably contributed to this. However, there is no doubt more to be said, for just as Almond noted that Victorian attitudes to Buddhism are probably more revealing of Victorian preoccupations than they are of Buddhism, so the change of preference from Buddhism to Hinduism speaks volumes about changing Victorian attitudes on religion. To suggest that Hinduism took precedence in people's minds merely as the predominant religion of the British Empire's main possession would be too simplistic.[40] Rather, I would suggest that the change reflects a new attitude towards religion. Buddhism's main attraction and feature was its highly developed ethical system.[41] In this regard, Hinduism could not compare (this attitude prevails even after Hinduism supersedes Buddhism as the preferred religion, see the Edinburgh Conference), and this reflects an interest in morality as the defining aspect of religion; Mill's popularization of the principles of utilitarianism at this time may be seen as indicative of this. Attitudes to religion were, however, to undergo a reform. The ecclesiastical changes associated with the Oxford and Cambridge Movements demonstrate an inclination towards reintroducing ideas of mystery into religion, while the rise of theosophy in the late nineteenth-century speaks of a need for esoterism. It might be said that there was a growth in forms of religion that went beyond seeing it merely as an aid to morality. In such a climate Hinduism, which had long been associated with idols, ceremony, and theological speculation, no doubt held a greater appeal than the pure morality of Buddhism. As this religion was popularly conceived, it was intellectually rather than religiously challenging.[42]

---

40   See Parsons, 1988(b), p. 283.
41   Almond, p. 112.
42   Parsons, 1988(b), p. 283.

Towards a Definition of Fulfilment Theology

The question as to what fulfilment theology is immediately encounters a very great problem, namely, the vast range of thought that has been classified under this title: 'Until the rapid rise of Islam in the seventh and eight centuries, it was the dominant Christian outlook toward other faiths. Today it represents the primary attitude toward other religions held by Roman Catholics as well as the conviction of many mainline Protestants.'[43] Hoehler is not alone in giving fulfilment theology such a broad range. Sharpe has noted the similarities between the teachings of Vatican II and Farquhar in this matter,[44] as has Race.[45] For his part, Whaling includes amongst the proponents of fulfilment theology, the seventeenth-century philosopher Lord Herbert of Cherbury, both Kant and Schleiermacher, as well as, more recently, Farmer and Eliade![46] This should give some indication of the difficulty of the task involved in any definition, and if reference is made back to what was said about the justifications given for fulfilment theology, this should come as no surprise. Essentially, anyone who acknowledges that the non-Christian religions answer to some religious need in man, are based upon some apprehension of the divine, however small, believe that Christianity offers a more complete answer to man's needs, offering a fuller apprehension of the divine, could be said to be propounding some form of fulfilment theology.[47] Indeed, in its broadest possible sense, i.e., that it recognizes the good in non-

---

43   Hoehler, p. 41 – it should be noted that he calls 'fulfilment theology' by a different title, that of 'preparationism', which, for reasons I will go into below, may well be a better term.

44   Sharpe, 1963, p. 2, he refers particularly to the teachings of *Ad Gentes* and *Alosta Aetate.5*

45   Race, p. 57.

46   Whaling, 1986, pp. 83 ff. It may also be mentioned in passing that the principle of fulfilment is not limited to Christianity, Whaling suggests it is present in the thought of Radhakrishnan and Sri Aurobindo and the Muslim thinker Muhammad Iqbal (ibid., p. 87), while a close similarity between the sort of fulfilment theology advocated by Farquhar and the thought of Vivekānanda in 'placing[...] Hinduism at the top of[... an] evolutionary ladder of religious developments' (Brockington, p. 178).

47   Indeed, most authors who refer to fulfilment theology make no attempt at a definition of what is meant by the term, apparently just assuming that some broad acceptance of what it is assumed. More will be said on this matter below.

Christian religions, but believes that Christianity is the 'highest' possible level of religion, then it would surely encompass practically every Christian who did not either see all other religions as wholly wicked and the work of Satan, or confirmed pluralists, who denied any exclusivist Christian claims as being the 'highest' form of religion.[48] Such a definition would be too broad to have any meaning; therefore some previously offered definitions of fulfilment theology will be considered next to see if a more adequate definition has been proposed.

Some Definitions of Fulfilment Theology

There is a marked reluctance amongst commentators to say what they mean when they use the term. While a number of writers are ready to define people as using 'fulfilment theology', or the principle of 'fulfilment', most do not attempt to give any definition of the term itself. Race, for example, includes both Farquhar and Rahner as people who use 'fulfilment theory', though he does not say what this theory is, beyond the basics of saying that it is a form of inclusivism.[49] In this he is representative of those who are ready to say who fulfilment theologians are,[50] or to say what particular people meant by the term 'fulfilment',[51] but are reluctant to define the limits of fulfilment theology itself. This is not intended as a criticism, and neither is it surprising. Attention has already been brought to the vast range of people across denominations, and two millennia of Christian tradition, who have been considered as standing within the tradition of fulfilment theology. However, some attempts at definitions have been made, and I will start by considering these.

I will begin by seeing what can usefully be gathered from the previous definitions,[52] which give some idea of what is included within the theory. Assent can be given to Race's suggestion that fulfilment theology is a form

---

48 Though of such people, it has been asked whether they are Christians at all (Hampson, p. 16, and see also, pp. 38 ff), though this matter is a wholly different question from that I wish to discuss here.
49 See Race, pp. 44, 52–55, 57 f, 68, and 75.
50 See for instance, Whaling, 1986, pp. 83 ff.
51 Such as Sharpe, see Fulfil, pp. 52 and 339.
52 Though, perhaps, I ought to say, non-definitions of fulfilment theology.

of inclusivism.[53] Sharpe's two definitions of what 'fulfilment' meant, to respectively, Monier-Williams and Farquhar, can also be examined:

> By 'fulfilment' Monier-Williams meant two distinct things: first, that 'lower religions are "fulfilled" by "higher" religions in the process of evolution'[...]; and secondly, that Christianity is the form of religion which satisfies, or "fulfills" the religious instincts and desires in the heart of every man, of whatever religion he may be[....]
> [...]Farquhar meant three distinct and yet related processes. First, Hinduism is 'fulfilled' by being replaced by Christianity: 'fulfilment' therefore means 'replacement.' Secondly, the 'truths' in Hinduism are 'fulfilled' by reappearing in a 'higher' form in Christianity. And thirdly, Christ 'fulfils' the 'quests' of Hinduism, by providing an answer to its questions, a resolution of its problems, a goal for its religious strivings.[54]

While this might cover the use of the term 'fulfilment' it does not tell us what the broader term 'fulfilment theology' means. Of other definitions, Hoehler offers little more than the following:

> Preparationism is grounded in the belief that God has not 'left himself without witness' in any time and place (Acts 14:17), that some knowledge of the Holy One is found in the world's faiths. To be sure, it is only in the Christian faith that God's revelation is fully disclosed. Yet other faiths are not to be rejected, for they possess the status of being preparations for the Gospel (*praeparatio evangelicae*), imperfect glimpses of the truth God has revealed decisively and incomparably in Jesus Christ.[55]

This description is extremely vague and generalized, giving little indication as to what the constituent factors are. The same may be said of Owen Thomas' definition, which he labels 'Development-Fulfilment':

> This approach sees the history of religion as a process of progressive development of evolution in which ever higher and purer forms emerge[....]Christianity is viewed as the highest stage of development in this process[....] It is thus superior to all other religions as the fulfilment of all that is implicit in them. The other religions are understood to be incomplete or preliminary stages of religious development which *may* function as preparations for Christian faith. When the idea of fulfilment is emphasized the other religions are seen to contain elements of truth which are drawn together and completed

---

53   As opposed to exclusivism, or pluralism, inclusivism entails, 'both an acceptance and rejection of the other faiths[....] On the one hand it accepts the spiritual power and depth manifest in them[....] On the other hand, it rejects them as not being sufficient for salvation apart from Christ[....]' (Race, p. 38).
54   Fulfil, pp. 52 and 339.
55   Hoehler, p. 41.

28

in Christianity, or they are understood to embody aspirations and longings which are satisfied in Christian faith.[56]

This definition offers rather more substance than Hoehler's, giving a better indication of what fulfilment theology involves, though the reservation may be noted that he sees the idea of preparation as optional, which, as is evidenced in Hoehler's definition, is a *sine qua non* of fulfilment theology. That preparation was a key feature of nineteenth-century fulfilment theology will be seen below and, I would venture to say, is part and parcel of most, if not all, forms of the doctrine that have been propounded. Certainly, it would be possible to use the term 'fulfilment' without reference to 'preparation', but it is, to say the least, normative within fulfilment theology for the two to go together.

Having noted these attempts, and the vast problems involved with a definition of fulfilment theology, I will, nevertheless, attempt to make one. The scope of this study, however, does not permit of a treatment of all the forms of 'fulfilment theology' that may be covered by the great list of proponents offered above. I will, therefore, attempt to define only what was meant by the term fulfilment theology as used by those figures who come within the scope of this work. Our aim here, then, is only to define nineteenth-century British fulfilment theology, and is, hopefully, a more manageable feat. From here on whenever the term 'fulfilment theology' is used, it will be the fulfilment theology of this particular period. It will, though, be necessary to make some observations which may be taken to have a more general application as to what fulfilment theology is. In examining this concept I will make some general observations on the way fulfilment theology was perceived at the time, before considering the central features that made up nineteenth-century fulfilment theology.[57]

---

56   O. Thomas, 1969, p. 22.
57   Using the term 'nineteenth-century' with the proviso noted above (see above).

It is unclear when the term 'fulfilment theology' first came into circulation. There does not appear to be any sense of an organized school or tradition.[58] There was some general sense of what was called, in Farquhar's day, a 'new attitude,' that is to say an assumption that there is good to be found within the non-Christian religions, rather than the traditional evangelical/missionary assumption that they are the work of the devil.[59] Thus, when someone is described as developing a 'fulfilment theology' it does not necessarily mean that they would have seen their work in these terms.[60]

Even with the above caveat, it is still possible to suggest that there was a common thread to the thought of the disparate group of individuals, whom we may term fulfilment theologians, which sums up the new attitude. The linking element is, of course, the concept of 'fulfilment', and what was understood by this term shall now be considered.

My definition of fulfilment will be essentially polythetic rather than monothetic, that is to say, rather than identifying a single essence I will give a set of shared characteristics and family resemblances.[61]

---

58   The closest thing being the liberal theological tradition at Cambridge, where fulfilment theology appears to have been part of an assumed world-view, which fitted in to the general tenor of their brand of Christian Platonism (see below, especially, chapters 2 and 5). They no doubt also saw themselves continuing the tradition of the early Church Fathers in this matter.

59   The term 'new attitude' was used particularly in the time following the publication of the *Crown of Hinduism* (see below, on the 'Indian Witness debate'). The term is also used by Sharpe, who speaking of the end of the nineteenth-century, said, 'Anticipated by Maurice in the 1840s, *a new attitude* to other religions was now beginning to be widely presented' (Sharpe, 1977, p. 19, italics my own). Wolffe notes that, 'This approach, which was focused particularly on Hinduism as the dominant creed of India, became known as fulfilment theology' (Wolffe, in Parsons, 1994, II, p. 26).

60   Likewise I shall use the term fulfilment theologian to refer to those who expound a fulfilment theology, but this is not meant to imply that it is a term that they would have recognized as applying to themselves, or that they were part of a school that can be recognized, with its members being fulfilment theologians. Rather, the term is intended to be merely descriptive. I follow Whaling in this broad use of the term (Whaling, 1986, p. 83: 'Fulfilment theologians from Clement of Alexandria to the present day[....]').

61   Urban, p. 139.

This is one of the key concepts of fulfilment theology, the idea being that there are different grades, or levels, of religion, each being an improvement on that below it.[62] The term may, though, lead to misunderstandings,[63] in that it might be read in terms of one of its meanings, in which the 'origination of species [of religion] conceived as a process of development from earlier forms, and not as due to "special creation".'[64] This reading would imply that there is a natural progression of religions, whereby, over time, mankind will, through his own powers, come to higher and higher understandings of the divine. The term is used in fulfilment theology with a sense of radical discontinuity, whereby only with a 'special creation', i.e. direct revelation, can the change occur, at least from the lower levels to the highest, that is from the non-Christian religions to Christianity.[65]

As will be mentioned below, evolution was a key idea in nineteenth-century thought; Illingworth went as far as to say, 'Evolution is in the air. It is the category of the age.'[66] Where the application of it to religion originates is uncertain, or, rather, there are several possible answers. Hegel's theory of 'Weltgeist', or 'world spirit,' posits a development in human thought,[67] while Schleiermacher developed a hierarchy of religions,[68] the 'idea of religions developing from simpler and more primitive to more complex and higher forms squared well with the Romantic stress on organic development or unfolding in the history of human spirit.'[69] While the idea was known in Germany well before this date, it has, nevertheless, been said of Newman's *An Essay on the Development of Christian Doctrine* that the 'idea of development as applied to this sphere was, for British theology, completely

---

62   See Fulfil, p. 52.
63   See section on Monier-Williams as an example of this.
64   *The Shorter Oxford English Dictionary*, '*Evolution: 3. Biol[ogical] c.*', third edition, 1983.
65   Whether a special revelation is necessary for evolution amongst the 'lower religions' is another question, which is, perhaps, never fully answered.
66   J. R. Illingworth, 'The Incarnation and Development', in Gore, 1890, p. 181.
67   See Halbfass, p. 88, as with the idea of evolution in fulfilment theology Hegel's 'Weltgeist' sees a development from the Orient to the Occident, culminating in Christianity (see Hegel, pp. 205 ff).
68   '*Editorial introduction*' in Smart et. al., 1988, I, p. 13 .
69   Ibid.

novel.'[70] Whatever the source of the idea it soon came into fairly widespread use in Britain in relation to all aspects of religion.

One final point should be made here, linked to the evolutionary ideal, which is that, mankind was meant to be evolving as well as religion, with each development of religion being suited to man at a different level of his development.[71] The idea of humanity developing through three stages, from childhood to youth, to maturity can also be seen in Frederick Temple's paper in *Essays and Reviews*.

Innate Religious Desire

Fundamental to fulfilment theology in any form is the idea that every religion responds to certain innate religious desires in man. Unless all religions appeal to the same sensibilities in mankind then there is no sense in which 'higher' religions 'fulfil' the lack left in man by 'lower' religions. Indeed, while it is often assumed that fulfilment theology considers the doctrines of the non-Christian religions to be fulfilled by 'superior' Christian doctrines, properly speaking, it is man's religious needs which are fulfilled.[72] These needs are thought to be satisfied in part by the teachings and practices of the non-Christian religions. However, it is only in Christianity or, more specifically, in the person of Jesus that the full satisfaction of these needs is said to be found.[73] In this there is often a distinction drawn between the doctrines of 'historical' Christianity and the 'religion of Jesus,' on which subject more will be said at various points throughout this study.

These ideas must surely have some basis in Schleiermacherian thought, for whom the basis of religiousness was feeling,[74] particularly, of course, for him the feeling of 'absolute dependence'.[75] His theory of feeling as the basis of religion will be seen as highly influential, though more particularly

---

70   Reardon, p. 146.
71   See Müller, 1873(a), p. 261.
72   See below, particularly in relation to Farquhar and his critics (chapters 7 and 8).
73   Farquhar's most notable contemporary critic, A. G. Hogg, based his attack upon this point, arguing that if Christianity *really* was the satisfaction to these supposed needs, then India ought to have been crying out for this revelation, which, he notes, it evidently wasn't (see chapter 8).
74   Gerrish, in Smart et. al., I, p. 125.
75   Ibid., pp. 135 f.

Coleridge's influence must also be acknowledged,[76] and although he saw feeling as primary, he opposed the non-rational basis of feeling which he saw in Schleiermacher,[77] and stressed the need for reason and understanding.[78]

Preparation(ism)

Once it had been accepted that the various religions of the world answer to man's religious needs, then the next question that would need addressing would be their ontological status. On this point the definition of fulfilment theology might be said to rest, for while one religion might fulfil another without any sense that the religion which is 'fulfilled' was somehow a *praeparatio evangelicae*, yet fulfilment theology carries this assumption. Indeed, fulfilment theology's alternative name, 'preparationism' makes it far clearer that this idea is central to the concept, and therefore might be regarded as a more descriptive term. The term 'fulfilment theology' carries no assumption that the non-Christian religions were actively prepared by God to lead men from their earliest days until they were ready for the final revelation.[79] The idea of fulfilment theology as a 'new attitude' has been spoken of above, and this entailed seeing the non-Christian religions as not coming from the devil, but from God, and so must be seen as part of His plan. One question that is left unanswered by this, is what is meant by 'preparation'. As will be seen in relation to the Edinburgh Conference, two distinct possibilities emerge. One is that the non-Christian religions, in as far as they demonstrate links between Christianity and the non-Christian religions, may be seen as preparations, i.e. a similarity of doctrine, might be held to suggest that they both point to some need in man which has caused this similarity to occur. A second notion is that similarities point to the fact that God has been involved in directing the development of the non-Christian

---

76   See especially chapter 2. However, amongst Romantics Coleridge was not alone in advocating the idea a common religiosity, William Blake's *All Religions are One* (Blake, p. 98) shares these sentiments, Blake in turn having been influenced by the neo-Platonists, especially Thomas Taylor (Raine, p. 103).

77   Welch, in Smart et. al., II, p. 7.

78   Ibid., pp. 7 ff.

79   The idea of evolution, and the development of mankind from its 'childhood' to 'maturity,' is implicit in this.

religions. The latter is the more usual view of confirmed fulfilment theologians.

Providence

This facet of fulfilment theology is essentially just a part of the last, but is worth mentioning in its own right. The reason for this is that the term 'Providence' speaks of a particular understanding of God's role in creation, whereby He actively orders and directs mankind's progress. With relation to this, a distinction may be made whereby it is possible to speak of particular thinkers having a 'high' or 'low' doctrine of Providence, meaning either that God is held to be directly ordering all aspects of life, or that God is supposed to be less involved with the ordering of things, intervening only in particular instances. In relation to fulfilment theology, this point is not entirely useful, as most thinkers, at least those considered here, even when they mention Providence, prefer to leave the degree of God's involvement as a mystery.

With regard to the last two points, Islam represents a particular problem for fulfilment theologians. Anteceding Christianity, it cannot be considered, as the pre-Christian religions are, to be a form of prior training. In fact, the problem is further exacerbated as part of Islam's raison d'etre, is that it specifically sees itself as transcending the Christian revelation, and denying the claims of traditional Christianity.[80] Nevertheless, fulfilment theology was propounded in relation to Islam.[81] The difficulties being explained away by suggesting that the Christianity found in Arabia in Mohammed's day was so debased that, in rejecting it, Mohammed was not really rejecting Jesus.[82] Rather, by purging a debased form of Christianity, and replacing it with a strongly monotheistic and legalistic religion, which it was believed, the people evidently needed, then it could be argued that Mohammed and Islam

---

80   It was noted at the Edinburgh Conference that Islam had to be viewed differently from Buddhism, Hinduism, or the indigenous Chinese religions, as the latter don't traditionally make reference to Jesus or Christianity, whereas Islam implicitly rejects the Christian teaching about Jesus (Ed. IV, pp. 138 and 243). There was also a lot of historical interaction between Christianity and Islam on the basis of military and political conflict which may have been influential (consciously or subconsciously) in the minds of some (Parsons, 1988(b), pp. 283, and 285 f).
81   Notably by Lefroy, and Benson (see below, chapter 6).
82   The high regard in which Mohammed held Jesus is often noted (see Ed. IV, p. 143).

were actually in accordance with the 'truths' of Christianity, and to be fulfilling God's will.[83]

Revelation and Natural Theology

Within the broad scope potentially covered by this point, there are a number of other points that need consideration. The reason I have grouped them all together is that they express the two extremes of thought that can be found in nineteenth-century fulfilment theology on the inspiration believed to lie behind the non-Christian religions. Essentially, the difference to be considered is whether natural theology is, or is not, to be considered authoritative as a form of revelation.[84] A further distinction might also be drawn between Revelation and revelation, that is to say, respectively, between God's final and definitive self expression of Himself in the person of Jesus, and the experience of man's response to God, as perceived in himself and in the world.[85] As I will suggest below, an appreciation of natural religion as a form of revelation is essential to a well balanced expression of fulfilment theology. However, there are a number of related points which must also be considered.

i) Primal Revelation

An idea commonly held by many evangelical and conservative Christians in the early nineteenth-century, and even into the latter half of that century, was that mankind had been vouchsafed a primitive and universal religion in its earliest days. According to Allen the idea first appeared in China in the seventeenth-century amongst Louis le Comte and the Jesuit 'figurists' who believed that the evidence of Chinese religion proved that there were

---

83   See Ed. IV, p. 140.
84   Indeed, at least since Schleiermacher's time, if not before, this dichotomy can be said to have marked the main dividing line between the conflicting tendencies in Protestant thought – in this century the distinction might be observed in relation to the differences of the Barthian and liberal schools of thought. It should be noted that I use the term natural theology in the sense it was used by Müller and others to refer not just to the knowledge of God that may be obtained through human reason (see, e.g., Cross, p. 940), but the knowledge also gained through experience.
85   See particularly Rowland Williams on this (chapter 2).

remnants of an original revelation still preserved amongst them.[86] Over the course of time mankind was held to have fallen away from, and lost, this early revelation.[87] The good points, which were then found in the non-Christian religions, were held to be 'truths' left over from this primitive revelation, which had been dimly remembered and continued, though now they often appeared in a distorted form.[88] Very few fulfilment theologians held this view,[89] and, indeed, as I shall suggest below, the theory is antithetical to the spirit of fulfilment theology.

ii) Logos Theology[90]

To convey the importance of this idea for fulfilment theology I will quote from Hoehler's study of Preparationism, who has noted that fulfilment theology has 'appeared within the framework of Logos theology:'[91]

> Christian thinkers have turned to the doctrine of the logos to express two distinct but connected ideas: (1) God's word made flesh in Jesus Christ (*logos ensarkos*); (2) God's seminal word not wholly limited to its incarnation in Christ (*logos spermaticos*). In other words, while God's logos – God's saving word and power – is made known unsurpassedly in Christ Jesus, those outside of the Christian faith are not left bereft.[92]

With regard to fulfilment theology's subsequent development in connection with Logos theology, he lists the following thinkers as those who have employed this paradigm: 'William Temple, Nathan Soderbloom, Rufus

---

86   Allen, pp. 41–3. Whether the idea reached nineteenth-century British evangelical thought from this source seems doubtful, though not impossible. With regard to this, the acceptability of this idea to conservative Christian thought lies upon its compatibility with the Biblical narrative of the tower of Babel – whereby the notion that mankind originally possessed a revelation, but lost it when God, in His wrath, divided mankind from one another, can be seen to have a scriptural forerunner.

87   Except, of course, for those within the Judaeo-Christian heritage.

88   See particularly Monier-Williams on this (chapter 3). Reference has already been made to Duff's use of this idea (see Duff, 1839(a), p. 179).

89   Monier-Williams and Banerjea being exceptions.

90   The importance of this conception has previously been observed by Bouquet, who also gives a good discussion of the history of the term 'logos' (Bouquet, chapter VI). Cracknell also stresses the importance of logos theology for his thought (Cracknell, pp. 98 ff).

91   Ibid.

92   Hoehler, p. 47.

Jones, Evelyn Underhill, H. H. Farmer, A. C. Bouquet, E. C. Dewick, R. C. Zaehner, Paul Tillich, Hans Kung, Karl Rahner, Raymond Panikkar, John Cobb, and Schubert Ogden.'[93] In view of these figures, and fulfilment theology's history, I would go further than Hoehler's assertion that the two have appeared together, and say that fulfilment theology is most characteristically, and also naturally, found in conjunction with Logos theology. Fulfilment theology cannot be seen as a doctrine separated from the rest of a person's theology. It needs a context, and to live, breathe, and develop naturally. In other words, fulfilment theology needs a congenial atmosphere. This, I will argue, is only provided in the world-view that is concomitant with Logos theology and, as will be seen during this study, not only was nineteenth-century fulfilment theology born in the bosom of Logos theology, but it almost axiomatically went hand in hand with this tradition,[94] and was most fully, and naturally, expressed in relation to it. Indeed, I will argue with regard to Farquhar that, while he gave the most famous account of fulfilment theology, his expression of it fails, precisely because he fails to place it in the context of a Logos theology.[95] It may be noted here that Müller suggests that Alexandrian-Christian philosophy (i.e. Logos theology) was not unknown in India.[96]

A New Religion

One idea, often found in conjunction with fulfilment theology, though not of itself essential, is that in an active encounter with the non-Christian religions, Christianity itself would itself be reformed.[97] This idea was propounded along a whole spectrum of degrees, from the mildest, in which it was recognized that Western forms of Christianity had not developed all the possible ranges of thought to the same degree as some of the non-Christian religions, so that an 'Eastern' form of Christianity would need to inculcate these ideas, and that

---

93 Hoehler, p. 48, see, pp. 47 ff.
94 I am here speaking of the Cambridge liberal tradition of theology which existed in the nineteenth-century.
95 See chapter 7.
96 Müller, 1902, p. 421.
97 See particularly, Müller, Miller, and Westcott on this idea (respectively chapters 3, 4, and 5).

Western Christianity might gain a pointer or two as to what aspects of thought lay undeveloped within it, to the most extreme, wherein the encounter with a new religion and culture, would, it was suggested, entail a total reshaping of the present form of Christianity, to take account of the new approaches found in the East.[98] While I have said that this idea is not essential to fulfilment theology it should, nevertheless, be seen as a natural outcome of the 'new attitude', for by actually taking the non-Christian religions as ordained by God, it would be necessary to consider what good could actually be found within them, and by taking the differences, not as signs of satanic corruption, but as positive aspects, it would be not unnatural to find areas in which another tradition might well supplement one's own.

An aspect of the above idea that often finds expression is the notion that each different race has its own specific genius,[99] which means that it develops a religion that accords with its own national character,[100] and, further, the idea that each nation has something unique, and important, to add to mankind's experience. Thus, only when the religious heritage of every nation has been explored and understood would it be possible, it was believed, for the highest form of religion,[101] to be attained.

Fulfilment Theology and Indian Christian Theology

Digressing somewhat from what should strictly be seen as a definition of fulfilment theology for the purposes of this study, the relation of fulfilment theology to Indian Christian theology should be mentioned. The question here, is what is the purpose of fulfilment theology, and in this regard D'Costa has raised an interesting point. Speaking of the fulfilment theology of Vatican II and many of the Indian bishops and theologians who promoted it there, he said:

---

98   Typically, it was suggested that, the Oriental religions, and in particular those of Indian, i.e., Hinduism, offered a more contemplative approach to religion, from which the 'active' West might learn something (see, e.g. Slater, chapter 4).

99   Which, taken in conjunction with the idea of Providence mentioned above, means seeing the different religions as part of God's plan.

100   In Müller and Westcott this idea became closely interlinked with the idea of language, race, and religion being part of one grand scheme (see below).

101   Which, it should be emphasized, means the highest form of Christianity.

The original inspiration for this school was the 'fulfillment [sic.] theology' of the early Church Fathers (rather than that of the contemporary Protestant thinkers), who used the thought of the ancient philosophers of Greece and Rome as the matrix for formulating their Christian faith in a theology of *chresis* or 'use.' What the early Fathers had done for ancient and medieval Christendom the Calcutta School dreamt of doing for Indian culture.[102]

D'Costa's point is that this Roman Catholic fulfilment theology aimed not at replacing Hinduism, but at Christianizing it, that is by adding (or making explicit?) the presence of Christ, leading towards the creation of a 'Christian Vedanta'; rather than fulfilling Hinduism by replacing it with a new Christianity. This idea was certainly not exclusive to Roman Catholic thought,[103] and as made clear in the last point, the idea of a new Indian Christianity was found in many thinkers at the time. However, D'Costa has picked up on an important point, that there is a difference in attitude between the fulfilment theologian who envisages fulfilment theology as leading to an Indian form of Christianity, and one who sees it leading towards a Christian Vedanta – indeed, the latter is, I would suggest, leading towards a new paradigm. The differences can, however, be spread through a whole range of degrees, but certainly there were fulfilment theologians with different aims in mind for the religion that would, they hoped, one day dominant India.

The 'Essence' of Fulfilment Theology

All of the above ideas can be found incorporated into expressions of what has been called fulfilment theology. Not all of them are necessary, and some represent a different form of fulfilment theology from that usually considered. However, from the above, three key phrases can be identified which sum up the quintessential foundation of any form of fulfilment theology. They are, a) 'progressive revelation', b) 'man as a religious animal', and c) 'Divine Providence'. To these I would like to add a fourth phrase, which, while not essential in one sense, does give coherence to the whole; that fourth phrase is 'Logos theology'.

---

102   D'Costa, in Ford, p. 458.
103   See particularly Westcott (chapter 5).

As has been noted, and will become yet more apparent in the historical survey, there is no single form of fulfilment theology in the period considered here, yet there are certain criteria lying behind all its forms.[104] Considering these criteria, which give fulfilment theology a sense of structure that can be discerned in its development, it may be possible to attempt some sort of standard definition of what fulfilment theology is. Farquhar's definition may be taken as, in some ways, definitive, not only being in accord with many earlier definitions, but also as the best known, and therefore, in this way, 'standard' form. Working then from Farquhar's paradigm, as well as from the general criteria, it is possible to define what may be termed a 'classical' form of fulfilment theology. However, it should be stressed that this is not a definition of Farquhar's formula, nor of any other individual's, but represents rather a generalized 'standard' taken from the most important figures involved in the history of fulfilment theology, taking all the essentials, but rejecting the individual accretions that mark out particular forms of the doctrine.

Fulfilment theology involves the belief that man has certain innate religious yearnings which can only be satisfied by the full revelation of God; however, it was necessary that mankind was first prepared for this revelation, so a series of lesser religions were given to man. These religions were

---

104   An analogy might be drawn with Ruskin's definition of Gothic architecture in 'The Nature of Gothic'. He identifies six elements of 'Gothic' architecture. According to him, most, but not all, of the six elements must be present for a particular form of architecture to be termed 'Gothic'. These six elements are savageness, changefulness, naturalism, grotesqueness, rigidity, and redundance. Other definitions of the term 'Gothic' have been offered, two contrasting ones are exemplified, on the one hand, by J. Thomas, who says that certain forms make architecture 'Gothic' (Thomas, 1998, pp. 1–2), while, on the other, Caröe argued that it is the spirit, not the form, that defines Gothic, and whereby it may be identified (Caröe, pp. 427 ff.). Evidently, 'Gothic', like 'fulfilment theology', is not readily defined, meaning slightly different things to different people (also, no doubt, at different times). Though, as has been suggested of the latter (see above), even without a precise definition people can identify it, the same is true of the former, for though, as Thomas notes, the original building of St David's College at Lampeter 'is a great work of synthesis,' he can still say that the 'building is clearly in a Gothic style' (J. Thomas, 1984, pp. 72 and 71).

themselves at different levels, and were made known to man as he became ready to receive them, with 'lower' religions being replaced by 'higher' religions, until, at last, the 'highest' religion became known. Each of these religions answered man's religious needs, though to differing degrees, and in this way they may be seen as 'evolutionary', in that there is a developing progression of religions from a lower to a higher form, each being more suited to man's needs. Further, each religion is held to be ordained by God for the purpose of leading mankind towards His final revelation.

This is, surely, not the only possible definition of fulfilment theology, and certainly, is not the only form of fulfilment theology. It represents, however, the most developed and widespread form of fulfilment theology that existed in the period under discussion. It might also be considered normative, other forms adopting 'unusual' variations, some of which will be noted below.

Variations of Fulfilment Theology

Two main differences may be observed between those who propound 'classical' fulfilment theology, and other fulfilment theologians. Each of these differences may be seen as bipolar, having two extremes, between which a range of options lies.

As will be seen, different writers on fulfilment theology give a different assessment of the teachings of the non-Christian religions. In as far as fulfilment theology represents a 'new attitude,' it typically sees the validity of the religious experience of the non-Christian holy men. However, as will be seen, some regard the religious experience of the non-Christian religions more highly than others. There is thus a gradation of differences from those who regard the teachings of the non-Christian religions as essentially negative, but redeemed either through some recognition of the need for God, or due to some primal revelation, through to those who are ready to speak of the religious experience of Hinduism and Buddhism as being on a par with Judaism, and who see the non-Christian saints as being comparable to the Christian saints. In this sense, fulfilment theology has a 'strong' and a 'weak' form in relation to natural religion, the 'strong' form being representative of the 'classical' form.

The second bipolarity appears between those who believe that the non-Christian religions have been created through the Providence of God, and represent part of His divine plan, and believe that they actively point, therefore, towards Jesus. The other extreme consists of those who would suggest that, while the non-Christian religions may have similarities to Christianity, and provide points of contact, these similarities are due only to the fact that there is a common religious instinct in man, and that God has not actually prepared the non-Christian religions as teachers for other nations. However, this does not mean that they cannot be seen, or used, as 'preparations' for Christianity, in that their teachings may be used as pointers to Christianity, but merely makes a statement about their ontological status. Again, we may speak of a 'strong' and a 'weak' sense in relation to Providence.

Neither of the two 'weak' viewpoints represents a 'classical' fulfilment theology; the main cause of differences between these and classical fulfilment theology is the absence of a Logos theology.

The Importance of World-View

I have stressed the importance that should be attached to a Logos theology for fulfilment theology.[105] I would now like to say something about its importance. However, the main argument for this contention rests on the historical study, where it is seen that fulfilment theology and Logos theology are intimately linked, not just in theory, but in its actual exposition.

Essentially, my claim is that fulfilment theology cannot stand alone, but needs a theological context.[106] This context must, for a 'classical' form of fulfilment theology, validate the religious experience of the non-Christian religions through an active divine principle immanent in the created order guiding the religious history of mankind. This is the background against which fulfilment theology makes sense. Without it, only an emasculated form of the doctrine is possible.

---

105   So far I have used the term 'Logos theology' without a definition. This would require a lengthy explanation of the world-view upon which it is based, and, rather than give it here, I refer the reader to the discussions of the Cambridge school of liberal theology who exemplify this world-view (see especially chapter 2).

106   In this it must reflect the 'new attitude' previously spoken of. While it is possible to have some form of fulfilment theology without this, such as Monier-Williams', for a truly healthy and full form of fulfilment theology, this 'attitude' is needed, as will be seen below.

The above assertion rests upon observation of the close connection of the two ideas,[107] coupled with the failure of those who do not propound a Logos theology to either attain to a full form of fulfilment theology, or to maintain a well balanced exposition of the same without it.[108] Unless a framework is provided, which gives a place for the reality of the religious experience of the non-Christian religions from a Christian standpoint, then the framework cannot succeed. Thus a compatible world-view is essential for fulfilment theology, and this form is ideally provided by the tradition of which Rowland Williams and Westcott form a part, as will be made apparent in the main study.

Finally, it should be noted that it is not essential for anyone to define themselves as a Logos theologian, or even to propound such a doctrine under this name, to be considered a proponent of some form of Logos theology. What is necessary is that someone has a world-view which entails a belief in the Divine and its activity that accords with the functioning of the logos, in the form of logos theology that can be seen to be operating in the thought of such figures as Maurice, Müller, and Westcott,[109] to be regarded as possessing a Logos theology for the purposes I have outlined here.

---

107   See especially chapters 2 and 5.
108   See especially chapters 3 and 7.
109   See most particularly Rowland Williams on this matter (chapter 2).

Part II: Beginnings

Introduction to Part II

Chapter 2 is dedicated to three works written by Anglican clergy, all of which, curiously, were written as the result of, a particular commission – two as prize essays, the other two being the publication of a series of lectures. The authors were, John Brande Morris (1812–1880), F. D. Maurice (1805–1872), Rowland Williams (1817–1870), and Richard Chevenix Trench (1807–1886), all four notable theologians.[1] It should be observed that after the publication of the three works in question no comparable book by a theologian of the stature of these men appears again in the nineteenth-century. Briefly, I would like to ask why this should be. Thomas suggests that, amongst theologians of the nineteenth-century, there was a general disregard for the non-Christian religions; Churchmen, he says, had no interest in them,[2] this, I would suggest, is not entirely true.[3] What can be said is that, amongst theologians, there certainly does not seem to have been a great interest in writing books on the non-Christian religions, but this is altogether different from saying they have no interest in the subject. The reason, I would suggest, was the growth of the science of comparative religion. With the growing knowledge and under-standing of the non-Christian, there could be few theologians ready to dedicate themselves to the necessary study to master the subject. Indeed, the only person truly to successfully bridge the gap between professional theologian and scholar of comparative religion is Rowland Williams. These three men stand at a time when serious knowledge of the non-Christian religions was just becoming available in the West, and when comparative religion was only beginning to establish itself as an area of study in its own right. The next chapter, however, will be dedicated to two men who may, more properly, be seen as students of comparative religion, Monier-Williams and Max Müller. It is worth noting though that while the study of comparative religion was yet still in its infancy a considerable knowledge of the non-Christian religions already existed.[4] Indeed, all these writers seem aware of

---

1   Most particularly the latter two.

2   Thomas notes that, 'hardly any theologians after Maurice and Williams paid any attention to other religions.' (Thomas, in Parsons, 1988(b), p. 293).

3   Interest in this topic is exhibited by, for instance, Westcott, whose thought will be looked at subsequently.

4   See J. J. Clarke, Part II.

the existence of many areas of similarity between Christianity and the non-Christian religions, and this it is suggested gives one reason for the reemergence of fulfilment theology. As was suggested in the first chapter some common understanding of how this was best explained might account for the three very similar accounts given by Maurice, Rowland Williams and Trench.

As a final point to this introduction, a clear distinction should be drawn between the thought of, on the one hand, Maurice, Trench and Rowland Williams, and, on the other, that of Morris. Morris' work is mainly included for the contrast it provides with the other two. Broadly speaking, the division is between the 'Cambridge school' of liberal theology (to which Maurice, Trench and Rowland Williams belonged), which 'was predominantly Platonic and Kantian,'[5] and the other schools of nineteenth-century theology.[6] The thought of this section of English liberalism will be seen to be very important in the development of fulfilment theology, therefore some brief account of certain tenets of its thought will be given here. One of the great figures of this school was Coleridge,[7] who profoundly influenced both Maurice and Rowland Williams, thus what shall be said of this school will be taken from Coleridge's thought.[8]

Coleridge believed that spiritual truth did not arise in the intellect, and was not addressed to that faculty,[9] however, religion was to do with the whole person not just the emotional aspect.[10] Further the chief business of religion

---

5   See Sanders, p. 14. Sanders distinguishes between two parties within 'liberal theology, the 'Oxford' and 'Cambridge' schools, both of whom were in favour of freedom of inquiry and supported the advances of Biblical criticism and the natural sciences, but whereas, as will be seen below, the 'Cambridge' school thought that it was necessary to go beyond mere intellect to intuition, what Coleridge called 'reason', the 'Oxford' school can be seen as predominantly 'Aristotelian', that is, inclined to see intellect alone as our source of knowledge. While Morris did not belong to the liberal party it will be seen that he does often use Aristotle in his work, in an Oxford sort of way.

6   The majority of people, in the period that concerns us in this chapter, would have belonged to the conservative and evangelical wings of the Church, such a person was Morris.

7   Elliott-Binns, 1946, pp. 292 f.

8   These points, while just sketched here, will be raised again throughout the chapter as they become relevant.

9   Sanders, p. 49.

10   Ibid., p. 65–6.

48

was to do with morality, and its purpose was to 'moralize the affections.'[11] The emphasis was therefore upon practical rather than theoretical reason;[12] Coleridge's religion was based not upon dogmas but was, 'a life; not a philosophy of life, but a life and a living process.'[13] The doctrines of religion were there to answer a need in man if they served any purpose, so, 'Any doctrine generally accepted by many nations in many ages was likely to be founded 'either in the nature of things, or in the necessities of human nature.'[14] He saw Christianity as the supreme religion,[15] and venerated the Bible the proof of which was its power over the lives of men,[16] which was, of course religion's main function to Coleridge. Yet he also looked elsewhere for truth,[17] feeling that Christianity was not hostile, but rather in tune with every truth;[18] in fact one of his great wishes was to bring all things into harmony.[19] Whilst opposed to all forms of party within the church,[20] and also because of this, Coleridge saw the Anglican Church as the best of all churches,[21] its greatest strength he felt was its toleration.[22] Seeing Christianity as the highest religion was for Coleridge perfectly compatible with his belief that man was continually progressing,[23] for Christianity was also capable of growth being described by him as being like 'a tree.'[24]

One final point with particular reference to this thesis that can be made is that, arguably, Coleridge was initially took a very high view of the value of Sanskrit literature seeing it, perhaps, as superior to much to be found in the West. Later however he was not so sure of its value, and attacks India and its

---

11   Coleridge, *Aids to Reflection*, p. 166, quoted in ibid., p. 67.
12   Ibid., p. 48.
13   Coleridge, *Aids to Reflection*, p. 233, quoted in ibid., p. 65.
14   Coleridge, *The Friend*, pp. 392–3, quoted in ibid., p. 51.
15   Ibid., p. 76.
16   Ibid., p. 83.
17   Ibid., pp. 59 and 82.
18   Ibid., p. 76.
19   Ibid., p. 72.
20   Ibid., p. 32.
21   Ibid., p. 87.
22   Ibid., p. 88. The same feeling was held by Williams, Maurice, and, perhaps more surprisingly, Müller, of which more shall be said later.
23   Ibid., p. 55.
24   Coleridge, *On the Constitution of the Church and State according to the Idea of Each*, p. 115 in ibid., p. 56

thought in his later works arguing for the superiority of Christianity.[25] This concludes what we need to say about Coleridge, and with it his influence upon the 'Cambridge' school of the liberals.

Chapter 3 goes on to consider the specific contribution made by two of the nineteenth-century's most prominent scholars of comparative religion, Monier Monier-Williams (1819–1899) and Friedrich Max Müller (1823–1900). Both were from very different schools of theology, and thus both, in their own ways, were to be very significant in determining the future course of fulfilment theology, particularly within missionary circles.

Also in the chapter the influence of German philosophical thought on Müller is discussed, and the influence of it upon Rowland Williams and Maurice is also touched upon.

---

25   Drew, pp. 185–6.

2 Commissioned Works

Frederick Denison Maurice

Maurice was probably the first person in the nineteenth-century who started to develop what can be called a system of fulfilment theology in his Boyle Lectures for 1846.[1] Unlike the later Müller and Monier-Williams, he was not an oriental scholar, and he did not make as thorough a study of the non-Christian religions as Rowland Williams. This has led to the quality of his scholarship being questioned.[2] In Maurice's defence it might be noted that his remit was far broader than that given to Williams, making the same kind of intensive study a somewhat weightier proposition. Maurice was also commissioned to deliver a series of lectures to a non-specialist audience, rather than write a learned essay for a university prize. Nevertheless, his work stands as the first movement in the development of fulfilment theology. Sharpe dismisses Maurice as just an 'isolated instance' in terms of his position amongst those who pioneered a more tolerant attitude to the non-Christian religions.[3] We should note, however, that the Boyle Lectures went through a number of editions, showing their popularity, and so they should not be dismissed as uninfluential as a source for fulfilment theology.[4] Further, it may be observed that Maurice's lectures were published in the year in which Williams wrote his prize essay at Cambridge, which shows a number of similarities to Maurice's work, thus begging the question as to how isolated a figure Maurice was. It should be remembered that these two men had similar influences, being members of the same school of thought. If they therefore reached conclusions that bear a striking resemblance, then it is not

---

1   Published in the year 1847 as *The Religions of the World: And Their Relations to Christianity*.

2   Sharpe, 1991, p. 147.

3   Fulfil, p. 44.

4   First edition 1847, second 1849, third 1852, fourth 1861, fifth 1877 (F. Maurice, I, p. xxiii), and the sixth 1886. The Boyle Lectures were regarded as his most popular work (ibid., p. 430).

unreasonable to assume that they represented a new attitude shared by others amongst their contemporaries. Before we discuss the contents of the Boyle Lectures, a few words would be of use on Maurice's theology, in order to contextualize him.

Liberal Theology, Christian Socialism, and the Logos

Firstly, like many in his day, he was influenced by Coleridge,[5] and was associated with the 'Cambridge School' of liberal theology. The relevance of this for a correct interpretation of his thought in relation to the non-Christian religions will be discussed further on in the chapter. Its importance to his thought generally will be seen, however, in the other aspect of his thought to which we now turn. Secondly, he was a member of the Christian Socialist movement.[6] In what is said below, it should be remembered that, for Maurice, 'the faith of the Blessed Trinity[... is] the key to Socialism.'[7] For Maurice, religion, specifically belief in the Trinity,[8] was the underlying unity behind all of his thought. This religious socialism is relevant to the way Maurice viewed the non-Christian religions. He wrote, 'I have endeavored [sic] to prove that if Christ really be the head of every man, and if He really has taken human flesh, there is a ground of universal fellowship among men.'[9]

Without knowing the context it would be impossible to say if this was an expression of a Christian Socialist or a fulfilment theologian. In this case it is the former. Yet, this striking example should help to demonstrate that the developing thought of Christian Socialism finds a close parallel in the more liberal attitude to the non-Christian faiths, as expressed in fulfilment theology, where it is essential that the unity of the whole body of mankind is seen.[10] Beyond this, the two movements show a striking correlation in their chronologies. There were many who were involved with both developments, from the time of Maurice through to Westcott and the younger William

---

5   Vidler, 1985, pp. 83–4.
6   Vidler, 1948, chapter VII.
7   Ramsey, p. 54.
8   See Welch, I, p. 249.
9   F. Maurice, 1884, I, p. 258, letter to the Rev. A. J. Scott, 20/2, probably 1839.
10   This theme is also mentioned by Cracknell (see especially Cracknell, 1995, p. 47).

Temple.[11] Another Christian Socialist, who must be mentioned in reference to fulfilment theology, A.M. Fairbairn,[12] was one of the influences on Farquhar, and was both a minister in Aberdeen when Farquhar lived there and later his tutor at Oxford.[13] The growing conscience of the British churches and the desire, as expressed above, to see all men as brothers, must surely have had some connection with the attitude taken towards the non-Christian religions – the number of Christian Socialists who were also involved in fulfilment theology suggests a strong link between the two.[14] As a final point it is worth noting that those who followed in Maurice's footsteps theologically, 'Hort and Westcott, Scott Holland and Gore and the late Archbishop Temple continued to expound and amplify[... the] interpretation of the Christian faith in the light of St. John's Gospel.'[15]

It is interesting that Higham traces his theological heritage in terms of those who followed him in the Johannine Christian tradition, ending with William Temple, because he, like Maurice, sees the passage in the prologue of St. John's Gospel that speaks of 'the true light, which enlighteneth every man'[16] as referring to the Logos, which is the spark of inspiration in the non-Christian religions: 'By the Word of God – that is to say, by Jesus Christ –

---

11   C. F. Andrews was also involved in both fulfilment theology (O'Connor, 1974, p. 36) and Christian Socialism (Chaturvedi, pp. 16–17). Andrews' work was closely linked to that of Gandhi in his efforts on behalf of, first, the Indian workers in South Africa, and then his political activity in India (ibid.; see also chapter 8 of this work).

12   Space does not permit Fairbairn's views to be discussed fully within this work. However, his influence was not seminal in the development of fulfilment theology, but he is mentioned in the introduction to chapter 5.

13   Fulfil, pp. 116 and 126 ff.

14   Incidently, the fact that one of the commonest complaints made by Christian missionaries against the followers of other religions was that they lacked the social conscience of Christians (see chapter 6) seems very ironic, in that such ideas were an innovation in the Christianity of that era. It may be observed that the emphasis upon social concern in the form of medical and educational missions was at its zenith at the time of the 1928 Jerusalem Missionary Conference, when, according to Sharpe, 'the culmination of the particular Christian literary movement launched by Farquhar, and the theories on which it was based' was reached (Fulfil, p. 13). This suggests a link between the development of ideas of social concern and the thought of fulfilment theology.

15   Higham, p. 122.

16   Jn. I: 9.

Isaiah, and Plato, and Zoroaster, and Buddha, and Confucius conceived and uttered such truths as they declared.'[17]

This linkage of Logos theology[18] and fulfilment theology, is a theme that will be repeated subsequently, both in this chapter and beyond. Having mentioned the tradition in which Maurice stands, it is time to consider the important features of his Boyle Lectures.

The Religions of the World

Maurice saw man as essentially a religious animal, saying, 'I ask nothing more than the Hindoo system and the Hindoo life as evidence that there is that in man which demands a Revelation – that there is *not* that in him which makes the Revelation.'[19]

Thus man has religious needs, and these needs are universal to all men. Here, speaking of Buddhism, he says, 'there must be something in it which has given it this wide diffusion. It must express some necessities of man's heart, some necessities of our own.'[20] The closeness of this to Maurice's earlier remark on Christian Socialism should at once be manifest. One of the essentials of fulfilment theology is that a basic unity of yearning is felt between all men, and so the desires that Christ fulfils for the Christian are the same as He fulfils for the Hindu, or any other person. As will become clearer, the sympathetic approach that fulfilment represents is very often a sympathy with the peoples of other nations rather than with their religion. The good in other religions is seen as a reflection of the divine origin of man, and his own innate spark of divinity. Not only did Maurice believe that there are certain feelings that must be common to all men, but these truths are met most fully in Christ: 'If we could not find that the great Mahometan truth[21] was asserted

---

17   Temple, p. 10. The linkage of Logos theology has already been observed. We may, however, emphasize its appearance here.

18   It should be mentioned that Maurice certainly does not have a fully worked out and realized Logos theology himself. It was to be the work of subsequent Anglican theologians, following the guidance of the early Church fathers in this matter, to formulate a more systematic presentation of ideas which Maurice and Williams were just starting to rediscover and understand.

19   Maurice, 1886 (hereafter Boyle), p. 55.

20   Boyle, p. 67.

21   That God is One.

more distinctly, mightily, lovingly in Christianity than in Mahometism, we did not feel that Christianity could ever be a substitute for Mahometanism.'[22]

Maurice's reference to 'the great Mahometan truth' relates to a distinctive idea, often found in conjunction with fulfilment theology, though not essential to it, that each religion has one particular 'truth' which forms its essential core. This belief will be found to be especially dominant in the thought of Müller and Miller, and is also to be seen in Williams' thought.[23] This idea is a commonplace of nineteenth-century, and even early twentieth-century, thought. It can be seen as linked to political ideas about national identity, and was not peculiar to Britain. To give an example of a twentieth-century religious thinker who gave spiritual overtones to this idea, we may note Rudolf Steiner. 'Steiner also followed his philosophical masters[24] in distinguishing national historical 'tasks', adding the piquant theory that each nation is guided from above by an archangel who is somehow also the folk-spirit of the nation.'[25]

It is interesting that this idea is to be found in such central figures of German philosophy, who influenced both the liberal school in England and Müller.[26] Another noteworthy feature in this reference to Steiner is the conception of national 'tasks'. This idea is found not just in later figures but also in Maurice, who speaks of 'that particular work which was assigned to the Jewish nation, of putting down wrong and violence, of asserting justice and judgement.'[27]

However, as so often with Maurice, his failure to present his ideas systematically means that it is not clear what, if any, tasks were assigned to other nations and what the 'great truth' of the other religions might happen to be. This is not in itself a major problem as the idea appears to be merely incidental to Maurice's thought. Still, I would venture to suggest that he sees the central idea of Buddhism to be:

> That profound feeling of reverence for the human spirit, which we have discovered in the Buddhist, his belief in the mighty capacities of this spirit,[...] his assurance that the spirit

---

22   Boyle, p. 165.

23   See next section on Rowland Williams who makes a passing reference to this idea.

24   Hegel and Fichte.

25   Washington, p. 164.

26   Further reference to this influence will be found in the relevant sections concerning Rowland Williams and Müller.

27   Boyle, p. 139.

in man cannot be circumscribed by the limits of time or space,[...] his conviction that the human spirit must, in some mysterious manner be divine.[28]

And of the Hindu he says, 'First, he has the deepest assurance that God must be an Absolute and Living Being, who can be satisfied with nothing less perfect than himself.'[29]

Maurice's vagueness on this matter leaves us unsure as to what to make of these ideas. Is each a form of training given by God for each people, or are they merely reflections of the national character? The answer is, of course, central to the value given to these ideas. What, however, Maurice is sure of is that they are 'truths'. For him each religion truly gives expression to some part of an eternal longing to be found in man. Each religion is, in itself, an answer, however imperfect, to the yearning that mankind has in its quest for God. Thus he can even go so far as to say – which even today some might find shockingly liberal – that, 'To abolish human sacrifice is good; but a blank will be left in the nation's heart even by the loss of such practices as these, which must be filled up, or we shall impoverish those we seek to reform.'[30] This is one of the fundamental tenets upon which the whole of fulfilment theology rests. In fulfilment theology the practices and beliefs of the non-Christian religions are not Satanic. Even those that may seem the worst to Western eyes have grown up in response to a need of the soul. How else, Maurice asked, could they have held such a great influence over the minds of men for so long?[31] The religious practices are not, then, just hollow or for show[32] but have a meaning for their followers, and provide an inner

---

28 Boyle, p. 197.
29 Ibid., pp. 60–1.
30 Ibid., p. 184. Advanced as Maurice's views may seem, it is worth noting that at the foundation of the London Missionary Society in 1795 the preacher, George Burder, had suggested that 'the custom of sacrifices, even human sacrifices, pointed to glimmerings of Christian understanding in even the South Sea Islanders' (Cracknell, 1995, p. 19). Burder based his ideas upon the notion of a primal revelation, speaking of the 'broken and mangled fragments of Gospel hope' (ibid.; see further George Burder, 'Jonah's Attitude to Nineveh', in *Sermons Preached in London at the Formation of the Missionary Society*, 1795, p. 31, part of which may be found in Pailin, pp. 281–4).
31 Boyle., pp. 66–7.
32 Though even by the time of the Edinburgh Conference there were still those who believed the native religions afforded no real religious consolation to their followers. See, for example, Ed. IV, pp. 10, 40, and 81.

spiritual life; so Maurice could say that to instil these people with only an outer faith, as a replacement for their old beliefs, would weaken their inner faith.[33] This would still be quite a radical stance even for Farquhar's era.

Maurice also heralds fulfilment theology by drawing out the similarities between the Christian and non-Christian faiths; though whether these are real or imagined is, of course, another matter.[34] After a long discussion on the idea of the twice-born, Maurice stated, 'Here then is a principle that is as characteristic of our faith as it is of the Hindoo.'[35] Maurice further says of the twice-born Brahmin that, 'Brahm is Wisdom or Light: the Brahmin is the reflection of this Wisdom or Light.'[36] This, he says, is connected to Christian teaching, for, 'The wise king or the wise prophet is ever spoken of in Scripture as having the Divine Wisdom, the Divine Word with him, nay in him.'[37] While recognizing a parallel here, Maurice saw a major difference in Hinduism in that it placed too much power in the human: 'All, Brahmanical acts, services, sacraments, imply an effort or scheme on the part of the creature to raise himself to God. All Christian acts, services, sacraments, imply that God has sought for the creatures that He might raise them to Himself.'[38] This tendency he sees even more strongly in Buddhism.[39] This leads Maurice to find another similarity to Christianity, in that 'the Buddhist affirms that there must be some person, and that a human person, in whom the perfect wisdom resides.'[40] Maurice believed that the Buddhist and Hindu developed these doctrines in response to their awareness of the Logos, but

---

33   Boyle, pp. 184–6. Later on, Maurice goes on to say something else that also sounds too modern for the 1840s, asking, 'Does it not sound like the idlest of all visions to talk of our converting Buddhists, when, judging from various indications, they are more likely to convert us?' (Boyle, p. 211). Perhaps he foresaw that much of the renewal of the inner life that would occur in the Western Church in this century would be borrowed from the Orient, though this trend now seems to have given way towards a rediscovery of the Christian spiritual heritage. After all, another feature of fulfilment theology is that the spiritual insights of the East will supplement, or correct, the leanings, or tendencies, of the West.

34   H. G. Wood, pp. 85 f.

35   Boyle, pp. 172–3, see pp. 166 ff.

36   Ibid., p. 173.

37   Ibid., p. 174.

38   Ibid., pp. 183–4.

39   Ibid., pp. 205 f.

40   Ibid., p. 199.

without Jesus' full revelation, which explains the error he finds in their teachings.

Another interesting, and indeed quite radical, aspect of Maurice's thought is that the non-Christian religions are not only supplemented by Christianity, but can also correct Christian faith where interpretations of it stray.[41] This willingness to perceive the good in the non-Christian religions is a foretaste of one principle of later theories of fulfilment theology, where it is stressed that we must always compare like with like; the best elements of Christianity with the best rather than the worst elements of Buddhism or Hinduism.[42]

Inspiration in the World's Religions

Having looked at the details of Maurice's thought, it is now time to consider what interpretation should be put upon them and whether the truths of the non-Christian religions are actually in the nature of a specific revelation or not. Certainly Maurice believed that the non-Christian religions were part of an authentic quest for God. He quotes the words of St. Paul to the Athenians on this subject, 'that they were ignorantly worshiping him.'[43] He also spoke of them containing certain 'truths'. However, interpretations have differed. Wood believed that he saw the non-Christian religions as having a 'revelation' of their own. Conversely, Terence Thomas argues that Maurice believed the non-Christian religions were purely human inventions,[44] contesting that, 'In terms of truth[45] Maurice seems to say that the Jews originally had it and lost it while the Muslims latched on to it for a time but were never really assimilated to the truth.'[46] Further, Thomas, describing Maurice's attitudes towards the religions of the Far East, says, 'His evaluation of Hinduism and Buddhism is even more negative. In both religions he finds analogies with Christianity[.... N]evertheless he sees no more revelation in

---

41   Ibid., p. 243.
42   Slater, 1903, p. 1, also Farquhar, 1930 (hereafter Crown), p. 119, etc.
43   Boyle, p. 220 (Acts XVII: 23).
44   T. Thomas, pp. 80–1.
45   By this Thomas means authentic knowledge of God, revealed from above.
46   T. Thomas, p. 81.

Buddhism than he sees in Hinduism.'[47] Wood, we may note, follows two earlier commentators on Maurice, Powicke and Stephen, in asserting this.[48] Cracknell concurs with the position maintained by Wood, though he does not cite him as an authority. For him, Maurice, 'laid the foundations[...] for a theology of the presence of Christ in other religious traditions.'[49]

In terms of language, Thomas is correct. Maurice finds nothing that he would call 'revelation' in Hinduism or Buddhism. While he acknowledges that both Judaism and Islam stem from the Old Testament religion yet, he says, they never realized its true potential. However, I would favour Wood's understanding of Maurice. In order to demonstrate why this seems to be the correct interpretation of Maurice's position it is necessary to consider certain general principles in his theology.

At the beginning of this section the Johannine, Logos-centric, side of Maurice's theology was mentioned, which is stressed by many commentators on Maurice.[50] However, more recent scholarship has argued that such an interpretation can be one-sided. This scholarship, while recognizing the influence of Platonism, also sees another aspect to his thought:

> The problem of Platonism is rooted in the recognition that, for Maurice, the Johannine writings are very much the clue to his understanding of the Bible as a whole. It might even be[...] that, within the Fourth Gospel, it is the prologue which is the key. Careful study, however, reveals that Maurice integrated Pauline and Johannine Christianity.[51]

This recognition, that Maurice saw the Pauline and Johannine writings as the culmination of the Bible, is not new.[52] Wolf has commented on the importance of Biblical revelation for Maurice in knowing God, in which the most important factor was the person of the Christ,[53] as Vidler also says, 'Maurice[...] believed that according to the New Testament "Revelation is[...] the unveiling of a Person – and that Person the ground and Archetype of men, the source of all life and goodness in men[....]"'[54] There is not, for Maurice,

---

47   Ibid., pp. 81 and 82.
48   Wood, pp. 73–4, and 86 f.
49   Cracknell, p. 39.
50   Notably Sanders, H. G. Wood, and Maurice's great interpreter, Vidler.
51   Wolf, pp. 76–7.
52   See, e.g., Vidler, 1948, pp. 39–40.
53   Wolf, pp. 73 ff.
54   Vidler, 1966, pp. 155–6, quotation from Maurice, *What is Revelation?*, p. 54.

a separate and equal root through natural religion to this knowledge. It is only through God's self-revelation and action in the historic episodes of the Biblical text that God is known as He is:

> Revelation can only mean God's making himself known, the bringing of light and truth in the place of uncertainty and confusion. We do – and we must – know God. The Bible declares to us what He is.
> Maurice's characteristic assertion about Scripture, therefore, was that the Bible is a book of facts – the facts of creation, redemption, the history of God's establishment of His Kingdom.[55]

Thus the Bible is revelation, and therefore outside of the Judeao-Christian tradition there is no revelation. Which is to say God's direct expression of His nature. However, as is acknowledged by Wolf, 'He [Maurice] never liked to call the Bible the Word of God as such. It was always the history of God's Word, by which the Word was to be discerned in life.'[56]

The Bible is then a guide to understanding the action of the Word, which Maurice believed to be operating before and outside of the Bible. Such then is Maurice's view of the Bible and revelation. To fit this into the context of Maurice's thought as a whole, and thereby to discern the way in which he saw the Word working in the non-Christian religions, it is necessary to turn to a dispute between him and Pusey.

The dispute was over the question of Baptism, and highlights the differences between, on the one hand, the world-view held by Maurice and others of his liberal school, and, on the other, broadly speaking, most of the other major English Christian theological traditions of this time. In this context I can do no better than to quote Ramsey's synopsis of the situation:

> To Pusey the context of Baptism was the sinful world on the one hand and the Church as the ark of salvation on the other: in Baptism we are brought from the sinful world into the Church, and are given a new nature by regeneration and we receive the infusion of the Holy Spirit. To Maurice the context was a world not ruled by the evil one but already redeemed by Christ: every child that is born is born into a world that is already redeemed, and in Baptism this truth is proclaimed and the child is put into relation to it.[57]

---

55   Welch, I, p. 255.
56   Wolf, p. 69.
57   Ramsey, p. 35.

For Maurice the universe was not a world alien to God's spirit, but was filled already with God's presence. God is thus already known about and yearned for: the non-Christian religions are not set up by the devil to lead people from God, but rather, 'all systems are feeling after Him [Jesus] as the common centre of the world.'[58] Thus, when we read these words of Maurice, their place within his thought should be clear:

> I have attempted to explain in my Boyle Lectures why I think the experiences of mankind respecting a Divine Spirit who awakens the thoughts, faculties, faith, hope, love in us, and directs them to an object above themselves, to a common object, in whom they find that which satisfies them, and which they are created to behold and enjoy, are altogether *distinct* from those respecting a Mediator – why, when they are *separated* from them or substituted for them, the result is... a priestcraft such as we see in Hindooism[....][59]

Here, Maurice clearly distinguishes between inspiration from a 'Divine Spirit' and the experience of a Mediator, which is to say Jesus Christ. This is his Pauline half stressing the need for the historical person of Christ, linked to God's self-revelation in Biblical history. Yet the Johannine half of Maurice is also present here. It stresses that our 'thoughts, faculties, faith, hope, [and] love' are already responding to the Logos which indwells creation. Though without the direct revelation of the Bible, which tells us about who God is, interpretations of this 'Divine Spirit' are apt to go astray. Thus in suggesting that Maurice sees 'merely human aspiration in Hinduism and Buddhism,'[60] I would argue that Thomas is mistaken. Maurice believed the non-Christian religions were responses to that 'Divine Spirit' awakening the minds and emotions of mankind, though lacking the revelation of God as person in Biblical history culminating in the person of Jesus of Nazareth. Certainly Maurice has no clearly worked out Logos doctrine in his Boyle Lectures, or even elsewhere. This might suggest that he saw no inspiration in the non-Christian religions, and certainly they are devoid of 'revelation' in his terms. However, from an understanding of his theology as a whole, based upon his Coleridgian heritage and of what he says elsewhere, a different reading of his thought may be gained.

---

58   F. D. Maurice, letter to his wife, 9/5/1840, in F. Maurice, 1884, I, p. 282.
59   F. D. Maurice, letter to R. H. Hutton, 8/1/1854, in ibid., II, p. 230.
60   T. Thomas, p. 84.

Maurice, interestingly, only uses the term 'fulfilment' (in any of its forms) to refer to the ancient Greek myths.[61] It is worth discussing here, briefly, the importance of terminology in fulfilment theology, and also whether Maurice can properly be considered to be in the line of fulfilment theologians, even if he does not always use the language that is associated with it.[62]

Although noting that he only uses 'fulfilment' in relation to Greek myths, it might be seen as significant that this usage occurs in the final lecture of the series, where he discusses all the religions. So it is not certain that only Greek myth is 'fulfilled.' Maurice had spoken earlier of the one who could answer the concerns of Hindus as being, 'not a destroyer, but a preserver.'[63] He is therefore using here another phrase typical of fulfilment theology, even if not using the term 'fulfil' itself. Maurice's limited use of the term does not mean that he only has a fulfilment theology in relation to Greek myth, but not, for example, Buddhism or Hinduism.

Having now considered Maurice's language it only remains to consider how far he went in developing his fulfilment theology. Essentially, most of what was later to become known as fulfilment theology can be found here. We may, therefore, feel justified in calling this its earliest exposition.[64] Most of the relevant themes have been noted above. One that hasn't however is the important question of how far the non-Christian religions were a preparation for Christianity. It was noted earlier that Maurice alluded to the idea of national 'tasks' but was very unclear as to what these were. Elsewhere he speaks of the non-Christian nations having roles, but not in the sense of preparing their devotees for Christ, rather:

> You say that Islam has not fallen before the cross. No, but Islam has become one of God's witnesses for the cross when those who pretend to bear it had really changed it for another standard. You say that Hindooism stands undisturbed by the presence of a triumphant Christian nation. Yes, for Hindooism has been wanted to teach this nation what it is very

---

61   Boyle, p. 221–2.

62   An analogous example would be Le Goff's argument that we cannot speak of Purgatory before 1170 because the word did not exist even though all the elements that made up this doctrine did (see Le Goff, p. 135).

63   Ibid., p. 59.

64   Its earliest nineteenth-century exposition of course.

nearly forgetting itself, very nearly forcing others to forget, that Christianity is not a dream or lie.[65]

There is thus a sense of Divine Providence directing the non-Christian nations and religions. Although, whether this has directed them to be preparations for Christianity, Maurice does not say.[66] The similarities that Maurice observed between the Christian and non-Christian religions were not used as indications of their being a preparation for Christianity. Whether or not the idea was in Maurice's mind, or whether it might be considered the natural outshoot of his work, he does not advance this proposition. However, that so much of what is later to become known as fulfilment theology is present in *The Religions of the World*, is a testimony to the tremendous depth of Maurice's thought. Speaking of Maurice's influence F. J. Powicke said, 'Am I wrong in thinking that this Boyle Lecture[...] did more than anything else to inspire that new attitude toward the non-Christian world which is now characteristic of the missionary and those who send him forth?'[67] Whether Maurice's lectures had the influence Powicke believed, he certainly attests to their continuing popularity, and their importance for later ages. Indeed, Wolf goes as far as to say of Maurice's work that:

It has[...] a surprising relevance for the continuing discussion of the Christian attitude towards the world's religions. It anticipates in some measure position's about the world's religions suggested in the documents of the Second Vatican Council and would add a dimension of understanding to the growing interest in the West in the non-Christian religions and in mysticism.[68]

Yet, while we must give all due respect to Maurice, he had a close contemporary in whose works can be found a fuller expression of fulfilment theology, and a greater knowledge of the religions of which he speaks. This was Rowland Williams, whose work we will now discuss.

---

65   Boyle, pp. 238.

66   Here I may refer again to Thomas who had suggested that belief in the activity of Providence amongst the non-Christian religions was a 'radical difference' between Williams and Maurice, the latter of course denying it (T. Thomas, p. 84).

67   Powicke, *Congregational Quarterly*, April 1930, p. 179, quoted in H. G. Wood, p. 74.

68   Wolf, p. 62.

Rowland Williams

Williams and Maurice

The year after Maurice's Boyle lectures were published, a prize essay was awarded in the University of Cambridge for 'the best Refutation of Hinduism, and Statement of the Evidences of Christianity in a form suited to the Hindús.'[69] This essay was to be the basis for Rowland Williams' Paraméswara-jnyána-góshthí[70] which was to appear nine years later. It may be noted that the prize was offered on the understanding that the initial essay be expanded to a larger work suitable for publication, with one fifth of the five hundred pounds prize money being initially awarded for the essay, with the remainder being due upon publication of the expanded work.[71] The intervening nine years between the writing of the prize essay and publication of the book (1847–1856) were busy ones for Williams. In 1850 he been appointed as Vice-Principal of St. David's College, Lampeter, and so he filled in work on his book as and when he could amidst his schedule.[72]

Before discussing Williams' attitude to Hinduism, it would be helpful to consider the position of his book in relation to Maurice's, especially in terms of the contemporary and subsequent reactions to it.

While Maurice's work, as observed above, has remained well known, Rowland Williams' has vanished into obscurity. Most references to Williams in works on nineteenth-century theology relate to his notoriety gained through *Rational Godliness* or *Essays and Reviews*. Even his biographer, Owain Jones, makes only a passing mention of it.[73] This is all the stranger considering Williams' own view of the book, '*Christianity and Hinduism*[...] is my chief work, and the one by which I should wish thoughtful critics to

---

69   John Muir, letter to the Rev. W. Whewell, 6/8/1845, quoted from E. Williams, I, p. 388.

70   Its full English title being *A Dialogue of the Knowledge of the Supreme Lord, in which are Compared the Claims of Christianity and Hinduism, and Various Questions of Indian Religion and Literature fairly Discussed*, though generally referred to by the shorter form, being the name which appears on the book's spine, *Christianity and Hinduism*, which will be used hereafter.

71   See R. Williams, letter to his father, 26/1/1848, in E. Williams, I, p. 140.

72   See R. Williams, letter to his father, 11/12/1850, in ibid., p. 187.

73   Jones, 1991, p. 44.

judge me.'[74] The work certainly had its admirers in its day. Dean Stanley referred to it as, 'one of the best manuals for dealing with the difficulties of heathen India.'[75] This obscurity is in many ways unfortunate. Maurice's work exhibited a limited knowledge of the subject, Williams' book, on the other hand, reflected the very highest scholarship, demonstrating a tremendous knowledge of the subject matter. The renowned Sanskrit scholar, Professor H. H. Wilson, suggested, 'the work would become a standard reference for the leading points of Hindú speculation, and the scope as well as history of their religious opinions.'[76] It was also praised by Professors Lassen and Bunsen amongst others.[77] Indeed, one of Williams' contemporaries, obviously an admirer of his work, writing in the year of his death, states that, to his knowledge, 'this greatest and fullest account of his teachings has never been attacked.'[78]

If such was the reaction to Williams' book we must ask why it never attained the circulation of Maurice's work. This is an important question, for Williams provides, as will be seen, a clearer exposition of fulfilment theology than does Maurice. Yet the latter seems to have had a greater influence upon subsequent thinkers. We will consider if there were any general qualities about the respective books which influenced this.

---

74   R. Williams, in E. Williams, I, letter to J. H. Rees, 18/2/1858, p. 399, see also p. 306.
75   Stanley, 1865, p. 257. See also Paul, pp. 242 f., and Owen, to whom we refer below.
76   Ibid., p. 315.
77   See ibid., pp. 309 ff. 'At the time of its publication,' Ellen Williams noted, 'it was said by competent judges, that it contained the best account of the rise and progress of the Buddhist religion which had been written in the English language, and that a knowledge of Hindú philosophy would be greatly facilitated to the English reader by the clear exposition which was here given of it' (ibid., p. 303, fn. 1). Also,' Of the Indian part it was said, that any one may learn more from it of the Hindú systems in a week, than he would ordinarily acquire in India in seven years. – *Col. Church Chronicle*, No. cxvi. p. 48.'
78   Owen, p. 63. In fact his scholarship was so thorough that Lampeter's first professor of Religious Studies, Cyril Williams, thought he had 'an astonishing grasp of Indian Religions' (Badham, 1997, p. 7). While the same amazement at Williams' depth of knowledge has been expressed to me by a notable contemporary scholar of Hinduism, Dr Gavin Flood, author of the now standard reference work for undergraduates, *An Introduction to Hinduism*.

Firstly, I would venture to suggest that, having noted the great many academic commendations for *Christianity and Hinduism*, this in itself would discourage the more general reader. Most people would not want a thorough discourse on Hindu philosophy; this would, of course, include many missionaries. Secondly, Thomas offers the opinion that interest in the non-Christian religions dwindled amongst theologians in the latter part of the nineteenth-century:

> The persons dealt with [notably Maurice and Williams...] represent a wider collection of clergy and theologians who were interested in the implications of the presence of other religions in the world for the Christian religion. Such clergy were more active in the earlier part of the nineteenth century. While Maurice's work continued to be reprinted, Williams' work was soon forgotten. In the aftermath of *Essays and Reviews* the contributors planned a second volume in the same critical mould. For the second volume Friedrich Max Müller was recruited to write on other religions. That venture came to nothing and hardly any theologians after Maurice and Williams paid any attention to other religions. Indeed, neither Maurice nor Williams integrated their work on other religions into their own theology. As far as the churches were concerned, the other religions, being the religions of subject races, were not worth any attention.[79]

Even if this were so, it offers no reason why Maurice's book should continue to be so popular while reference to Williams' disappears.

Why is it then that later books make reference to Maurice rather than Williams?[80] In citing *Essays and Reviews* Thomas may have hit upon at least part of the answer. Following the publication of this contentious work, Williams' name would have been marred in the eyes of at least part of his potential readership; missionaries and those interested in such matters[81] who would now regard any work of his with suspicion. Thomas notes that this

---

79   Thomas, in Parsons, 1988 (b), p. 293.
80   In Sharpe's *Faith Meets Faith*, for instance, considerable mention is made of Maurice's opinions on the world religions. In contrast, Williams' work, specifically on Hinduism(!), is not mentioned. Again, in Louis Jordan's history of comparative religion, of 1905, it is Maurice rather than Williams who is mentioned. See also Neufeldt in Coward, 1990, p. 33. Indeed, it seems only recently that any interest in Williams' book has reappeared; Thomas mentioning him alongside Maurice, in his discussions of nineteenth-century attitudes to non-Christian religions (see T. Thomas, chapter 3, and T. Thomas in Parsons, 1988(b)).
81   That a conservative evangelical brand of Christianity prevailed amongst the missionary societies is a fact that will be seen in a later chapter dealing with the spread of fulfilment theology in India.

work received little attention after 'his fall from grace over *Essays and Reviews*.'[82] More importantly, Maurice's book was, in certain ways, more conservative. Williams' work is deeply theological and discusses Biblical criticism. He also concedes that the Hindus have 'revelation'. Maurice, on the other hand, does not explain the thinking behind his thought in his presentation; Williams admits openly that at which Maurice only hints. Of course, saying that there is some form of revelation amongst the Hindus would have been anathema to the evangelical and conservative wings of the Church.[83] To another possible audience, the student of comparative religions, the book may still have looked too much like a straightforward work of Christian apologetics.[84] Though, of course, we have seen that a number of liberally minded thinkers evidently read and approved of it. Yet we must bear in mind Thomas' words about the lack of interest in the non-Christian religions amongst the clergy, and ask how many of them would read a detailed book upon Hinduism. Three factors, then, would seem to account for the reason why Williams' book lacked the influence of Maurice's. First, it was too scholarly for the general reader, second, it was too liberal for the conservatives and, third, its presentation was too conservative for the liberals.[85] Nevertheless, it certainly had a readership in its day. While it may not have had a wide readership, no doubt a fair number of liberally minded and scholarly churchmen would have read it, and been influenced by it.[86]

---

82   Thomas, in Parsons, 1988 (b), p. 293. It might be objected that the same would be true of Maurice, but his work, as we noted above, was of a more popular nature. Having been circulated more widely it would have had a chance to have established itself as a standard reference work before the time of his trial for heresy.

83   Writing to Bunsen, Williams observes that the Bishop of Calcutta, Daniel Wilson, referred to his book as 'metaphysical, neological, and almost pantheistical' (R. Williams, letter to Bunsen, 1/5/1859, in E. Williams, I, p. 314). Incidently, it was during Wilson's episcopate that the Bishopric of Calcutta was made Metropolitan.

84   Though it is reasonable to suppose that Müller read this work, for Bunsen wrote to him praising it highly, even going so far as to say, 'No German could have written it.' Which Ellen Williams suggests is intended as 'the highest praise' (quoted by E. Williams, I, p. 314.)

85   I purposefully say its 'presentation' rather than its contents, for, as will be seen in a later chapter, even such a figure as Müller is not as radical as he was perceived to be by his critics.

86   I suggest this because, as we will be seen in a later chapter, towards the end of the nineteenth-century fulfilment theology is rapidly assimilated by a number of thinkers in the Church of England. Williams' book may well have played a part,

Having considered the relative reception of *Christianity and Hinduism* and Maurice's Boyle lectures, we will now turn to consider Williams' attitude towards Hinduism, as exhibited both in this work and elsewhere in his writings.

Christianity and Hinduism

i) Introduction

The work takes the form of a dialogue between two English priests, some natives of India, and a European materialist.[87] Of the two priests, the younger one, named Blancombe, who does most of the debating, represents Williams' own views.[88] The older man, known as Mountain, presents a more traditional view of Christian belief.[89] While there is some difference between these two in their views, Williams did not make the difference as great as he had originally intended.[90] It is also worth noting that Williams says that the character of Blancombe showed great respect for Mountain.[91] Unless stated otherwise, all speech quotations from this work should be assumed to be spoken by Blancombe. The dialogue is said to have occurred in 1854,[92] and is related by a non-Christian Indian, who, while not embracing Christianity, at least contemplates it.[93] No doubt this is part of Williams' apologetic method, having an impartial – in the eyes of Hindus – person to relate the dialogue, who, while not being seen to convert, does nevertheless underline

---

for it gives a far clearer foretaste of the future fulfilment theology than is to be found in Maurice.

87   The Indians are all representatives of a particular Hindu tradition, and are: Sadánanda, a Vaishnava Sānkhyast; Vidyáchárya, a Śaiva Vedāntist; and Saugata, a Nepalese Buddhist. Williams regarded Buddhism as a sect of Hinduism, a common belief in those days. This raises issues to which we shall refer again, associated with the imposition of Western interpretations, especially the classifications of religions into particular 'isms' (Thomas, in Parsons, II, p. 292). The European is named Wolff.

88   See E. Williams, I, p. 305.

89   Ibid., II, p. 398.

90   Ibid.

91   Williams, 1856, p. 1.

92   Williams, 1856, p. 239.

93   Ibid., p. 559.

that there is, from Williams' point of view, much that is attractive in Christianity. Indeed, it was part of Muir's stipulations that the essay should undermine rather than directly attack Hinduism, for he realized that this would not be helpful to the missionary.[94] Indeed the narrator of the dialogue says that he finds Blancombe attempting to search for a common ground with those he is debating with.[95] While Williams no doubt believed he was being very conciliatory there is still a great deal that he attacks.[96]

One notable feature of the work is Williams' preoccupation with history.[97] Several chapters are devoted to showing that the chronologies of Indian history, especially those found within its sacred literature, are flawed, whereas the Bible, by way of contrast, is held to be relatively free from historical error. However, it was Williams' application of historical criticism to the Hindu sacred books that made him believe that he had also to apply the same treatment to the Christian literature if his comparison was to be fair; thus the main impact of Williams' book was not to be as part of the history of improving Christianity's understanding of Hinduism, rather in helping Christianity to a better understanding of itself through Williams' advocacy of Biblical criticism.[98]

As a final point here, we may consider what one commentator on Williams has considered to be the main propositions of *Rational Godliness*, and see how far they are reliant on, and integrated with, his work in *Christianity and Hinduism*:

(1) Revelation is a progressive unveiling of God as love and as Spirit; (2) there was a preparation for the Gospel among the Gentiles as well as among the Jews; (3) the Word of God is not to be identified too literally with the Bible as a whole, and the human element in Scripture, where secular matters are concerned, must be frankly acknowledged; (4) the Old Testament Prophets do not refer directly to the coming of Christ, their

---

94   John Muir, letter to W. Whewell, 6/8/1845, in E. Williams, II, pp. 390–1. That Muir was aware at this time of the need of a more conciliatory approach is a great credit to him, for such a realization came much later to most missionaries; as will be seen below in relation to Slater and Farquhar.

95   Williams, 1856, pp. 1–2.

96   Yet the same is just as true of Farquhar writing over fifty years later (see the discussion on this matter in chapter 7).

97   T. Thomas, p. 83.

98   See E. Williams, II, pp. 395–6, and Sambrook, p. 451. Is this not, perhaps, a general truth; that a truly deep and sympathetic understanding of another religious tradition will inevitably lead one on to a greater understanding of one's own religion?

immediate reference is to people and events in Jewish history; (5) questions of the date and authorship of the different books of the Bible are legitimate subjects for reverent enquiry; (6) the Gospel miracles are to be viewed as examples of divine beneficence rather than of mere power.[99]

Points three, four, and five are obviously related to what was said above about Williams' growing conviction that if he applies criticism to Hinduism he must do the same to the Bible. Number six can be seen as akin to an argument he adduces in favour of Christianity in *Christianity and Hinduism*, that the Gospel miracles are qualitatively different to those found in the Hindu sacred literature as they all have a purpose in being acts of divine compassion, or they have some teaching purpose rather than being merely gratuitous examples of omnipotence.[100] The relation of point two should be obvious.[101] Point one is related towards the method by which Williams allows a form of revelation to be active in Hinduism, of which more will be said below. Indeed, it is worth relating that these ideas are to be found in Williams' works outside of *Christianity and Hinduism*, as they help to show how they fit into his theology as a whole, whereas in the case of Maurice it was necessary to work more from inference to show how the non-Christian religions were related to his theology generally.[102]

ii) Fulfilment

Before going on to look at how Williams understood the way in which Christianity fulfils Hinduism, it is useful to note some of the examples where Williams believes Hindu conceptions are fulfilled by Christian conceptions. We can start with a correspondence that is used over and again in fulfilment

---

99 Scott, p. 119.
100 Williams, 1856, p. 358.
101 Incidentally, in 1857 Williams published a Greek mystery play, *Orestes and the Avengers*, which showed 'the religious feeling underlying heathen forms of worship' (E. Williams, I, p. 318).
102 On this point I would take issue with Thomas, who asserts that, 'neither Maurice nor Williams integrated their work on other religions into their own theology' (T. Thomas, in Parsons, II, p. 293). While this, as has been seen, is fair comment upon Maurice, Williams' own theology was influenced by his study of Hinduism, and, as noted above, he held *Christianity and Hinduism* to be his central work. Therefore, his views on the non-Christian systems, specifically Hinduism, were of necessity integrated into what he there says of Christianity.

theology, and has, for many people, not just advocates of fulfilment theology, formed one of the major links between these two religions; the doctrines of avatar and incarnation.

Concerning avatars, Williams says that whereas the Hindu myths are fables, the Christian myth of Jesus' incarnation is a fact, and is that which the Hindu myth foreshadows, 'Whatever then your poets have fabled of the Divine preserver's becoming incarnate in Ráma or Crishna, seem to me shadows of the truth, that the thought of the eternal Spirit must come to fulfilment in act[....]'[103]

Jesus' incarnation was necessary, Williams tells us, for us to 'know the counsel of Him whose thoughts are not as our thoughts[.... Else] we may bewilder ourselves in speculations about that which is above our senses.'[104] Further, Jesus' incarnation and death allowed him to express the divine love. Also, 'Jesus fulfilled by dying, not only the thing meant in ancient sacrifices, but the martyr-type, or the character of all godlike sufferers for the right and the good.'[105]

Williams' thought here is close to that of later fulfilment theologians, and this similarity extends further when he suggests, 'it is quite conceivable that by exhibiting the Divine thus clothed in humanity the supreme Íswara might have given us such an image of Himself, as would be a true medium of conceiving him, and as a blessed substitute for the idolatry which degrades.'[106] A similar sentiment is expressed by Farquhar and others.[107] This raises the question as to whether there is a transmission of this idea from Williams through a succession of later writers. Certainly there is no evidence to suggest this. However, in the context of fulfilment theology, the idea seems natural enough; thus it is not unreasonable to suggest that anyone could have come up with it. We may, however, bear the question in mind.

The other points suggestive of fulfilment to Williams need only be mentioned in passing. They are the notion that Jesus' resurrection is a fulfilment of the aspiration that man's faculties of reason and conscience may be 'raised' from a base level to a higher spiritual level.[108] Related to this is his

---

103   Williams, 1856, p. 359.
104   Ibid.
105   Ibid., p. 362.
106   Ibid., pp. 227–8.
107   See later chapters.
108   Williams, 1856, p. 524.

suggestion that the Sānkhya notion of spiritual bodies is actually a foreshadowing of the resurrection body.[109] Again, there is the notion of the trinity being related to the Hindu trimūrti, which in *Christianity and Hinduism*, he says, are only related by the coincidence of number,[110] yet in *Rational Godliness* he expands this idea to say that, 'the human mind is ever driven, by a kind of necessity, to something which at least resembles the Christian Trinity.'[111] The religious bath of the Hindus is mentioned (though only in parenthesis) as offering similarities to baptism.[112] Also, Williams suggests that the Hindu, specifically Advaita Vedāntin, belief that the human soul and Divine Spirit are one can be seen 'as obscurely meaning the great nearness of the Father of our spirits to all those who approach him in prayer, together with the true feeling, that every human excellence comes in a way of the Spirit of God.'[113] A final point, to be dealt with at greater length later, but which may be mentioned here, is what Williams sees as the correspondence of the Christian Logos to the Hindu vâch.[114] Having identified these areas of fulfilment in Williams' thought it is now necessary to understand what the nature of this fulfilment is.

Williams' understanding of fulfilment theology has many of the elements that come to be associated with the later expressions of this theory. In this regard his thought, while not systematically laid out, is far clearer than Maurice's.

Firstly, Williams states that God has made it natural for people to pray to him.[115] Concomitant with this is his belief that men innately need religion.[116] This belief is found from Maurice to Farquhar, and is one of the essential ideas of the nineteenth-century.[117] It is therefore an essential part of

---

109   Ibid., pp. 167–8.
110   Ibid., p. 293.
111   Op. cit., p. 276. In a contemporary review of Williams' work it is observed that other writers of his day had seen the trinity as an essential, even universal, feature of religion (Anon., 1857, p. 384).
112   Williams, 1856, p. 502.
113   Ibid., p. 295.
114   Ibid., pp. 100–1, and see below.
115   Ibid., p. 300.
116   Ibid., p. 549; see also Williams, 1855, p. 259, sermon XVIII, 'The Witness of God', preached in Cambridge, Advent Sunday, 1854.
117   See section on Morris.

true religion that it answers this need.[118] Indeed, it is partly from the constitution of man that religions develop:

> By the Spirit of God, then, I say, the ancient heroes founded kingdoms, and legislators devised laws, and the fair fabric of every science was reared, having had its twin foundations long ago laid, partly in the constitution of nature, and partly in the unfolding recesses of the human mind[....] Their very fables were born of this instinct. The Muse of the old poets, sacred as they deemed her, the Nymph who taught Numa his laws, the whispers in which father Jove counselled Scipio Africanus[...] are all more or less conscious witnesses to the same principle. Think not that all these things were, as bad men conclude, judging from themselves, gross impostures; but although the ill-trained aspirations settled down into religions so imperfect that we rightly call them false, still recognize in them some approximation to the truth.[119]

Here Williams reminds us of Maurice's words of there being 'that in man which demands a Revelation.'[120] Before looking at the way Williams sees 'revelation' operating within this system it will be useful to see what else he has to say on the concept of fulfilment.

Williams describes Hinduism as a 'sort of training,'[121] saying that God has raised up teachers in every land.[122] Also, he suggests that God undoubtedly scattered elements of truth throughout the world,[123] further suggesting God may have put 'good thoughts' in the minds of many men.[124] Thus, he can say that most men in the world are not opposed to God, but that they may be seen as his 'representatives.'[125] He is also ready to see developments within Hinduism as coming from God. As an example of this he says that Hindus were led away from blood sacrifices by a 'Divine' source.[126] Further, he says that all that is best in India should lead people to

---

118   'With whatever eloquence our platforms may ring, the Churches of England and Rome will ultimately stand or fall in proportion as they satisfy or disappoint the religious instincts of mankind' (R. Williams, letter to the Editor of the Evening Mail, 1851, E. Williams, I, pp. 189–90).

119   Williams, 1855, p. 217, sermon XV, 'The Spirit's Operation', Lampeter, 7/6/1851.

120   Boyle, p. 55.

121   Williams, 1856, p. 302.

122   Ibid., pp. 291 and 311.

123   Ibid., pp. 525 and 543.

124   Ibid., p. 540.

125   Williams, 1855, p. 212, sermon XV.

126   Williams, 1856, p. 320.

Christianity,[127] saying of the Hindu vâch that it is, 'not opposed to Christianity, but might rather prepare you for what we read in St John[....]'[128]

Finally, it is necessary to see how Williams compares Hinduism with Judaism as a form of training. Williams uses St Paul to compare Judaism to Hinduism, saying:

> He [St Paul] would speak of all caste and sect, as he spoke of the separate sanctity of the Jews[....] He would compare all your ancestral traditions to those of Moses, and deny that they give you a true righteousness of God[....]
> If you would read St Paul, comparing things that correspond among the Hindús and Hebrews, as for instance the old Brahmanical caste with the Levites, and the overgrown Law of Moses with your traditional system, and the new spiritual life which Christ breathed into the world with the attempts of reformers in India,[129] you would find St Paul's reasonings with the Jews apply often to yourselves.[130]

Beyond this Williams can say, '[....]Yet he would find many things in your religion leading up to a higher faith, or containing germs of it.'[131]

Yet Williams poses one further question, for while Judaism leads, in his mind, inevitably on to Christianity, he asks if the same is true of Hinduism?[132] His answer is that is does not lead there as surely as Judaism. His argument here is too long to be followed in detail, but is essentially that the whole history of Judaism is a steady development upwards. Hinduism, on the other hand, is marked by various false starts and changes, and so does not present a smooth and continuous demonstration of Divine Providence guiding it to a spiritual fulfilment.[133] The argument ranges over several discussions from chapter nine to the conclusion. This is entirely consistent with his Coleridgian belief in man's progress, for Coleridge himself believed that:

> The progress of the species neither is nor can be like that of a Roman road in a right line. It may be more justly compared to that of a river, which, both in its smaller reaches and its larger turnings, is frequently forced back towards its fountain which cannot otherwise

---

127   Williams, 1856, p. 353.
128   Ibid., p. 553.
129   He speaks particularly highly of Madhva, one of the main figures of Dvaita-Vedānta (ibid., pp. 177–8, 181, 198, and 267–8).
130   Ibid., pp. 379–80.
131   Ibid., p. 380.
132   Ibid., p. 387.
133   See, for instance, ibid., pp. 389, 443 f., and 534 f.

be eluded or overcome; yet with an accompanying impulse that will ensure its advancement hereafter[....][134]

iii) Revelation

In the previous section we noted the opinion of Terence Thomas that Maurice saw no trace of 'revelation' in the Indic religions. Just as I argued there that this is a misrepresentation of Maurice's thought, so I would suggest that unless carefully considered, Williams' assertion that Hinduism contained 'revelation' might also be misconstrued. The term 'revelation' when applied to Hinduism does not, for Williams, mean quite what it does in relation to Christianity. Thomas observes that, 'Williams did believe that other religions contained divine revelation, *though the meaning he gave to revelation may be deemed less than orthodox according to the norms of his age.*'[135] I would suggest that Williams' views are, in many ways, similar to Maurice's. However, we find the relation of these ides to Hinduism more clearly expressed by Williams. The similarity in this matter is undoubtedly due to the shared influence of Coleridge[136] and Hare.[137]

In examining Williams' understanding of revelation we begin with a passage near the beginning of the dialogue, where Williams makes the following point:

It is only, indeed, with some belief in revelation that we in Europe associate the term *religion*; though we do not deny that much natural piety may exist without such a belief; but then we should call any opinion respecting the Deity in this case a philosophy rather than a religion.[138]

To determine whether revelation resides within Hinduism, it is necessary to look at Williams' idea of revelation. Here we should consider his indebtedness to Coleridge and his ideas of religion as an inward faculty.[139]

---

134   Coleridge, *The Friend*, p. 362, quoted from Sanders, p. 56. These words describe most accurately Williams' beliefs about the progress of Hinduism.

135   Thomas, in Parsons, 1988 (b), p. 291, italics my own.

136   In particular *The Confessions of an Inquiring Spirit* and *Aids to Reflection*, (Owen, p. 59).

137   Jones, p. 43.

138   Ibid., p. 26.

139   See Sanders, pp. 48 ff.

Williams was also well acquainted with the German liberal tradition stemming down from Schleiermacher.[140] Thus, while much of *Christianity and Hinduism* is taken up with demonstrating the fallibility of the Hindu scriptures and defending the Christian, it is not in texts that Williams finds true revelation to reside.[141] Rather, Williams finds a new interpretation for revelation, new at least to many of his readers, so one of the characters in the dialogue is made to enquire if Williams views are as they appear, 'But still it is not clear to me, whether you have not shifted the idea of Revelation from its usually positive sense into a kind of spiritual growth, or something more nearly resembling some Indian theories of a Divine spirit pervading and elevating humanity.'[142] While Williams hints in other places that this is the doctrine of revelation he prefers, he also clearly states that he has adopted this interpretation. In a letter, relating to this book, Williams wrote '[I have made] *revelation* appear a more inward and mental process than we generally conceive it to be.'[143] What Williams said about Hindus having been led from blood sacrifices by 'Divine guidance'[144] is of relevance here, for this is an example of the 'Divine spirit pervading and elevating humanity' which has

---

140   Speaking of Schleiermacher Mackintosh says for him, '"You reject," we can hear him say, "the dogmas and propositions of religion. Very well reject them[....] You are right; we are children no longer; the time for fairy-tales is past. Only cast off as I do faith in everything of that sort, and I will show you miracles and revelations and inspirations of quite another species[....] What is revelation? Every new and original communication of the Universe to man; and every elemental feeling to me is inspiration. The religion to which I will lead you demands no blind faith, no negation of physics and psychology; it is wholly natural, and yet again, as the immediate product of the Universe, it is all of grace"' (Mackintosh, pp. 43–4).

141   In *Rational Godliness* Williams observes that the Bible is not the foundation of the Church but rather its 'creature,' (op. cit., p. 309, sermon XIX 'Servants of God Speaking as moved by the Holy Ghost', preached in Cambridge, Second Sunday in Advent, 1854) and also that, as there was a time when the Bible was not, it cannot, therefore, be necessary to salvation (ibid., p. 289). It was for denying the normative definition of Biblical inspiration that Williams was tried for heresy in the wake of *Essays and Reviews* (Parsons,1988(a), pp. 40 ff).

142   Williams, 1856, p. 522, Wolff speaking. Thomas points out this is not denied to suggest that it is therefore Williams' own view, (T. Thomas, p. 84) and elsewhere refers to this passages as evidence of what 'is believed to express Williams' own view of revelation' (Thomas, in Parsons, 1998(b), p. 291).

143   R. Williams, Letter to the Editor of the 'Journal of Sacred Literature', 26/11/1856, in E. Williams, II, p. 396.

144   Referred to above.

led not just Christians, but also non-Christians, in a continuing path of revelation. In relation to this we may note that in his *Psalms and Litanies* Williams translates (interprets) the Nicene Creed as saying, 'And I believe in the Spirit which is holy, supreme and life giving[...] which speaks by all holy men[...]'[145] Referring to this passage Jones says:

> The substitution of 'holy men' for 'prophets' is deliberate. Mindful of Clement's statement that philosophy was the pedagogue which brought the Greeks to Christ, as was the Law for the Jews, he still wanted to include the gentiles in the sphere of revelation, and this included Hindus.[146]

Divine inspiration is, then, to be found in all 'holy men'. It is not a particular aspect of the Judaeo-Christian heritage, nor did God direct the prophets and evangelists to write down His very words in a divine message to mankind.[147]

To answer the question as to whether this universal 'Divine inspiration' is 'revelation'[148] it is necessary to understand fully Williams' thought in this matter. This is a digression from the main work of this study; this account will therefore be very brief, just sketching over the surface of his thought. The answer to our question has a three-fold aspect, relating to his recognition of a Divine teaching within Hinduism, his Coleridgian heritage, and also his work on Biblical criticism. In terms of these three reasons I shall start with the last and work backwards.

Firstly, once the fallibility of the Bible was recognized,[149] there was a need for a new understanding of revelation from that common within the nineteenth-century, i.e. that revelation was, so to speak, a direct dictation from God to the Biblical authors. If the Bible was not, de facto, the 'words' of God, the process of revelation must have entailed some spiritual truths being transmitted to the Biblical authors, which they then expressed in their

---

145   R. Williams, op. cit., quoted in Jones, 1991, p. 76.
146   Jones, 1991, p. 77.
147   This question takes us beyond the scope of this work on to Williams' essay in *Essays and Reviews* and his other teachings on Biblical criticism.
148   It may be useful here to give a brief definition of revelation as generally conceived, 'In Christian theology the word is used both of the corpus of truth about Himself which God discloses and of the process by which His communication of it takes place[....] Traditionally, Protestants have held that all revelation is sufficiently contained in the Bible, Catholics that part is also found in the tradition of the Church' (Livingstone, p. 438).
149   See, Jones, 1991, chapter III, for an account of Williams' thought in this matter.

own words, according to the knowledge of the day.[150] Secondly, while Coleridge believed that the Bible contained all the truths necessary for salvation,[151] he also looked outside of the Bible (as well as the Church) for spiritual truth,[152] a point with which Williams would agree. Williams, realizing that there was a time before the Bible came into being felt impelled to say that it was, therefore, not necessary for salvation.[153] For Williams it was a continual process. Revelation was not to be found in books but in man's own inner life. Thus, the saints of the Christian Church were recognized to be messengers of revelation as well as the Bible.[154] Thirdly, if revelation was the preserve of all holy men, and did not just refer to what is found in the Bible, then it follows that Hindu holy men also had revelation. Revelation was therefore, 'the use of the intuition, or the 'reason' of Coleridge and Kant, as a means to perception of truth.'[155] It was, therefore, the natural prerogative of all men. This returns us to a distinction, mentioned already, between the world-view of the neo-Platonic liberals and, essentially, all other parties within the Church. To say that Maurice believes that non-Christians have revelation, in Williams' sense of the term, should almost to be taken for granted; for it is but the shared Coleridgian belief that man has a direct perception of the Spirit of God which dwells in man.[156] However, the revelation to Hinduism is, certainly for Williams and, also, it can be said, for Maurice, of a limited kind. While it may be 'revelation,' it is not as great a revelation as that given to the Jews,[157] nor is it the final revelation, given only in Christianity, i.e. the knowledge and experience of Jesus. Where Williams does differ from Maurice is that the former allows that God may be guiding mankind Providentially through revelation, while there was no suggestion in Maurice that there was any special pattern of preparation in the revelation amongst the non-Christian religions.

---

150   See, e.g., Williams, 1855, p. 297, sermon XIX.
151   Sanders, p. 82.
152   Ibid., p. 59.
153   Williams, 1855, p. 289, sermon XIX.
154   This is, I believe, an important part of what Sanders means when he says that Coleridge's purpose was to 'Catholicize Protestantism,' (Sanders, p. 33) he acknowledged the validity of tradition as an equal authority to the Bible, if not giving it a higher position.
155   Sanders, p. 14.
156   Boyle, pp. 195 ff.
157   See above.

Having seen, then, that Williams believes that there is revelation amongst the Hindus, it is now time to look at what Williams says of the Hindu.

iv) *Vâch, Logos, and the Holy Ghost*

Williams not only sees the Hindu vâch as an example of fulfilment, but appears to see it as one of Hinduism's highest doctrines. He first describes the Hindu doctrine of vâch and then says:

> While Vidyáchárya was uttering the last three or four sentences, Blancombe appeared to be listening most attentively, and yet to be lost half in wonder;[158] for he exclaimed to himself unconsciously, yet half aloud so that I could hear him, 'How wonderful! wonderful alike in its resemblance, and in that resembling so nearly, it still differs so much!'[159]

Further on in the dialogue he says, 'All that has been said about Vâch, as the voice of God creating, and about Máyá, as being the representation of the Divine thought by nature, appeared to me not only grand but credible, so far as it traces the visible world justly to creative Mind.'[160] Then, finally and most importantly, he says:

> Again your parable or history, of Vâch coming forth from Brahmá, is not opposed to Christianity, but might rather prepare you for apprehending what we read in St John, that the Word was with God, and was God, and that through the Word all things were born, and without it nothing began to be[....][161] With submission at least to wiser people, I do not think it a greater tampering with mixture of distinct systems, than the early Church doctors permitted themselves in setting forth the life of Christ after the phrase of Plato, if I say that your Vâch appears *a prophecy*, or expression, of the everliving Word of God.[162]

---

158   Perhaps, here we can imagine that Williams is describing his own first reaction to discovering the doctrine of vâch, fascinated and awed.

159   Williams, 1856, pp. 100–1.

160   Ibid., p. 215.

161   It may be mentioned in passing that the words Williams puts into Vidyáchárya's mouth concerning vâch, 'Besides Him nothing was yet, which since has been,' (ibid., p. 100) sound very similar to the words of St John's Gospel, 'without him was not any thing made that was made' (Jn, I: 3, Authorized Version). Without copying the exact pattern of the words Williams may have intended this to echo the language of the evangelist.

162   Ibid., pp. 553–4, italics my own.

Williams' reference to John's Gospel is worth noting, for Thomas suggests that his ideas of revelation imply some form of a Logos doctrine.[163] The importance of this for the development of fulfilment theology has already been referred to. However, while Williams certainly has something similar to a Logos theology, the term is, I believe, a misnomer in Williams' case. The reason for this is that while later Logos theologians say that it is through the Logos that the holy men of the non-Christian religions were inspired, the same is not true of Williams. Certainly he speaks of vâch as being 'a prophecy' of the Logos, but does not say that it is a description of the Hindu *experience* of the Logos.[164] It was noted above that Williams regarded non-Christian holy men to be inspired by the Holy Spirit.[165] Further, in *Rational Godliness*, when discussing the gifts of the Holy Spirit, he says that the first five (fear, wisdom, understanding, counsel, and ghostly strength) have been given to all good men,[166] but 'this sixth gift of right knowledge is reserved for those, who have known the light of the only-begotten Son.'[167] Williams seems, then, to have kept a distinction between the activity of the second and third members of the Trinity, the third member acting in the non-Christian religions, the second being known only to Christians, though foretold in prophecy.[168]

---

163   T. Thomas, p. 83. I have, of course, already argued something similar above with regards to Maurice.

164   Williams, 1856, p. 554.

165   See the reference to *Psalms and Litanies* above.

166   Op. cit., pp. 219 ff.

167   Ibid., p. 222.

168   There are certain implications in this, for while Williams, in a way, means much the same as many future Logos theologians, i.e., that while non-Christians have direct experience of God they do not know the person of Jesus Christ as the revealed Son of God in human form. He says that their knowledge is only of the Holy Spirit, while Logos theology says that there is a direct connection between non-Christian holy men and Jesus, in his form as the Word of God. This could result in a major difference if the Logos theology is placed in a system in which salvation is seen as being apart from the need for acceptance of certain dogmas, so no conscious acceptance of Jesus as God's son and in his atoning death is required; where salvation is seen to lie in being the experience of God's presence, and in following his will. Also, depending upon how it is interpreted, a true Logos theology might be seen as indicative of taking the religious experience of the non-Christian religions more seriously. While many may suggest that the non-Christian religions lack any true moral or spiritual power in their devotee's live, (see above), a Logos

It has been seen above that Williams considers there to be a revelation in Hinduism, the purpose of which is as a training for Christianity. The vehicle for this revelation is Williams' 'Logos' theology. This, however, only provides a limited revelation, and having so far emphasized what Williams has to say positively about Hinduism, we should now turn to look at what he sees as its negative aspects.

v) Criticisms of Hinduism

The question of the negative aspects of Hinduism need not be dwelt on at length. Only the major features of Williams' thought need consideration. While recognizing the presence of revelation, Williams is still content to say that Hinduism is a 'false' religion and Christianity a 'true' one.[169] He can also speak of the non-Christian religions as being essentially human products, 'One might say that Buddhism went before Christianity as a sort of rude prophecy of the methods by which the Truth should conquer, or as *a tentative groping of mankind* in the direction in which God was about to open for them a new and living way.'[170] Likewise, the Vedas were seen as a picture of a human searching for God.[171] As we noted above, Williams was prepared to say that God 'may have put good thoughts in the minds of many of your people,'[172] but that is all. For Williams, God did not direct Hinduism to the same degree as Judaism; what good there was being but scattered fragments. Thus Williams' 'Logos' theology can be called 'embryonic'. There may well be a universal religious sense, and the Holy Spirit may act through all men,

---

theologian accepting that the non-Christian has an experience of Jesus might be more willing to concede that this can give the necessary spiritual force to his life. However, it is by no means certain that this would be conceded. When compared to, for example, William Temple, Williams' theology is effectively no different from a Logos theology, therefore, I hope that it will not be considered inappropriate if, rather than use an equivalent term such as 'Spirit theology' (which could well be misunderstood), I shall refer to Williams as having a 'Logos' theology. Although I use the term with qualifications. Also, I shall in future chapters classify him as a 'Logos theologian' because, as can be seen by Thomas' reference to him as having a Logos theology, this is how he is generally perceived, and so, even if not technically correct it is how he has been understood.

169   Williams, 1856, p. 556.
170   Ibid., p. 530, italics my own.
171   Ibid., p. 541.
172   Ibid., p. 540.

but it does not inspire and give validity to the non-Christian religions as far as Williams is concerned. In considering Hinduism's merits Williams looked for two things, for there 'are chiefly two kinds of proof possible for a religion as Divine. One is external authority; the other, inward excellence.'[173] As noted, Williams believed that Hinduism fails on the first account.[174] As to the second, he observes that while there may be aspects of man's innate religious sense and signs of God's Spirit: 'He may in his unsearchable wisdom have taught mankind a more excellent way.'[175] Thus we come to, what is, for Williams, the essential difference between Christianity and Hinduism, a difference that is held to exist almost universally by all the writers we will consider. To quote further from the passage already quoted above, in which Williams sees Buddhism as a 'rude prophecy' of Christianity: 'You have noticed the resemblances; but do not forget the differences. Remember that we invite you to worship the living God; we show you in Christ the way of coming to Him, and promise you the help of His holy breathing to animate you in treading it.'[176] The same assertion is repeated elsewhere that only Christianity has 'regenerating' power to alter men,[177] Williams asserting:

> You acknowledge its [Hinduism's] weakness as a moral instrument, by your despair of improving men of low caste, or of unteaching them even idolatry. But that fancied wisdom in which you look down upon the ignorant, without effort to teach them, leaves your own souls barren, with the sensuous richness of the popular faith stript away, and with cold abstractions instead[....][178]

Like many of those who came after him, Williams did not believe that any religion, besides Christianity, had any genuine moral power to live in men's hearts and control their lives.[179] This, for Williams, was a central tenet of his Coleridgian belief system, 'In place of the external evidences he reiterates the

---

173 Ibid., p. 299.
174 Ibid., pp. 299 f.
175 Ibid., p. 300.
176 Ibid., p. 530.
177 Ibid., p. 449.
178 Ibid., pp. 552–3.
179 We may forgive this more readily in Williams than those such as Farquhar, Slater and Monier-Williams, all of whom had direct experience of the religious life of the Indian people. Williams, like many later fulfilment theologians, does admit that the non-Christian religions have some power in peoples lives, but there is never believed to be the same power there as is found in Christianity (see ibid., p. 548).

axiom of Coleridge that the true evidence of Christianity consists in its life-giving power.'[180]

However, we have already noted that Williams believed that non-Christians were, through the mediation of the Holy Spirit, given a certain 'ghostly strength,'[181] which acts:

By[...] touching our conscience, and by thus informing us both of our strength and weakness, – our strength when working with God, and our weakness when following lawless desires, – the Spirit becomes our Comforter and our fountain of ghostly strength.[182]

Yet he says that this gift of 'ghostly strength' is better seen as the 'earnest endeavour to seek it.'[183] Thus, while both Christian and non-Christian may struggle to follow God's will, only the Christian can truly succeed. The difference lies, so Williams believed, in the person of Jesus, whom we have seen Williams says is only accessible to Christians, 'For the religion of Christ is a living power. It is an unveiling to the soul of that which constitutes strength.'[184]

vi) Final Considerations

It would not, however, do to stress too heavily the negative aspects of Hinduism. Williams acknowledges that the rapid spread of Buddhism was no doubt due to some good in it.[185] While Buddhism and Hinduism may have many flaws, there is, to Williams, much in them that responds, even if only in a limited way, to man's innate religious needs. Williams is also ready to acknowledge the worth of other aspects of Indian religion and culture: he is happy to use the Indian term Īshvara to talk of God;[186] is ready to speak of the good qualities of certain Hindu practices such as building water tanks and planting trees for the benefit of travellers;[187] and he even acknowledges that

---

180   Jones, 1991, p. 46. See Sanders, pp. 48 ff.
181   See above.
182   Williams, 1855, p. 221, sermon XV.
183   Ibid.
184   Ibid., p. 236, sermon, XVI, 'Good Works Hitherto', Lampeter, 6/6/1852.
185   Ibid., p. 166.
186   See, e.g., ibid., pp. 189 and 235.
187   Ibid., p. 231.

many of Hinduism's metaphysical speculations 'might stand very well with Christianity, which is not hostile to any kind of truth.'[188] In allowing these points we may see Williams as expounding a form of proto-inculturation, which is very liberal for its day, especially as regards the last point.[189]

As a further example of Williams' fairness in dealing with Hinduism he does allow various criticisms to be levelled by the native religionists against Christianity.[190] However, as Thomas observes, all of the criticisms are made against a Calvinistic style of Christianity, and these criticisms are readily answered by Williams as being misinterpretations of what Christianity really teaches.[191]

There is one more point of particular interest in Williams' thought that should be mentioned. This is a theme which recurs both in Müller and Miller, where, particularly in the latter, the theory takes a more prominent role. The idea is that each of the non-Christian religions has its own particular genius which can all be harmonized within the mantle of Christianity:

> For it [Christianity] mediates and harmonizes between them [the non-Christian religions], adding to the strong belief of the Hebrew, something of the largeness of thought of the Hindú and of the heroic humanity of the Greek, while it sobers these with the household virtues of the Roman, and with the deeper sense of truth and right, which the Hebrew had in his consciousness of having to answer before the Judge of the whole earth.[192]

The same idea is alluded to in *Rational Godliness* where he suggests that Providence has guided history and literature, such that:

> [.... T]he ancient Greek manifested the sensitiveness of his organization and the activity of his mind by a literature moulded in beauty and full of speculation; and as the Roman, whose mission it was to civilize the world with law, spoke the firm language of history

---

188   Ibid., p. 553. This attitude of mind is one he attributes to St Augustine, 'No discovery can hurt Christianity; for whatever is true is Christian, as St. Augustine often taught' (R. Williams, *Hebrew Prophets*, volume II, p. 287, quoted in E. Williams, II, p. 225).

189   It will be seen in relation to Farquhar that he is much less tolerant of the fancies of Hindu metaphysical speculation. The question of how far Christianity should be made indigenous will be a theme we see repeated in the thought of many later fulfilment theologians.

190   See Williams, 1856, chapter XII.

191   Thomas, in Parsons, 1988 (b), p. 292.

192   Williams, 1856, p. 349.

and manly virtue; so the Hebrew, having been wonderfully trained, laid the wisdom of the Egyptians at the feet of Jehovah[....][193]

Quite what significance this has for Williams' thought as a whole is left unclear. Certainly he does not imply, as does Müller, that the characteristic of each religion will all add up to form a new religion. Indeed in *Christianity and Hinduism* he seems to suggest that all of these properties are fulfilled in Christianity; whatever is best in each of them is found in Christianity alongside the best of the other non-Christian religions. The idea can be seen as having its origin in Hegelian thought, where the genii of particular religions are the thesis and antithesis which come together in the synthesis.[194]

Conclusion

A great deal of what was to become known as fulfilment theology was seen to be present in Maurice. These elements are, if anything, even clearer in Williams. It has also been observed that Williams considered Hinduism as a form of training, which is one of the essentials of the classical exposition of fulfilment theology. Further, Williams' fulfilment theology can definitely be seen as 'evolutionary' in the way that Sharpe suggests is necessary for Farquhar's fulfilment theology.[195] For Williams, Hinduism represents a 'lower' religion which finds its tenets transcended by a 'higher' religion, i.e. Christianity, and also Christianity meets far more successfully and fully the needs of the man as a religious animal. Williams, then, predates Monier-Williams' exposition of fulfilment by at least twenty or thirty years.[196] Also Williams, like Farquhar, recognized the need for sound historical groundwork[197] and so predates Farquhar as not only the first proponent of what may be called a fully developed fulfilment theology, but also in combining fulfilment theology with the highest level of scholarly knowledge available. Certainly, this method of apologetic is not Williams' aim; the main

---

193   Williams, 1855, pp. 295–6, sermon XIX.
194   See, e.g., Hegel, pp. 88–9. See previous chapter, on Hegel's connection to evolution as a concept in fulfilment theology.
195   Fulfil, pp. 52, 189 f., and 200.
196   Whom Sharpe suggests is the first exponent of fulfilment theology (Fulfil, pp. 52–3).
197   Williams, 1856, p. 238.

concern is to show the reliability of the Christian scriptures over those of the Hindus in historical terms, but he gives a full enough account of what has become known as fulfilment theology.

The main difference between Williams' work and that of later fulfilment theologians is, I would suggest, more to do with the usage of critical language. We should bear in mind that *Christianity and Hinduism* was intended for use as a missionary work,[198] in this its purpose was to undermine rather than directly assault Hinduism.[199] However, as we have noted, Williams nevertheless feels free to say that Christianity is true and Hinduism false,[200] language which Slater or Farquhar would have never dreamt of employing for fear of causing offence, especially later on in the face of the Hindu revival. The fact that he was writing in the days of the Hindu renaissance,[201] Rām Mohan Roy it should be remembered had been dead for twenty-three years when *Christianity and Hinduism* was published, meant that Williams' apologetic would be different to Farquhar's. It can be seen that while the characters in the dialogue are not in favour of abolishing caste and idolatry, they make no argument in favour of the latter,[202] and Williams feels able to say, 'All moralists or philosophers allow, that prayer to one eternal and life-giving Spirit is better than idolatry[....]'[203] While Farquhar is not any more in favour of idolatry, he needed to emphasize its purpose in his fulfilment paradigm, rather than to say openly with Williams that Hindus should shun 'the idolatry which degrades.'[204] Despite the differences, then, *Christianity and Hinduism* can be seen as almost a first draft of *The Crown of Hinduism* but written fifty years earlier. Its emphasis is different but the ideas behind it are very similar, and it is, in its own right, a scholarly work of the highest

---

198 See R. Williams, letter to the Editor of the *Journal of Sacred Literature*, 26/11/1856, in E. Williams, II, p. 398.
199 Ibid., pp. 390–1.
200 Williams, 1856, p. 556.
201 It should be noted here that throughout this work I will use the term Hindu renaissance to refer to the mid to late nineteenth-century when the influence of such movements as the Brahmō Samāj were at their height, and the Hindu revival to refer to the later part of the nineteenth and early twentieth-century when the theosophists and Vivekananda were most influential. The thought and influence of these two periods will be considered in chapter 4.
202 Williams, 1856, p. 226.
203 Ibid., p. 547. Quite conceivably a reference, at least in part, to the leaders of the Hindu Renaissance.
204 Ibid., pp. 227–8.

order. Although, as Thomas notes, it has gone unacknowledged as an early expression of fulfilment theology.[205]

Richard Chevenix Trench

It is not my intention to dwell at length upon Trench's theology. He belonged to the same tradition of Cambridge men as Rowland Williams and Maurice.[206] His thought in this matter lacked the popularity of Maurice's, or the depth of Rowland Williams', so I shall just dwell upon it briefly; though saying this, I do not wish to undermine its importance. The fact that he wrote as he did gives further evidence of the defusion of such ideas in the Cambridge school of the mid 1840s. Also, at least one important later figure acknowledges him as a source for their ideas.[207] In view of the above we may ask the question here, already implicit in what has been said; how far the early Cambridge writers on fulfilment theology influenced one another? It is a question we can only speculate on, but is worth bearing in mind.

Trench's writings upon this matter are to be found in his Hulsean Lectures for 1846. These have the most revealing title, *Christ the Desire of all Nations, or the Unconscious Prophecies of Heathendom.*

In the first lecture he says that he wishes to leave aside the preparations to be found in Jewish revelation,[208] concentrating instead on 'the implicit expectations which were in the heathen world... for a redeemer.'[209] Hopes which, he says, could only be met in 'the true Redeemer.' Jesus is only conceived of 'worthily', he says, when we see him, 'as "the Desire of all nations" – the *fulfiller* of the world's hopes.'[210] Yet he wishes to stress that mere parallels between Christianity and the non-Christian religions are 'groundless and mythical'[211] when used to show that the teachings of the

---

205   T. Thomas, p. 85.
206   See Cross, p. 1373.
207   Lefroy, see chapter 5.
208   Trench, pp. 2–3.
209   Ibid., p. 3.
210   Ibid., p. 19.
211   Ibid., p. 9.

Christian faith were to be found previously in other religions. This is a ploy often used, he says, by the Church's enemies.[212] Instead of being signs that Christianity is not unique he argues that the 'expectations', as he calls them, show 'the transcending worth and dignity of the Christian revelation not being diminished by their existence, but rather enhanced.'[213] That Trench feels the need to make this point can be taken as evidence that the sorts of parallels exploited by himself, Maurice, Rowland Williams, and others were not merely something acknowledged by those who wished to show that Christianity transcended the non-Christian religions. That conservative thinkers such as Morris and Duff[214] also acknowledge the similarities, indicates that the knowledge and influence of the non-Christian religions was exerting a considerable influence by this time.[215] The idea that 'parallels' were becoming part of the common intellectual property of the 1840s explains the appearance of these works. Perhaps also why they share similar views, was that such ideas, we may deduce, had been discussed and in circulation, orally at least, for some while previously.

Trench reserves comment on whether prophecy be reserved for the Jewish hope alone, saying of the 'expectations' of other nations that, 'we may call them the world's divination at the least.'[216] Trench barely discuss specific examples, speaking mainly in general terms of 'the hope which the world has cherished of redeemers and saviours.'[217] Where he does use examples, he gives them but brief mention to make particular points. That the Greek gods are portrayed in human form is, he says, a realization 'that if God did reveal himself, it would be as man,'[218] and, interestingly, he speaks of this as being a prophecy of the Incarnation, though the gods, he says, are only 'weak prophecies.'[219] Like Maurice and Rowland Williams, Trench appears to believe that 'revelation' was available outside of the Jewish and Christian traditions. Although he speaks cautiously of this matter, he is not prepared to

---

212   Ibid., p. 5. He notes Celsus, and the historian Gibbon, as examples of those who use such tactics.
213   Ibid., pp. 3–4.
214   Duff, 1839(a), pp. 179 ff. For Morris, see next section.
215   See J. J. Clarke, Part II, who demonstrates the often unacknowledged influence of Eastern religious thought on the West.
216   Ibid., p. 25.
217   See ibid., pp. 26 ff.
218   Ibid., p. 49.
219   Ibid., pp. 49–50.

say that such 'revelation' is equal to that of the Jewish tradition. Another example he uses is the worship that was offered to the Persian king, being indicative of the idea that God's presence would be known, and that he would not be distant.[220] Speaking of this as exhibiting man's needs, Trench observes, 'Humanity, however it craved a God for its deliverer, yet craved just as earnestly a man.'[221] To develop the theme of man's needs being answered by Christianity, Trench stated that the Gospel met and gave expression to man's religious desires.[222]

Trench not only saw Christianity answering to man's heart-felt wants, but also saw the non-Christian religions as offering prophecies of divinations of the God who was to come.[223] The whole fitted in his thought in an evolutionary schema:

> We have asked ourselves whether we could not discern an evident tendency of men's thoughts and feelings and desires in one direction, and that direction the cross of Christ, – a great spiritual current, which has been strongly and constantly setting that way, so that his bringing forth of his kingdom into open manifestation, if in one sense a beginning, was in another, and in as true a sense, a crowning end.[224]

Although just speaking generally, Trench does, nevertheless, provide a clear example of a form of fulfilment theology, speaking of mankind's desires and religions all finding their culmination in Christianity and the person of Jesus. We may end with one last quote which aptly sums up all of his thought in this matter:

> And it shall seem to us then, as if that Star in the natural heavens which guided those Eastern sages from their distant home, was but the symbol of many a star which twinkled in the world's mystical night, but which yet, being rightly followed, availed to lead humble and devout hearts from far off regions of superstition and error, till they stood beside the cradle of the Babe of Bethlehem, and saw all their weary wanderings repaid in a moment, and all their desires finding a perfect fulfilment in Him.[225]

---

220   Ibid., p. 51.
221   Ibid., p. 57, see also p. 45.
222   Ibid., p. 111.
223   Worth quoting in this regard are his words, 'I have undertaken to trace the yearnings of this whole world after its Redeemer, the presentiments of Him which it had' (ibid., pp. 85–6).
224   Ibid., pp. 147–8.
225   Ibid., pp. 169–170.

John Brande Morris

Introduction

Jack Morris[226] sits rather incongruously besides Maurice, Rowland Williams and Trench in this chapter, not just in his approach to the non-Christian religions, but also in his life and beliefs. While the other three are best described as liberal Broad Churchmen,[227] Jack Morris was very conservative in his theology.[228] He belonged to the Tractarian party, becoming, in time, a convert to Rome,[229] though he wrote the work to be considered here while still within the Anglican Church.[230] He lacks the standing of Rowland Williams or Maurice as a theologian, yet this is not to demean his abilities in that direction, as we are comparing him alongside, arguably, the two greatest figures in nineteenth-century English theology. We should note that Newman, the only other English theologian of the period to rank alongside Maurice and Williams, wrote highly of him to Archbishop Cullen:

> He was the first Syriac scholar in Oxford, and one of the first Hebraists. He is a man of genius – besides a great talent for languages, (for I think he knows French, Italian, and German, perhaps Welsh [!], besides the classical languages) he is a metaphysician, a poet, a carpenter, and a chemist.[231]

---

226   As he was generally known (see, e.g., J. H. Newman, letter to F. Wilfrid, 21/8/1850, in Dessain, p. 47, or Faber, p. 417).

227   We may note that Maurice in particular did not wish to see himself as the member of any party within the Church (Sanders, pp. 11 f.). Whether what has become known as the 'Broad Church' formed a party in any meaningful sense is a moot point (ibid., pp. 7 ff.).

228   In contrast to the 'heretical' Biblical critic Williams, Morris refers to the Christian scriptures as being, 'infallibly true' (Morris, p. 23).

229   He converted on the 16th January 1846 (*Dictionary of National Biography*, p. 100).

230   Speaking of his gaining this prize essay, one writer refers thusly to him, 'Mr. Morris, of Exeter College, a gentleman of great learning whose subsequent defection to Church of Rome we have had to lament' (Anon., 1857, p. 363).

231   Op. cit., 28/4/1851, in Dessain, p. 267.

The range of Morris' learning can be seen in the prize essay to be considered here, where, in the published form, over half of the text of the entire book is given over to his copious notes. The essay was originally submitted containing the references alone, the bulk added for publication.[232] It is fair to say that he is now little more than a footnote in the history of the Oxford Movement, perhaps best remembered for his eccentric views and, at times, excessive behaviour. Beyond being regarded as a member of 'the extreme section of the so-called Tractarian party,'[233] he was, 'Eccentric in appearance and manner, he was brimful of genuine and multifarious learning, but so credulous that he seriously believed in the existence of the Phœnix.'[234]

As to his behaviour, he was keen upon a strict religious discipline, verging on self-mortification, and so it is recorded:

> During his [Newman's] absence Jack Morris[...] had taken the pulpit at St. Mary's. 'What does he do' complained Newman to Bowden 'on St. Michael's day but preach a sermon, not simply on angels, but on his one subject, for which he has a monomania, of fasting; nay, and say that it was a good thing, whereas angels feasted on festivals, to make the brute creation fast on fast days: so I am told. May he (salvis ossibus suis) have a fasting horse next time he goes steeple-chasing.[235]

In accordance with these ideas he once, with a colleague, determined to eat nothing but dried peas, soaked in a little water until just soft enough to eat, throughout Holy Week. So it was that towards the end of the week he was found collapsed and unconscious in his room.[236]

Turning to the work to be considered here, *An Essay Toward the Conversion of Learned and Philosophical Hindus*, it had neither the popularity of Maurice's nor the profound and scholarly knowledge of Hinduism shown by Williams'.[237] Neither is it a foreshadowing of what would

---

232   Morris, pp. vii–viii.
233   *Dictionary of National Biography*, p. 99.
234   Ibid.
235   Faber, p. 417.
236   Boase, p. cli.
237   However, it 'displays both learning and ability' (*Dictionary of National Biography*, p. 100) even if not the sympathy and understanding of Hinduism in Williams. Referring to it, Williams seems to imply that it did not meet the mark expected of it in regard to its being a learned work on Hinduism, 'A similar prize (i.e., that awarded to Morris) had before been given to the University of Oxford; but the result

later become known as fulfilment theology.[238] Indeed, Morris' essay might be seen as the antithesis of the two later works, as will be seen below. However, it is for this reason that it is of interest to us, for it holds 'traces'[239] of ideas found in fulfilment theology that we will see recurring in later writers.

Morris' essay was intended to be written with the aim of converting 'learned and philosophical' Hindus, and to this end Morris, like Williams after him, used the form of a dialogue. There are four dialogues, between two figures, Laurence, who is not introduced to us,[240] and Ra'dha'ka'nt[241] whom Laurence tells us is a Brahman.[242] The text appears as a straight conversation in which Laurence does most of the talking, the other mainly asking questions.[243] Having introduced Morris' essay, the main themes, of relevance here, will now be considered.

---

had not satisfied the munificent donor. I must *try* to be more successful; and, indeed, I do hope and intend (if possible) to make it a regular standard work, which men shall read for ever' (R. Williams, letter to his father, 26/1/1848, in E. Williams, I, p. 140). The donor of this prize was anonymous, it being offered through the Bishop of Calcutta. However, it may be surmised that the donor could have been John Muir, who offered the prize to Cambridge University (the prize Williams gained), as he desired to offer this prize through the Bishop of Calcutta (see J. Muir, letter to W. Whewell, 6/8/1845, in E. Williams, II, p. 388). In this letter Muir states that he wants 'to procure the composition of a *really good Treatise* on the Evidences of Christianity, in a form suited for Hindús, together with a refutation of their own erroneous tenets' (ibid., italics my own). Muir's insistence upon a first rate piece might also be suggested as indicative that *he* was unsatisfied with the response to *his* first prize). If being, as Williams notes above, unhappy with the first essay from Oxford then he may well have offered a second prize to Cambridge. Also, we may note that as Williams was aware that the donor of the first prize was unhappy with the Oxford essay, it might suggest that he knew something about this anonymous donor's wishes and thoughts, which, if the person were in India, as the offering of the prize through the Bishop of Calcutta would suggest, then this also may suggest to us that it would be Muir. However, this remains speculation, my enquiries to Exeter College, Oxford, have revealed that they have no further information on the prize other than that on the frontispiece of Morris' essay.

238   Just how Maurice and Williams 'foreshadow' fulfilment theology will be seen in the next two sections.
239   To echo Morris' own language.
240   Though presumably an English missionary.
241   Spelt later on in the dialogue as Rádhákánt.
242   Morris, p. 3.
243   In all quotations herein from Morris' work it is Laurence who is talking.

Like many people in the nineteenth-century, Morris believed that mankind had originally had one religion. This was preserved by the people of Shem,[244] i.e. the Jews, while other nations fell away from this. This explains why, for Morris, in many instances, the same belief is found scattered amongst the world's religions, such as the belief in there being but one God.[245] This theory is somewhat different from what is generally meant by fulfilment theology, i.e. as Farquhar uses it, for the beliefs shared in common are not a form of training or schooling from God given to each nation, and placed in the minds of men to prepare them for Christianity, rather they are half remembered fragments of an original revelation.[246] So, for example, Hinduism is not itself a religion built around certain truths which is itself a preparation for Christianity, but is rather a shadowy and faulty form of a revelation which men have forgotten or fallen away from. While this can be put into the context of fulfilment theology, as Monier-Williams does, it is a different form of fulfilment theology from the 'classical' expression of Farquhar. However, these similarities are not used in this way by Morris, for while he says that particular angels have intervened to ensure that certain fundamentals are preserved,[247] he also says that evil spirits are responsible for inserting other semblances to the true doctrines.[248] Thus similarities, far from being a training for the truth, might rather be there to pervert the minds of men:

> [T]hey [the evil spirits] seem to have been specially careful to put into men's minds sundry doctrines of incarnations throughout the world[....] Of these, that of Chrishna has in it certain points calculated to deceive[.... W]hich bear a rude likeness to the accounts of Him who was really incarnate.[249]

---

244   Morris, p. 152.
245   Ibid., p. 25.
246   See chapter 1.
247   Ibid., p. 22.
248   Ibid., p. 152–3.
249   Ibid., p. 153. He continued by saying, 'Other things might also be mentioned; but I am afraid of comparing things sacred to me, even in this way, with things which to me, of course, when so compared, cannot be else than profane.'

Morris believed that the evil spirits needed to base all the errors upon some truth.[250] This is indicative of the idea common to the fulfilment theologians that man is an innately religious animal. Thus, for any truth to take hold upon a person, it must answer some inbuilt need. Indeed, Morris even suggests that:

> Neither do I know that it would be wrong to think that where he [Satan] found he could get no hold of some virtuous heathen, he may have left him unmolested with the purpose of letting him serve the better to deceive others, who should mistake such a man for the true Messiah, the great pattern of all holiness.[251]

Thus similar concepts are at work here, which were common currency in the nineteenth-century. However, we must note that the understanding of this idea is radically different.

Two further instances in which Morris sees certain truths expressed – again in the form, or so Morris believed, of false doctrines – should be mentioned. The first of these two is metempsychosis. This, according to Morris, is an expression of the truth that whenever a man commits an evil action he is more prone so to sin again.[252] Yet this similarity is not, for Morris, a devilish trick, as he believed the Hindu doctrine of incarnation to be, rather, he says:

> Your own doctrine of metempsychosis is but one great and cumbrous expression of the plain truth, that the commission of sinful acts entails upon a man a necessity of sinning again, unless there be a very vigorous exertion of moral principle upon his part.[253]

Indeed it would be a perfectly natural use of the term to say that Christianity 'fulfils' the idea of metempsychosis in Morris' thought.[254] Yet, as I have noted, Morris is not suggesting a scheme of fulfilment theology as it is generally perceived.[255] However, what he says here would not be out of place

---

250   'Still, as far as I know, all error depends upon some truth for its subsistency' (ibid., p. 343).
251   Ibid., p. 161.
252   Ibid., p. 355.
253   Ibid.
254   Christianity providing within itself, so Morris would feel, a less 'cumbrous expression of the plain truth.'
255   Fulfilment theology of course requires the notion that this idea is placed as a 'preparation,' for Christianity, which is why I suggest the sometimes used term 'preparationism' instead of 'fulfilment theology' is, perhaps, less of a misnomer.

in the work of a fulfilment theologian, for while he does not say this conception exists as a form of training, it could come close to that. Yet, still, there is a subtle difference, for this doctrine does not, in Morris' system, reveal a religious truth, but it rather expresses a fact of psychology;[256] bad habits enforce themselves upon us, and it is thus not a preparation for a certain doctrine of Christianity. Rather, it is the expression of a certain matter of experience, which he believes finds a more straightforward expression in the Christian West.[257] There is, then, some limited sense of 'fulfilling' here, but there is no suggestion of 'preparation' as the purpose of the concealed truths. If anything quite the reverse: 'These great doctrines of which I have been speaking [i.e. the doctrines of Christianity], are the more marvellous because there are traces of them throughout the world, and because when known they show upon what truth these diabolical imitations were founded.'[258]

One further doctrine can be mentioned, which is related to metempsychosis, and which is man's pre-existence. The truths Morris believes lie behind this, though they are 'disguised by the evil spirit, the father of this error'[259] and are, firstly, that God chose the saved before creation,[260] and secondly, the knowledge of the fall.[261] I mention this doctrine because of what else Morris has to say about it, for this reflects his attitude as a whole. Pre-existence, Morris says, is 'too perfect a theory to be a true theory.'[262] What he means by this is that it is an attempt to explain the differences in men's positions in the world, some better off, some worse off. This, he obviously believes, it does well, but, or so he says, experience teaches us that we can't know everything about anything, and he invokes Aristotle to says that the vastness of creation means that we cannot have any all encompassing

---

256 This idea is found in Aristotle, here we may recall what was said in the introduction to this chapter about the difference between the Cambridge Platonists and the Oxford Aristotelians (see, Aristotle, Nicomachean Ethics, II, i, and III, v, 16–19).

257 As will be seen in Farquhar and others reincarnation is seen as expressing the idea that people suffer for their sins, and is therefore seen as being fundamentally religious (see Crown, pp. 135–6).

258 Morris, p. 368–9.

259 Morris, p. 343.

260 Ibid.

261 Ibid., p. 344.

262 Ibid., p. 187.

theory to explain things.[263] It is, he says, an attempt to form rules for the world and is therefore, in effect, blasphemy.[264] There is in this a certain anti-intellectualism, which goes against the spirit of his contemporaries Maurice and Williams.[265] All three acknowledge certain similarities between Christianity and the non-Christian religions, but Morris' response is to fight against Hinduism, and place it into a preconceived category, as a false religion. Whilst, as we have seen, both Maurice and Williams saw the non-Christian religions as essentially 'false.' This judgement is made on very different grounds, and they mean something very different despite using the same phrase.

One important point to be noted here, is that fulfilment theology shared with conservatives, such as Morris, certain common ideas of the nineteenth-century,[266] in a way doing little more than putting a more favourable gloss

---

263   Ibid., p. 188, and p. 255 (note 89) where he says, 'Aristotle, in his Metaphysics, p. 993. b. 6,[...] notices the vastness of the system of things, as creating such difficulties.' Again we may note Morris' reference to Aristotle.

264   Ibid., p. 336.

265   As well as, I might add, fear. The impression given is that he recognizes in pre-existence an answer to a problem which Christianity cannot give, hence his vehement diatribe against it, the idea of a theory being 'too perfect' to be true suggests a certain desperation, as well as acknowledging that he cannot find flaw in it. Whereas elsewhere he seeks reasoned arguments, of greater or lesser success, against Hinduism, here, he seems to feel that Hinduism has the high ground, and so his answer is a flight from reason to blind assertion and ignorance.

266   I.e., that there are similarities between religions, or, as noted earlier, the need for any viewpoint to be grounded in a certain amount of truth. To give another example of ideas shared in common, we may note that Morris says that, to him, the strongest argument for any religion is the effect it has upon the lives of its devotees (Morris, pp. 356–7). The same will be seen in both Maurice and Williams, and continues to be repeated throughout the nineteenth-century, and, indeed, into the twentieth by many Christian commentators on the non-Christian faiths. This 'common view' cannot, however, be said to be used in a very 'liberal' sense in fulfilment theology, in that it is often used to 'prove' the superiority of Christianity over the non-Christian religions which were felt to lack the power that Christianity had to change lives and truly infuse its devotees with moral strength. This point, mentioned in relation to Williams, is one repeated constantly, see, for instance, the reports of the Edinburgh conference in which this is a constant factor (Ed. IV, e.g., pp. 72, 78–79, 81, and 90 ff.). However, it should be borne in mind that some limited spiritual power was generally held to reside within the non-Christian religions, and thus the argument that the spiritual life of a religion proved its worth could be used by 'liberals' as a counter to those who said that the non-Christian religions were utterly

upon certain ideas that more conservative thinkers would be happy to accept.[267]

From what has been said above it might be supposed that Morris' essay was wholly negative in tone and character, but he says his aim is to 'enter into your [i.e. Hindu] ways of thinking.'[268] Indeed, in places he does show a surprisingly leniency, notably towards India's holy men, for speaking of them, he says:

> You have seen, Rádhákánt, how it may be that in your ancient books there is kept up a part of an ancient tradition, which contains the true doctrine, more or less disfigured: and one reason why so much of it has kept up in India, doubtless was the austere habits of your ancient seers[....] I have said that your ancient sages, through Tapas, attained to the sight of much holy truth, being fitted for the transmission of it from the discipline they observed, and able to see and understand it.[269]

Generally the austerities of India's sadhus were frowned upon by Christian writers,[270] but we have already noted Morris' own penchant for fasting and penance.[271] Thus, while others looked at such things in disgust, Morris found something admirable in the self-sacrifice and discipline of these men.[272]

---

corrupt (see, ibid., pp. 282 and 283).

267   See particularly the chapter on Farquhar in which it is argued that he was essentially an evangelical conservative in his thought.

268   Morris, p. 15.

269   Ibid., p. 143.

270   Consider, for instance, Farquhar (Crown, p. 295).

271   See above.

272   The idea of ascetic discipline was reintroduced by High Churchmen such as Morris,having fallen by the wayside in English Christianity by the nineteenth-century, as the response to Pusey's 'temperately and persuasively argued' Tract on baptism shows, 'The Tract was received with a good deal of indignant or derisory criticism. "I was not prepared" wrote Pusey to Newman[...] a few days after its appearance "for people questioning, even in the abstract, the duty of fasting; I thought serious minded persons at least supposed they practised fasting in some way or other. I assumed the duty to be acknowledged, and thought it only undervalued." Dr. Arnold was much alarmed by the Tract. He thought that fasting belonged "to the antiquarianism of Christianity – not to its profitable history"[....] More insidious was a comment of the Provost of Oriel. Pusey, who had been ill all winter, was due to preach on January 19 in the Cathedral. He was unable to appear in the pulpit; his sermon was read for him by the Archdeacon. "He must," said Hawkins, "have been fasting too much"' (Faber, pp. 353–4). If even the suggestion of moderate fasting was seen as perverse it is not surprising that many English

There is little else that we need remark upon in Morris. His condemnation of idolatry[273] is to be expected, and the similarities he finds between Moses' Law and that of the Hindus needs no extra comment.[274] Morris also observes that all nations have some 'traces' of the doctrine of the trinity.[275] As a final note we may observe that, amongst the non-Christian religions, Morris regarded the religions of the Chaldeans, Persians, Indians and Chinese as being the closest to Christianity; the Chinese holding, he says, a better system than the Indian. However, most interestingly, Morris goes on to say, in contradistinction to many others, for instance Rowland Williams (who sees the Buddha as a great reformer of Hinduism), that:

> Your country [India] it was who corrupted all the nations with the doctrines of Buddha, – doctrines that have been, and perhaps I may say are, in one way or another, the basework of the most pernicious heresies that were ever wielded by the evil spirit against the kingdom of GOD and His Christ.[276]

In conclusion, Morris, while not figuring in the history of the development of fulfilment theology, does, nevertheless, provide some important comparisons with those who do. The similarities, as well as the differences, should help to highlight some of the facets of nineteenth-century thought that lead to the development of fulfilment theology.

Christians were shocked by the Indian austerities, however, such practises as fasting would become more commonplace as the influence of the Oxford Movement spread. Few, however, would take it to the extremes of Joseph Lyne (better known as Fr Ignatius), in whose semi-monastic community penances were harsh, 'The women were to lie prostrate in ashes on the chapel floor; the elder men were to present themselves before the congregation carrying a stinking candle made of 'tallow dip'; and the younger men were to be publicly caned by Ignatius on the altar steps[....]

[.... The] penance for breaking the solemn silence... [was] to trace a cross on the ground with their tongues' (Palmer, pp. 217 and 218). We may observe, however, that Fr Ignatius did face something of a mutiny over the imposition of the last penance mentioned (see ibid.).

273   See, Morris, e.g., p. 160.
274   Ibid., pp. 27 f.
275   Ibid., p. 365.
276   Ibid., p. 370.

3 Comparative Religion

Monier Monier-Williams

Monier-Williams, perhaps surprisingly for a scholar of comparative religion, was throughout his life a staunch evangelical Christian.[1] He was not, though, as hostile to the non-Christian religions as some others of this persuasion,[2] It has, however, been suggested that, later on in his career, he repudiated all he had previously said or written that expressed a positive attitude towards the non-Christian religions.[3] The validity of this suggestion, which I would dispute, will be considered towards the end of this chapter. Whatever the case, it was his positive assessment of the non-Christian religions that were to be influential for later fulfilment theologians.[4] This influence was of a distinctive character. Before discussing Monier-Williams' thought, his particular significance in the history of fulfilment theology should be mentioned.

Where Monier-Williams differs from such figures as Rowland Williams, or Maurice, was in being a known evangelical. He could therefore propagate the theory of fulfilment to a much wider, and wholly different, audience. As Sharpe observes, 'Monier-Williams[...] did much to introduce a more sympathetic attitude to Hinduism into areas in which it was previously little known,'[5] areas which would generally be hostile to the liberal tradition.

---

1   Fulfil, p. 49.
2   Thus even the evangelical Monier-Williams was criticized by the evangelical party. One reviewer of his book *Indian Wisdom* wrote, 'a student wholly ignorant of India would with difficulty gather that the religion of India is, and has been for many centuries, naked idolatry of the most gross and vulgar description, little superior to that of savages in Central Africa' (quote from the *Church Missionary Intelligencer*, V (N.S.), 1880, p. 220 in Fulfil, p. 28).
3   It is related that at the Church Missionary Society meeting at which he is generally considered to have announced this fact (see Fulfil, pp. 52–3, and below) that a 'roar of delight' (quoted from Stock, III, p. 303) burst forth at the end of his speech.
4   Fulfil, p. 54. More will be said below on the reasons for this change.
5   Fulfil, p. 49.

Propounded by Monier-Williams 'liberal' thought could penetrate conservative circles.[6] Having now mentioned Monier-Williams' particular influence, we will discuss his thought.

Evolution

First, we need to look at the concept of 'evolution'. Monier-Williams, Sharpe suggests, gives the final form to fulfilment theology with the concept of 'evolution', in that he envisions religions giving way to one another in an evolutionary process.[7] I will, however, suggest below, his usage is not something new. Evolution, along with the historical-critical method, were the two keystones of all the developments of Victorian thought. Both were important in the development of a more tolerant attitude towards the non-Christian religions, but it is the idea of evolution that concerns us here.[8] We have already quoted from Sharpe's assessment of what Monier-Williams meant by fulfilment theology,[9] but here we may quickly recapitulate. Monier-Williams, Sharpe says, gave two meanings to 'fulfilment'. First, that it was evolutionary, 'higher' religions replacing 'lower' religions; and, second, that Christianity, as the highest religion, is that which satisfies the needs of all men. Sharpe ends this description with the words, 'There can be no doubt that here we have a primary source of the missionary theory of the later 'fulfilment school' in India.'[10]

Before discussing Monier-Williams' thought further, something should be said about the use of the term 'evolution' in the context of fulfilment. In evangelical circles the term gave rise to considerable misgivings, suggesting

---

6   Although, as will be noted below evangelical thought did become more open to such ideas throughout the nineteenth-century.

7   Fulfil, pp. 51–2.

8   The importance of both is discussed in Sharpe, 1991, pp. 25 ff. Elsewhere he says, 'These two – evolution and historical criticism – were the keys with which the late nineteenth century believed would unlock every door' (Fulfil, p. 41).Though both are deeply intertwined, for the new science of comparative religion necessarily involves both; in comparison it utilizes the historical methodology, which is only possible because of the presupposition that all religions are essentially of the same type and are linked in an evolutionary development.

9   See chapter 1.

10   Fulfil, p. 52.

that Christianity was on a par with other religions. To allay such misgivings, Monier-Williams, in his later writings, emphasized that there is 'a bridgeless chasm which no theory of evolution can ever span' between the Christian and non-Christian religions.[11] However, at least amongst the vast majority of the missionaries and other thinkers who used this phrase,[12] there was never any suggestion that Christianity was anything other than a separate revelation. While it had points of contact with the non-Christian systems due to the innate needs of mankind, Christianity was, nevertheless, entirely separate. For Monier-Williams the non-Christian religions offered merely the strivings of men in answer to man's needs, though containing, at their best, some memory of a primitive revelation.[13] A revelation allowed by God that men would be ready for His final revelation, Christianity, or rather, Christ.

Monier-Williams' theory of evolution was the concept that all religions provide an answer to man's deepest needs (though some better than others), with Christianity as the highest pinnacle. In response to Sharpe's assertion that this is something new in Monier-Williams' fulfilment theology, we should note that this idea was already present in Maurice's and Rowland Williams' thought.

It should be emphasized that while Monier-Williams believed that, although transcending other religions in a form of evolution, Christianity was of an inherently different type of revelation from all other religions. This is an important point to bear in mind, for the difference between those who are for, and those who are against, fulfilment theology, is often based upon a misunderstanding of this point, rather than there being a difference of belief involved. Fulfilment theology is the old thought in new clothing; but this is a point that will be examined later.[14]

---

11   Monier-Williams, *The Holy Bible and the Sacred Books of the East*, p. 19, quoted in Fulfil, p. 53.

12   Or, even if not using this term, made use of this conception.

13   See below. Thus Monier-Williams' theory leaves room for the idea of a praeparatio evangelicae. Though as mentioned in the first chapter not in the sense that would normatively be expected in fulfilment theology.

14   There were, of course, those who saw the non-Christian religions as the work of Satan and who have no contact at all with the fulfilment theologians. So when I say it is the old thought in a new guise I mean this simply as between those who emphasize the good versus those who emphasize the bad in the non-Christian systems.

Turning now to Monier-Williams' fulfilment theology, he believed that religion was an instinct of man, and so could say:

> [A]nd is it not a proof of the Divine origin of Christianity, and its adaptation to humanity in every quarter of the globe, that some of its grandest and most essential dogmas, and, so to speak, its root-ideas, do indeed lie at the root of all religions, and explain the problems of life which sages and philosophers in all ages of the world have vainly attempted to solve? Is it not a fact that all the gropings after truth, all the religious instincts, faculties, cravings, and aspirations of the human race which struggle to express themselves in the false religions of the world, find their only true expression and fulfilment – their only complete satisfaction – in Christianity?[15]

There is thus some common ground between Christianity and the non-Christian religions, based upon the 'root-ideas.'[16] It should be mentioned here that Monier-Williams believed that all religions give a partial answer to man's innate religious needs, but it is only within Christianity that these needs can be fully satisfied.[17] Sharpe suggests that Monier-Williams may have got this idea from Max Müller.[18] As noted previously, this belief was accepted by Morris, Maurice and Williams, the theory being a common one in the late nineteenth-century.[19]

The 'root-ideas' mean, for Monier-Williams, that within the non-Christian religions there will be intimations of Christianity. The following passage is worth quoting in this context:

> When I began the study of Hinduism, I imagined that certain elementary Christian conceptions – such as the Fatherhood of God, the Brotherhood of God, and the Indwelling of God in the human heart – were not to be found there, but a closer examination has enabled me to detect not only these, but almost every other rudimentary idea of our holy religion.[20]

---

15   Monier-Williams, 1887, p. 234.
16   Ibid., pp. 233–4.
17   Monier-Williams, 1875, p. xxxviii.
18   Fulfil, p. 51.
19   See previous chapter.
20   Monier-Williams, 1887, p. p. 234. These ideas, Monier-Williams continued, 'ought to be eagerly searched for by the missionary as the basis for his own superstructure.' These words foreshadow much of the later thought at Edinburgh. See, for instance, Ed. IV, pp. 27, 57, 118, especially, pp. 177–187, on Hinduism.

This develops the concept of religion answering to man's needs further than Maurice and Williams, in that Monier-Williams explicitly states that virtually all the central doctrines of Christianity are found in Hinduism. It may be noted, however, that this is a relatively late work, and various treatises on fulfilment had already been written by missionaries in the field when this was published, so this is not necessarily an original idea of Monier-Williams'. Yet, while noting the similarities between Christianity and Hinduism,[21] Monier-Williams' works on fulfilment theology, unlike those of Slater and Farquhar, do not expand upon these instances. Brief mention is made of certain doctrines in relation to their Christian counterparts, such as between the ceremony of the sacred thread and baptism,[22] but none of his books can really be considered, primarily, as works of fulfilment theology. So, while influential in stimulating the spread of fulfilment theology, Monier-Williams was not, himself, someone who really developed the idea.

As Sharpe suggests, however, Monier-Williams may have been one of the early influences on Farquhar.[23] All aspects of his thought are of interest to us here, particularly as regards which aspects of his thought correspond, and which do not correspond, to Farquhar's own thought.

As already mentioned, Monier-Williams held to the view that there had been an original revelation, which all the non-Christian religions had fallen away from.[24] This should not surprise us, if we remember that, although a student of comparative religion, Monier-Williams was also an evangelical. Yet, although he believed all religions[25] to have been in a process of decay, he nevertheless stipulated that it was needful to seek for the good that is

---

21 He mentions the stories of creation, and of the deluge, the doctrines of revelation, original sin, belief in the gradual depravement [sic] of the human race, sacrifice and sacrificial acts, and many more (Monier-Williams, 1875, p. xxxvii).

22 Monier-Williams, 1887, p. 201.

23 Though, as Sharpe observes, no direct influence can be shown. However, he does argue that Farquhar was far more likely to have been influenced by Monier-Williams than Müller. Even if this is so, there is no reason to believe that his ideas on fulfilment are based upon what he read in England, for he arrived in India in 1891, and his works on fulfilment theology only began in the early part of this century.

24 Monier-Williams, 1875, pp. 2–3, where he speaks of finding 'traces of the original truth imparted to mankind.'

25 Barring, of course, the Judeao-Christian tradition.

concealed within them,[26] his reasoning here, I would suggest, being apologetic expediency. The good, he believed, being remnants of the primal revelation. Thus he stated, 'They all [the non-Christian scriptures] begin with some flashes of light, and end in utter darkness.'[27]Attention should here be drawn to two distinct aspects Monier-Williams sees in the non-Christian religions, 'light' and 'darkness'. These mark, for him, the distinction between revelation and natural religion.[28] With regard to this, we may mention that Monier-Williams saw Christianity as a religion guaranteed as true by revelation, whilst Hinduism and the other non-Christian religions had only human failings to go on:

> Here, then, we may note the distinction between the Christian and the Hindū idea of revelation. We Christians believe that a succession of sacred books, and not a succession of fallible men, constitute the repository of our faith, and that God communicated knowledge to inspired writers, permitting them at the same time to preserve the peculiarities of style, incident to their respective characters as men.[29]

Another aspect of Monier-Williams' fulfilment theology that should be mentioned was his belief in the infallibility of historical Christianity.[30] He 'insisted on the absolute supremacy of historical Christianity and, indirectly, of the Western civilization with which it was closely allied.'[31] However, while holding to these views, he still believed, at least in theory, in the need for an Eastern form of Christianity:

> Depend upon it, that when the fullness of time arrives, and the natives of India everywhere accept Christianity, they will construct for it a setting of their own. And bearing in mind that our religion originated in the East, and that the Bible itself is a thoroughly Eastern

---

26   Monier-Williams 1875, pp. 3–4. Monier-Williams believed that, the 'original truth... should be diligently sought for in every religious system, however corrupt, so that when any fragment of the living rock is discovered, it may (so to speak) at once be converted into a fulcrum for the upheaving of the whole mass of surrounding error'

27   quote from M. Monier-Williams *The Holy Bible and the Sacred Books of the East*, p. 11, quoted in Fulfil, p. 53.

28   Mention has already been made to this dichotomy previously, and it will be discussed in relation to this chapter below.

29   Monier-Williams, 1861, p. 24. The distinction between Monier-Williams' thought here and Williams' views of revelation are plain.

30   Fulfil, p. 50.

31   Ibid.

book, we shall not only expect, but joyfully acquiesce in an Indian framework for Indian Christianity.[32]

In this, Monier-Williams is in accord with Farquhar, Slater, and the general tendency of other fulfilment theologians, who suggested that Christianity needs to find an indigenous form. However, it is not clear quite how Monier-Williams believed this indigenization should be realized. His suggestion that Christianity needed to be indigenized was made after he had visited India, no doubt in response to missionary needs, yet what aspects of Eastern thought are to be used is unclear. He recognized that native language would have to be used,[33] but, beyond this, it is unclear how he feels that Christianity should be made indigenous. A clue might be seen in a reference he makes to the success of Roman Catholic missions:

> [The] chief successes of Christianity in India have been hitherto achieved by Roman Catholics who offer to the Hindū mind a kind of Hindūized Christianity, or, at any rate, present him with the images, symbols, processions, decorations, miraculous stories, marvelous histories saints, and imposing ritual of which his present mental condition appears to stand in need.[34]

However, elsewhere he makes it clear that, although successful, he does not have a high regard for the practices of Roman Catholicism. Speaking of their mission churches, he says:

> The interior aspect of these churches appeared to me, I deeply regret to say, very little different from that of the adjacent Hindū temples. The images of the Virgin in one might do duty for those of the goddess Bhāvanī in the other. Such images are carried in procession through the streets of towns in a similar manner. Services in which the laity are spectators only, worship of saints, ceremonies for the dead, fastings, holy water, prostrations, genuflections, noisy music, ringing of bells, illuminations, incense, symbols, pictures, decorations, rosaries, votive offerings, satisfy the lower cravings of humanity under both systems; while the asceticism of Romish priests, their shorn heads, their mode of life in the midst of the peasantry, and their style of preaching, harmonize with the corresponding points in the character of Hindū religious leaders and teachers.[35]

---

32   Monier-Williams, 1887, quotation from an address delivered at a Missionary Congress, Oxford, May 2nd, 1877.

33   Monier-Williams, 1861, p. 54.

34   Monier-Williams, 1887, pp. 205–6.

35   Monier-Williams, 1878, p. 271.

What he does say, however, is that:

> I fear that our severely purified Anglican system, cut into an European shape and deprived of Asiatic flexibility by strict rules of ecclesiastical uniformity – found to be scarcely suited to all varieties of character even among our own people – has at present little prospect of making itself acceptable to the generality of our Indian fellow-subjects.[36]

In the quotation above, Monier-Williams spoke of the Indian's 'present mental condition', and earlier he had spoken about Christianity inculcating a better state of mind, suggesting that Indians have a 'feeble condition of brain.'[37] Considering these comments, it seems evident that he lacked great respect for the peoples of the Indian subcontinent.[38] Further, if we regard this in the context of his assertion that, 'some may doubt whether, if religion is an ingredient of civilization, the Hindūs have ever possessed any true civilization at all,'[39] then quite what form of indigenization he envisioned is even more unclear, when his view of Indian culture is so negative. However, having noted this problematic aspect in his thought, we may move on, as it is not strictly relevant to this study, yet provides an excellent insight into Monier-Williams' attitude.

The Merits of Buddhism, Hinduism and Islam

Having now discussed the major aspects of Monier-Williams' fulfilment theology, one further aspect of Monier-Williams thought that deserves mention, are the alterations he made to his opinions on the relative merits of the non-Christian religions over the years. In this respect a certain difference between Müller and Monier-Williams should be observed While the former dedicated himself to textual analysis and translation, the latter took a more phenomenological approach, and visited India himself.[40] It appears not to be

---

36   Monier-Williams, 1878, p. 271.
37   Ibid., p. 205.
38   Though such comments were not untypical in the nineteenth-century, (L. James, p. 180) and even later (see ibid., pp. 503 ff, where the negative attitudes of Anglo-India towards the native population that existed well into this century are discussed, especially as portrayed in fiction).
39   Ibid., p. 225.
40   T. Thomas, 1988, p. 88.

too much of an over-simplification to say that Monier-Williams' visit to India was responsible for his changing his ideas on this subject. He reacted strongly in response to what he saw as, 'the hideous idolatry witnessed in the temples of Viṣṇu and Śiva.'[41] Writing in 1875, before visiting India, he suggested that 'Brāhmanism' was the closest religion to Christianity, followed by Buddhism and Islam.[42] Only two years later, after his first visit to India, he had reversed the order, putting Islam as the highest religion, followed by Buddhism, with Brāhmanism as the lowest.[43] To understand Monier-Williams' hostile reaction to Hinduism we should consider his evangelical faith. Considering the context of the day, the Low Church attitude that characterized his faith would have had, along with much else, a corresponding detestation of overt ritual of any form.[44] He preferred a more sober and thoughtful atmosphere for religious worship. So, just as he detested the 'hideous idolatry' of Hinduism, he approved antithetically of 'the severe anti-symbolism conspicuous in all the surroundings of Muhammadan mosques.'[45] Further, concerning the worship he observed in the mosques, he said:

> I felt that there was nothing in the outward appearance of either building or worshipers incompatible with the spirit of Christian prayer. Nay more – I felt as I watched the devout Muslims, that I also might have prayed in the same place in my own way, and even learnt from them to pray with more solemnity and reverence of manner than I had ever before practiced.[46]

There were, though, differences between the theory and practice. These can be seen in the following passage, written, perhaps significantly, before he visited India, where he says, 'Notwithstanding its gross polytheism and idolatry, the points of contact between Hindúism and Christianity are more

---

41   Monier-Williams, 1887, p. 238. This is not to say that Müller disregarded the practices of the non-Christian religions in his assessment of them. He too, like Monier-Williams, was appalled by the idolatry of everyday Hinduism (see below).

42   Monier-Williams, 1875, p. xxxvii. Monier-Williams had said the same earlier regarding the relative merits of Hinduism and Islam (Monier-Williams, 1861, p. 60, fn).

43   Monier-Williams, 1887, p. 253.

44   Reference may be made to Monier-Williams views on Roman Catholicism expressed above.

45   Ibid., p. 238.

46   Ibid.

numerous than between Christianity and Islám, and on this account the missionary has always more hold over Hindús than Muhammedans.'[47]

I would venture to suggest that it may not have been just the idolatry itself which so offended Monier-Williams' sensibilities, but the associated noise and bustle, which are attendant at any Hindu temple, and may well have rankled in the mind of a Victorian Low Churchman.

Further, he altered his views in this area again, though this time not in response to the ritual and worship of a 'religion', but due to its thought. If a date for this change must be given, then a series of lectures he gave in 1888 on Buddhism can be seen as the turning point.[48]

In these lectures he once again speaks of Buddhism as being in many ways an improvement on Hinduism.[49] However, he goes on to talk of Buddhism as being in no way comparable to Christianity, for it is, he says not a religion. This might seem to make a distinct break from his earlier views, if he is suggesting that the non-Christian faiths should not even be seen as religions, as Christianity is. In this regard it would be useful to follow his argument.

In *Buddhism*, Monier-Williams does allow that there are points of contact between Christianity and Buddhism: 'We are bound to acknowledge that Buddhism, as it extended to other countries, *did* acquire the character of a theistic religious system, which, though false, had in it some points of contact with Christianity.'[50] However, he follows this up, echoing almost word for word his phrase of two years earlier, by saying, 'it will be easy to show how impossible it is to bridge the yawning chasm which separates it from true religion.'[51] However, after noting various connections, for instance in ethical systems,[52] he admits its religious aspects:

> it taught the existence of unseen worlds; it permitted the offering of prayers to Maitreya and other supposed personal saviours; it inculcated faith and trust in these celestial beings, which operated as good motives in the hearts of many, while the hope of being born in higher conditions of life, and the desire to acquire merit by reverential acts, led to the

---

47   Monier-Williams, 1861, p.60, fn.
48   Published as *Buddhism* in 1889.
49   Monier-Williams, 1889, pp. 551 f.
50   Monier-Williams, 1889, p. 541. Here he is speaking specifically of Buddhism, but the same attitudes seem to underlie his opinions of all the non-Christian religions.
51   Ibid.
52   Ibid., p. 550.

development of devotional services, which had much in common with those performed in Christian countries. Nay, it must even be admitted that many Buddhists in the present day are deeply imbued with religious feelings.[53]

Yet still he says:

But if, after making all these concessions, I am told that on my own showing, Buddhism was a kind of introduction to Christianity, or that Christianity is a kind of development of Buddhism, I must ask you to bear with me a little longer, while I point out certain other contrasts[....][54]

After speaking, yet again, of 'how impassable is the gulf,'[55] he goes on to list what he sees as all the differences between Christianity and Buddhism. There is no need to list them here, but the tone of the whole work is deeply antagonistic.[56] However, we must not conclude that Monier-Williams repudiated his previous views on fulfilment theology. Rather, he came to conclude that Buddhism[57] was not a religion, but a philosophy. In a later work, his *Hinduism*, published in 1894, a further understanding of this can be gained, for he says:

Brāhmanism *is* a religion and may be described as all theology, for it makes god everything, and everything God. Buddhism *is no religion at all*, and certainly no theology, but rather a system of duty, morality, and benevolence, without real deity, prayer or priest.[58]

Here, he reiterates the words of his 1888 lectures, that Buddhism is 'no religion,' but by this he means only that it is a form of a philosophy. Unlike Hinduism, it does not satisfy the criterion he lays down for a religion.[59]

With regard to this matter, digressing from our main theme for a moment, the following passage deserves inclusion as a most informative

---

53   Ibid., p. 552.
54   Ibid.
55   Ibid.
56   To give but one example he refers to, 'the feeble utterances[...] the tedious diffuseness, and I might almost say 'the inane twaddle' and childish repetitions of the greater portion of the Tripiṭaka' (ibid., p. 558).
57   Except, perhaps, in as far as it adopted a theistic form (see above).
58   Op. cit., p. 74.
59   See Monier-Williams, 1890, p. 539.

statement upon Monier-Williams' religion, and that of some of his contemporaries:

> The late bishop of Calcutta[60] once said to me, that being in an outlying part of his diocese, where Buddhism prevailed, he asked an apparently pious Buddhist, whom he happened to observe praying in a temple, what he had just been praying for? He replied, 'I have been praying for nothing.' 'But,' urged the Bishop, 'to whom have you been praying?' The man answered, 'I have been praying to nobody.' 'What!' said the astonished Bishop, 'praying for nothing to nobody?' And no doubt this anecdote gives an accurate idea of the so-called prayer of a true Buddhist. This man had not really been praying for anything. He had merely been making use of some form of words to which an efficacy, like that of sowing fruitful seed in a field, was supposed to belong. He had not been praying in any Christian sense.[61]

In response to this quotation, I would like, briefly, to say a few words regarding whether the bishop was correct to state that this man had not been praying in the 'Christian sense'. The following is most informative in this respect:

> Meditation is not the time for words, however beautiful and sincerely phrased. All our words are wholly ineffective when we come to enter into this deep and mysterious communion with God whose own Word within us is before and after all words. 'I am the Alpha and the Omega,' says the Lord.[62]

Such a view is not new to Christianity, or, even, something unknown in nineteenth-century British theology. Commenting upon Hindu contemplative disciplines Slater acknowledged, 'Periods of solitude and secret prayer, silent spaces wherein the soul may give itself up to intense communion with God are the means of heightening, broadening, deepening, the spiritual life.'[63] Having noted this point, it would be an appropriate time to turn to consider Sharpe's suggestion, that Monier-Williams repudiated his views on fulfilment theology late in life.

---

60   No doubt Robert Milman, bishop of Calcutta 1867–1876.
61   Monier-Williams, 1889, p. 540.
62   Main, p. 19.
63   Slater, 1897, p. 61, see also in this regard, Larsen.

Sharpe suggests that Monier-Williams' speech of 1877 to the Church Missionary Society represents a change of opinion regarding fulfilment theology. However, all that he said at this meeting was that there is no connection between the Christian and non-Christian scriptures,[64] a suggestion which would not have been out of place in his earlier writings. For him, the only revelation – barring, of course, the primal revelation – is the sole concern of the succession of books that are accepted by (Protestant) Christianity.[65]

Further evidence to suggest that Monier-Williams did not repudiate his earlier views at this time can be found in his book, *Modern India and the Indians*. This was completed after the speech to the Church Missionary Society of May 1877,[66] and, in it, he still speaks of the truth in the non-Christian religions.[67] Moreover, it speaks of the need to indigenize Christianity,[68] as well as the suggestion that Christians can learn from the non-Christian religions.[69] Monier-Williams was, most certainly, often harsh on other religions. In an article published in 1879, referring to Islam – at this time reckoned by him the best of them – he speaks of it as liable to fall into polytheism and pantheism, and as being 'adulterated with Hindūism.'[70] Yet, however harsh, he never totally condemns other religious traditions. In a series of articles published between 1877 and 1879[71] (of which the article on Islam quoted above comes from), there does not appear any outright condemnation of the non-Christian religions. Later, there is still no sign of a change of view. Further editions of Monier-Williams' *Religious Thought and Life in India* still use his 'positive' view towards the non-Christian religions.[72]

---

64   Stock, III, p. 303.

65   Monier-Williams, 1861, p. 24.

66   The work contains extracts from, and references to, speeches he delivered in May and October of 1877, and was thus still being edited after his CMS speech.

67   Monier-Williams, 1887, pp. 233 f.

68   Ibid., p. 235.

69   Ibid., p. 260.

70   Monier-Williams, 1879(b), p. 849.

71   See Monier-Williams, 1878, 1879(a), and 1879(b).

72   See the introduction to the third edition where he quotes the Earl of Northbrook and commends his views (Monier-Williams, 1887, pp. v–vii, also in the earlier editions, Monier-Williams, 1883 and 1885).

Finally, it remains to say something on the fundamental difference between Monier-Williams and other fulfilment theologians. In a sense, Monier-Williams' thought can be seen as foreshadowing the attitude of dialectic theology towards the non-Christian religions, whose basic premise is the utter difference of the Christian revelation to all other faiths. The proponents of dialectical theology are ready to speak of 'the often all-too-human element in Christianity in its historical development and reality, often as degrading as the baser elements in other religions.'[73] This form of theology sees a difference between the revelation of Jesus and natural theology, rather than between Christianity and non-Christian systems as Monier-Williams was inclined to do.[74] Both Monier-Williams and the followers of dialectic theology, are, however, agreed on the point that natural theology represents a merely human searching, and this is where they differ from the liberal proponents of fulfilment theology. The whole world-view of the two parties was, and, indeed, still is different. However, as was seen in the last chapter, in relation to Morris, while we may distinguish between 'conservative' and 'liberal' attitudes, there is much common ground shared by those in both camps. Often, it is only the emphasis which distinguishes them. These points should be born in mind especially when we come to look at Farquhar, for, although seen as the definitive writer on the 'liberal' concept of fulfilment theology, he, nevertheless, shared much in common with his conservative forebears.

Friedrich Max Müller

Like Monier-Williams, Max Müller was a devout Christian.[75] However, by many, he was seen to be an enemy of Christianity in the 'war' with the non-Christian religions, particularly by the evangelical wing of the Church.[76] Sharpe suggests that it is more likely that many of the later missionary writers

---

73   Kraemer, 1947, p. 108.
74   It is worth noting that the division between Jesus' revelation as opposed to historical Christianity is seen in the later developments of fulfilment theology.
75   He was a member of the Church of England.
76   Neufeldt, p. 11.

would find their inspiration in Monier-Williams than in the 'heretical' Müller.[77] However, even amongst missionary circles, Müller's influence can be seen.[78] Certainly, as the nineteenth-century progressed, missionaries could not ignore the growing knowledge of, and change of feeling expressed towards, the non-Christian religions. This was largely engendered by the new science of comparative religion, and Müller himself was particularly influential in this regard. In making knowledge of Hinduism and other faiths more widely available, the negative and iconoclastic attitudes of previous ages – in which the non-Christian religions would be condemned out of hand – were less tenable. In particular, we should mention Müller's role in editing the Sacred Books of the East series.[79] This growing knowledge did not always induce a more positive reaction towards them: 'Some[...] told me that they had been great admirers of ancient Oriental wisdom till they came to read the translations of the Sacred Books of the East. They had evidently expected to hear the tongues of angels, and not the babbling of babes.'[80] The following is worth quoting here, where Müller, speaking of the Vedas as, 'the dawn of the religious consciousness of man' and, 'one of the most inspiring and hallowing sights in the whole history of the world,' nevertheless, says, 'yet not without its dark clouds, its chilling colds, its noxious vapours.' [81]

Even if Müller's notoriety rules him out as being a direct influence upon many extreme evangelicals and conservatives, he was, nevertheless, read by those on, what may, somewhat incongruously, be termed the liberal wing of the evangelical party.[82] Certainly, we should not be too doctrinaire in saying that no conservatives would have read him. He was a friend of Edward Pusey,

---

77 See, Fulfil, p. 122. He did, however, have his defenders, one of whom, referring to his publication of the Sacred Books of the East series, said, 'I have been roused to indignation by the accusations I found taken up by almost everyone I knew, that in this signal service to religion he had only wished to discredit Christianity' (Lady Welby, quoted in Müller, 1902, II, p. 65).

78 See e.g., Slater, 1897, p. 1, etc.; also Maw, 1990, p. 18, who notes that Müller had an ambivalent reputation amongst such circles (ibid., p. 125).

79 Fulfil, p. 54.

80 Müller, 1884, p. 1005.

81 Müller, 1969, I, Preface, p. xi.

82 Sharpe observes that, 'it was the emergence of a new type of Protestantism (Liberal Protestantism or Liberal Evangelicalism) which enabled J. N. Farquhar to make his distinctive contribution to Protestant missionary thought and practice' (Fulfil, pp. 34–5).

who has already been mentioned in antithesis to Maurice.[83] Pusey, it may be noted, supported Müller in the contest for the Boden Professorship of Sanskrit against the more orthodox Monier-Williams.[84]

We should now turn to consider previous assessments of Müller's position in the history of fulfilment theology, in a recent book Müller is identified as a forerunner of Farquhar in terms of his fulfilment theology, the only difference was that, whereas Farquhar saw Christianity as being victorious, Müller envisaged a new religion as fulfilling those of the past.[85] Maw, however, in his study of fulfilment theology, largely ignores Müller's contribution to fulfilment theology,[86] concentrating upon his 'Aryan race' theory.[87] However, his contribution to fulfilment theology must rank

---

83   See Beckerlegge in Wolffe, p. 190, reference to M. Müller, *My Autobiography – A Fragment*, London, Longmans, Green, 1901, p. 291.

84   Ibid., p. 203. Beckerlegge notes that, 'Pusey's support is interesting, because he had little sympathy for Müller's "broad" attitudes and therefore it is reasonable to view his contribution as a judgement on the academic calibre of the candidate who, he believed, would be most able to further the missionary cause.' Possibly rivalries between Pusey's High Church friends and the Evangelical party represented by Monier-Williams may have had some influence upon his support for Müller. Pusey most certainly did not see eye-to-eye with him on all matters, as Cantwell Smith recounts, 'It is interesting to note that when Müller's "friends first submitted to the Delegates of the University Press at Oxford [his] plan of publishing... all the Sacred Books of the East," one of the delegates, the substantial scholar and prominent clergyman E. B. Pusey "strongly supported the plan, only stipulating that the Old and New Testaments should not be included;" Müller tried to persuade him otherwise, arguing for his own wish, "very near to my heart," that "these two, the most important Sacred Books of the East" should indeed be in the set, but '[in] vain[...] I had to give up [that] wish[...] in order to save the rest." Yet almost half a century later, shortly before his death, he was still hoping that "the gap thus left" would eventually be filled and the two Testaments "find their proper place in [the] collection" – Müller, *Auld Lang Syne – second series: My Indian Friends* (London and Bombay: Longmans, Green, 1899), p. 87' (Smith, 1993, p. 244, fn 4).

85   Bennett, p. 48. Whether this is a fair assessment of Müller's position will be considered shortly.

86   Though he does note that the idea was present in his thought (Maw, 1990, p. 27).

87   The theory was a popular one in the nineteenth-century. It suggested that the Aryan peoples had a common origin, the peoples of Europe and India being of one root race. For Müller, however, the theory was based upon the notion of a common language rather than being racial in content (Maw, 1990, pp. 124–5). The theory formed the basis of K. M. Banerjea's fulfilment theology (see next chapter). Maw suggests that the theory offers a racial analogue to fulfilment theology (ibid., p. 15).

alongside that of Monier-Williams, and it should be mentioned here that there are areas in which future fulfilment theologians, such as Farquhar, were closer to Müller than they were to Monier-Williams. Both should be seen as exercising a substantial influence upon the growth of this doctrine.

Müller's Theology and Influences

Before going on to look at Müller's fulfilment theology, two points need raising. First, mention should be made of Müller's own theological beliefs. Here Müller stands within the tradition of immanentist theology.[88] The preface to St. John's Gospel was, for him, the most important part of the Bible.[89] He outlined this system in the paper he sent to the World's Parliament of Religions, saying, 'There is nothing new in all this, it is only the earliest Christian theology restated, restored and revived.'[90] This theology is the Johannine/Alexandrian theology which emphasizes the presence of the Logos throughout the world to be found in all men at all times.[91] For Müller, all the world's religions were intimately related, and he saw 'a pattern of religious progress running from the Vedic hymns to the Christian philosophy of Alexandria.'[92] In this, the Logos is the uniting factor and source of revelation. While he can be placed within the context of the British theological scene, most of his thought in this area was developed while he was still studying on the continent.[93] Nevertheless, it appears that he may have owed a debt to Rowland Williams, Trench and Maurice as the following quotation illustrates:

> I thought I was simply following in the footsteps of the greatest theologians of our time, and that I was serving the cause of true religion by showing... what St. Paul, what the Fathers of the Church, what mediaeval theologians, and what some of the most learned of modern divines had asserted again[....][94]

---

88   Fulfil, p. 45.
89   Trompf, p. 212.
90   Müller in Barrows (hereafter WPOR), II, p. 936.
91   In this he owes much to Schelling and Burnouf.
92   Trompf, p. 201.
93   See references below.
94   Müller, 1892, p. v.

115

It does not seem unreasonable to suppose that 'the most learned of modern divines' may refer to Rowland Williams, Trench and Maurice, whom he may well have read.[95] However, what influence they may have exerted upon him is uncertain. This is probably also a reference to Newman, whose work Müller goes on to praise.[96]

Much of the thought upon which Müller bases his fulfilment theology was gained during his studies on the continent. Hegel, Schelling,[97] and Burnouf were all influential sources for him. The idea that a religion could be developed from the different facets of previous religions came from Hegel.[98] Schelling taught that 'Christianity must[...] have been present in Heathenism,'[99] and that natural religion was really an experience of the divine.[100] The importance of Alexandria in Christianity, and the central role of the Logos, was imprinted into him by Burnouf in Paris.[101]

This contrasts with Rowland Williams and Maurice, who were influenced by Coleridge. Rowland Williams was well read in the teachings of the German liberals, and so Hegel and Schelling may well also have influenced him. While we can only speculate on their importance, Maurice, in the introduction to his Boyle lectures, pays tribute to the influence of both Hegel and Schlegel.[102] Therefore, the influence of German philosophical thought should not just be seen as entering into British ideas of fulfilment theology through Müller, but is also present in the developing Cambridge

---

95   It was noted above that Bunsen recommended Williams' book to Müller. Also, the Boyle lectures were Maurice's most popular work, and, being a well known work by a renowned author, Müller may well have read this work which would have been one of the few books published in England at this time in his field of interest.

96   See Müller, 1892, pp. vi–vii, and see also the section on Newman herein (chapter 5).

97   Whom he called, 'one of the profoundest thinkers of Germany' (Müller, 1873(a), p. 145).

98   Trompf, p. 204.

99   Ibid., p. 209.

100   Ibid., p. 210.

101   Ibid., p. 212.

102   Boyle, p. xix. To quote Maurice's exact words he says, '[....] I should be ungrateful if I did not say that the passages on India in the Mythologies of Baur and Windischmann, and still more in Hegel's *Philosophy of History*, with the little book of Frederick Schlegel, called *Die Inden*, have illuminated many dark and dull reports, and have enabled me to feel the connection between the thoughts of other periods and countries and those which characterise our own times.'

tradition of fulfilment theology. It would be useful to say something of Müller, qua a student of comparative religion, to further consider the pre-understandings that he brings to his studies of religion.

Comparative Religion in Müller's Thought

The basis of the science of comparative religion was historical-critical study. Müller believed in applying these rules to the study of all religions,[103] such that no religion would be given a privileged position.[104] According to Sharpe, in this new system:

> Revelation tended to be ruled out *a priori*, or reinterpreted; every historical religion was treated in the same terms, without any attempt at evaluation (at least ostensibly, though the postulating of an evolutionary scale could not well take place without the passing of value-judgements).[105]

This historical method of the late nineteenth-century, was, of course, what inspired Rowland Williams in his work. Interlinked with this was the quest for the 'historical Jesus,' whereby the accretions of the Church were removed to reveal the 'real' Jesus, and his 'real' teachings.[106]

That all religions should be regarded equally was the basis of comparative religion, and why it was considered to be so dangerous for Christianity. In Müller's writings there is little sense of a difference between the Christian and non-Christian religions, except in terms of degree; all

---

103   Müller, 1873(a), p. 9.

104   Ibid., pp. 25–6.

105   Fulfil, p. 40. This was certainly Müller's belief, see Neufeldt, p. 11.

106   It was believed 'that Jesus 'is to-day more studied and better known as He was and as He lived than at any period between now and the first age of the Church' (A.M. Fairbairn, *The Place of Christ in Modern Theology*, p. 3, in Fulfil, p. 43). The same 'quest' continues today, though whether it is any closer to reaching any 'truth' is, of course, another question. As one of the most famous scholars involved in the pursuit today, Crossan, has noted, a 'number of competent and even eminent scholars [are] producing pictures of Jesus at wide variance with one another' (Crossan, p. xxvii).

religions were essentially of the same nature.[107] For Müller, however, there is always an extra dimension away from the strict rules of comparative religion, which sets Christianity apart, the person of Jesus, as the Christ. Jesus is seen as the final revelation, that which separates Christianity from other religions: 'The critical step which some of the philosophers of Alexandria[108] took, while others refused to take it, was to recognize the perfect realization of the Divine Thought or *Logos* of manhood in Christ, as in the true sense the Son of God.'[109]

Natural Religion: True or False?

It was observed in the previous section that Monier-Williams referred to the non-Christian religions as 'false religions,'[110] whereas, for Müller, all religion comes from man's apprehension of the infinite. For him: 'There never was a false god, nor was there ever really a false religion, unless you call a child a false man.'[111] He can also say:

> I hold that there is a Divine element in every one of the great religions of the world. I consider it blasphemous to call them the work of the Devil, when they are the work of God, and I hold that there is nowhere any belief in God except as a result of a Divine Revelation, the effect of a Divine Spirit working in man.[112]

Müller's Logos theology can be clearly discerned in this. The indwelling Logos, was, for him, what validated natural religion. Commenting upon this subject, he said, 'What I have aimed at in my Gifford Lectures on Natural Religion is to show that all religions are natural.'[113]

What Müller meant by this was that all religions begin with a perception of the sacred within the confines of our perceptions of the world, 'in

---

107   See Müller, 1900, I, p. xxi, and Müller, 1902, pp. 147 (letter to M. Renon, 21/4/1883) and 459 ff. (letter to Mrs Max Müller, 9/1902, from the vicar of St. Giles', Rev. H. S. Bidder, expressing F. M. Müller's views).
108   Clement and Origen.
109   Müller in WPOR II, pp. 935–6. The reference to the Logos may be noted.
110   Monier-Williams , 1887, p. 234.
111   Müller, 1902, p. 141 (letter to the Rev. M. K. Schermerhopn, 6/3/1883)..
112   Ibid., p. 491.
113   Müller in WPOR, II, p. 935.

perceiving the finite we always perceive the infinite also.'[114] An essential part of Müller's thought in regard to this is that God is at work in the mind of man.[115] This means that all the essential truths of religion can be arrived at by means of human reason and natural religion.[116] There is no need for any special revelation; man's religious beliefs are part of an internal revelation of God working within men's minds.[117] Yet this must be seen in the light of Christianity, which, while all its truths may be known by natural revelation, still has another aspect:

> [The] development of philosophical thought in Greece[... is] perfectly compatible with the religious and moral doctrines of Christianity[....]
> [W]hat was the highest result of Greek philosophy[...]? It was the ineradicable conviction that there is Reason or *Logos* in the world[....]
> [.... T]he whole world assumed a new aspect. It was seen to be supported or pervaded by reason or *Logos*, it was throughout teleological, thought and willed by a rational power. The same divine presence had now been perceived for the first time in all its fullness and perfection in the one Son of God, the pattern of the whole race of men, henceforth to be called 'the sons of God.'[118]

Again we return to the central role of the Logos. In accepting that before the coming of the Christian messiah the non-Christian philosophers already had knowledge of the Logos and, more than this, *experience* of the Logos, Müller establishes that the difference between religions is largely a matter of degree. All that separates Christianity is knowledge of the Logos as an incarnate human being. For Müller this perception is the basis of all religion.

The same thought was present in both Maurice and Rowland Williams. Yet, although they both accept a Logos type doctrine regarding the inspiration of the non-Christian religions, they are still both ready to call them 'false' religions.[119] It should be asked, in regard to this, how different Müller's

---

114   Müller, 1899, p. 123; see Neufeldt, p. 9. This is an important difference between Müller and Monier-Williams, for where for Monier-Williams other religions are 'false,' for Müller all religions cannot be other than true, for they 'perceive the infinite.' This point will be developed below.

115   See Müller, 1902, pp. 277 and 464.

116   See ibid., p. 290, Müller, 1892, 'Preface'. This is an idea Müller took from Schelling (see Trompf, p. 210).

117   Fulfil, p. 45.

118   Müller in WPOR, II, pp. 935 and 936.

119   See below.

thought really was in this respect. To answer this question, it should be considered how far he is ready to concede the good in other religions; portraying him as someone who would indiscriminately praise the non-Christian religions would be to do him an injustice. He stated:

> The worship of Śiva, of Vishnu, and the other popular deities, is of the same, nay, in many cases of a more degraded and savage character than the worship of Jupiter, Apollo, and Minerva; it belongs to a stratum of thought which is long buried beneath our feet: it may live on, like the lion and the tiger, but the mere air of free thought and civilized life will extinguish it.[120]

Here, we should remember that Müller was a nineteenth-century British Protestant. Despite the differences, he shared with Monier-Williams a belief that religion should be pure and spiritual, devoid of the need for external images.[121] His support for the Brahmō Samāj can be seen as indicative of this.[122] Certainly, Müller was more liberal in his views than Monier-Williams but, nevertheless, he was still a child of his own times. What he saw as acceptable in religion still fell within certain proscribed limits. Within these limits he was, however, more ready to see the 'good' within the non-Christian religions, rather than the bad. Therefore, he could say: 'Holding that opinion, I do not wish to see the old religions destroyed. I want to see them reformed, reanimated, resuscitated by contact with Christianity.'[123] Even though he may have been revolted by certain religious practices, he still believed that all religions are good, and just needed reviving. The false accretions of centuries of superstition had to be wiped away, so that the pure Logos centered core may be revealed. We should note, that, although in the quotation above, Müller appears to be suggesting that Christianity will only be one future religion amongst many, this is not the case, as will be seen below.

---

120   Müller, 1873(b), pp. 36–7. It should be noted here that Müller split the world's religions into two categories, missionary and non-missionary. The former vital and alive, the latter dead and dying. The three missionary religions were Christianity, Islam, and Buddhism (ibid., pp. 25 ff).

121   Something of this matter was said in discussion of Morris, and of the problems faced by the Tractarian movement in their desire to introduce further ritual usage into Anglicanism (see, for instance, Palmer, chapter I, Gilley, section II, etc.).

122   Of which more below.

123   Müller, 1873(b), p. 37.

It has been mentioned above that Müller believed all religions to be 'natural',[124] but he still placed Christianity in a different category. Yet, by holding all religions to be subject to historical-critical research, he was held to be reducing this distinction.

Evolution and Fulfilment

Müller, in common with so many other nineteenth-century thinkers, saw religion as an answer to man's need for God.[125] He had innate religious desires, but, unlike Monier-Williams, it was not historical Christianity that, for Müller, was the fulfilment of all other religions, but rather, he believed, Jesus' revelation is the ideal religion and this fulfils the longings of mankind. In so far as the person of Jesus was seen as a manifestation of the Logos at a particular time in history, Christianity was, for Müller, given a unique status. At the same time, in so far as Christianity was an historical religion, it was as possible to study it on a par with any other. Further, because Müller believed the Logos lay not just at the heart of Christianity, but of all religions, it placed Christianity in a distinct relationship to them. To follow the theme of Müller's argument in his *Introduction to the Study of Religion*, he spoke of:

> [...] the sundry times and divers manners in which, in times past, God spake unto the fathers by the prophets; and instead of recognising Christianity as coming in the fulness of time, and as the fulfilment of the hopes and desires of the whole world, we have brought ourselves to look upon its advent as the only broken link in that unbroken chain which is rightly called the Divine government of the world.[126]

Here Müller criticizes the attitude of those who fail to see the Divine Providence ordering the 'spiritual education' of mankind. The comparative study of religion, he believed, revealed this truth: 'Nay, it shall teach us more;

---

124   Müller, 1873(b), pp. 132–3.
125   Müller, 1900, I, p. xxvii, 'there is in all religions a yearning after the true, though unknown, God.' A certain difference may be noted here between Müller and other fulfilment theologians. He speaks of religion not so much as being an innate need of man, but as the direct influence of God at work in man. For Müller, God's interaction is a part of the natural workings of man's reason.
126   Op. Cit., p. 222.

it will enable us to see in the history of the ancient religions, more clearly than anywhere else, the *Divine education of the human race.* '[127]

The reason for the continual development that Müller believed was occurring is that each religion is, he said, suited to the needs of mankind at the time:

> [W]e shall see that there is not one [religion] which is entirely false; nay, that in one sense every religion is a true religion, being the only religion which was possible at the time, which was compatible with the language, the thoughts, and the sentiments of each generation, which was appropriate to the age of the world.[128]

There was a close connection for Müller between the religion of a nation, its language, and its people.[129] Each race had its own religion.[130]

One question raised by Müller's thought, is whether, in the course of mankind's religious development, Christianity itself would be transcended. Speaking elsewhere of this, he says:

> It gives us at the same time a truer conception of the history of the whole world, showing that there was a purpose in the ancient religions and philosophies of the world, and that Christianity was really from the beginning a synthesis of the best thoughts of the past, as they had been slowly elaborated by the two principal representatives of the human race, the Aryan and the Semitic.[131]

This idea, though in a different form, was to be a key theme of many later writers on the non-Christian religions, in that Christianity needs to absorb the best of the other religions within itself. In the form in which Müller uses this idea, it is, of course, derived directly from Hegel.[132] An important factor in this, stressed by later writers on fulfilment theology, but which is often obscured in Müller, is that there is nothing more to add to the religion of Christ; it is only historical Christianity which stands in need of correction

---

127   Ibid., p. 226.
128   Ibid., p. 261.
129   Ibid., p. 43, see also lecture III. Comparison may be drawn here with Westcott's ideas which were very similar in this regard (see chapter 5).
130   Ibid., p. 216, more will be said on this below.
131   Müller, 1873(a), p. 216.
132   Trompf, p. 204.

when national prejudices have taken Her off course.[133] Müller expresses this idea, however, by saying that he expects the development of a new religion, of which he says: 'The true religion of the future will be the fulfilment of all the religions of the past.'[134] In this, he seems to imply, as we noted Bennett alleging earlier, that Christianity is to be supplanted in the evolutionary process, but this misrepresents him. In his paper to the World's Parliament of Religions,[135] he makes it clear that what he is looking for is 'a complete revival of religion, more particularly of the Christian religion.'[136]

For Müller, Christianity was 'the fulfilment of the hopes and desires of the whole world.'[137] He does, for instance, see the Bible as being 'tremendously ahead of the other sacred books,'[138] even saying that, 'Our religion is certainly better and purer than others, but in the essential points all religions have something in common.'[139]

Later fulfilment theologians were prepared to admit that the contribution of the non-Christian religions would be to correct the faults of historical Christianity; the idea that Hinduism can supplement Christianity becomes, as will be shown, a commonplace observation in Christian thought.[140] Müller's

---

133   Instance upon instance of this could be cited. However, as this is not the place to discuss it I shall note just one example, which may be seen as representative. This is taken from the Rt. Rev. L. G. Milne, a bishop of Bombay, in Bishop Montgomery's book *Mankind and the Church*, in which seven bishops air their views as to what the peoples of particular nations and creeds have to offer to the Church. Milne says that the English Christian may learn from Vedantic Pantheism a greater appreciation of 'the speculative side of religion.' This is, he suggests, alien to the Anglo-Saxon nature, 'It is towards this trend towards Materialism that I believe that Hindu thought can so assist the English mind' (Milne in Montgomery, 1909, pp. 311–12. This notion that the Indian mind differs from the European is, of course, one of the factors influential in the realization of the need for, and the development of, a specifically Indian Christian theology. This subject will be touched upon elsewhere.

134   Müller, letter to Rev. K. M. Schermerhopn, 1902, p. 141.

135   Given in absentia.

136   Müller in WPOR, II, p. 935.

137   Müller, 1873(a), p. 148 f. See Müller, 1900, I, p. xx.

138   Müller, 1969, I, p. xiv.

139   Müller, 1902, p. 383 (from a religious paper, probably the Christian World, 1897).

140   To note one recent example, we may refer to the thought of Father Bede Griffiths for whom 'Hinduism and Christianity should be seen as revelations in relation to one another' (Brookman, p. 65). He suggests that the Holy Spirit can be seen as, '*Sakti*, the power, immanent in all creation, the *receptive* power of the Godhead'

vision does seem, though, somewhat more radical. While placing Christianity in the primary position, he, nonetheless:

> Foresaw Christianity becoming more and more synthetic, extracting sweetness and light from all kinds of theology, reconstituting these essences within its own body. Thus as the Aryan had transfigured Semitic conceptions of the Christ, so India would transform current Western comprehension of the Divine. The alteration had already begun. Keshub Chunder Sen's work as leader of the Brahmo Samaj and founder of the Church of the New Dispensation was considered by Müller to be an outrider of the greater faith to come.[141]

He thus stretched the idea of what constituted Christianity beyond the boundaries within which most of his contemporaries would have felt comfortable. He emphasized a broad theism, with some reference to the person of Jesus. Müller certainly felt a profound respect for the Brahmō Samāj and felt that it was practically a form of Christianity already.[142] What

---

(Griffiths, 1983, p. 191).

141   Maw, 1990, pp. 33–4.

142   Müller even tried to persuade the Brahmō Samāj to join the Church of England! (Müller, letter to Mr Mozoomdar, 30/10/1899, 1902, pp. 411 ff.). He believed that it could be a positive source of spreading Christ's message. In this matter he was not alone, Farquhar wrote in 1889 that, 'The Brahmo-Samaj, which owes so much of its primal influence to Missions, and especially to educational Missions, has done more to spread reverence for Christ and His teaching amongst the educated classes, and to enable them to understand what spiritual religion is, than any other single force' (Farquhar in Goodall, pp. 26–7 (probably from a London Missionary Society report). Others also expressed these views, 'For a long time there were Christian missionaries who regarded the Brahmo-Samaj less as a rival and alternative to Christianity than a movement through which the claims of Christ would be brought home in a characteristically Indian fashion to the Indian mind and heart' (ibid., p. 26). In saying this I think Goodall rather over-stretches the degree to which the acceptance of Christ by the Neo-Hindus was welcomed by Christian missionaries. While the influence may have generally been perceived as positive, there is never any suggestion that such movements are a separate and acceptable form of 'Christianity.' It is seen, rather, as a Hindu sect which has absorbed some good. Müller, gives us a somewhat different picture, 'In the eyes of our missionaries this religious reform in India has not found much favour: nor need we wonder at this. Their object is to transplant, if possible, Christianity in its full integrity from England to India[....] They do not deny the moral worth, the noble aspirations, the self-sacrificing zeal of these native reformers; but they fear that all this will but increase their dangerous influence, and retard the progress of Christianity, by drawing some of the best minds of India, that might have been gained over to our religion, into a different current. They feel towards Keshub Chunder Sen as

may be surprising though is that Müller did believe in missions.[143] He did, though, lack faith in the majority of missionaries:

> I have not much faith in missionaries, medical or otherwise. If we get such men again in India as Rāmmohun Roy, or Keshub Chunder Sen, and if we get an Archbishop at Calcutta who knows what Christianity really is, India will be Christianized in all that is essential in the twinkling of an eye.[144]

Athanasius might have felt towards Ulfias, the Arian Bishop of the Goths; and yet, what would have become of Christianity in Europe but for those Gothic races, but for those Arian heretics, who were considered more dangerous than downright pagans?' (Müller, 1873(b), p. 48). Whether missionaries generally looked upon the Brahmō Samāj as the early Christians would have looked on the Arians, as aberrant Christians, rather than as pagans, seems to me doubtful. However, this is not the place to discuss this matter, attitudes towards the Hindu revival will be discussed at greater length elsewhere. In Müller's thought, there is an odd parallel to Maurice. He 'entered the Church of England because he had become convinced that in the historic Catholic Church with its God-given constitution men could be brought together and held together in a unity out of their own ideas or notions. The Church was a deliverance from all sects and parties[....] So he maintained that each of the main divisions of Christendom, and each of the parties in the Church of England, and indeed each secular philosophy and movement too, stood at bottom for a true principle or at least a valid quest: their mistake was to assert their own truth exclusively against others' (Vidler, p. 84). While Müller wrote, 'I am, myself, a devoted member of the English Church, because I think its members enjoy greater freedom and more immunity from priestcraft than those of any other Church,' (op. cit., p. 413) in his letter to Mr. Mozoomdar. Both saw the Church of England as being a broad Church free from narrowness of teachings in which all men could come together in universal brotherhood.

143   He even saw his Sacred Books of the East series as of special importance to missionaries, for whom detailed and accurate knowledge of the non-Christian religions was 'as indispensable as a knowledge of an enemy's country is to a general' (Müller, 1902, p. 10, from the Prospectus to the Sacred Books of the East). Indeed he saw missionary activity as a sign of vital life in a religion (Fulfil, p. 47).

144   Attributed to Müller, 1902, p. 310, in Fulfil, p. 47, but not found there or elsewhere. Emphasis should be put on the second part of Müller's quotation, that India will be, 'Christianized *in all that is essential*,' which for Müller would appear to be an acceptance of Christ and his precepts as the highest revelation, no matter what system they are attached to, or what other beliefs attend them.

Finally, the following quotation from Müller should help to show the essential difference that lay between him and Monier-Williams in this matter. Speaking about the World's Parliament of Religions, he said, 'It has been established once for all[...] that the points on which the great religions differ are far less numerous, and certainly far less important, than are the points on which they all agree.'[145] Anyone having read Monier-Williams' *Buddhism* would have been left with quite the opposite impression, that there are only a few points of agreement, and that these are highly disputed as to details, while the points of divergence were legion and all of the most exaggerated kind![146] The differences between these two men and, indeed, between all those who stand on either side of the two contrasting schools of thought that have been mentioned so far in this work,[147] can neatly be summed up in the following words of Rowland Williams:

> [I]f we ask the followers of the two tendencies[...] for their watchwords, one will reply the infallibility of the Bible; but the other will say the truth of Christ[....] The one then pays its principle allegiance to the Scripture, which is true; but the other to the Truth, which is also written.[148]

Conclusion to Part II

The previous two chapters have laid the foundations of the background to fulfilment theology in modern British thought. A definite tradition of fulfilment theology can be seen to have been developing at Cambridge, which, as will be seen in later chapters, continued and become dominant. Meanwhile the research undertaken by scholars of comparative religion made

---

145   Müller, *Last Essays*, series II, p. 335, in Sharpe, 1977, p. 17.
146   Op. Cit., pp. 522 ff.
147   I.e. conservative and liberal nineteenth-century Christians.
148   R. Williams, 1855, sermon XXIV, 'The Spirit and the Letter, or the Truth and the Book', p. 386.

the position of the non-Christian religions something which had to be addressed. Indeed, as can be seen from the contributions of Monier-Williams and Müller, those in both the evangelical and liberal camps had to deal with this same problem, and in each case the answer given was fulfilment theology, though definitions of what this entailed varied.

All the foundations of fulfilment theology had been laid in the thought of the figures we have considered so far. How these different strands of fulfilment theology developed will be seen more clearly in the next part.

Part III: Acceptance

Introduction to Part III

Chapter 4, along with chapter 5, will help to uncover the truth behind Farquhar's position regarding the spread of fulfilment theology. Far from being the popularizer of this school of thought, he was merely one in a long chain of writers propounding these ideas, which had received a wide audience, as well as acceptance, well before his time. For two reasons, the focus of this chapter will be India. First, it will, of course, provide the background and context for Farquhar's thought, and, second, it was in India, and particularly in relation to Hinduism, that fulfilment theology first became widely used and really flourished. This statement I take to be a truism. While it was used in relation to other religions, Max Müller, for example, saw fulfilment as a general rule applicable to all religions, as did Maurice, yet Müller's work was primarily concerned with India, as, too, were Monier-Williams' and Williams'. While these ideas were applied in other missionary fields, and in relation to other religions,[1] even from an early date,[2] it was nevertheless in India that these ideas were given the most widespread and systematic treatment. That it was not just British missionaries who were expounding these ideas is something else that may be mentioned and Cracknell's exploration of the figures R. A. Hume,[3] and J. P. Jones[4] should again be mentioned.

A number of different figures have been chosen for inclusion in this chapter, either for their importance in the history of fulfilment theology or because they demonstrate a particular point, either in their thought or in their life. Firstly, the thought of the Hindu Renaissance, as seen in the work of Ram Mohun Roy, and Keshub Chundra Sen, will be considered, as their work is very influential in the development of fulfilment theology in India. Next,

---

1   See Martin and Jersey, both of whom employ concepts of fulfilment theology in relation to Buddhism. Mention may also be made again of Timothy Richard, who, 'During his first eight years as a missionary[...] had decided that Christ had not come "to destroy but to fulfil", and he was never to tire of citing Matt. 5.17' (Cracknell, 1995, p. 128).

2   See J. F. Clarke's article of 1869.

3   Cracknell, 1995, pp. 132 ff – but particularly pp. 138–9 on his ideas of fulfilment and preparation.

4   Ibid., pp. 144 ff.

three Indian Christian writers will be studied, most particularly Krishna Mohan Banerjea (1813–1885), the others being Nehemiah Goreh (1825–1895), and Brahmabāndhab Upādhyay (1861–1907).[5] Then the work of four missionary writers will be looked at, John Robson, G. Mackenzie Cobban, William Miller (1838–1923) and, most importantly, Thomas Ebenezer Slater (1840–1912). To these could be added many more names, if we only wanted a list of figures involved with fulfilment theology, such as F. W. Kellett,[6] to name but one whose work has been considered significant.

Before proceding with the chapter, the reasons for including the particular figures to be discussed should be mentioned. Banerjea, who was converted in 1833 and ordained in 1837,[7] has a double significance. Firstly, his was the earliest book to be published in India expounding fulfilment theology, and, as might be expected, much of his thought is found repeated in later Indian writers. Secondly, he is himself an Indian Christian and thus stands as a significant character in the development of an indigenous Indian Christian theology, by virtue of his early date.[8] Banerjea's ability as a scholar was noted at the time.[9] Goreh is included as having insight into the thought of the Oxford Mission to Calcutta, the significance of which will be discussed more fully in the next chapter. He was baptized in 1848, and travelled to England to study theology at the Islington College of the Church Missionary Society, before returning to India, where, in 1870, he was ordained.[10]

---

5   It may be noted that a new book by Lipner on Upādhyay has recently been published though too late for its insights to be incorporated into this work. The details are given in the bibliography.

6   See Fulfil, pp. 105 f. It may be noted that Kellett was an evangelical, though like many others of this wing of the church who chose the missionary path, was an able academic; thus the idea that missionaries can easily be divided into two camps, evangelicals who were ill educated and untutored and liberals advancing more 'progressive views' should not be entertained (Bebbington, p. 138).

7   See his entry in Buckland, pp. 25 f.

8   In the first edition of his book, An Introduction to Indian Christian Theology, Boyd specifically mentions Banerjea's thought as an important omission, which is corrected in the second edition. His omission does tell us that evidently Banerjea is not the most influential figure in terms of Indian Christian theology as a whole, but he is certainly a prevailing influence on fulfilment theology in India.

9   He was from 1852–68 Professor at Bishop's College, Calcutta (Buckland, p. 26). Philip notes that, he was one of 'the outstanding scholars of his time in Sanskritic literature' (Philip, 1982, p. 94).

10   Buckland, p. 172.

Upādhyay is mentioned as he is a very significant figure, although, as a Roman Catholic, he does, technically, stand apart from this study.

Miller's thought provides an interesting alternative slant on the standard presentation of fulfilment theology, while Slater is the most significant figure we have to deal with. He is the only person whose fulfilment theology will be dealt with in a comprehensive way, being, as Maw describes him, as, perhaps, 'the only systematic exponent of fulfilment theology in the sub-continent' before the arrival of the Cambridge Mission to Delhi.[11] Indeed, Slater foreshadowed all that Farquhar was to say in terms of the theory of fulfilment theology.

Robson is significant, not so much for his writings, which do, nevertheless, provide an early instance of fulfilment theology in India, but for the testimony he provides as to the spread of the concept.[12] Next, mention will be made of Cobban, who is not so important for what he thought, but rather how he was misunderstood, and how this has led to a misapprehension concerning the acceptance of fulfilment theology in the latter part of the nineteenth-century.

This chapter should demonstrate that Farquhar did not popularize these ideas – they were common currency well before his day.

In chapter 5 the adoption and utilization of fulfilment theology by missionaries in India is discussed. The early limited approval, and suspicion, it received was observed, as well as its later widespread adoption by many missionaries, including leading figures in the Indian Anglican episcopate. In this chapter attention turns from the mission field to the home front to show that fulfilment theology was not just popular and accepted by the missionaries themselves, but that it was also well regarded by the ecclesiastical establishment at home. The use of fulfilment theology by some major figures will be studied as examples. These are Brooke Foss Westcott (1825–1901), Bishop of Durham, Arthur Penrhyn Stanley (1815–1881), Dean of Westminster, John Henry Newman (1801–1890), Archbishop of Westminster, Charles Gore (1853–1932), Bishop of Oxford, and Edward White Benson (1829–96), Archbishop of Canterbury. There will also be seen to be a host of supporting characters, in greater or lesser favour of these ideas. In addition to

---

11   Maw, 1990, p. 51.
12   We may observe in passing that he was Moderator of the Synod of the United Presbyterian Church of Scotland in 1899–1900, having retired from missionary work due to ill health in 1872 (Buckland, p. 362).

those mentioned here there were many others, whom, for reasons of space, cannot be included, such as R. W. Church,[13] J. R. Illingworth,[14] and Benjamin Jowett.[15] Amongst those whose work is not explored here, A. M. Fairbairn is, perhaps, the most important.[16] While he did not propound fulfilment theology at length, he influenced both Farquhar[17] and Slater.[18] Fairbairn also visited India,[19] where he was warmly received by the Hindu community[20] We are reminded here of the difference noted between Müller and Monier-Williams, the former who never visited India, and the latter who did and found his views subsequently altered.[21] The idea that an experience of the non-Christian religions was important, rather than just having theoretical knowledge, was

---

13   He can be seen as in many ways similar to Stanley, both were contemporaries in the liberal Oxford tradition. All Church has to say, that is informative for us here, can be found in two lectures which he delivered in St. Paul's in 1874, published as *The Sacred Poetry of Early Religions*. In the preface he acknowledges his debt to Müller (Church, 1874, p. vii.). Certainly Church felt that the non-Christian religions did approach, instinctively, towards God (ibid., pp. 23, 26, 35, and 47), and suggests that, 'the Gentiles had much that was needful, perhaps as much as was possible' (ibid., p. 35. See Müller, 1873 (a), p. 261). From the few comments Church makes we cannot, however, discern whether he believed the non-Christian religions to be providentially ordained preparations for Christianity, rather than being just man's instinctive yearnings, the result of natural religion.

14   His contribution to *Lux Mundi* provides one example, but see also Supple, pp. 121 ff.

15   A good discussion of Jowett's changing views can be found in Supple, pp. 48 ff. His writings upon this, and many other matters, would be well worth exploring at greater length.

16   See Cracknell, 1995, pp. 71 ff, also Fulfil, pp. 126 ff., and also Fairbairn, N.D., pp. 75 ff.

17   See chapter 7.

18   Cracknell, 1995, p. 117.

19   Selbie, p. 352 f.

20   According to Selbie, 'Thoughtful Hindus recognised in him one who was something more than the ordinary apologist for the Christian faith. He was that, but they found in him at the same time a student of religions who had some claim to understand their own position, and who had real sympathy with the ideas that underlay it[....] They appreciated the fact that he spoke as one who knew; and his criticisms of their position left no sting because they were based upon principles which they themselves could understand and appreciate. They were profoundly touched by the keen sympathy for them and their fellow countrymen which the lecturer's whole attitude implied, and which frequently found expression in his words' (ibid., pp. 352–3).

21   Chapter 3.

something Fairbairn believed in.[22] He studied the non-Christian religions deeply,[23] and exercised a wide influence: 'By his writings and through his speeches, as well as by his teaching and example, Fairbairn moved theologians within his own denomination and elsewhere in the direction of justice and fairness, courtesy and sympathy as they evaluated other religious traditions.'[24]

However, it was not just Churchmen and theologians who propagated this idea. The statesman Gladstone also propounded a form of fulfilment theology. In his work *Juventus Mundi, the Gods and Men of the Heroic Age*, Gladstone suggested that Christ was foreshadowed by Apollo, the Virgin Mary by Latona, Satan by Ate, and the Trinity by a combination of Zeus, Poseidon, and Hades.[25] His biographer sees this as an aberration in the 'great man.'[26] However, in the context of this study, Gladstone's theories can be seen alongside other similar thought of his day.

The first section of this chapter will deal with B. F. Westcott, examining his thought, and, also, arguing against Maw's assertion that: 'Fulfilment [theology] had begun as Westcott's private creed.'[27] Here I will just observe that, in considering the great number of eminent figures who will be dealt with in this chapter, it is impossible to conceive that they all owe their influence in this matter to Westcott. Rather, I would refer back to the earlier chapter on Maurice and Williams, where I suggested that the similarities

---

22   See Cracknell, 1995, pp. 78 ff.

23   According to Cracknell, 'Fairbairn was the first theologian in Britain to use the scientific studies of the new scholars of religion, entering into their labours far more deeply than had Westcott' (ibid., p. 75). I think this perhaps an exaggeration, while he may have studied this area more deeply than Westcott – who, as we shall see, did not regard himself as an expert in this area – many others had used the new science of comparative religion before. One who studied the area in great depth was Rowland Williams. See Selbie, p. 351 in this regard who says that Fairbairn was one of the first to use 'Muir, Tiele, Max Muller, and Chantepie de la Saussaye, [etc].'

24   Ibid., p. 81 – that Cracknell notes that Fairbairn influenced people in the direction of 'justice and fairness[...]' is a point we may note, that his role was more in laying foundations for an attitude in which fulfilment theology could flourish rather than being himself a major propagator of the idea.

25   Magnus, p. 220.

26   Ibid.

27   Maw, 1990, p. 253.

between these two could, possibly, be attributed to their belonging to a common tradition, of which, it will be seen, Westcott is also a member.

The next section deals with the work of the Cambridge Mission to Delhi. This discussion is included here, rather than in the previous chapter on missionary work, as its fulfilment theology can be seen as springing directly from the Cambridge tradition, rather than from the usual missionary context. Most missionaries adopted fulfilment theology as a response to the situation in India, while the Cambridge Mission to Delhi was founded specifically to propagate it.

The final section covers a wide range of thinkers to seek to show that fulfilment theology was not just known within the context of the Cambridge tradition, but within the wider Christian community, and, that, it was, if not whole heartedly embraced, then at least known and accepted. The majority of these figures are from Oxford, as opposed to the Cambridge tradition exemplified by Westcott and the Cambridge Mission to Delhi. Each may be seen, in some way, as representative of a tendency within various parties in the Church to accept more 'liberal' views towards the non-Christian religions. Indeed, in the Church in the later part of the nineteenth-century, the liberal perspectives pioneered by Rowland Williams and Maurice were becoming more acceptable generally, as Knight observes:

> By 1870 the reading list for ordinands in Ely, a diocese that was still six years away from founding its own theological college, contained a mixture of the old and new. Many of the authors had been familiar for decades – Butler, Paley and Pearson – but some newer scholars were also being recommended, reflecting a more liberal and critical tone, among them A. P. Stanley and B. F. Westcott.[28]

---

28   Knight, p. 115, reference to *Ely Diocesan Calender and Clergy List* (1870), pp. 17-
        18.

4 Missionary Usage

Banerjea, Indian Christians, and the Hindu Renaissance

While this section will focus on K. M. Banerjea, there is a larger theme, which is to demonstrate the way in which the thought of Indians contributed to the development of fulfilment theology. There is a twofold aspect to this; firstly, seeing how Indian Christians such as Banerjea related their new faith to the religion in which they were brought up, and, secondly, considering how the writings and thought of Indians were used in developing the theory of fulfilment theology. These factors are of vital importance for the missionaries in India, as they needed to develop a method of evangelism that would appeal to the native population. While, in previous chapters, the development of fulfilment theology can be viewed as something of a theoretical intellectual exercise, this chapter will dwell upon those who used it as a practical method. This first section will show how fulfilment theology was a response to the way Indian converts perceived the relationship between Christianity and Hinduism. It will also be argued that developments within Hinduism led many missionaries to the belief that the adoption of fulfilment theology was the best approach to this religion.

The Hindu Renaissance and Fulfilment Theology

Both Sen and Roy felt a deep devotion to the figure of Jesus,[1] and represent, arguably, the phase of India's religious development when Western (Christian) influence was most evident. This is not the place to enter into a discussion of the influences on the theology of these two figures, nor of the Brahmō Samāj generally. However, it should be noted that one Indian commentator, writing in 1894, observed that sixty years previously a number of English educated Bengalis were very much opposed to Hinduism

---

1   Gupta, p. 1435.

generally, while thirty years previously a great many had turned to Bráhmanism,[2] and within the last fifteen years the trend had been towards Neo-Hinduism.[3] Both may be seen as coming from the first phase into the second.

Roy will be considered first. While, in some ways, he is the more significant figure as the founder of the Samāj, he does not contribute so much to the development of fulfilment theology as Sen, but rather he laid the foundations of it. He opposed many of the institutions of traditional Hinduism, such as idolatry[4] and suttee.[5] Indeed, one recent commentator has said that, 'Rammohun Roy, the founder of modern Hinduism in theory rejected nearly everything that was essential in Hinduism.'[6] Most importantly, in attacking Hinduism, he stated that he belived Jesus' teachings to be more conducive to morality than Hinduism.[7] Obviously these words, from a leading figure such as Roy, would have been eagerly greeted by many missionaries. Indeed, it is worth noting that Zaehner considers that it is through the Brahmō Samāj that a social conscience first entered Hinduism.[8] Many Christians did, indeed, welcome Roy's work,[9] but there was opposition to his reforms from certain missionaries.[10] The details of this do not concern us, but what should be noted is that Roy was seen as an example of one of those Hindus who found that his ancestral faith was no longer up to the challenges posed by the West.[11]

Finally, it must be mentioned that Roy believed that it was necessary to return to the Vedas to regain a pure Hinduism,[12] and in this he was followed

---

2   By which term he means the Brahmō Samāj.

3   Bose, p. 85.

4   Richards, p. 5.

5   Ibid., p. 16 ff.

6   A. Eschman, in Sontheimer, p. 116.

7   Ibid., p. 8. The importance Roy attached to Jesus' moral teachings is discussed by M. M. Thomas, 1969, pp. 8 ff.

8   Zaehner, 1990, p. 155. This point will be referred to again in considering subsequent missionary attitudes towards Hinduism.

9   Fremantle, pp. 67 f.

10   See Gupta, p. 1438, and M. M. Thomas, 1969, chapter 1. These critics were opposed by Müller (see Müller, 1873, p. 48 f.).

11   Fremantle, p. 80. This is an important point for Christian missionaries, which found an airing as early as Williams, and will be seen again in the thought of later writers.

12   This idea was taken up by K. M. Banerjea, see below.

by many later reformers including Sarasvati,[13] founder of the Arya Samāj. Thus, in the nineteenth-century, for many Hindus the Vedas became the yard-stick by which all doctrines should be judged. For later Christian writers, particularly Banerjea, it became important to show that the Vedas pointed to Christianity, rather than modern day Hinduism. It may be observed in passing that this Hindu desire to return to a pure religion of the Vedas makes a parallel to the nineteenth-century search for the pure religion of Jesus. I would suggest that there were both similar and divergent causes at work. Simply put, the Hindu Renaissance was largely the result of an Indian response to Western education and criticism, due to which many recoiled from what were seen as late abuses of what was considered the original religion of India. As already mentioned, Rowland Williams, when applying historical criticism to Hinduism, felt it necessary to apply the same methods to Christianity, and so in the light of modern criticism much of the form of Christianity was swept away to reveal what were believed to be Jesus' original teachings. The similarities lie in the response of both religions, in the face of new critiques, to return to some supposed original religion. The differences lie firstly in the origin of the assault, on Hinduism from outside of itself, on Christianity from within its own Western cultural setting, though, of course, the Hindu reformers then take the criticisms and apply them to their own religion. Secondly, while there is a certain similarity in the position of retreat, the Hindu response is to take refuge in a revealed text and to use its authoritative status to determine what doctrines may be held, whereas for the Christian, in the light of New Testament criticism, the response is to dissect the 'revealed' text to see what parts are genuine and which parts are later interpretations. Both of these reactions only represent one response of each religion, there being different traditions which deal with the matter in different ways.

Next we will consider the, for us, more important figure of Sen, whom Boyd observes developed a number of important concepts in Indian Christian theology.[14] He has been regarded as the greatest Indian of his time,[15] and, according to Farquhar, helped lead many Hindus at least some way closer to Jesus.[16] Many thought that he would in fact convert to Christianity.[17]

---

13   Webster, pp. 2–3.
14   Boyd, 1979, p. 27.
15   Ibid.
16   Farquhar, 1918, p. 22
17   See in this regard, M. M. Thomas, 1969, pp. 69 ff.

However, it has been doubted if his thought was as thoroughly Christ-centred as certain Christian writers have claimed.[18] Perhaps, with hindsight, we might say that the failure of the Church at the time to be truly indigenous was what held Sen back from conversion. Before passing judgement on the eisegesis of Western observers, it should be observed that many Hindus believed that he had become a Christian.[19] One contemporary writer sees the Brahmō Samāj under Sen offering a place to both Christianity and Hinduism.[20] The question of Sen's beliefs are not pertinent, but how he was understood, and how he provided opportunities for the future development of fulfilment theology, are.

Sen called Jesus, 'the Prince of Prophets.'[21] While this phrase places Jesus only on a human level, Boyd has noted that Sen's beliefs concerning Jesus' role moved closer to Christian orthodoxy throughout his life.[22] Noteworthy is that, while Roy's thought had been essentially monistic, one contemporary commentator saw that the main bar to seeing him as a Christian thinker were his 'unitarian' views,[23] Sen's thought was Trinitarian. Here he propounded one of his most insightful correspondences, which was to equate the Christian trinity, not with the Hindu trimurti, Brahmā, Vishnu and Śiva, but with the attributes of Brahman as saccidānanda.[24] He was the first person to propound this idea,[25] which was taken up by Upādhyay, who claimed that the Advaitic understanding of God/Brahman as being-consciousness-bliss was essentially the same as Neo-Thomistic understandings of the trinity.[26] While most of the fulfilment theologians to be considered draw parallels between trimurti and trinity, it is nevertheless significant that Sen saw the trinity as present in Hinduism. Later writers could change the emphasis and thereby use this for apologetic ends, saying that Hindus recognized a trinity which would, in their eyes be a preparation for the Christian trinity. Beyond just equating the Hindu and Christian concepts of trinity, Keshub developed his Christology so that Jesus became identified with the Logos, the second person

---

18   See Devdas, p. 14. It has been said of him that he 'was particularly adept at synthesizing the varying strains of Hindu-Muslim-Christian religion present in mid-nineteenth-century India' (Ashby, p. 32).
19   Boyd, 1979, p. 27.
20   Wilkins, p. 359.
21   M. C. Parekh, *Bramarshi Keshub Chunder Sen*, p. 33, in M. M. Thomas, p. 58.
22   Boyd, 1979, p. 30.
23   Fremantle, pp. 70–1.
24   Boyd, 1974, p. 21.
25   Boyd, 1979, p. 34.
26   Lipner, in Coward, 1987, pp. 308–9.

of the trinity, of whom he was the incarnation.[27] In the light of such opinions, Farquhar's assertion that, 'in the latter part of his [Sen's] life, his deepest theological beliefs were full Christian,'[28] does not seem unreasonable, and is an idea endorsed by others of his time.[29]

So far Sen's devotion to Christianity and, along with this, his turning to Christian orthodoxy, have been considered. From this alone the missionary could find evidence that, for western educated and intelligent Indians, no firm foundation could be found in Hinduism, but rather that they must turn to Christianity.

Yet, Sen's thought went further than this. He was deeply nationalistic, and wanted to bring his belief in Jesus' teachings to an Indian audience, for this, he believed, was necessary to show that Jesus' message was not alien to the Indian ethos. He therefore presented Jesus as an Asian.[30] Most significantly, he said:

> Behold, Christ cometh to us as an Asiatic [...] and he demands your heart's affection [....] He comes to fulfil and perfect that religion of communion for which India has been panting [....] For Christ is a true Yogi, and he surely help us to realise our national ideal of a Yogi.[31]

Sen's words here are pure fulfilment theology and would not be out of place in Farquhar's *The Crown of Hinduism*; their importance cannot be overstated. A leading Hindu presenting Jesus as the fulfilment of the Hindu religious ideal.[32] Further, Sen expounded a form of Logos theology, saying:

> Christ is already present in you. He is in you, even when you are unconscious of his presence [....] For Christ is 'the Light that lighteth every man that cometh into the

---

27   See M. M. Thomas, 1969, pp. 64 ff.

28   Farquhar, 1918, p. 66 f.

29   See Fremantle, p. 68. This observation has been made by Parrinder, p. 99.

30   See Bose, pp. 150–1.

31   K. C. Sen, *Lectures in India*, I, pp. 388 and 389, in Boyd, 1974, p. 20.

32   It may be mentioned that Halbfass has suggested that Sen saw himself as fulfilling Hinduism as a Messianic figure responsible for establishing a new dispensation (Halbfass, p. 226). Certainly Sen's later splinter group from the Brahmō Samāj, the Church of the New Dispensation, was seen as fulfilling the Old and New Testaments, (Boyd, 1979, pp. 26–7) but there is no indication that Sen saw himself superseding Jesus. While it is possible to concede Halbfass' point that Sen saw himself as introducing teachings that would fulfill Hinduism, it probably is not possible to correctly speak of Sen himself as the fulfiller of Hinduism.

world'[....] He will come to you as self-surrender, as asceticism, as Yoga, as the life of God in man, as obedient and humble sonship.[33]

Sen, thus, identified man's religious sense with Jesus as the Logos. Whether his inspiration comes from Christian sources, or whether he is merely giving a Christian gloss to ideas gathered from other sources, is uncertain. While Sen never converted to Christianity, and he certainly did not draw on Christian sources alone, I feel compelled to agree with Boyd's words that, 'Sen's eclecticism cannot be disguised but he himself makes it clear that it is what he calls 'Christian eclecticism', in which Christ himself becomes the touchstone by which every doctrine or practice must be tested.'[34] Sen turned further to Christian practice as well as belief in later life. In a lecture in 1870, he said:

I found Christ spoke one language and Christianity another[....]
There are some persons who believe that if we pass through the ceremony of baptism and sacrament, we shall be accepted by God, but if you accept baptism as an outward rite, you cannot thereby render your life acceptable to God, for Christ wants something internal[....][35]

When, however, Sen formed the Church of the New Dispensation in 1882 he introduced the rite of Baptism, as well as a form of the Eucharist.[36]

That two of the earliest and best known Hindu reformers should base their teachings so heavily upon the figure of Jesus is undeniably important when viewing later missionary activity. While it is easy for us today to view the beliefs and attitudes of the missionaries as arrogant and colonial, when considered in the context of their times, where two of India's greatest sons had already conceded so much to Christianity, the claim that Jesus fulfilled the needs and desires of Hindus was to say no more than one of Hinduism's great reformers had already said. Whatever one may think of missionary methods of fulfilment theology, they had already been endorsed by a Hindu.

One point worth noting in Sen's thought, which might, at first glance, seem antinomic, is the equation of his patriotism with the suggestion that it

33   Ibid., in Boyd, 1979, pp. 37–8.
34   Boyd, 1979, p. 36.
35   K. C. Sen, 'Lecture on Christ and Christianity', in Müller, 1873(b), p. 61.
36   Zaehner, 1990, p. 154.

is providential that India be placed in England's hands.[37] This should not, though, be seen as a contradiction, for I suggest that Sen's meaning is that it was providential for India to be placed temporarily in England's hands in that knowledge of Jesus and his teachings could be spread. The colonial situation, however, may be felt to have reached an end of its usefulness. While absorbing much from the West in terms of religious ideas, the Brahmō Samāj did, nevertheless, mark Indian's first moves towards ideas of a national identity (and therefore, inevitably, of independence).[38]

Before passing on, Bose's analysis at the beginning of this section should be remembered, in that the height of the Brahmō Samāj's influence had been in the 1860s, and that from about 1880 onwards Neo-Hinduism was coming to dominance. It should thus not be considered that in the period in which fulfilment theology came to dominance in Indian missionary circles, that all the traffic, in terms of Hindu thought, was heading in the pro-Christian direction. Even in 1866 it was observed that the Brahmō Samāj was opposed to Christianity, although Sen removed this stigma.[39] The significance of Roy and Sen, and of the Brahmō Samāj as a whole,[40] was possibly given far more weight than it deserved by Western, specifically Christian, commentators at the time. Thus it may be noted that at the World's Parliament of Religions two members of the Brahmō Samāj represented Hinduism,[41] which had by this time rather lost out to Neo-Hinduism.[42] Even Neo-Hinduism, however, had a place for Jesus,[43] and it was Christianity rather than the person of Jesus they were opposed to. Roy and Sen introduced new ideas into Hinduism, and in the process their thought, and Hinduism itself, was changed.[44] Many

---

37   See quotation in Fremantle, p. 75. While he does not attribute the quotation, he does later attribute the ideas contained in it to Sen (ibid., p. 80).

38   Flood, 1996, p. 254.

39   Fremantle, p. 68.

40   It may be mentioned that the thought of Roy and Sen do not necessarily represent the Brahmō Samāj as a whole, particularly after Sen's second schism to found the Church of the New Dispensation when the majority of the movement did not join his new group (see Collet, pp. 730 and 736).

41   The two speeches are given in Seager, pp. 433 ff., and 440 ff., neither of which, it is worth noting, give any special place to Jesus beyond that of any other religious teacher.

42   Bose, p. 137; see also Farquhar, 1918, p. 65.

43   Devdas, pp. 13–4.

44   We may note Halbfass' assertion that Sen's soteriology was no longer Indian in character.

Western notions were integrated through their work, which would help lead to the introduction of an indigenous form of Christianity.[45] Their importance in this study is that their thought provides substance to, and also leads the way towards, many future developments in fulfilment theology.

Krishna Mohun Banerjea

Banerjea can be seen as the first major Christian interpreter of Christianity into Indian terms in the subcontinent itself. Maw has interpreted Banerjea's thought in terms of the Aryan race theory,[46] and certainly the first three chapters of his best known work *The Arian Witness*[47] do attempt to show that the Aryan races had a common homeland in Media. However, Banerjea's thought in this matter could have had another source, coming not from a reading of 'a relatively new and potentially radical theory'[48] but from his evangelical Christian training, as he was one of Duff's converts.[49] Already in Morris and Monier-Williams the theory that the light in every religion comes from an original common revelation has been seen. Duff, Maw notes, had no problems with the theory, as it 'was a quasi-empirical proof of the Mosaic record.'[50] Rather he used the theory to show the difference rather than the similarities, '[Duff] reasoned that all societies originated from the Aryan homeland: yet homogeneity no longer prevailed, because the West had received Christ and had articulated the miracle of the Incarnation[....]'[51]

Banerjea argues along similar lines, although he diverged from Duff in stressing what was good in Indian thought, while Duff went on to use the idea to pursue a theory that India should be Anglicized.[52] That Banerjea does make use of aspects of the Aryan race theory is undeniable. He uses it very much to show that the Vedas are part of a primordial revelation, and so was not

---

45   See M. M. Thomas, 1969, p. 56, and Boyd, 1974, p. 20.
46   The idea that the Indian and European peoples share a common ancestry; see the section, in chapter 3, on Müller, also, Maw, 1986, pp. 45 ff., where he discusses Banerjea.
47   Banerjea used the spelling 'Arian' to mean what we normally term 'Aryan'.
48   Maw, 1990, p. 45.
49   Boyd, 1979, p. 280.
50   Maw, 1990, p. 42.
51   Ibid., p. 43.
52   Ibid., pp. 42 ff.

pursuing a particularly radical agenda in his theories.[53] However, his raison d'être in writing was to make an answer to the growing nationalism of the Samājs in India, where he was the first writer in India to propound the idea that certain Hindu teachings were forerunners of Christianity in terms that made an appeal to Indian thought.

It would be useful to expand further on the influence of nationalism on Banerjea. Like Sen, Banerjea had believed that it was providential that India had been be placed under British rule to cleanse its own social abuses. Later in life, however, he altered these views, becoming more nationalistic in his thinking.[54] His views on his Indian heritage also underwent a change. It is generally suggested that up until his retirement in 1867, as a Professor at Bishop's College, Calcutta, he had largely dismissed his Hindu heritage.[55] After this time his ideas changed,[56] although it appears that he had taken a more positive stance to Hinduism by 1863.[57] He had personal contact with the Brahmō Samāj,[58] however it is generally considered that the Arya Samāj was more influential on him, with its especial interest in the Vedas.[59] As noted earlier, Roy, too, had seen the Vedas as the sole source of Hinduism. The Arya Samāj should not be seen as the only source of these ideas, but it was more militantly nationalistic than the Brahmō Samāj,[60] and it was perhaps more than anything the growing national movement that led Banerjea to return to his Indian heritage. One of the essential points that he makes in the *Arian Witness* is that they are not traitors to India:

> [A]n idea often broached against Hindoo Christians [is] that they are rebels against the *sanātana dharma* of the country, and apostates from the faith that has animated the Hindoo mind, and the rule of life that has governed Hindoo practice, from time

---

53　See, for instance, Banerjea, 1875, p. 3, where he speaks about sacrifice being antediluvian in origin, and kept up by Noah, who was, for Banerjea, as will be noted below, identical with the Indian Manu. We may note that in an early work Banerjea referred to the Hindu trimurti as a problem, and suggested it was due to 'a relic of some primitive revelation, of which a distorted tradition had probably reached our ancestors' (Banerjea, 1861, pp. 522–3).

54　See Lipner, in Coward, 1987, p. 304.

55　Boyd, 1979, p. 280.

56　Boyd, 1979, p. 281.

57　See Maw, 1990, p. 49.

58　Baago, 1969, p. 42.

59　See Baago, 1969, p. 42, Maw, 1990, p. 46, and Boyd, 1979, p. 281.

60　Zaehner, 1990, p. 159.

immemorial. This essay aspires to the patriotic honor of proving that[...] Hindoo Christians can alone have the satisfaction of knowing that the fundamental principles of the Gospel were recognized and acknowledged[...] by[...] the Brahmanical Arians of India[... who] would[...] recognize the Indian Christians[...] as their own descendants.[61]

His aim then was certainly polemical against the Arya Samāj and others who recognized the Vedas, but did not accept Christianity. It was also apologetic, to show that Christianity was not an alien religion to India. He is therefore important most as an influence on missionary writers, especially Slater,[62] who, in the closing years of the nineteenth and early twentieth-centuries, sought to couch Christianity in terms acceptable to Hindus. Banerjea, as an Indian, could be seen as a good guide showing what would appeal to the native mind.

Banerjea never developed a particularly expanded fulfilment theology, and as has been mentioned, it relies upon the notion of a primordial revelation, rather than a Logos theology. He also attempts to tie up the Biblical and Vedic accounts, showing, for instance, the similarities between the flood stories,[63] and attempting to show by philological means also that the figures of Noah and Manu in the two stories are the same person.[64] Again he seeks to show the similarities of the accounts of creation.[65] Most of the book follows this pattern, containing very little fulfilment theology. The only significant example to be found is in his discussion of Prajāpati, an idea that crops up again in Slater.

Sacrifice was an essential element in Banerjea's thought, mentioned throughout his work,[66] and the main area in which he describes fulfilment occurring. He identifies it as the core of Christianity,[67] and he seeks to show its vital place in Indian tradition as well.[68] In fact, he suggests, the Vedas have the closest approximation to Old Testament notions of sacrifice of any

---

61   Banerjea, 1875, p. 10.
62   Baago, 1969, p. 15 and Maw, 1990, p. 51.
63   Banerjea, 1875, pp. 153 ff.
64   Ibid., pp. 157–8.
65   Ibid., chapter IV.
66   See Lipner, in Coward, 1987, p. 305, referring to his Ordination address, Banerjea, pp. 2 ff, and chapters VII and VIII; also Fulfil, p. 93, on his later work, *The Relation between Christianity and Hinduism*, p. 6.
67   Banerjea, 1875, p. 2.
68   Ibid., pp. 194 ff.

nation.[69] He mentions three elements of Vedic sacrifice, which he sees as vital, which link it to Jewish, and, thereby, Christian notions:

(1) The mystical identification of the sacrificer with the victim, which is the ransom for sin; (2) Sacrifice the great remedy for the ills of life – the ship or ark by which we escape sin and all worldly perils. (3) Sacrifice the instrument by which sin and death are annulled and abolished.[70]

For Banerjea this ideal was found supremely with 'Prajāpati [who] coincided precisely "with the meaning of the name and offices of the historical reality of Jesus Christ."'[71] Indeed, he says of Prajāpati: 'The Vedic ideal of *Prajāpati*, as we have seen, singularly approximates to the above description of our Lord, and thereby remarkably confirms the saving mysteries of Christianity.'[72] However, he says: 'The gold has become dim by the alloy which has been mixed up by unholy and impure hands.'[73] So the original doctrine of sacrifice became misunderstood and lost with the passing generations. Even the proof of the Vedas showed, he felt, that the Aryans in India had originally been followers of Jesus, who was identified with the

---

69   Ibid., p. 194.
70   Banerjea, 1875, p. 206.
71   Maw, p. 48, quoting from Banerjea, *The Relation Between Christianity and Hinduism*, p. 2.
72   Banerjea, *The Relation Between Christianity and Hinduism*, text in Philip, 1982, p. 193. Indeed it is worth quoting from what Banerjea says immediately before this at some length, for having looked at the notion of prajāpati he continues,'Without going further with these quotations[...] I may now undertake to declare that the first of the two propositions, with which I commenced this discourse, is proved, viz.: '"That the fundamental principles of Christian doctrine in relation to the salvation of the world, find a remarkable counterpart in the Vedic principles of primitive Hinduism in relation to the destruction of sin and the redemption of the sinner by the efficacy of sacrifice, itself a figure of *Prajāpati*, the Lord and Saviour of the Creation, who had offered himself a sacrifice for that purpose."
'All that has just been shown appertaining to the self-sacrifice of *Prajāpati* curiously resembles the Biblical description of Christ as God and man, our very Emmanuel, mortal and immortal, who "hath given Himself for us, an offering and a sacrifice to God for a sweet-smelling savour," of whom all previous sacrifices were but figures and reflections, who by His sacrifice or death hath "vanquished death, and brought life and immortality to light through the Gospel"' (ibid).
73   Banerjea, 1875, p. 216.

Divine Purusha.[74] He thus followed Sen, in seeing Jesus as the fulfiller of Hinduism, but he also makes reference to Müller in the *Arian Witness*, and, with his evangelical background, may well also have known of Monier-Williams' work. We cannot, therefore, trace his fulfilment theology to any particular source, although there are some indications which will be mentioned below.

Two further instances of Banerjea's fulfilment theology are worth mentioning. First, when discussing the concept of avatars he says, 'that to the Mosaic narrative of the Fall must be attributed the great idea with which the incarnation of Ráma was fraught, that it was necessary for a divine person *to be made flesh*, and assume human nature, in order to encompass the destruction of *the Devil and his works.*'[75] Evidently, he does not follow Müller and Sen in their Logos theology. This is not an idea inherent in man, as fulfilment theology would normally state, but rather the knowledge comes from revealed scripture.

The second is not strictly speaking a case of fulfilment theology, as such, while he sees the cult of Krishna bearing 'curious testimony to the Christian doctrine of *faith* as opposed to ceremonial works.'[76] He suggests that it was directly inspired by Christianity,[77] so, again, it is not the Hindu tradition which gives rise to this tradition, but it is copied from Christianity. The implication should be taken that the human being as a fallen creature relies upon external revelation, and cannot rely upon his own experience. Banerjea follows Duff's assessment, that Hinduism since the time of the Vedas has been one long descent into darkness, the light being the fragments of an ancient revelation.

In the light of what has been seen above it should not surprise us that a conservative evangelical like Duff endorsed his work.[78] The same response came from George Cotton, Bishop of Calcutta, who arranged for him to give a talk in 1864, in which 'faint shadows of the truth' were demonstrated, from

---

74   The terms 'purusha' and 'prajāpati' may be used inter-changeably in the context in which they are seen in *The Relation Between Christianity and Hinduism* (see Schuhmacher and Woerner, 1989, pp. 273–4, and 282, Flood, 1996, pp. 45 and 48–9, Lipner, 1994, pp. 87–8, and Zaehner, 1988, pp. 8 ff.).

75   Banerjea, 1875, p. 152.

76   Ibid., p 227.

77   Ibid., p. 235.

78   Maw, 1990, p. 48.

Banerjea's point of view.[79] There appears to have been no dissent.[80] It evidently was acceptable to missionaries even of the 1860s to suggest that there were fragments of good in the Hindu system(!), a point to be born in mind in the following sections of this chapter. Even when people disagreed with his arguments there appears to have been no hostility, a reviewer of *The Arian Witness* calling his ideas fanciful, and saying he builds a lot upon few foundations, but not dismissing his ideas altogether.[81] When Banerjea's sequel came out in 1880, *Two Essays as Supplements to the Aryan[82] Witness*, more had been done to promote fulfilment theology, both Robson and Slater had published their first works, and Monier-Williams had visited India, so it should not surprise us that a review of this work in the same journal suggests that Banerjea is 'largely successful' in propounding his ideas.[83] Also he refers to Banerjea's earlier work as that 'well known but 'curious book,''[84] suggesting that what he says is not considered usual.

In the light of his theology, and presentation of fulfilment theology, I would suggest that Monier-Williams would be a more likely source for these ideas, rather than Sen or Müller, although it is possible to show that he was at least familiar with the thought of these two figures. However, as an person educated in an evangelical Christian environment it is, I would suggest, absurd to say that he would not have known, at the very least, of Monier-Williams' work, even if he had not actually read any of it.

The two most significant factors to be taken from Banerjea are, first, his witness that fulfilment theology could be acceptable in evangelical Christian circles from a very early date, and, second, the influence he was to have on later writers, particularly in the way he, as an Indian, could suggest that it was possible to speak of Christianity as fulfilling certain aspects of Hinduism and Hindu desire.

---

79   Ibid., p. 49.
80   Maw takes this as evidence that the Aryan race theory was widely known and accepted by Protestant missionaries. However, as already indicated, even if such ideas, which would have been very new at this time, were widely known, they would no doubt have only been a confirmation of the conservative Christian position that there was a common antediluvian revelation.
81   Anon., 1876, pp. 262–3.
82   This latter work adopts the more normative spelling apparently.
83   Anon., 1880, p. 226.
84   Ibid., p. 225.

Two figures whose work is insightful will be mentioned here, but only briefly, for they stand to one stand of the general development of fulfilment theology.

First, is Nehemiah Goreh, who, like Banerjea, was converted into evangelical Protestantism, but once a Christian found a greater sympathy for Tractarianism.[85] He was impressed by the asceticism of the movement, and even served a novitiate with the Cowley Fathers,[86] who started missions at Bombay in 1874.[87] The asceticism of the Oxford Movement has already been mentioned in relation to Morris, and while the importance of this to mission may not be immediately apparent, for missions to India it is, nevertheless, a point of vital significance in the development of Indian Christian theology. While it may be seen as not relevant to fulfilment theology, it rather should stand side by side with it as another aspect of the attempt to make Christianity indigenous to India.[88] As will be seen in the next chapter the ideal of the simple life was for the Cambridge Mission to Delhi a practical expression of the intellectual commitment to fulfilment theology.

Goreh has been seen as a very conservative figure, the 'Indian champion of orthodox western Christianity.'[89] Undeniably, his theology was almost entirely Western,[90] and his best known work was an attempted refutation of the major schools of Hindu philosophy.[91] While taking whole-heartedly to the

---

85   Boyd, 1979, p. 42.

86   Ibid.

87   Slade, p. 25

88   C. F. Andrews may be mentioned as a particular case in point, of whom more will be said later. The cultural differences as to what would be considered ascetic are very different. The basics of Western society are not those of the East, as Father Bede Griffiths notes in the changes that took place in the development of his Christian ashram, 'I had a Western habit, I wore shoes and socks, and we had tables and chairs and spoons and forks. We thought it was very simple but it was still Western[....]

     '[....] We began wearing the *kavi*[.... W]e began to adopt normal Indian customs – like sitting on the floor, sleeping on a mat, eating with the hands, and so on' (Swindells, p. 73).

89   Boyd, 1974, p. 22.

90   See Boyd, 1979, pp. 40 ff.

91   Ibid., pp. 42 ff.

Western expression of Christianity, he remained firmly committed to Indian culture.[92]

Indeed, I would suggest that his expression has led to some misunderstanding. He had little influence,[93] unlike Banerjea, and it has been suggested that he had little sympathy for Hinduism.[94] He was actually far more sympathetic to Hinduism than Banerjea, though he still had reservations on several points.

Goreh sought to show that 'the Christian faith fulfils the needs and longings of the Indian mind and heart.'[95] While he never set out a systematic view of fulfilment theology, he did make references to the idea in his books. He follows Sen in seeing saccidānanda as a foreshadowing of the trinity:

> May we, the sons of India, say, that the unity of God, Whom our fathers delighted to call 'Sat, Chit [sic], Ananda Brahman', after which they ardently aspired, but in a wrong sense[...] God has granted us their children to realise in a right sense? Was that aspiration and longing[...] a presentiment of the future gift? I indeed have often delighted to think so.[96]

Further he said:

> Providence has certainly prepared *us*, the Hindus, to receive Christianity, in a way which, it seems to me, no other nation – excepting the Jews, of course – has been prepared. Most erroneous as is the teaching of such books as the *Bhagavadgita*, the *Bhagavata*i, etc., yet they have taught us something of *ananyabhakti* (undivided devotedness to God), of *vairagya* (giving up the world), of *namrata* (humility), of *ksama* (forbearance), etc., which enables us to appreciate the precepts of Christianity.[97]

The difference to Banerjea exhibited in this passage is clear. Goreh did not attribute all that is good in Hinduism to a primordial revelation, rather he used a type of Logos theology, in that he allowed that the experience of the Hindu is of worth, and man is not seen as utterly fallen and evil. The importance of this is that it shows the pervasiveness of these ideas within Tractarian thought,

---

92   Ibid., p. 54.
93   Fulfil, p. 93.
94   Lipner, in Coward, 1987, p. 300.
95   Boyd, 1979, p. 40.
96   N. Goreh, *On Objections against the Catholic Doctrine of Eternal Punishment*, 1868, pp. 41–2, quoted in Boyd, 1974, p. 22.
97   N. Goreh, *Proofs of the Divinity of Our Lord*, 1887, p. 75, quoted in ibid., p. 55.

though this may well be due to Goreh's influence in propagating these teachings. Moreover, even if he gained his ideas from Sen and his own acquaintance with the Brahmō Samāj,[98] it shows that the teachings of fulfilment theology were acceptable within Tractarianism. That the origin of these ideas lay with what is known as the Cambridge School of liberal theology has already been argued. As mentioned earlier, the distinction is somewhat artificial, and Goreh stands as proof that such ideas were present within Tractarian thought by the mid to late nineteenth-century.[99]

His attitude to Hinduism was not as positive as that of some later thinkers. Boyd detects a certain negativity in his assessment of the great bhakti saints, saying that he did not see them as reformers, as they added nothing new, rather they merely revived what was still the same 'false' practise which had previously existed.[100] This is perhaps too harsh a critique. Boyd compares him to Appasamy who sought to develop a Christian bhakti,[101] yet he was born but four years before Goreh died, and a span of approximately half a century separates their writings.[102]

Finally, mention should be made of Brahmabāndhab Upādhyay. A Catholic thinker, he is very significant in the development of Indian Christian theology, and also demonstrates many of the points made above, although expressed in a different tradition. He was led to Christianity by Sen,[103] and developed, far more than Goreh ever did, the notion of the trinity as a parallel to the Hindu saccicdānanda.[104] Indeed, his aim was far more radical, to show that what scholasticism had been for Christianity in the West, so the Vedanta could be in India.[105] He also suggested that missionaries should search for the truths to be found in Hinduism,[106] and suggested that the two religions agreed in all their essentials.[107] To explain this, he expanded a theory of natural and

---

98   Boyd, 1979, pp. 43 f.
99   This will be developed more fully in the next chapter.
100   Boyd, 1979, pp. 45–6.
101   Boyd, 1979, p. 45.
102   Appasamy's main work on this topic was published in 1926, whose work then was still pioneering (see Francis, 1992, pp. v ff.).
103   Lipner, 1999, chapters 3 and 4.
104   See Boyd, 1979, pp. 69 ff.
105   M. M. Thomas, 1969, p. 100.
106   Lipner, 1992, p. 4.
107   Lipner, in Coward, 1987, pp. 308–9.

supernatural revelation,[108] whereby the truths of Christianity are held to be supernatural, while, 'The truths in Hinduism are of pure reason illuminated in the order of nature by the light of the Holy Spirit.'[109]

This is clearly a type of Logos theology, and in suggesting that Hinduism had formed precursors of Christian doctrines, clearly has links to fulfilment theology. His aim was not to expand a theory to show how Christian doctrines were superior, and 'fulfilled' Hindu ones, but rather to develop a theology based upon Vedantic philosophy, using native Indian concepts to replace the thought patterns of the West. He therefore went a step beyond fulfilment theology, starting to develop Westcott's dream of an Indian Christian theology, and working along similar lines to A. G. Hogg, as will be seen later.

He was deeply nationalistic, and argued that Hinduness (or Hindutva) did not depend upon following particular doctrines,[110] and described himself as a 'Hindu Catholic.'[111] He felt it very important that Christianity should not be seen as denationalizing, and became more involved with radical nationalism as the years passed.[112] He recognized the importance of asceticism, becoming a mendicant himself,[113] and his ideas of an ashram were fulfilled by Monchanin and Abhistikananda,[114] who were followed by Bede Griffiths,[115] to whom reference has already been made, as someone who has continued the interpretation of Indian Christian theology. He had in turn been influenced by the author and academic C. S. Lewis[116] who wrote to him in 1954, saying:

> I suspect that a great going-to-meet-them is needed not only on the level of thought but in method. A man who had lived all his life in India said, 'That country might be Christian now if there had been *no* missionaries in our sense but many single missionaries walking

---

108   See Ibid., p. 308.
109   Upādhyāy in *Sophia*, January 1895, quoted in ibid.
110   Lipner, 1992, p. 5.
111   M. M. Thomas, 1969, p. 107.
112   Lipner, in Coward, 1987, pp. 309 ff.
113   Ibid., p. 307.
114   Ibid., p. 310.
115   See Spink, pp. 120 ff.
116   He had been his tutor at Oxford, and the two stayed in contact afterwards (see Griffiths, 1979, pp. 32 and subsequent chapters).

the roads with their begging bowls. For that is the sort of Holy Man India believes in and she will never believe in any other.'[117]

Thus the Catholic tradition in India, at least starting with Upādhyāy, has much in common with the Protestant tradition. It is, then, perhaps, not surprising that we see the two traditions merge in the above example. I think it fair to say, that everything that is said of Upādhyay above, finds a parallel in the thought of Banerjea and Goreh.

Thomas Ebenezer Slater

Thomas Ebenezer Slater is, without doubt, the most influential and important of the missionary fulfilment theologians before Farquhar. As early as 1876 his first work, *God Revealed*, had explored this area. The date of this book is not, I would suggest, accidental; Monier-Williams had made a tour of India in 1875–6.[118] Slater's book was not the only one to be published at this time, Robson, who will be discussed below, is a good example. Worth noting, also, is that, in a letter, written at the end of 1876, Slater mentions that he had met with and discussed these ideas with Monier-Williams.[119] It would be naive to suggest that Monier-Williams' tour was the first that these missionaries knew of his ideas. That Slater, when he had to defend his work, called upon him as a witness, shows that, at any rate in the London Missionary Society, Monier-Williams was a known and respected figure. Also to assume that, for no reason, these missionaries had decided to adopt the academic theory of fulfilment, would seem equally naive. Rather, it seems likely that Monier-Williams' theories provided a response felt by the missionaries to see the good in the philosophical aspects of Hinduism, and to answer the concern expressed by Slater during 1876, that educated Hindus didn't listen to

---

117   C. S. Lewis, letter to Bede Griffiths, 1954, quoted in Spink, p. 115.
118   In his work *Modern India and the Indians*, Monier-Williams records his first experiences of India when landing in Bombay on November 10th 1875, op. cit., pp. 27 ff.
119   Slater, letter to Mullens, 14/12/1876 (London Missionary Society archives), in Fulfil, p. 101.

antagonistic assaults upon their faith. The need for missionaries to take a more conciliatory role towards Hinduism is something that is explored below, and for which 'fulfilment' provided an intellectual framework, which in their hands is further developed. Slater obviously felt that there was a need for these ideas to be examined more closely, and he published the first fully thought out manifesto of missionary fulfilment theology in 1901, *The Higher Hinduism in Relation to Christianity*. That views such as this were not seen as anathema to many, even most(?), missionaries has already been seen, and when Slater's first work detailing the fulfilment idea was published, it appears that it was largely welcomed by his fellow missionaries.[120] There were, however, some critical voices who, anonymously it seems, questioned Slater's orthodoxy.[121] Thus, we should never over-emphasize the idea of missionaries as progressive liberals. The majority of missionaries would be drawn from conservative evangelical circles who were, perhaps, merely less vocal; an issue which will be dealt with later. Though here we may note the following observations made by Sharpe:

> The perpetuation of traditional Evangelicalism was also assisted by the conservatism of the missionary societies in the West.[122] The principles on which the societies had been formed permitted of no relaxation; impeccable orthodoxy was required of all missionary candidates. Liberal views, unless skilfully revealed, would automatically disqualify a man from missionary service;[123] and when expressed by an active missionary, could place that missionary in a difficult position.[124]

Yet the adoption of more liberal ideas by missionaries in the field was to become vital, so that toleration of Hindu thought became a part of the missionary's approach. Not only did missionaries adopt liberal ideas from Western scholars but from now on there is a sense in which certain

---

120   Fulfil, p. 98.

121   Ibid., p. 98 f. More will be said of this below

122   [fn 4]: 'One important reason for this was that in virtually all cases societies were dependent for their support on public support from churchgoers, who were not in a position to keep up with developments in the scholarly world [see Glover, *Evangelical Nonconformists and Higher Criticism in the Nineteenth Century* (1954), pp. 161 f., 217, 287....]'

123   [fn 5]: Sharpe here refer sto a case that occupied the London Missionary Society from 1897–1900, over a certain E. Evans, 'a brilliant scholar,' which was made 'a test case on the freedom of men to hold modern theological views.'

124   Fulfil, pp. 33–4.

missionaries, at least, start to lead the field in terms of developing positive attitudes to the non-Christian faiths.[125]

In this section I will deal chiefly with Slater's thought as developed in *The Higher Hinduism in Relation to Christianity*, for although he doesn't present any new thought in it, it does present in 'a connected system the lines suggested in'[126] his previous works. However, before going on to examine this work, Slater's background, and something of the development of these ideas, should be sketched.

Slater has been described as 'one of the most brilliant non-graduates ever recruited by the L.M.S,'[127] though Maw notes that his career would better be described as sucessful rather than 'outstanding.'[128] Slater's missionary work was, at the time, highly unusual. His brief from the L.M.S. was to work exclusively amongst higher caste Hindus who had finished their college education, and already knew something of Christianity.[129] Many of these people would have been to colleges influenced by William Miller –of whom more later – which sought to 'diffuse' Christian ideas rather than seeking converts.[130] All Slater's missionary career was spent in educational establishments or in ministry to the educated classes.[131]

Working amongst the higher caste, Slater was more likely than many other missionaries to come in touch with the so-called Higher Hinduism.[132] Thus he was separated from the bulk of missionary workers who were active amongst the lower castes, and were largely unaware of the aspects of

---

125   One is reminded here of an incident in the life of Gandhi, in which he berated a group of Canadian missionaries for their bigotry and intolerance, and told them that if they wanted to have an effect they should rather study Hindu religions and Indian history and literature. The missionaries humbly listened to the great man without making any reply, but afterwards remarked they wouldn't have minded the berating at all if it wasn't for the fact that they probably knew far more about the history of India's religious life and culture than Gandhi did (reference unknown).

126   Fulfil, p. 103.

127   Oddie, 1974, p. 64.

128   Maw, 1990, p. 51.

129   Ibid., p. 94 ff. The call for someone to undertake such work came at the Madras Missionary Conference of 1874, and Slater volunteered for the job (Cracknell, 1995, p. 109).

130   Fulfil, p. 95.

131   He spent his first five years at the Bhowanipur Institution in Calcutta where he would, thirty years later, be followed by Farquhar (Cracknell, 1995, p. 109).

132   Fulfil, p. 101.

Hinduism with which they were not in daily contact with.[133] Slater, however, did not come into contact with a Hindu tradition centred primarily upon idol worship and sacrifice,[134] but upon the return to a pure 'Vedic' religion as advocated by such figures as Ram Mohun Roy, and Keshub Chundra Sen.[135] Not only was there this factor, but also, 'the growth of Neo-Hinduism and Indian nationalism, often so closely interwoven as to be virtually indistinguishable from each other, created a climate of opinion in which the old attitude was worthless as an apologetic weapon.'[136] This was not fully recognized when Slater was first writing, and it was only in the beginning of this century that it became commonplace to say that a hostile attitude to the Hindu faith was damaging to the missionary cause.[137] This, I would suggest, is a major reason why Slater remains relatively unknown while Farquhar's work has become so influential.[138] Slater was simply ahead of his times,[139] or at least ahead of his contemporaries, who might be seen as being behind the times in failing to appreciate the crisis that was developing by the staunch

---

133   Ibid., pp. 32–3. See also pp. 101 and 104.

134   Whether, of course, Hindu veneration of idols is worship of the idol itself or of the god or power behind the idol is another matter, this however is how it was perceived by the missionaries of this period. Sen makes the point that, 'image worship and idolatry are not necessarily the same thing, though most Western observers seem to have treated the two as identical' (Parrinder, p. 60). And elsewhere he says, 'In religious ceremonies the images of gods may help to focus devotion, but in theory they represent nothing more than imaginative pictures of the infinite aspects of one all-pervading God[....]

    '[W]e should emphasize that the significance of these ceremonies can be appreciated only with some imagination, for without the Hindu philosophical background the rituals are not very meaningful' (ibid., pp. 35–6). Of course we can still ask how much of the 'philosophical background' would be known to the low caste devotee of the nineteenth-century, it is quite possible that the assumption of idolatry was often well founded.

135   See above, also Parrinder, pp. 98 ff.

136   Fulfil, p. 100.

137   It should, however, be pointed out that the rise of Indian nationalism only became an important factor in the 1890s (Doss, p. 7), so only affecting Slater's later work. However, in recognizing the need for a more open attitude to Hinduism he seems aware of the undercurrents that would lead to this, and many later problems may have been avoided if more people had followed the same path.

138   'He was a layer of foundations: and it is commonly the fate of foundations to remain hidden' (Fulfil, p. 104).

139   Ibid.

refusal to let go of the old approach of attack and antagonism.[140] Showing his awareness of these trends, Slater wrote in 1876: 'If you adopt a denunciatory and authoritative tone, they [educated Hindus] simply will not listen to you, and would consign any book written in such a style to the flames.'[141]

Maw emphasizes Slater's use of the evolutionary motif, suggesting that in his works he relied upon secular theorists of evolution, particularly Alfred Russel Wallace and Herbert Spencer, both of whom were cited in a work published in 1898.[142] From this standpoint Maw, therefore, comes to the conclusion that Slater confounded 'the religious and biological terminology of ascension.'[143] In this, Maw, however, neglects the fact that evolutionary ideas were not unique to Slater, being common currency in religious thought at this time, an idea to be developed particularly in the next chapter, and already seen in relation to figures such as Monier-Williams and Müller. Furthermore, the principle of religious evolution and development are found in Slater's earlier works, that is before Maw finds traces of the influence of Wallace and Spencer. In *The Philosophy of Missions*, for instance, he mentions a number of religious thinkers who develop the idea of evolution.[144]

---

140   Sharpe relates how an increasing antagonism between Indians and Christians meant that, 'Standard missionary methods were seriously disturbed' (Fulfil, 209 ff.) in the period following 1902. While this is referring to the situation in Bengal, where Farquhar was (Slater worked in Madras) he also, as shall be shown, recognized the need for adopting a 'new attitude' towards Hinduism.

141   Slater, from letter to Mullens, 14/12/1876 (London Missionary Society archives), in Fulfil, p. 101.

142   Maw, 1990, p. 60.

143   Ibid., p. 73.

144   See, op. cit., pp. 114 ff, for references to Eaton, Fairbairn and others, and as will be seen he was also greatly influenced by Müller, and also Maurice. The following line, appears unattributed, and appears almost to be plagarism, bears testimony to this, 'there is ample evidence of that in man which *demands* a revelation, but not that in man which *gives* the revelation' (ibid., pp. 125–6). Compare with Maurice, 'there is that in man which demands a Revelation – that is *not* that in him which makes the Revelation' (Boyle, p. 55).

Given these factors, we shall see, briefly, how they are reflected in *God Revealed*. Firstly, he refused to say anything attacking Hinduism, claiming, 'If there happens to be error, falsehood, evil, in what a man calls his religion, it may be owing to ignorance and want of light; and such a man is an object for pity and for help, and not for reproach and condemnation.'[145] So he adopted the approach that was to characterize missionary fulfilment theology: not attacking the faith of those you were seeking to convert, so Christianity would not be seen as opposed to the native faith, but rather to be in harmony with it. Fulfilling not replacing:

> Not to present Christianity as an antagonistic Religion among other Religions of the world, not a voice sounding the knell of doom to non-Christian nations, but, in the firm persuasion that they are all *by nature* Christians, to hold it up as that in which Hindus would find realised and satisfied the noblest and earliest ideas of their sages, and the truest sentiments and yearnings of their hearts.[146]

Thus he saw the basic principle of contact between Christianity and Hinduism as being 'not an aspect of antagonism but of consummation.'[147] As already mentioned, this viewpoint was generally well received, though there were those who questioned his orthodoxy. The main contention does not seem to have been that Slater should not have taken a conciliatory attitude toward Hinduism, but whether his views on such conceptions as the Atonement were orthodox.[148] The complaints against him were anonymous, being signed 'True Friend of Missions', and in one he was accused of being a Unitarian.[149] Slater contended that his views were orthodox and there seems no reason to doubt this, as Maw notes the letters did not just attack Slater and appear to have been written by someone with a grudge against the London Missionary Society.[150] For our purposes, what is of the most interest amongst all of this is that, in defence of his position, Slater made reference to the fact that his views were in accord with those of Monier-Williams, and the letter in which

---

145   Slater, 1876, p. 2.
146   Ibid., p. iii. Is this an early foreshadowing of the 'anonymous' Christian concept?
147   Ibid., p. 8.
148   Fulfil, pp. 98 f.
149   Ibid., p. 99, fn 8.
150   Maw, 1990, pp. 63–4.

he informed his superiors of this was taken 'as an adequate assurance of Slater's theological *bona fides.*'[151] From here we may move briefly on to discuss a later work of Slater's, *Studies in the Upanishads*, published in 1897.[152]

What might first strike one about this book are the several references to Müller in the opening pages. This is, in part, only natural, because Müller had published the translation of the Upanishads from which Slater worked.[153] It can also be seen as a signifier of something else. Slater's readiness to refer to Müller, rather than Monier-Williams, indicates that the concept of fulfilment had now gained a certain general acceptance, not by any means a universal acceptance as the protest that Farquhar received will serve to testify.

Not only does Slater quote from Müller but he readily accepts a number of his theories, in his opening paragraph quoting a number of lines from Müller concerning the Vedas:

> we watch, as Professor Max Müller says, 'the dawn of the religious consciousness of man;' 'one of the most inspiring and hallowing sights in the whole history of the world;' yet 'not without its dark clouds, its chilling colds, its noxious vapours.' Indeed these constitute 'the real toil and travail of the human heart in its first religious aspirations,' which give birth to 'the intensity of its triumphs and its joys.'[154]

There are a number of ideas here, some, such as the suggestion that man has innate 'religious aspirations' common to the tradition, others that the Vedas are 'the dawn of religious consciousness' peculiar to Müller. As will be seen below, Slater has a more pessimistic attitude as to the 'purity' of the original Vedic experience of Natural Religion. However, just because Slater is prepared to accept the scholarly opinion of Professor Müller on the antiquity of the Vedic literature, does not mean that he accepted all his ideas on

---

151   Fulfil, p. 101. He quotes from two letters in the London Missionary Society archives, Slater, letter to Mullens 14/12/1876 and Mullens, letter to Slater 16/2/1877, footnotes 2 and 1, which should be 1 and 2 respectively.

152   The work is composed of a series of five lectures delivered in Bangalore towards the end of 1896 (op. cit., p. 1, fn), and if the internal evidence of the work is to be believed, to an audience of Indian Christians, for he says, 'If a study of *your* Upanishads can recall you to a higher ideal, I would urge you, *as a Christian*, to study them; for I find in all their best and noblest thoughts a true religious ring, and a far off presentiment of the Christian truth' (ibid., p. 15, italics my own).

153   Slater, 1897, p. 3.

154   Ibid., p. 1, quoting Müller, *The Upanishads*, vol. I, p. xi.

fulfilment. It is, though, enough for us here to show the direct influence of Müller on Slater, whose ideas will in turn influence Farquhar.[155] The thought of this work is essentially the same as that of *The Higher Hinduism*.[156]

The Higher Hinduism in Relation to Christianity

i) Attitudes to Other Religions

Twelve years before Farquhar published *The Crown of Hinduism*, Slater's major work on fulfilment theology was published.[157] There is very little to separate the two books, except that whereas the former was, and still is, accepted as the definitive work, the latter has not been well remembered. Possible reasons for this were observed above, though, at the time, at least in India, Slater was a well known figure. In order that the two may be compared, it is necessary that the details of Slater's scheme of fulfilment theology as outlined in this book should now be described.

Something has already been said of Slater's reasons for adopting this approach. Brief note may, though, be made to the fact that early on in the book Slater feels the need to say, 'We shall never gain the non-Christian world until we treat its religions with justice, courtesy, and love.'[158] There is much in Slater to suggest that he did have a genuine appreciation for, at least parts of, Hinduism, and he said that the Upanishads were the highest spiritual writings outside the Bible.[159] Yet, even if the Upanishads did reach certain spiritual heights, they were still found lacking:

---

155 See Fulfil, p. 208, especially fn 8.

156 He observes there that the Upanishads mark the high point of Hindu thought upon which he bases his critique (op. cit., pp. 25 and 60).

157 Although Slater's work had first been presented two years earlier at the Saxon Missionary Conference at Leipzig, in 1899 (Barrows' preface, p. v, in Slater, 1903).

158 Slater, 1903, p. 2. The words Slater uses here, it may be noted, mirror the title of Cracknell's book on this area (Cracknell, 1995).

159 Ibid., p. 78. However, while he said this I suspect, though I cannot, of course, prove it, that he had a higher regard for certain Christian devotional writings. This is mostly presumption, but as shall be seen below he does condemn portions of the Upanishads and sees certain Hindu ideas finding their culmination in the writings of Christian mystics.

Christ will yet satisfy the spiritual hunger and thirst to which the great religious ideas of the East only gives expression; and India[...] will surely find the enlightening revelation of the Gospel to be in *complete accord* with the best sentiments of her best minds, the true realization of the visions of her seers, the real fulfilment of the longings of her sages.[160]

Thus Slater saw Hinduism reaching up to the truths of Christianity, and said of it that it is, 'destined for a diviner purpose than to be swept away as vestiges of evil.'[161] Indeed, in his papers for the Edinburgh conference he suggested that, 'we should *lead the people by such light as may be found in their own Scriptures and hearts* to the fuller light of ours.'[162]

He saw the process of Christian renewal already at work in the internal reforms of Hinduism, whereas he saw Christian ideas being taken over and adopted by the reformers.[163] Yet he saw Hinduism being, at best, a one-sided approximation to Christianity,[164] so there is no sense as there is in Müller that all Hindus need to do is to accept Christ, as his asking the Brahmō Samāj to join the Church of England indicates.[165] Here Farquhar is more in line with Slater in suggesting that Hinduism needs to be totally reformed, rather than just having Christ tacked on to the old system, 'Hinduism must die in order to live. It must die into Christianity.'[166] Here we should mention the major difference between Slater and Farquhar,which is that Slater, like Monier-Williams, is quite happy to speak of Hinduism being fulfilled by Christianity, without making the distinction that it is Christ, not historical Christianity, which is the fulfilling principle, whereas Farquhar's views on this are more in line with those of Müller.[167] This is important, for, as we have seen, many

---

160   Ibid., p. 291.
161   Ibid., p. 3.
162   EDMS, Slater # 229, p. 54.
163   Ibid., pp. 15 ff and 82–3. As one example of the need for Christianity he notes the attempts to disband caste which he asserts are only possible within a Christian framework (ibid., p. 119). How far these assertions are valid is beyond the scope of this work, but that there were definite Christian influences on the Indian reformers is beyond doubt (see Webster, pp. 2 ff.).
164   Slater, 1903, p. 3.
165   See chapter 3.
166   Crown, p. 51.
167   Baago sees this as the only development between Slater and Farquhar which he attributes to the latter's 'emphasis upon the historical Jesus and the ethical contents of his message' (Baago, 1969, p. 74). Slater does certainly see a moral dimension to the contrast of Christianity and Hinduism, but he does not lay the same stress upon Jesus' moral teachings as Farquhar does, as we will see below.

Hindu reformers were opposed to the institution of Christianity,[168] but wanted, 'the lowly and meek and gentle teachings of Christ, not because we do not have them now, but we want more of them[....] Seeing the selfishness and intolerance of the missionary not an intelligent man will accept Christianity.'[169] This change in emphasis from Christianity to Christ is reflected in another change. While Farquhar held that we had to judge each religion by the best that it had to offer, saying, 'Like Hinduism, Christianity must be judged by its principles, not by the vicious lives of those who refuse to obey it,'[170] Slater said that it is not possible to judge a religion fairly solely on the merits of its founder and greatest thinkers, but also on the daily life of its practitioners to judge its results.[171] Farquhar's paradigm reflects his interest in the figure and teachings of Christ, while Slater's paradigm is based upon comparing the whole of Christianity.

ii) Attitudes to Hinduism

Now we shall turn to some general points that Slater makes about Hinduism and India. First, he regards all parts of Indian culture to be imbued with religion.[172] This is important for Slater and Farquhar, so that in offering a critique of Indian culture and social customs they can at the same time, show the flaws of Hinduism. Slater notes, quite rightly,[173] that there is no such thing

---

168   See Baago, 1969, p. 72.
169   Dharmapala in WPOR II, p. 1093. Although, speaking as a Buddhist, he reflects the views of many others (see ibid., pp. 1095–6, for the opinions of one missionary, R. A. Hume, on the need to become more like Christ, and Seager, pp. 436 ff., for the views of a member of the Brahmō Samāj, B. B. Nagarkar, who contrasts Christ's 'meekness of purpose' with the 'Christian fanatics and dogmatists' (p. 438), from W. R. Houghton, ed., *Neely's History of the Parliament of Religions*, Chicago, Neely Publishing Company, 1894, pp. 742–47).
170   Crown, p. 119.
171   Slater, 1903, p. 1.
172   Slater, 1903, p. 4.
173   Lipner, 1992, p. 2. Though he notes that many, even Indian academics, have written 'as if Hinduism is a monolithic phenomenon comprising a hierarchical structure, with 'animism' at the lowest levels, followed progressively by polytheism, incarnational and non-incarnational monotheism, and monism at the top' (ibid.). He also observes W. C. Smith's argument in *The Meaning and End of Religion*, where he says, Smith 'has argued – and shown, I believe – that the designations 'Hinduism,' 'Buddhism,' 'Christianity' etc., especially as established from the

as Hinduism as a single comprehensive entity.[174] Yet, while noting that it is no single religion, he does treat it as such, and accuses it of being inconsistent for holding a multiplicity of ideas:

> whether we are to regard ourselves as God or not God[...] Hinduism lets us take our choice, and tolerates discordant sects. But a system that includes both[...] Advaitic and Dvaitic[175] thought, that declares *with one voice* that the human and Divine Soul are identical, and with another that they are distinct, is surely a distinction in something more than terms, and can scarcely be considered a safe guide.[176]

Yet in another place, he tells his readers to be careful not to confuse Vedānta and polytheism, because they are separate things.[177] While we can criticize Slater for such inconsistencies he is partly resolved from blame, because in setting up the different sects and traditions into a hierarchy, and seeing them as being all part of one giant Hindu system, he is in accord with the thought

---

nineteenth-century onwards, are classic instances of the western tendency of 'reification,' viz. 'mentally making religion into a thing, gradually coming to conceive [of] it as an objective systematic entity' (Lipner, 1992, p. 2, quote from Smith, op. cit., p. 51). Smith notes that: 'Each community has what modern outsiders have tended to call its religious system' (Smith, 1978, p.53). Of course, some scholars have argued that Hinduism is a single religion, such as Weightman, 'It is Hindu self-awareness and self-identity that affirms Hinduism to be one single religious universe, no matter how richly varied its contents' (Weightman, p. 192). This was certainly the view that Slater would have gained from his knowledge of Neo-Hinduism, which, with its links to Indian nationalism, sought to promote a view of Hinduism as being one vast system, though containing many different forms within itself (see, e.g. Fulfil, pp. 246 ff.). Figures as Ram Mohun Roy and Vivekananda always refer to Hinduism as though it were one system (see Richards, pp. 4, 8, 79 ff., etc., alsor, Lipner, 1994, chapter 1, and Flood, 1996, pp. 6 ff.). Lipner gives a brief history of the use and development of the term 'Hindu' noting that the term was appropriated by the Indian intelligentsia in the nineteenth-century (Lipner, 1992, pp. 7–8, fn. 7).

174   Slater, 1903, p. 5. Though he does, as will be shown, conceive of it in terms of the 'hierarchical structure' outlined by Lipner (see previous footnote).

175   Non-dualism and dualism respectively.

176   Slater, 1903, p. 194 (italics my own). I would suggest that to criticise such a vast animal as Hinduism on these grounds, would be akin to condemning the whole Judaeo-Christian-Islamic tradition for internal consistencies, or at the very least to suggest that the differences between Protestant and Roman Catholics demonstrate internal contradictions in some supposed over arching religion of Christianity (see W. C. Smith in fn 173).

177   Ibid., pp. 86–7.

of the Hindu intelligentsia of the reform movement, who, though seeking a return to the Vedānta, tried to envisage a Hinduism which could embrace all these ideas:

> From the spiritual flights of Vedantic philosophy, of which the latest discoveries of science seem like the echoes, the agnosticism of the Buddhas, the atheism of the Jains, and the low ideas of idolatry with the multifarious mythology, each and all have a place in the Hindu's religion.[178]

Also like Müller and the Neo-Hindus[179] Slater saw Hinduism as being a decline from an ancient religion,[180] which for him reached its high point, as mentioned above, in the Upanishads.[181] He saw Hinduism as having three stages, first, Vedism; second, matured Brāhmanism; and third, the debased 'modern Hindūism.'[182] He also saw Hinduism as being of three main types, Vaishnavism, the dominant faith, whose form was bhakti-mārga, Śaivism, whose form is karma-mārga, and the highest form of philosophical Hinduism, as expressed in the Upanishads, whose form is jnānā-mārga.[183] There is also a fourth, debased, tradition to be found: 'In Tantrism or Saktism – though even this claimed to have an esoteric side – Hinduism arrived at its worst stage of medieval and modern development.'[184]

---

178   Vivekananda in WPOR, II, p. 968. Though in the early days most reformers were opposed to idolatry (Parrinder, p. 98). Though in later years all aspects of Hinduism were accepted, as seen in Vivekananda's quote above, and this was also an important tenet of the Theosophical society whose influence was increasing (Fulfil, p. 144), this was probably due to the rise of Indian nationalism, which was closely linked to the religious revival (ibid., pp. 144 ff.), 'McCully has pointed out that one of its [Neo-Hinduism's] main tenets was that the regeneration of India was dependent upon the restoration of Hindu culture' (ibid., p. 247; see also McCully, pp. 253 ff.).

179   The Hindu revival was much indebted to the work of the Western Orientalists, especially Müller (Fulfil., p. 145).

180   Slater, 1903, pp. 6 ff.

181   Ibid., p. 60.

182   Ibid., p. 23.

183   Ibid., p. 33.

184   Ibid., p. 34. More recent research on this 'esoteric' side has reassessed this view. Thus, one of the most revered of contemporary Christians in India, the late Father Bede Griffiths, has said: 'The Tantras were really a sacramental system, by which external rites – mantras (sacred words), mudras (sacred gestures) and yantras (sacred designs) – were used as methods of meditation so as to bring the whole

In seeing the philosophical system of the Vedas as the perihelion of Hinduism, Slater regards it as having left the great mass of devotees in darkness,[185] having only idols[186] while the true religion is left to the philosophers.[187] Yet here he seems to be forgetting the dictum of Vivekananda:

> But if a man can realize his divine nature with the help of an image, would it be right to call it a sin? Not even when he has passed that stage that he should call it an error. To the Hindu man is not travelling from error to truth, but from truth to truth, from lower to higher truth.[188]

Slater saw Hindu idolatry as a partial truth, and referred to it as 'of a distinctly spiritual kind.'[189] This sums up Slater's general attitude towards Hinduism, so we shall now say something of the theory upon which his fulfilment theology was based, as outlined in *The Higher Hinduism*.

iii) The Theory of Fulfilment

Slater believed that Christ was the 'Light' of every pagan saint.[190] But there is no historical revelation in Hinduism,[191] which means that it is based purely upon natural religion, being the innate religious wants of every man:

> the deepest evidence of all the Divine teaching is in the intimations and cravings... to be found in Hinduism; in that hoping in the Divine mercy as exhibited in Vaishnavism; and in the remarkable words of the Bhagavad-Gita[...]: 'Renouncing all Dharmas, come unto me as your sole refuge. sorrow not, *I will release you from all sins.*'[192] Whatever a

---

	being into union with the divine' (Spink, p. 177).
185	Slater, 1903, p, 10.
186	Ibid., p. 9.
187	Ibid., p. 124.
188	Vivekananda in WPOR II, p. 976. In this point of view the peasant before his idol is not left in darkness, but only a lesser light, and, oddly enough, the last sentence quoted would have been just at home coming from Slater talking of man's religious journey from Hinduism to Christianity!
189	Slater, 1903, p. 9.
190	Ibid., p. 2.
191	Ibid., p. 34.
192	Gita XVIII, lxvi. The translation here uses somewhat loaded terminology, in the use of the word 'sin,' whereas Zaehner's translation reads: 'Give up all things of law (*dharma*)

philosophical system may say to the contrary, those words express the longing of the heart, and foreshadow that truth of Divine Forgiveness and Restoration which appears in all its fullness in the Christian Gospel.[193]

Not only are human wants answered, to some degree, in Hinduism, but also, Hinduism has a place in mankind's religious life. Each religion, he says, 'being the manifestation of a human *want*, has a *raison d'etre*, a place to fill, and a work to do, in the great evolutionary scheme.'[194] This idea is very reminiscent of Max Müller, who saw the religion of the future being the culmination of all the religions of the past. Slater certainly goes on to say:

> The questions raised by the Vedānta will have to pass into Christianity if the best minds of India are to embrace it; and the Church of the 'farther East' will doubtless contribute something to the thought of Christendom of the science of the soul, and of the omnipenetratrativeness and immanence of Deity.[195]

Unfortunately Slater does not develop these ideas very far here; the idea that India would help correct the materialism of the West was in circulation already, as has been mentioned above, and it is not unreasonable to suggest that this could have been in Slater's mind when he wrote these lines.[196]

Like many earlier fulfilment theologians, Slater believed that the doctrines of religion answer to needs innate in man, and that they can be

---

'Turn to Me, thine only refuge,
'[For] I will deliver thee
'From all evils; have no care' (Zaehner, 1988, p. 324; see also Monier-Williams' work *Indian Wisdom*, pp. 145–6).

193   Slater, 1903, p. 217.
194   Ibid., p. 2.
195   Ibid., p. 291.
196   Thus, he says,'Indian Christianity should contribute something very beautiful and true, on the side of meditative worship, to the overactive, bustling life of the West. 'Vedāntic thought is so thoroughly Indian that the *Indian Christianity* of the future will of necessity take a Vedāntic colouring' (Slater, 1903, pp. 262 and 290). That the Vedānta philosophy could be Hinduism's main bequest to an Indian Christianity, and to Christianity generally, is a view found very often in thinkers of this period (see, for example, Andrews in Edinburgh, report iv, p. 178, and the Rev. T. J. Scott in WPOR II, p. 22, who notes that Rome produced law and the civil life, Greece had art, China practical piety and patient industry, and India discovered God's immanence; see also, Rev. R. A. Hume in ibid, p. 1275, and Mylne in Montgomery, pp. 310 ff.).

discovered by reason alone. His thinking here is in accord with Müller's thought on this. Slater says:

> The Hindu doctrine of Karma is just as reflective [as the Christian Gospel] and philosophical minds perplexed with the problems of existence, would reach it, *apart from the Gospel*; and so true is it that the Christian religion, while recognizing all the truth that other systems hold in common with itself, has *something more* to give – something more that the Divine Father has revealed, as man has been able to receive it.[197]

There is, however, a difference, for Müller saw this knowledge as coming from a direct interaction between God and human reason.

Slater, in the quotation above, interprets Karma as a truth held 'in common' with Christianity. What this means will be discussed below, but what is important here is that he sees 'the truth' that Karma reveals as known through reason, but then added to by Christianity. Also, in the above quotation, through the phrase 'as man has been able to receive it' he points to another facet of fulfilment theology, and that is that the non-Christian religions are 'preparations' for Christianity, that make certain truths known to man so that he is ready to hear them in the Christian Gospel. The two terms can be seen as partly interchangeable, Christianity only 'fulfils' a particular doctrine or religion because it had already 'prepared' the way for it. This idea leads into the last part of Slater's theory of fulfilment and that is that, while all non-Christian faiths seek after certain solutions to man's innate religious cravings, these are satisfied in the Bible.[198] The difference between Christianity and the non-Christian faiths is that, while the latter show man seeking after God, Christianity shows God in search of man.[199] So he can say:

> The Christian Gospel thus offers all that the Vedānta offers, and infinitely more. So true is it that every previous revelation flows into the revelation we have in Christ, and loses itself in Him. Christ includes all teachers. All 'other masters' are in Christ. We do not deny the truths they taught; we delight in all. We can give heed to all the prophets; but every truth in every prophet melts into the truth we have in Christ.[200]

For Slater it is only in Christianity that God, as Christ, comes into the world to answer man's wants. This is reminiscent of Maurice's dictum, 'that there

---

197   Slater, 1903, pp. 217–8.
198   Slater, 1903, p. 53.
199   Ibid., pp. 76 and 182.
200   Ibid., p. 277.

is that in man which demands a Revelation – that there is *not* that in him which makes a Revelation.'[201]

Perhaps the clearest expression of Slater's views on this matter are found in his papers for the Edinburgh conference, where he says: 'If[...] Christ has always been the Spiritual Light of the world, and the Source of such truths in other faiths that have nourished the best souls[...] then we can only regard such truths as *akin* to those of Christianity, and as a Divine *preparation* for it.'[202]

iv) Examples of Fulfilment Theology

While there had been many who saw Christianity as the fulfilment of Hinduism, what really sets the works of Slater and Farquhar apart is the amount of space they give to demonstrating which Hindu ideas are fulfilled by Christianity, and how they are fulfilled.[203] This is done by showing both similarities and contrasts, and suggesting the innate religious needs that these ideas respond to. For these two thinkers, this was not an idle academic exercise, but of practical value for the missionary, who would need to show both converts and adherents to other religions how Christianity responded to the religious questions asked in their native religion.[204]

---

201   Boyle, p. 55. Cracknell notes that apart from direct borrowings there are many 'echoes' of Maurice's theology in Slater and, he says, 'It is apparent... that Slater had drunk deep from the well of Maurice,' and goes on to claim that one passage 'in *The Philosophy of Missions* could have been written by Maurice, had he lived until 1882' (Cracknell, 1995, p. 113 – the passage he cites is from Slater, op. cit., is pp. 47–8). While Slater no doubt used Maurice, I feel that from this Cracknell may over estimate his importance to Slater, as will be seen below. He also lifts passages from Banerjea's work as well. So while Cracknell sees his fulfilment theology as coming mainly from Maurice (Cracknell, 1995, p. 116), we must remember that Slater drew from other sources, such as Banerjea. He may well, also, have known Rowland Williams' and Trench's work (which Cracknell does not mention at all in his study). He most certainly used Müller. When Cracknell describes certain aspects of thought as 'Maurician' it must be remembered that, such ideas can equally well be attributed to many others, contemporary with Maurice.
202   EDMS, Slater #229, p. 58.
203   In one of his works on Farquhar Sharpe observes that Slater's main work is the only book similar to *The Crown of Hinduism* (Fulfil, p. 329).
204   Hence the stress laid upon the idea of preparation at the Edinburgh Conference (see chapter 6).

The first example Slater uses is the Avatara doctrine, which he argued shows the need for a personal God.[205] He says that, in Hinduism this ideal is flawed, because the union of God and man is not complete. After the avatar's time on earth the human body is laid aside, so this is different from Christianity.[206] The same need is, Slater says, reflected in idolatry:

Idolatry, as opposed to pantheism,[207] foolish and degraded as it is, lays supreme stress on a vital truth – a truth which the human heart will never surrender – the Personality of God. It witnesses to man's natural craving to have before him some manifestation of the Unseen – the Unknowable – to see, in fact, a humanized God[....][208]

Here we see an important point, in that, although Slater has said the Upanishads represent the highest form of Hinduism, he also sees important truths outside of the Upanishadic system. Theistic 'truths' are to be found that are not in the pure monism of the Vedānta. Slater saw pantheism as being explicitly taught in the Upanishads.[209]

For Slater, the perfected form of the 'humanized God' is to be found in Christianity, whereas this doctrine is 'in Hinduism a necessary evil.'[210]

The question of personality is an important difference for Slater between Christianity and Hinduism, both in terms of the advaitic 'God', who is expressed in terms of negatives, and so is different from the Christian perception,[211] and also in terms of man's personal survival after death. He

---

205   Slater, 1903, p. 31.
206   Ibid., p. 32.
207   Slater believed pantheism lead inevitably to polytheism (ibid., pp. 120 ff).
208   Ibid., p. 123.
209   (Slater, 1897, p. 17.
210   Slater, 1903, p. 123.
211   Ibid., pp. 97–8 and 156. In saying this Slater seems entirely ignorant of the whole Christian tradition of the via negativa: '"But if God is neither goodness nor being nor truth nor one, what then is He? He is pure nothing: He is neither this nor that.* If you think of anything He might be, He is not that," In accents of the ancient negative or *apothatic* theology of Alexandria and Dionysius, Eckhart remarks that God "is beingless [weselôs] being"' (Woods, pp. 50–1, quotations from Meister Eckhart, Walshe's translation, no. 54, p. 72 and no. 62, p. 115). Here a certain distinction may be struck between Non-Conformists such as Slater and Farquhar for whom these ideas are based upon missionary need and evolutionary thought, and the liberal Anglicans of the Cambridge Mission who saw their fulfilment ideas going back to the early Church and Alexandria in particular (see O'Connor, 1974, p. 20).

says that the belief that man will eventually lose his individual identity is an 'assumption... unwarranted and unsupported by any evidence.'[212] Further, he says this idea flies in the face of human nature, 'the desire for non-existence, so utterly contradicted by human nature at its best, is to be looked at as the outcome of despair.'[213]

Thus we can see from this that where Hindu ideas can be seen to have some accord with Christianity[214] they are seen to be reflections of man's innate wants and desires, but where there is discord they are seen to be based upon false premises of human psychology. There is, then, no process of self refection going on here;[215] what can be tacked on to the old system is what is not is rejected. This is why, as I said earlier, fulfilment theology is really only the old thought in a new guise, there is no reappraisal of the merits of Hinduism and Christianity, the same standards for truth and falsity are set, and more things are seen as true rather than false.[216] In the end, the 'Christian understanding' must replace other understandings. Fulfilment is merely a Christian interpretation of what is wrong with Hinduism.

However, there are examples of a personal God in Hinduism which Slater acknowledges; for instance, the passages in the Rig Veda where Indra is described as, 'the most fatherly of all fathers.' And, again, as one who is 'easy to approach, even as a father to his son.'[217] Much as this may be a foreshadowing of Christian teaching, it is criticized because the conception of deity with goodness is not found here as it is in the Old Testament.[218] However, the main distinction for Slater is to be drawn between Krishna and Jesus, where he notes the great contrast between the Christ of the Gospels and

---

*A phrase that in this context is strikingly similar to the Hindu 'neti neti,' 'not this, not that.'

212   Slater, 1903, p. 191.
213   Ibid., p. 192.
214   Or rather, we should say, Slater's interpretation of Christianity, evangelical Protestantism.
215   One could say he exhibits no 'dialogic reflexivity'.
216   Or, at least, to echo Vivekananda, more things are seen to be a lower truth rather than merely error.
217   Rig Veda IV, 17, 17, and I, 25, 10 in Slater, 1903, p. 42.
218   Ibid., p. 43.

the Krishna of the Gita and the Bhāgavata Purana.[219] Here, he mentions the distinction of moral conceptions between Jesus and Krishna.[220] He says:

> the fundamental defect of the Gita, therefore, from the Christian standpoint is that it nowhere exhibits any sense of the real evil of sin as a violation of moral government, and makes no provision whereby sin may be forgiven and its thraldom and guilt removed.[221]

Nevertheless the Gita does show, 'a high level of religious experience – trustful and ardent attachment to an object represented as Divine.'[222] Certainly, but an unpassable chasm[223] exists between those who trust something 'represented as Divine' and those who know the Divine. He believed that 'Hindūs will yet learn to transfer their allegiance from Krishna to Christ.'[224] Thus, Slater's fulfilment is not a case of ordinary evolutionary progress, Hinduism will not develop into Christianity, it must be replaced by it. More will be said on this matter when we discuss Farquhar. As a final point on the Gita it may be observed that Slater said that it 'contains nothing good that is not found in Christianity.'[225]

Another important aspect of Christianity's fulfilling Hinduism lies in the area of sacrifice, where Slater's thought should be compared to Banerjea. For what follows is a restatement of a view that had already been expressed by K. M. Banerjea in his *Arian Witness*. Slater says, the great sacrificial act of the Vedas was the death of Prajāpati:

> The idea exists that *Prajāpati*, begotten before the world, becoming half immortal and half mortal, offered himself mystically in a body fit for sacrifice, thereby making all

---

219   Ibid., pp. 136–7.
220   What Baago, quoted above, referred to as the difference between Slater and Farquhar; Slater does stress the moral element.
221   Slater, 1903, p. 137. The second part of the quotation is of interest in that it seems to contradict the passage Slater quoted elsewhere from the Gita (XVIII, lxvi) where he notes Krishna takes our sins away. The explanation for this is simply that Slater did not believe the Gita, this was an expression of need not power, like all Hindu scripture it is purely natural not supernatural religion.
222   Ibid., p. 141.
223   I purposefully echo Monier-Williams's language here to emphasise the point made above, that this is a Christian assessment of Hinduism, where, whatever may be said in praise of Hinduism, it is still the case that Christianity is seen as being 'true' and Hinduism 'false.'
224   Slater, 1903, p. 146.
225   Ibid., p. 147.

subsequent sacrifice a reflection or figure of himself. And there was a profound truth in the belief that sacrifice was 'a *good ferrying-boat* for getting over the ocean of sins.'[226]

However ,this knowledge was lost, and sacrifice degenerated into 'empty *acts of slaughter.*'[227] But Slater asserts that the need for sacrifice is inbuilt in man, so the idea re-emerged, thus 'material sacrifices[...] offered to manifold deities have continued, in one form or another, down to the present day, and must continue in India and other non-Christian lands till Christ, the great *Fulfiller* of sacrifices is understood and accepted.'[228]

As a further point on sacrifice, Slater says the Old Testament God is superior to others because he does not demand material sacrifice, quoting Micah that He only requires his devotees 'to do justly, and love mercy, and walk humbly with God.'[229] While this is certainly one aspect of the Old Testament God,[230] more often than not the Old Testament speaks of the need for sacrifice.[231] Here Slater can hardly be said to be offering a fair comparison. Other example Slaters proposes are the ideas of karma and transmigration, which he says offer the greatest hindrance to the acceptance of Christianity,[232] yet even these answer to a human need. The truth of karma, he says, is to be found in Christianity, as long as it is not tied up with transmigration.[233] This truth is the knowledge of the hold of sin, 'If sin is unreal,[234] its *penalties* certainly are not, if we may judge from the hold that the

---

226   Slater, 1903, pp. 65–6.
227   Ibid., p. 66.
228   Ibid., pp. 66–7. Worth noting is that the account Slater gives, here, of Prajāpati's sacrifice, and the subsequent decline, renewal, and future fulfilment of the idea comes, almost word for word, from what he had said previously in his *Studies on the Upanishads*, pp. 12 f.
229   Micah VI, 8, in Slater, 1903, p. 57.
230   See Jeremiah XXXIII, 18, and Hosea VI, 6 for instance.
231   See, to mention but a few examples, Leviticus VII, 12, Deuteronomy XVIII, 3, II Kings XVII, 36, etc.
232   Slater, 1903, p. 190.
233   Ibid., p. 197.
234   The position, he says, of the 'pantheistic Vedāntists' (ibid., pp. 194–5). This denial of the reality of sin is echoed in the thought of one of the most extreme examples of English Idealism, the 'New Theology' of R. J. Campbell, who said: 'To think of all human life as a manifestation of the eternal Son renders it sacred. Our very struggles and sufferings become full of meaning. Sin is but the failure to realize it; it is being false to ourselves and to our Divine origin' (Campbell, p. 109). And elsewhere: 'However startling it may seem, sin itself is a quest for God – a

doctrine of *Karma* has upon the mind of all Hindūs.'[235] We have noted above that Slater disregards the words of Krishna in the Gita as promising release from sin, recognizing only the agency of Christ as salvific:

> The Christian religion, therefore, while fully admitting the truth of Karma – the persistence of the past – has something *more*, and something priceless to offer, which Hinduism has not – even that Gospel of God's Atoning and Forgiving Grace by which the sinner, subdued and penitent, and filled with a sacred affection, is *clothed anew with moral power*, through the inspections of the Father's love.[236]

This is a truism for Slater, that while Hindus have to rely upon their own strength 'the Gospel throws them on the strength of *another*.'[237] This is another example, if another is needed, that while Slater's ideas may stem from an evolutionary perspective, this doctrine is, for Slater, one of substitution, where an infinitely higher religion replaces a lower religion. There is an absolute otherness between Christianity and all other religions despite what some may have felt the use of the term 'evolution' may imply.

It is worth noting in passing that Slater felt the term 'Karma' was quickly becoming absorbed into the English language.[238] As for transmigration, Slater suggests that Hindus only believe this because they have heard of it from their

---

blundering quest, but a quest for all that. The man who got dead drunk last night did so because of the impulse within himself to break through the barriers of his limitations, to express himself, and to realize more abundant life. His self-indulgence just came to that: he wanted, if only for a brief hour, to live a larger life, to expand the soul, to enter untrodden regions, and to gather to himself new experience. That drunken debauch was a quest for life, a quest for God' (R. J. Campbell, a Sermon delivered 31 January, at the City Temple,Clements, p. 32). This echoes the Hindu view. Mention is made elsewhere of connections between Idealism and Vedānta. Also, the thought that underlies Campbell's thought here can be seen to have strong links with fulfilment theology; that, at the heart of man is a religious nature which will always seek after God. The presence of this idea in Campbell can be seen as a reflection of how widespread it was, but here, I would suggest, the idea may be linked to Campbell's position as a socialist, reflecting his concern with the wants and aspirations of the man on the streets, rather than in Slater's, where his concern is the non-Christian. Both can be traced back to Maurice. I would suggest that the liberal concern for others fostered by Christian Socialism, while not the cause, is another symptom of this attitude, or world-view.

235   Slater, 1903, p. 196.
236   Ibid., p. 216.
237   Ibid., p. 212.
238   Ibid., p. 197.

youth,[239] but that once theistic belief spreads through India 'belief in transmigration will die out.'[240] Rather, I would suggest that belief in transmigration has, arguably, spread far more rapidly in the West than Christianity has in India.

Another of Slater's contrasts is between what he sees as the self-introspection of the East, and the turning outwards of Christianity to a higher being.[241] A loving being is necessary, he asserts, to uphold any system, and criticizes Hinduism's lack of any moral absolutes.[242] The pantheistic system, he suggests, does not solve the problem of 'moral evil.'[243] And he follows Caird in saying that the pantheistic system is responsible for all the faults of the caste system, as there is no inspiration to seek for justice.[244] He quotes Vivekānanda to support this, 'our evil is of no more value than our good, and our good of no more value than our evil.'[245] He sees the Hindu system as being based upon metaphysics, whereas Christianity is based on morality.[246] Also, while the Neo-Hindus may seek to do away with caste, they can only do so with the aid of Christianity.[247]

In this pantheistic system, man's identity is lost, of which Slater's views were noted above. So, he says, one difference is that whereas Hinduism interprets man through nature, Christianity does the opposite, saying that only through the personal can nature be understood, for when seen in this way, the intellect and the moral can be seen in nature, that is to say, God is seen in nature.[248] To someone lacking Slater's preconceived notions it might be suggested that one will see in nature what one looks for in it. As a further point, Slater tries to show the illogical nature of pantheism by reference to the Hindu proverb 'Tat Tvam Asi,' 'Thou Art That' by saying that 'That' and

---

239   Ibid., pp. 222–3.
240   Ibid., p. 225.
241   Ibid., p. 181.
242   Ibid., pp. 181 and 182.
243   Ibid., p. 181.
244   Ibid., pp. 117–8, his reference is to Caird's, *The Faiths of the World.*
245   Vivekānanda from *Brahmavādin*, 19/1/1897, in ibid., p. 117.
246   Ibid., p. 224.
247   Ibid., p. 119.
248   Ibid., pp. 103 ff.

'Thou' must refer to separate things and therefore the whole system is internally contradictory.[249]

From this standpoint Slater goes further to say that Eastern thought sees matter as evil.[250] While we are here examining what Slater believed, rather than the correctness of his ideas, it does seem necessary, at this point, to say that this reading of Eastern thought on Slater's part shows a highly unsympathetic reading. I would suggest that Slater is reading a part of his own Christian heritage into Eastern thought here, whereas in the extreme versions of Platonic and Gnostic traditions, the world, within which the spirit is trapped, is evil. In Eastern thought, when the illusory nature of the world is stressed, it is always within the monistic context where the world is a part of the divine anyway.[251] However, in making these criticisms, Slater cannot just be seen as an 'ignorant missionary' for he was conversant with the works of Müller and Monier-Williams, and his misconceptions reflected the misunderstanding that existed, and still does, between the Orient and Occident. For instance, reference has already been made to some of the 'negative' attitudes both Müller and Monier-Williams held towards the non-Christian scriptures. With these caveats to hand I will now proceed.

Slater saw the Eastern idea of the world as evil as being the cause of its ascetic morality, which sought to destroy the individual.[252] He even says: 'The austere type of the Buddha's self-renunciation... – that of a homeless beggar, a mendicant friar – finds no counterpart in the more cheerful West.'[253]

---

249   Ibid., pp. 173–5. How far his criticism holds up is, perhaps, an endlessly debatable point. So, even within Hinduism there were the three traditions of dualism, non-dualism, and qualified non-dualism.

250   Ibid., p. 115.

251   See Sen, pp. 82 ff, where he discusses the thought of Śankara, Rāmānuja, and Madhva on this point.

252   Slater, 1903, p. 117.

253   Ibid., p. 187. What we may ask of the mendicant friars of the Western Church, the Franciscans, and then there is of course, the example of the Desert Fathers, and then again the words of Jesus: 'And Jesus said to him, "Foxes have holes, and birds of the air have their nests; but the Son of man has nowhere to lay his head"' (Mt. VIII, 20). A passage quoted by Mr. Mozoomdar, of the Brahmō Sāmāj, at the World's Parliament of Religions where he said: 'Those orders of Christians who, like the Roman Catholics, have adopted this principle of renunciation, have made the greatest impression upon Asiatic communities' (Mozoomdar in WPOR, II, p. 1089). While Slater obviously had little time for the idea of renunciation the development of Ashrams became a major feature of Indian Christianity, and so a chapter of

However, he does see the idea of renunciation as being similar to the Western idea,[254] and he suggests the yogic idea of dying to the self is essentially Christian,[255] but sees the yogin's path as being a mistaken idea of true self-sacrifice.[256] He also criticizes what he sees as the one sided nature of Indian spirituality, saying that religion needs activity, not just meditation.[257] It should be remembered, though, that while we see him attacking Indian forms of spirituality in this instance, we have seen that Slater does see the possibility of Indian spirituality as contributing something positive to the West.[258]

v) Further Observations on Hinduism

The above outlines all the main examples of Christian fulfilment of Hinduism that Slater noted. There are, however, a few points he makes that are worth mentioning.

Slater observed a parallel between the Hindu paramatman, which means breath, and the Hebrew term 'ruah', which can mean both spirit and breath.[259] What importance he attaches to this is unclear.

Echoing sentiments already expressed by both Müller and Monier-Williams, Slater observes that while there is much that is good in the Upanishads, and of a deep spiritual nature, there is equally a lot of material that is silly, or absurd.[260] But here Slater is prepared to allow for an explanation, that he feels does not put the East in such bad light compared to the West. Quoting from Müller, he says:

we must try to imagine what the Old Testament would have been had it not been kept distinct from the Talmud[...] or the New Testament if it had been mixed up with the

---

Rethinking Christianity in India is given over to the subject for instance. More recently, concerning Christian monasticism in India it has been suggested that: 'Through a Christian form of *sannyāsa*, India will eventually discover Christ in the Spirit and his message will then penetrate her heart. India awaits Christ; he is the fulfilment of her spirituality' (Teasdale, p. 333).

254   Slater, 1903, p. 102.
255   Ibid., p. 269.
256   Ibid., pp. 170–1; see also, p. 262, where he says yoga points to a great truth and it is only by seeing this truth that the error can be overcome.
257   Ibid., p. 265.
258   See above.
259   Slater, 1903, p. 76.
260   Ibid., pp. 73–4.

spurious gospels or with the wranglings of the early Church Councils, if we wish to understand the wild confusion of sublime truth with vulgar stupidity that meets us in the pages of the Sacred Books[.... Therefore] we must learn to look up to their high points and down into their stony tracts, in order to comprehend both the height and depth of the human mind in its searchings after the Infinite.[261]

Further, he differentiates the Vedas and the Bible by saying that the former lacks any Divine promises as does the Old Testament.[262] Also, he says, the fact that in Hindu thought the scriptures were deemed to be transcended when knowledge of the truth was gained shows their unsatisfactory nature.[263]

In view of the flaws he sees in Hinduism, Slater declares that Christianity is the only religion suited to the modern world,[264] and the reason for this is:

In Christ[...] we can be *sure of God* – of His real Being. We are not left to derive our idea of Him from the dreams of a disordered fancy or from 'an infinitely extended photograph of ourselves, begotten of insatiable vanity[....] God is like Christ[.... This] truth will remain changeless and eternal – God *is*, and God is *Father*.
And it is the best *working* conception of God that the world can have – the conception that best meets its sorrows and its sins[....] With such a God, *prayer*, which is instinctive in the human heart, finds its highest place; whereas in the Vedānta there is no place for prayer. Let the energy of these two truths once enter into a man's heart – that in everything we have to do with a *living* God, and that our God is the *Christ*-like One – and they are enough to revolutionize a man's entire life.[265]

---

261   Müller, 1969, I, pp. 15 and 20, in ibid., p. 74.
262   Ibid., pp. 51 f.
263   Ibid., p. 160.
264   Ibid., pp. 283–4.
265   Ibid., pp. 164–5.

William Miller

William Miller was the principal of the Madras Christian College[266] and contributed a distinct development to the growing concept of fulfilment in India. Miller's thinking in these matters was not scholarly, and in this he stands in utter contradistinction to Farquhar, seeking to settle the matter in broad generalizations about differing racial contributions. Saying, during a series of lectures given to his students at the college – these lectures caused quite a stir in Madras at the time, a number of missionaries protesting, and even some suggestions that Miller should resign as principal[267] – that:

> Some of you are likely to say at this point that[...] you must have a profound acquaintance both with Hinduism and Christianity, and that long years of study are indispensable[....] It is very far from being so. Meditation and prayer and free scope to the thoughts that spring from them – these are indispensable. Not so with study. Hindu learning and Christian learning have their own places, but their place is subsequent and secondary. For that commencement of which India and the world have need, not much equipment is required. The Hindu ideal is in you now. It is bred with you. It is the basis of your character[....] And it is not with Christianity, it is with Christ alone, you have to do[.... Y]ou may, and also you may not, be called to read widely and to think deeply of how ideals have been wrought out in actual and imperfect practice upon both sides.[268]

This is clearly an alternative approach to the likes of Slater and Farquhar, who go to great lengths to show how particular ideas are fulfilled, and how these ideas are worked out. Nevertheless, Miller's ideas are based upon the same general premises of evolution and fulfilment.

Miller is best known for suggesting that conversion is not necessary: 'there were Hindus who had the call of God to be baptized, but there were many others who were not called, at least not called by God, to be baptized, but who would and should remain non-Christians, following Christ in their own way and in their community.'[269] He sought, instead of baptism, a

---

266   Described by Goodall as 'that outstanding achievement in Christian higher education' (Goodall, p. 76).

267   Baago, 1969, p. 77.

268   Miller, 'The Place of Hinduism in the Story of the World', *Madras Christian College Magazine*, 18/4/1895, in Baago, 1969, p. 196.

269   Baago, 1969, p. 77.

diffusion of Christian knowledge amongst Hindus.[270] Certainly such ideas had a place in Miller's thought, but while this may have been his immediate aim it does not do justice to his views. While Miller stated that the work of Christian education should not be judged upon the number of baptisms achieved, this was because of the way he saw his work affecting Hinduism, and the practical problems of the work of conversion.[271] Miller uses an analogy of heating up a portion of metal. The area directly adjoining the heat source is heated quickly, and the rest is left cold, versus the effect of heating a mass of water where the whole is heated more or less evenly, taking a longer time to achieve a great heat, but when this temperature is reached it will affect the whole rather than just a portion – the water, Miller suggests, is analogous to Hinduism.[272] What he thus seeks is, 'a change of thought and feeling, a modification of character, a formation of principles tending in a Christian direction, which has begun from our institutions to leaven the whole lump of Hinduism.'[273]

This leavening process 'will show itself in due time in many individuals,'[274] but until this time, it is necessary to remember that Hinduism 'has woven itself into custom and thought and feeling – into the very texture of men's minds – that has poured its spirit into and expressed itself by means of the whole framework of society, as no religion has done elsewhere – as to this day most certainly Christianity has not done among those who nominally yield allegiance to it.'[275] There is thus a great strength to the Hindu corporate life, which it is very hard for him to pull away from.[276] While there certainly

---

270   Fulfil, p. 84.
271   Miller, 1878, p. 29. The Madras Christian College certainly never aimed at achieving direct conversion. See Miller, *The Madras Christian College Magazine*, pp. 20 f., in Fulfil, p. 84. Also see Stock, III, p. 496, where, with reference to 'The Place of Hinduism' and Miller' aims, the work of the college is given a favourable reaction, 'he [Miller] dwelt upon the immense importance of *preparatory work*, the results of which, though slow, would be sure. This is a consideration to be recognized to the utmost, and whether or no the Madras College has aimed at conversions as definitely as some other institutions, it may be doubted whether it has not achieved results as distinct as theirs, and as clearly tokens of God's blessing' (ibid).
272   Miller, 1878, p. 30.
273   Ibid.
274   Ibid.
275   Ibid., p. 9.
276   Ibid., p. 10; see, also, Miller in Baago, 1969, p. 186.

180

are instances of conversions: 'Some few have been led[...] to Christ so fully as to separate from their people, and to be baptized in the Redeemer's name. That is one precious result.'[277]

But this is just the tip of the iceberg, and the great mass of the work is spreading the knowledge of Christ, that will in time slowly seep into Hindu ways of thought so that the many may come to Christ:

[Baptism] is the fully developed fruit[....] But it is a fundamental law of our Master's kingdom – we have it from His own lips – that His kingdom is like the seed growing in the earth, which 'bringeth forth first the blade, then the ear, after that the full corn in the ear.' When that full corn really appears, we are to rejoice with exceeding joy; but if we have one particle of our Master's spirit in us, we shall rejoice and be thankful too when either blade or ear appears[....][278]

Because of this emphasis Miller found that he has often been misunderstood, 'On this I have dwelt unhesitatingly and often, and I have found my doing so represented as meaning that I did not believe in conversion, did not labour for it, and did not want it.'[279] He goes on to say that direct evangelism is a vital second stage in the process that he begins with education.[280]

Aside from the direct question of Miller's views on fulfilment, a few words could usefully be said about his beliefs on the effect of education on Hinduism. Miller sees the findings of modern Western knowledge as being utterly incompatible with Hindu belief,[281] and says that, even without the influence of Christianity, it would destroy Hinduism, and this would lead to secularism, materialism, and atheism.[282] Therefore the Christian influence is needed, saying of education, 'but if the 'crowning element' of Christian influence and Christian thought be present in sufficient quantity, it is positively useful.'[283] The use of the term 'crowning element' is of mild interest prefiguring, in a way, the title of Farquhar's main work. Of more interest is Miller's suggestion that if 'a state of avowed atheism or of contented materialism and worldliness' set in, then 'that would make the

---

277   Miller, 1878, p. 29.
278   Ibid.
279   Ibid.
280   Ibid., p. 32 ff.
281   Ibid., p. 21.
282   Ibid., pp. 22 f and 32.
283   Ibid., p. 23.

Christian effort barren and hopeless through many a dreary age.'[284] This foreshadows the belief of many future missionaries that the final contest will not be between Christianity and the non-Christian faiths, but between Christianity and unbelief.[285]

In what has been said above of Miller's thought, no mention has been made of fulfilment theology. However, it was necessary to clear up one misunderstanding concerning Miller, to set in context another aspect of his thought, and also to see that he believed that Christian thought[286] will infuse Hinduism; bringing Hindus, eventually, to conversion. This is important in order to understand his views on fulfilment. While Miller has been seen to stray away from the thought of Slater,[287] in view of what has been said before, such differences as do exist will be seen as being not quite as significant as they appear at first sight.

To understand Miller's thought on fulfilment we return to themes brought up in the opening quotation of this section in 'The Place of Hinduism in the Story of the World', in which the main themes of his fulfilment thought were discussed. Miller believed that Hinduism 'like Greece, like Rome, like Israel' has its own particular truth which it has to contribute to the mass of human knowledge.[288] Each of these is, taken by itself, one-sided and in need of perfection.[289] The Hindu ideal may be expressed quite briefly:

---

284   Miller, 1878, p. 32.
285   See Slater, in WPOR, II, pp. 1172–3, Barrows in New York I, p. 357, and Hocking, p. 29, where we see the idea that all the world's religions should unite versus the common foe of materialistic atheism.
286   That is to say, thought based upon the ideal of Jesus.
287   Baago, 1969, p. 75. Baago sees two streams of fulfilment theology, one typified by Slater and Farquhar in which Hinduism is 'fulfilled' by being replaced, the other the line followed by Miller and Bernard Lucas, (on the latter, see chapter 8) where fulfilment is seen in terms of development towards a new religion. The distinction between the Monier-William's and Müller's types of fulfilment, though he does not use this paradigm (see Fulfil, p. 87: 'Miller's use of the term [fulfilment] was not quite that of, for example, Monier-Williams, though it approaches that of Max Müller'). However, the influence of both flows into Miller's thought.
288   Miller, *Madras Christian College Magazine*, 18/4/1895, in Baago, 1969, pp. 186–7. This idea is reminiscent of Maurice who spoke of 'the great Mahometan truth,' etc (Boyle, p. 29 and elsewhere). See above concerning Slater, where it was mentioned that there seems to be a general conception that there is a Hindu ideal, as there is an ideal for each religion.
289   Ibid., p. 187.

There is the thought of the irresistible power that dwells somehow in the universe, a power which man can never change, to which it is his only wisdom to submit. There is the thought that God, that the divine, is not merely over all but in all, that the whole being of the world and those who dwell in it is the expression of divinity. There is the thought that all men, or all men within the Hindu pale, are inseparably linked, are responsible for one another, must in no circumstances part from one another.[290]

However, Miller in no way suggests that this, or that the ideals of any other nation, are to be found only within that place, but the world has been ordered[291] so that, in each part, one ideal will predominate, giving it the power to influence those beyond that nation's shores.[292]

To bring each of these national ideals to their fulfilment, a new ideal is needed, a perfect ideal, which is the ideal of Jesus.[293] This ideal is that:

Not only for a nation or a people but for each individual man, the loving God has care. Each man may know for himself that God loves him. each man may live on earth and amid all earth's sin and sorrow knowing as one of the contents of his own experience that a loving all-comprehending Being is taking the guidance of his life and making it serviceable for inconceivably noble ends. That each man should thus see God for himself, should be taught, strengthened, guided, in personal intercourse with God, that he should be set to work – for the good of men, knowing that he is working in God's way and for God's end: that was Christ's ideal of human life.[294]

Under the influence of this ideal the other, lesser, ideals which 'produced in isolation are mingled and therefore are beginning to bear their perfect fruit.'[295] Miller says this does not involve making India into a 'Christian nation,' a concept which he sees as, 'a stage, and an important stage, but it is obviously and infinitely far from being the final stage of the training of mankind.'[296] This is a very important point, because it entails a criticism of historical

---

290   Ibid., p. 186.
291   Miller does not explicitly say so but he seems to imply this is by Divine Providence.
292   Ibid., p. 188.
293   Chetty, p. 49 f.
294   Miller, *Madras Christian College Magazine*, 18/4/1895, in Baago, 1969, p. 189–190.
295   Ibid., p. 194.
296   Ibid. Miller describes a 'Christian nation' as one in which some people accept Christ's ideal, and it affects some parts of society, but still leaves many untouched (ibid., pp. 192 ff).

Christianity as it has developed and been put into practice.[297] His religion of the future is, nevertheless, a form of Christianity, though not in the form it is now known, for he says: 'Some nations came to be what is called 'Christian.' This nominal acceptance of the new ideal, and its heartfelt acceptance by the few, gave new life to what was good in the old ideals.'[298] His criticism is of what these so-called 'Christian nations' are in practice, and by implication, of Christianity as practised therein, rather than of Christianity as the religion infused with Christ's principles. While he is reluctant to use the term Christianity in the lectures we have been looking at, he certainly does use the term after his return to Scotland,[299] suggesting that his aim in this place may have been apologetic in speaking to his audience of Indian, and primarily Hindu, students. He is therefore suggesting, as does Müller, that a new form of Christianity will emerge from all the old religions under Christ's influence. We must ask how this differs from Slater's view, who said that the Hindu ideal would not only create a separate Indian Christianity, but would also affect Western Christianity by correcting some national tendencies. However, I would not want to suggest that his thought was indistinguishable from, say, Slater or Monier-Williams on this matter, for he does speak of the intermingling of the national ideals as being 'the means of advancing our race further than it has advanced as yet towards its pre-determined goal.'[300] This will be towards not just a new Indian Christianity, but a new Christianity altogether, which is the blending of all national ideals under the ideal of Christ. The difference, then, is partly one of degree, for with Miller the influence of the Hindu ideal upon Western Christianity will be much greater, creating a new world-wide faith, built up from all national ideals, and applicable to all peoples. In this he is very much in line with Müller. In seeing Christ, rather than historical Christianity, as the fulfilling principle he is in the same camp as Müller and Farquhar, as opposed to Monier-Williams and Slater. However, as will be seen above, Farquhar's view of how Hinduism will affect the development of Christianity is far more in accord with Slater's.

---

297   Sharpe observes that, 'he makes it clear that it is not historical Christianity which occupies a position of absolute supremacy over against Hinduism; it is Christ' (Fulfil, p. 87), and Baago notes that, 'it was not the historical Christianity which Miller considered to be the fulfilment of Hinduism' (Baago, 1969, p. 76).
298   Miller, *Madras Christian College Magazine*, 18/4/1895, in Baago, 1969, p. 192.
299   See Chetty, pp. 80 f.
300   Miller, *Madras Christian College Magazine*, 18/4/1895, in Baago, 1969, p. 195.

Therefore, as Baago suggests, Farquhar and Slater should be seen to be in a different camp from Miller.

As a final note, despite his rather unusual views, Miller was responsible for spreading the knowledge of the principles of fulfilment theology throughout Southern India.[301]

Before passing on, a comparison may be drawn between Miller and one of the most significant missionary figures of a century earlier, Alexander Duff. Duff's attitude to Hinduism was wholly iconoclastic,[302] and, on leaving India he became in 1851 the moderator of the General Assembly of the Free Church of Scotland.[303] He was to be followed in this post, nearly fifty years later, by Miller, who was elected to the role in 1896.[304] Perhaps we should not read too much into this, but it seems fair to say that if for the mid-nineteenth-century Duff's views were not too extreme, by the late nineteenth-century Miller's views were not seen as too liberal to debar him from holding such an office.

The Spread of, and Attacks on, Fulfilment Theology

John Robson

The year before Banerjea's *The Arian Witness* appeared in India, a book that was to run to three editions was published in Britain, that expounded fulfilment theology. Its author was a missionary of the Free Church of Scotland, formerly of Ajmer,[305] who largely endorsed Müller's ideas.[306] The missionary was John Robson, whose contribution to fulfilment theology

---

301   Fulfil, p. 87.
302   See for instance, Duff, 1839(a), pp. 179 ff, 1839b, pp. 45–6, or 1851, pp. 99–100, and 145–6.
303   Cross, p. 425.
304   Fulfil, p. 86.
305   See Fulfil, p. 54, and Robson, 1874, frontal.
306   Fulfil, pp. 54 f.

seems to have been largely ignored.[307] Certainly he does not seem to have had any direct influence upon Farquhar, or any later figures,[308] His work does not stand out as a major contribution to the development of an Indian Christian theology, nor as a systematic exposition of fulfilment theology. However, there are signs in it that he was a far more theological capable thinker than most later fulfilment theologians.[309]

While Robson was an admirer of Müller,[310] he stills seems to use the evangelical idea of there being a primitive revelation,[311] from which he says there is a gradual deterioration.[312] Certainly, he does follow Müller in allowing that there is a religious faculty in man which transforms 'a dead statement of doctrine into a living power,'[313] and this faculty is to be found in all religions.[314] However, this admission should not be seen as a statement of Logos theology; Robson's thought is closer to Banerjea's. In mentioning Banerjea it should be asked if the two had any contact. Both place great stress upon sacrifice, and mention the figure of Prajāpati. However, Robson, stationed in Ajmer, just to the south of Jaipur, was on the opposite side of the country to Banerjea. As to whether Banerjea read Robson's book,it must remain unknown.[315] The differences between the two, Banerjea's reliance on the Aryan race theory, and the failure of Banerjea to mention a number of key features of Robson's work,[316] suggest that there was no direct link. Banerjea's

---

307   Sharpe gives him but a couple of brief mentions (Fulfil, pp. 54 f, and 106 f), while Maw makes no mention of him at all.
308   Though the fact that his book ran to three editions suggests that there were many who read his work.
309   The figures associated with the Cambridge Mission are, of course, notable exceptions to this general rule.
310   His monograph of 1876 on the relevance of what he calls the 'Science of Religion' gives ample evidence of this.
311   Robson, 1874, pp. 269 ff.
312   Ibid., pp. 22 f.
313   Robson, 1876, p. 70.
314   Ibid., p. 74.
315   That he did so prior to beginning work on *The Arian Witness* is, I would suggest, highly unlikely. Remembering that it would take a considerable time to reach India by sea, the idea that a copy, hot off the press, was shipped straightway to India, where it was read at once by Banerjea, who, then, inspired, got immediatly to work on the preparation of his book and finished it ready for printing that same year, seems implausible, to say the least.
316   E.g., the difference of Levitical and Brahmanical sacrifices, vicarious atonement being expressed through transmigration, and the stress laid upon human nature.

fulfilment theology was suggestive of Monier-Williams, while Robson's is definitely tempered by Müller's thought.

Robson is most distinctive and original in what he says about sacrifice, and as this helps to show his theological acuity, I will take the liberty of quoting him at length:

[The] Brahmans attached to their sacrifice a significance not very different from that which we now attach to the old Levitical sacrifices. Still more startling is the point of difference between the two. The latter was typical, the former sacramental. The utter impossibility that 'the blood of bulls and of goats should take away sins,' is a truth that must be felt by every one who realizes what sin is[....] The Hebrews felt more than any others its utter inadequacy, and at the same time[...] persisted in a simple observance of it[...] without attempting any explanation of its hidden meaning.[317]

Robson goes on to say that, without putting any further meaning onto the sacrifice, the Jews kept up the practice, despite the protests of the Psalmists against, 'an ordinance of God which it [the human mind] cannot understand,'[318] until at 'length, in the death of Christ on Calvary, the whole course of Jewish sacrifice was fulfilled.'[319] Thus Jewish sacrifice was seen, in the fullness of time, to be a type of Jesus' sacrifice. However, Robson suggests that the case is different with Brahmanical sacrifice:

But well-nigh a thousand years before the coming of Christ, the Brahmans of India had felt, and in their own way expressed, this truth. Conscious seemingly that the animal sacrificed could not of itself bear the sin[...] they boldly declared that God Himself was in the animal sacrificed, and that thus it was efficacious.[320]

Thus, says Robson, the sacrifice was sacramental, as it was held to be an outward expression of a spiritual, and inner act, which he compares to the understanding of the host in the Eucharist of the Roman Catholic Church, going on to quote the following passage:

Prajapati is this sacrifice. Prajapati is both of these two things, uttered and unuttered, finite and infinite. What the priest does with the Yajus text, with that he consecrates the

---

317   Robson, 1874, pp. 41–2.
318   Ibid., p. 43.
319   Ibid., p. 43.
320   Ibid., pp. 43–4.

form of Prajapati which is uttered and finite. And what he does silently with that he consecrates the form of Prajapati which is unuttered and infinite.[321]

Whether one agrees with Robson's argument or not, it cannot be denied that he enters into a much subtler, and more theological assessment of Hinduism, than Farquhar ever does. Also, interestingly, he does not suggest that this doctrine is 'fulfilled' in Christianity, as he says Jewish sacrifice was. He does however talk of Christianity 'as the fulfilment of what is best in the old religion of India.'[322] In fact he never explicitly speaks of any doctrine being 'fulfilled,' but rather says that what is met in Christianity, are human needs; an idea already seen in past expressions of fulfilment theology.[323] So Robson speaks of, 'principles of human nature which Hinduism has ignored.'[324] These 'principles' he says, 'are the auxiliaries to which we have resort in pressing on them the religion of Jesus. In recalling them to their manhood we are calling them to Christianity.'[325] This is clearly seen in a paper Robson wrote on, as he called them, the 'differentia' of Christianity. Robson here notes three main 'differentia'; first, baptism in the name of the Father, Son, and Holy Ghost; second, remission of sin's in Jesus' name;[326] and third, the conception of God.[327] It is the last of these that will concern us here. The trinity, he says, 'responds with complete fulness [sic] to the aspirations of man's heart after God.'[328] He sees each member of the Trinity as meeting a different need in man's psyche, each having a role equivalent to some earthly model, and says:

Christianity teaches not only the *Fatherhood* of God, but also the *Brotherhood* of God and the *Companionhood* of God; the threefold relation of God to man, which fully responds to man's religious needs, the absence of any one of which leaves a blank that craves to be satisfied.[329]

---

321   Ibid., p. 44.
322   Robson, 1874, p. 286.
323   See below.
324   Robson, 1874, p. 313.
325   Ibid., pp. 314–5.
326   Robson, 1898, p. 552.
327   Ibid., and p. 555.
328   Ibid., p. 552.
329   Ibid.

188

Robson asserts a priori that these are needs of man, and so can say in the light of this, that Christianity 'responds to man's religious aspirations as no other religion does.'[330] Further, in regard to Hinduism, Robson notes that it fails to meet the needs of consciousness and conscience,[331] that it is to say he believes that it disregards man's personality, and also his sense of the presence of sin, which must, he feels, be emphasized as 'antidotes to the subtle pantheistic poison' of Hinduism.[332]

It is important that Robson stresses this aspect of fulfilment theology, which is found later in Farquhar, for it is on just this point that Hogg attacks Farquhar's fulfilment theology, saying that it is not specific doctrines, but rather human needs, which are met. Robson, unlike Farquhar, never speaks of specific doctrines being fulfilled, although both would agree that it is the essential human need behind them which is *really* what is fulfilled. I mention this particularly for there are certain similarities between Robson and Hogg, and it is even possible that Hogg was influenced by Robson's writings on fulfilment theology. As will be seen below, Hogg himself, while a critic of fulfilment theology, does use a form of fulfilment theology which bears marked similarities to Robson's model. To outline the similarity of Hogg and Robson, it will be necessary to consider one specific need or expression of human yearning, on which they both lay great stress, which is sin.

According to Robson in Hinduism, 'sin is not made exceedingly sinful, but merely a misfortune, differing accidentally from virtue,'[333] so it is not, he observes, such a pressing need for the Hindu, who cannot see man as essentially sinful, and in violation of God's law, 'Hinduism[...] is debarred from this conception, for it denies a personal God; denying Him, it can have no place for His holy law, and consequently sin as such is excluded also[....] It ought to have no place in the Hindu religion at all. But it has a place[...]'[334]

Robson also originated another novel expression of fulfilment theology, which is that man's innate sense of the need for vicarious atonement, first met by sacrifice, was in later Hinduism answered by the idea of transmigration.[335]

---

330   Ibid., p. 558.
331   Robson, 1874, p. 313.
332   Ibid., p. 314.
333   Robson, 1874, p. 254.
334   Ibid., p. 249.
335   Robson, 1874, p. 253.

One possible reason why Robson was not such an influence on later fulfilment theology is his mode of expression at times. In dealing with Slater and Farquhar, the need for a conciliatory tone with regards to Hinduism will be stressed, whereas Robson suggested that the missionaries' attitude should be one of 'intolerance.'[336] While he appears to mean by this only that the missionary should not take an unduly lenient attitude, that is not to say that all forms of belief are equally valid, which he calls Hindu 'tolerance'.[337] However, to those like Farquhar this language would be seen as too provocative.

Finally, the difference between Robson's earlier and later editions of *Hinduism and its Relations to Christianity* should be noted, as they give valuable witness to the change in attitude towards Hinduism. In the preface to the third edition of 1905, he refers back to the first edition, saying: 'When that edition was published, thirty years ago, the difficulty was rather to convince people at home that in Hinduism there was a real yearning after God, and an embodiment of many of the truths which are at the basis of all religions.'[338] Robson thus suggests that the beliefs which underpin fulfilment theology were commonly accepted in England by the turn of the century.

The Misunderstanding of Cobban

John Mackenzie Cobban was a missionary with the Wesleyan Methodist Missionary Society, who deserves a mention, not because of any great contribution to fulfilment theology, but rather because he demonstrates both how widely accepted fulfilment theology was, and yet how carefully it had to be expressed. In particular he deserves attention because his example has been held to mean the opposite of what it does, in fact, tell us.

Sharpe has suggested that Cobban's treatment shows that in the 1880's fulfilment theology, indeed, any positive attitude towards Hinduism, was generally not acceptable in missionary circles, and he says:

[At] the Protestant Missionary Conference held in London in June 1888[...] Cobban[...] was censured for opinions expressed in a paper on 'Christianity in Relation to Hinduism'.

---

336   Ibid., p. 291.
337   Ibid., p. 292.
338   Robson, 1905, p. iii.

Cobban had claimed that the method of the missionary must be discriminating and intelligent. Everything in Hinduism is not of the devil; God and spiritual truth are not confined to the Hebrew and Christian sacred books. The immediate reaction was that the Acting Secretary of the Conference declared: 'I can only say that if I were prepared to concede as much as our friend does, I should not be prepared to leave home and country to preach the Gospel anywhere.'[339]

More than this, Cobban was not even allowed to finish his paper,[340] though Sharpe notes that one missionary, John Hewlett, did take Cobban's part.[341] However, his was not a lone voice. In the following papers, not just Hewlett, but another missionary, John Ross, as well as a member of the Free Church of Scotland's Foreign Missions Committee, Principal Brown of Aberdeen, all mentioned Cobban by name to defend him.[342] While several others spoke out for a positive approach to Hinduism,[343] only one person spoke against him, though not mentioning Cobban by name, who asked whether liberals preach salvation through Jesus, or by some 'spiritual truth,'[344] though he was interrupted by Principal Brown, with the authoritative words, 'That was not said this afternoon.'[345] Hewlett and his colleagues appear to have convinced the audience that they had condemned Cobban too soon, and that he was not saying that elements of Hinduism could replace Christian doctrines.[346] Thus Cobban was allowed to speak again in extended time, where no objection was raised to his saying: 'And when I meet spiritual truth yonder, either on the lips of a Hindu or in a Hindu book, I say this has come from God, and I rejoice[.... Also, that] Christianity finds a line of approach to the Hindu heart by these truths which are already there.'[347] Unfortunately a full copy of Cobban's speech is not given as it was sent to an unspecified journal,[348] which would perhaps explain why it was

---

339   Fulfil, p. 55, quoting B. Broomhill, in Johnston, p. 89.
340   Johnston, p. 93.
341   See Fulfil, p. 55, fn 5.
342   Johnston, pp. 93, 95, and 96.
343   J. Kennedy (ibid., p. 92 f.), and K. F. Junor (ibid., pp. 94 f.).
344   See ibid., pp. 93 f.
345   Ibid., p. 93.
346   Ibid.
347   Ibid., pp. 97 and 98.
348   Ibid., p. 89.

misinterpreted. However, in a later article, Cobban gives an account of the beliefs of the Śaiva Siddhānta,[349] which he evidently regards as religious truths which look forward to Christianity, to be 'used' by the Christian missionary 'to bear witness for Christ.'[350] It is unnecessary to expound them here, for it will only repeat what has been said already, and will be said in the works of those fulfilment theologians discussed at length. What is worth noting is what he says of those who play down these truths. They are generally recognized, he suggests, but he notes: 'There is[...] a natural tendency to minimise truth outside the Christian area[....] Phrases like the following – "unaided human reason," "unaided human resources" – are in themselves inaccurate.'[351] Yet not only does Cobban oppose those who do not accept that a divine presence is to be found in the non-Christian religions, he also says, 'Nor is the statement that these other religions are "a preparation for Christianity" at all adequate to describe either their *raison d'être* or their contents.'[352] This attitude will, he says, do Christianity no favours, rather a greater openness should be exhibited. This attitude bears a similarity to Hogg's suggestion that fulfilment theology is inherently patronizing. Cobban, then, denies the meta-narrative of fulfilment theology but endorses its practical application. That is to say, he denies that Hinduism was given by God as a form of training for Christianity, but the truths that are known of God by man, can, nevertheless, be used as tools by the missionary to indicate that Christianity teaches higher truths. Cobban, then, rejects the idea of providence, but whether he sees the change as 'evolutionary' is unclear. To what degree he does, in fact, hold a fulfilment theology is therefore unclear. His rejection of the term 'preparation,' it is worth noting, is based upon apologetics, that any suggestion of Christianity taking such a stance would alienate Hindu opinion.

This article was warmly greeted, at least in certain quarters, a glowing review appearing in the *Madras Christian College Magazine*.[353]

---

349   Cobban, pp. 857 ff.
350   Ibid., p. 863.
351   Ibid., p. 861.
352   Ibid.
353   Anon., 1895.

5 British Theological Usage

Westcott and the Cambridge Tradition of Fulfilment Theology

Westcott and the New Alexandria

It should come as no surprise that, amongst those who endorse fulfilment theology, a great many were been educated at Cambridge, and thus immersed in the Platonist tradition that inspired Rowland Williams and Maurice.[1] Bishop Westcott was such a man. Of all the leading theologians in Britain in his day, Westcott appears to have been the only one to write at any length on fulfilment theology, and he will thus be the main figure considered in this chapter. It should be noted, however, that he, along with Lightfoot, Hort and Stanton, were all supporters of the Cambridge Mission to Delhi, indeed all taking a leading role in it, we may surmise that they were all in sympathy with the fulfilment theology upon which it was based. This is not to suggest that they would have agreed in every particular with what will be said here of Westcott's own particular fulfilment theology. Whilst Westcott was a central figure, it should be pointed out that he is not, as Maw suggests, almost single handedly responsible for promoting fulfilment theology.[2] Maw is closer to the mark than Sharpe, who sees Westcott as being utterly opposed to fulfilment theology, and suggesting that he saw no relation between Christianity and the non-Christian religions.[3] His work *Christus Consummator,* (surprisingly,

---

1 This is not to suggest that they were natural allies, they were both professors at Cambridge, but they did not get on, though after having read his biography after his death Westcott noted that he felt a great sympathy with Maurice (Norman, p. 167). We may note that Cracknell observes that Westcott often 'echoes or reflects' Maurice, but with regard to this we may repeat the same proviso, made in relation to Slater, that Cracknell reflects the wider tradition of fulfilment theology to be found in Rowland Williams, Trench, Müller, etc (see Cracknell, 1995, p. 60).

2 See Maw, 1990, p. 12, and chapter III.

3 Fulfil, p. 15, fn. 4.

perhaps, considering the title) is not a work of fulfilment theology in a broad sense,[4] being limited to the Hebrew prophets, though there is one reference to Plato, whose vision, Westcott says, 'found its confirmation and fulfilment' in Jesus' life and teachings.[5] Again, the passage Sharpe takes from *Christian Aspects of Life* is taken out of context. The Gospel of which 'there is no anticipation'[6] refers only to God's self-sacrificing love in Jesus, whereas earlier he had spoken of the non-Christian sacred books as showing, 'the Divine plan in the education of the world.'[7] At the other extreme, Maw calls fulfilment Westcott's own 'private creed'[8] and that having *developed* it, he then spread it widely to all who came into contact with him. While he recognizes both Trench and Maurice as expounding somewhat similar ideas,[9] and rightly places Westcott within the same Platonist tradition, Maw fails to recognize that fulfilment theology was far more widespread. While he knows the work of Banerjea, he treats it essentially as an example of the Aryan race theory inspired by Müller, rather than as a work of fulfilment theology,[10] though he notes that Müller's thought was essentially fulfilment theology.[11] He does acknowledge that there was an independent tradition of fulfilment theology, exemplified by Slater,[12] whom he calls 'the only systematic exponent of fulfilment theology in the subcontinent' before the arrival of the Cambridge Mission to Delhi.[13] Certainly it has been seen that a school of fulfilment theology was flourishing in India. Regarding the British scene, whilst a number of those to be looked at certainly were in contact with Westcott, and may have been influenced by him,[14] there remain certain

---

4   Though it does expound upon Westcott's understanding of 'fulfilment' in a broader sense (Cracknell, 1995, p. 62).

5   Westcott, 1890, p. 84.

6   Op. cit., p. 171.

7   Ibid., p. 164.

8   Maw, 1990, p. 253: 'Fulfilment had begun as Westcott's private creed.'!!!

9   Ibid., pp. 156–7.

10   Ibid., pp. 45 ff.

11   Ibid., p. 127.

12   Ibid., p. 325.

13   Ibid., p. 51.

14   Maw observes that Westcott was a close friend of Benson, and inspired Gore's fulfilment theology (ibid., pp. 132 and 255). There is no doubt that Westcott had a profound influence on many of those whom he taught as evinced by Scott Holland's short monograph in memory of him, in which he recalls the way he held his students enthralled (Holland, pp. 8 ff). Also, it is worth mentioning that, in

difficulties in suggesting that fulfilment theology was in some way Westcott's own 'private creed.' Westcott's interest in fulfilment theology, as exhibited in his writings, should be seen to begin only in the 1890s. Combined with this there are many earlier figures, whom Maw is apparently unaware of, who endorse, or mention, similar ideas, to whom reference shall be made later in this chapter. Westcott, although he expounds upon fulfilment theology at a greater length than his peers, is not a leader, but, rather, a follower of contemporary thought in this area.

In putting Westcott as just one amongst many expounding fulfilment theology at this time, it should be considered that these ideas would not be considered unusual to those immersed in the Cambridge Platonist tradition. Much has been written on Westcott's Platonist leanings;[15] the importance of such ideas to fulfilment theology have already been discussed in relation to Williams and Maurice. Therefore, having noted Westcott's relation to this tradition, it is unnecessary to discuss the matter further in itself, as doing so would merely repeat much of what has already been said, though naturally aspects of his Platonism will be discussed in relation to his ideas as they arise.

One particular aspect of Westcott's life that should be noted is his connection with the Cambridge Mission to Delhi, in the setting up of which he was particularly involved,[16] which will be discussed more thoroughly in its own right below. It was to be in Westcott's vision a 'new Alexandria.'[17] According to him: 'At Alexandria in the first ages the Faith found its widest and most philosophic expression through Origen and Athanasius; as we are encouraged to do, we therefore welcome the past as the omen of the future.'[18]

---

relation to his speeches in the Christian Socialist movement, at the end although no one could recall the substance of what he had said, everyone was inspired by the speech itself (A. Westcott, II, p. 16; see also Maw, 1990, p. 150). He was certainly a man capable of guiding other men's minds, but this does not mean that he lead men to their beliefs in every sphere.

15   See especially Newsome, 1969, also Newsome, 1974, pp. 79 ff, and Maw, 1990, pp. 137 and 144 ff.

16   See A. Westcott, I, p. 383. The mission realized that 'it was to his inspiring influence and suggestion that the Cambridge Mission owed its origin' (General Letter, signed by S. S. Allnutt on behalf of the members of the Cambridge Mission to Delhi 12/8/1901 (USPGCMD #87)).

17   Westcott, Letter to Lefroy, 15/1/1884 (USPGCMD #92). This phrase was often used by Westcott, even before the foundation of the Cambridge Mission to Delhi, see Westcott, 1873, p. 41 and Westcott, 1882, p. 7.

18   Westcott, 1882, p. 7.

According to Maw, through the Cambridge Mission to Delhi, Westcott hoped to reassert Alexandrian theology,[19] meaning, in this particular context, that it should not just be a centre of learning, but also the means whereby Christianity could be interpreted into the terms of Indian philosophy and thought. Despite being a mission, Westcott wanted its work to be confined solely to education.[20] Westcott believed that past missionary work had been too traditional and dogmatic,[21] faults which he felt 'academic coöperation would tend to remove.'[22] Indeed, he believed the Universities to be providentially ordained for the task,[23] as part of a divine scheme in which England had been 'fitted as a people and as a church to be missionaries of the world,' more than this, Westcott continued, they were 'to be interpreters of the East to the West, and of the West to the East.'[24] The last phrase of this passage is of the most interest to us, for it is the key to the most interesting feature of Westcott's fulfilment theology, which is most certainly not unique to him, but to which he gives his own particular spin. Put simply, it is the need for the Eastern world to develop its own particular form of Christianity which will then, according to Westcott, contribute to the expanding whole of Christian understanding. For Westcott, the role of the Cambridge Mission to Delhi in this was to form a base from which a less Westernized Christianity could be taught, an intellectual centre in which Indians could be educated so that they would then, in the light of this benevolent institute of liberal thinking, be able to propagate an Eastern version of Christianity, having been freed from the strictures of Western dogmatism. More specifically, Westcott believed that India alone could offer the first full interpretation of the fourth Gospel.[25] Westcott's central ideas will now be looked at more closely.

A number of Westcott's ideas will be very familiar, particularly the first, that all religions are an aspiration after God:

> Even the rudest demon-worship contains the germ of this feeling by which the worshipper seeks to be at one with some power which is adverse to him. It is a witness to something in man by which he is naturally constituted to feel after a harmonious fellowship with all

---

19   Maw, 1990, p. 159.
20   Bickersteth Letter to Carlyon, 10/5/1883 (USPGCMD #92).
21   Westcott, 1873, p. 31.
22   Ibid., p. 30.
23   Stanton, p. 25.
24   Westcott, 1873, p. 28.
25   See Lefroy, 1907(b), p. 78, also Boyd, 1979, p. 1.

that of which he is conscious, with the unseen, and with the infinite, no less than with the seen and the material.[26]

Each one of these needs is met in Christianity as the highest, and universal, religion.[27] As already mentioned, as well as being expressions of man's religious yearnings, the non-Christian religions were also, for Westcott, providential as part of man's education,[28] and he states explicitly that the Logos operated within these religions.[29] Making in his commentary on St John's Gospel the point that: 'It does not follow that everyone that is guided by Christ [i.e., as the Logos] is directly conscious of his guidance.'[30] Westcott does not expand explicitly upon the question of fulfilment. The most he says, here in relation to Greek philosophy, is:

> The end of Philosophy is Truth; not in one region but in all; Truth apprehended, if it may be, in its highest unity. The name of Christianity is Truth; and I think that I have shewn that the first great writer [Origen] who endeavoured to face the question affirmed, with unquestioning belief, that Christianity is the fulfilment of Philosophy.[31]

The detailed exposition of fulfilment theology was something found only in India. Presumably it was only felt necessary to do so there, where such work would have a practical purpose. Westcott acknowledges the contribution of Justin Martyr, Clement of Alexandria and other fathers of the Church, 'particularly men of the Alexandrine School,'[32] to this type of thought, and we may note that many of his courses at Cambridge made special reference to St.

---

26   Westcott, 1892, pp. 96–7. See also Westcott, 1873, pp. 28–9.
27   Westcott, 1892, p. 121.
28   Westcott, 1897, p. 171.
29   Westcott, 1892, pp. 118–9, where he refers to Clement of Alexandria.
30   Westcott, 1887, p. 202, commentary on Jn XIV: 6. Cracknell says of this line that it 'was to prove seminal for Anglican thought on the significance of other religions, for the idea that the guidance of Christ need not be 'conscious' functions as undergirding for all 'inclusive' Logos Christology when it is used to make sense of the faith of people who are not Christians' (Cracknell, 1995, p. 61). While I cannot disagree with Cracknell on the importance of the idea I do not feel that he can call its appearance here 'seminal'. The centrality of Logos theology for fulfilment theology is something stressed throughout this study, and has already been discussed in relation to the earlier part of the Cambridge tradition, and was seen in Müller.
31   Westcott, 1891, p. 251.
32   Westcott, 1892, p. 116.

John the Evangelist and the Alexandrian philosophers.[33] The whole Logos tradition, especially as interpreted through the Neo-Platonism of Alexandria, suffused his thinking.[34] Just as these men had interpreted Christianity into the language of Greek philosophy, so Westcott felt it necessary for Christianity to be clothed in Indian philosophy in the East, which was to be the task of the universities;[35] hence his new Alexandria. There was also a missionary aspect to the indigenization of Christianity in India, as Westcott believed that if Christianity could be shown to be an Eastern religion then it would triumph in India,[36] a belief shared by Westcott's contemporaries at Cambridge, such as Lightfoot, 'Indian Christianity can never be cast in the same mould as English Christianity[....] We must become Indians to the Indian, if we would win India to Christ.'[37] Lightfoot, too, was deeply involved with the Cambridge Mission to Delhi.[38] Moreover, Westcott had a vision akin to that of Miller in India, in which there would not just be an Indian Christianity for India, but the insights of the East would, in turn, then alter Western Christianity, just as the writings of Origen and the other members of the Alexandrine tradition had transformed Christianity in the early centuries, and alter it in a similar way to the Alexandrians.[39] For Westcott any interpretation of the Gospel was always partial.[40]

Westcott spoke of the services offered by the different nations,[41] each religion having a different national characteristic.[42] Speaking of what he refers to as the three 'præ-Christian Book-religions' he says: 'We may say with justice, speaking broadly, that the Chinese (Turanian) religions are impressed

---

33   Maw, 1990, p. 134.
34   In relation to this, Newsome suggests that Westcott is more properly speaking a Plotinist, rather than a Platonist, i.e. that he is one of those who follows the later interpretations of Plato as opposed to a follower of the Plato of the Dialogues (Newsome, 1969, p. 9).
35   Westcott, 1873, pp. 29 ff.
36   Maw, 1990, p. 142. The connection of this to Sen's thought may be noted here, for he, too, tried to show that Christianity was an oriental religion, whether Westcott relies upon Sen as his influence cannot be known (see previous chapter on Sen).
37   Lightfoot, pp. 91–2.
38   See 1889 *Cambridge Mission to Delhi Annual Report*, p. 15 (USPGCMD #131).
39   Ibid., pp. 32–3.
40   Chadwick, 1961, p. 8.
41   Westcott, 1908, p. 210.
42   Westcott, 1892, pp. 108–9.

with the stamp of order, the Aryan with that of nature, the Shemitic [sic.] with that of history.'[43]

Westcott notes that the recognition of the 'special office of Gentile nations in the divine economy' is something to which the Alexandrian school 'did not rise to the apprehension of.'[44] Westcott felt that it was necessary for all the peoples of the world to be brought within the Church for it to be complete,[45] not least because other races could add facets to the faith which the Western world was not capable of uncovering.[46] This fits into the general scheme of Westcott's own thought, in which all of creation in its diversity is united ultimately in, and through, the person of Jesus as the incarnate Son of God[47] – the special characteristics of all the nations finding their consummation in Christianity. It should be mentioned in this regard that Westcott followed Maurice in the tradition of Christian Socialism where, as has been seen, it is essential to see the inter-connectedness of all people.[48] Many commentators have noted Westcott's love of paradox,[49] and here we see one example, where the unity and diversity of man is both affirmed and denied, for although all men are linked together through Christ as one, yet at the same time it is only in the combination of their differences that Christianity can become complete. Both were essential in Westcott's world-view.

In pursuit of the ideal of Indian Christianity, Westcott's theology suggested a dialogue with the non-Christian religions in which the role of language was all important.[50] Westcott followed Müller in seeing each language as having a direct correlation to the national religion,[51] which he sees as part of the divine plan, 'it can hardly be an accident that each of the three great families of speech offers collections of sacred books which present in a form capable of a direct analysis the faiths which correspond with

---

43   Ibid., p. 123.
44   Ibid., p. 116.
45   Westcott, 1897, pp. 144 ff.
46   Westcott, 1901, pp. 155–6.
47   See Westcott, 1890, p. 103.
48   'He [Jesus] is shewn to stand essentially in some ineffable yet real connexion with all finite being' (ibid.). See chapter 2 where Maurice is discussed.
49   See, e.g., Chadwick, 1961, p. 3, also Newsome, 1969, pp. 11–12.
50   Maw, 1990, pp. 162 ff.
51   Westcott, 1892, pp. 103–5.

them.'[52] Such was the degree to which Westcott saw providence guiding the world, that, as Maw notes, 'Platonically, he reasoned that God, via the Logos, had stocked creation without waste or repetition.'[53] So each language had a purpose in being best able to reveal different aspects of each religion and the national characteristics it represented.

Westcott's fulfilment theology has much in common with Müller,[54] as well as, of course, Williams, Maurice, and Trench. It is interesting that Maw suggests that those such as Slater who derived their fulfilment theology from sources independent of Westcott had a vision 'of the "fulfilled Church"[...] somewhat different from his.'[55] There are, though, many similarities between the fulfilment theology that was developing in the mission fields of India, and that which existed in academic circles in Britain. Although it is possible to speak of two separate strands of fulfilment theology, both feed from the same sources, and it is impossible to speak of certain aspects that are found in one and not in the other.

Commenting on Westcott, Maw makes a number of criticisms of his scheme of fulfilment theology, to which it is necessary to make some reply. Maw's criticisms, though valid to some degree, fail to appreciate quite what Westcott's position was. Maw accused Westcott of reducing the world to a 'condition of language.'[56] and turning 'complicated societies into emblems.'[57] Further, Maw says: 'On the face of it, it seems unlikely that someone so intelligent should not have realized their error.'[58] Maw's portrait of Westcott is of some dreamy academic stuck far away in some ivory tower, too out of touch with the real world to realize his error. Indeed, he often refers to Westcott's view of India as his 'imagined empire.'[59] He accuses Westcott of an idealism which demanded a passive India, which would just accept his

---

52   Ibid., p. 120. The three groups are the Chinese, Aryan, and Semitic, already mentioned above.

53   Maw, 1990, p. 164.

54   Westcott certainly knew of Müller's work, referring to his *Introduction to the Science of Religion* in his discussion of the relationship of language and religion in *The Gospel of Life* (op. cit., p. 103, fn 1).

55   Ibid., p. 325.

56   Maw, 1990, p. 253.

57   Ibid., p. 223.

58   Ibid., p. 224.

59   Ibid., e.g., p. 165.

fulfilment theology without reacting.[60] The criticisms are all based upon the supposition that Westcott felt that his fulfilment theology and writings on India, based upon a Platonic world view, were the final and definitive statement. This, however, was not the case, as I will show in relation to each point.

Firstly, regarding language, Maw appears to think that Westcott believed that language was the key to the spiritual thought of the non-Christian religions in a very literal way, 'an understanding of words gives one an insight into *the* Word: Platonically, if it were possible to identify and investigate its every manifestation, one might be able to define the Idea conditioning any part of the universe.'[61] Certainly, Westcott felt that much could be gained by a careful study of language. Relevant to this is the fact that Westcott, in collaboration with Hort, were the key people involved in creating the Revised Version of the Bible, and devoted years to studying the Greek text of the New Testament. At the same time, Westcott believed that we must 'recognize the inadequacy of human language to express infinite truth. Nothing for Westcott could be more important than that recognition.'[62] Related to this is the charge that he simplified India, making it submit to his linguistic scheme. If we admit that Westcott did not believe that he could fully grasp what India had to offer in language, then this charge is partially refuted.

Secondly, we must consider what he was doing in setting up the Cambridge Mission to Delhi. We have seen that its purpose was to train people to be able to formulate an Indian theology. He did not believe that what he said was the encapsulation of India, that all it had to offer was contained in a few trite phrases. His work was but some brief preliminary guidelines at the most, to the work that had to be done in India. Westcott did not, then, have in his head some 'imagined empire' which he thought was India. Maw attacks Westcott for never having visited India, suggesting that he thought he could know all he wanted by sitting at home in England. Talking of such a visit, Maw says: 'Westcott[...] felt very little need for personal contact with it [India]. The absurdity inherent in a scholar ignoring a primary subject did not trouble [him]. Westcott seems never to have considered it.'[63] The unjustness of this criticism is evident. Westcott believed personal contact with India essential,

---

60   Ibid., p. 224.
61   Ibid., p. 163.
62   Chadwick, 1961, p. 7.
63   Maw, 1990, p. 16.

this was part of the reason for the mission. Westcott himself never saw this as his main subject of study, his only work to deal with it in more than passing, the *Gospel of Life*, dedicates just two out of ten chapters to the subject of Christianity's relation to the non-Christian religions as a whole.[64] Continually Westcott makes clear that the East has something distinctive to offer, which the West cannot grasp by itself, yet the few tentative steps that he makes towards giving a broad outline of Eastern thought are taken by Maw as Westcott saying *exactly* what India is.

The final point that Maw makes, that Westcott saw India as passively receptive to ideas imposed by the West, is surely contradicted by what he says elsewhere, that '[i]nstead of imposing Western theology on the Orient, missionaries should engage in a dialogue.'[65]

That Westcott did not regard India in this way is to miss the point; he helped found the mission for the purpose of this dialogue to take place. Indeed, Maw's picture of Westcott as a dreamer does not ring true when we consider that he founded this mission, and, as Bishop of Durham, he showed his capabilities as a practical man in bringing a resolution to the coal strike of 1892,[66] and, as has been noted by Edwards: 'He could be down-to-earth.'[67] He may have presented in too idealistic a fashion, but that may have been his aim. Speaking here of another matter, he nevertheless makes a point that may also be pertinent here: 'It will be said that this is an unattainable ideal. But, in any case, unattainable ideals are the guiding stars of life. They convert movement into progress. If we acknowledge them we fix our goal, and enable us to strain towards it with undistracted and unwasted effort.'[68] It seems not unreasonable to suggest that his writings on fulfilment theology had a similar purpose in mind, to inspire the members of the Cambridge Mission to Delhi towards an ideal, of which they would have to work out the day to day details and practicalities. Indeed, it is now to the Cambridge Mission to Delhi that we turn our attention.

---

64   Though elsewhere he does give more space to discussing the relationship of Greek philosophy to Christianity (especially Westcott, 1891).

65   Maw, 1990, p. 162.

66   Edwards, p. 229.

67   Ibid., p. 228.

68   Westcott, 1901, p. 308.

i) The Aims of the Mission

As mentioned in the previous section, the Cambridge Mission to Delhi was established very much with the premise that it would put fulfilment theology into practice. Maw refers to it as Westcott's 'ideals embodied in an organization.'[69] Its importance lies in three factors. First, the number of illustrious theological names associated with it at Cambridge – Westcott, Lightfoot, and Hort, to name Cambridge's great triumvirate[70] – while other notable theologians such as Professors Stanton and Swete were also associated with the mission.[71] Westcott expounds his own belief in fulfilment theology in several places, and while the others do not, it must be assumed that in their various positions as chairmen and presidents of the mission over the years that they were at least in sympathy with this essential tenet of its work. It has already been noted that with Williams, Maurice and Trench all expounding upon this idea in the 1840s, it must have had some circulation in Cambridge at that date, from this, and also considering Westcott's example and the evidence of the mission and its supporters, then we are led to deduce that it certainly seems to have been the generally accepted belief in Cambridge in the later part of the nineteenth-century. Perhaps even so common that it deserved no special attention or comment! Related to this is the fact that the mission's leading members themselves rose to prominence in the church, showing that evidently their fulfilment theology was not considered incompatible with mainstream Anglican thought. Bickersteth, the mission's first leader, became Bishop of Japan,[72] while Lefroy, a later head of the mission, became Bishop of Lahore, and later Bishop of Calcutta and

---

69   Maw, 1990, p. 130.

70   The 1892 *Cambridge Mission to Delhi Annual Report* mentions the close association of all these three with the mission, p. 3 (USPGCMD #131).

71   Stanton took over as chairman on Hort's death (1892 *Cambridge Mission to Delhi Annual Report*, p. 4 (USPGCMD #131)), while Swete was on the executive committee (1893 *Cambridge Mission to Delhi Annual Report*, p. 19 (USPGCMD #131)).

72   Henderson, p. 5.

Metropolitan of all India.[73] Second, and to be dealt with briefly below, were the problems encountered in practising fulfilment theology and the practical attempts made. Third, is the fulfilment theology taught by members of the mission, principally Lefroy.

The first point has already been considered above, noting the support of Cambridge's leading men, and the esteem in which the mission members were held. Therefore, the second of the points above will be considered. The main question to be asked is how far fulfilment theology was employed as a practical scheme, which is to say, what attempts were made at creating an indigenous Indian Christian theology and how far the mission's work used native models, or whether, in fact, Western models were still employed. The question needs only a brief mention, as a side issue to the main intent of the study, looking more, as it does, at problems of missiology, and education, rather than contributing to the development of the theory of fulfilment theology. However, it is important to consider the practical implications as bearing upon the ways in which it may have influenced thinking on fulfilment theology, as well as demonstrating in concrete form quite what various thinkers envisaged as its aim.

The first question that should be asked is what was the practical purpose of this 'New Alexandria', in its attempt to give Christianity an Indian clothing. This might not be what we would expect, for, writing in the 1893 *Cambridge Mission to Delhi Annual Report*, a Mr. Cunningham, laments the poor standard of students on entry, goes on to observe of the MA students: 'But work with them is a real pleasure; four years at college seems to make something after the type of the English gentleman. The contrast with the rough material of the early years is encouraging.'[74] With regard to this, it should be observed that Lefroy's assessment of the moral character of the Indian, to be discussed below, was none too high, sentiments which were common at the time.[75] The point should be taken that even the Cambridge

---

73   The following testimony on Bishop Lefroy shows the high esteem in which he was held, 'He was certainly one of the greatest missionaries our Church ever had in India. So highly respected was he by the Mohammedans, that he was sometimes invited to discuss the truths of our religion in the precincts of their mosques' (Chatterton, p. 339).

74   B. F. Cunningham, Letter on 'Work in College' in the 1893 *Cambridge Mission to Delhi Annual Report* (USPGCMD # 131).

75   See later chapters.

Mission to Delhi, which, being run purely by liberal scholars from Cambridge, was, nevertheless seeing its aim as moulding the Indian character into the Western type. Thus, we must not be led into reading a more modern liberalism into the words they use, for while they may talk of creating a purely indigenous Indian Christian theology, there is still a heavily Western biased agenda dictating what is, and what is not, correct. There are two factors which might be taken into account to suggest that the mission members were aware of the Western bias of their approach, but felt forced into it out of necessity.

First, there was a shortage of funds,[76] which meant that the mission had to rely upon books that could be got cheaply, rather than ones which were considered more suitable, so that even by 1909 Indian boys were still being given copies of *Tom Brown's Schooldays*, in what was considered, 'an exercise in irrelevance.'[77] Secondly, Western models were no doubt just adopted as the only practical option, as the newly arrived graduates from England could hardly be expected to develop an Eastern form of education overnight, opting instead for the familiar form of the English public school.[78] In this regard it should be remembered that most saw the project as being essentially something to be pursued in the long term. Lightfoot had expressed what he thought to be the governing principle in the following words, 'I have one word of advice only – it sums up everything – patience, inexhaustible patience.'[79] Another problem for the Cambridge Mission to Delhi was the fact that they clashed continually with the Rev. Winter whose work they were meant to be supporting in Delhi.[80] The problems, according to Maw, reduced

---

76   Maw, 1990, pp. 197–8.
77   Ibid., p. 197.
78   Ibid., pp. 196–7.
79   Lightfoot, letter to Westcott, 22/4/1887 (USPGCMD # 92). See also Jex Blake in the 1888 Annual Report, p. 20, quoted from the *Mission Field*, December 1888 (USPGCMD # 131), and Maw, 1990, pp. 199–200.
80   Bickersteth wrote to Westcott saying that he could not 'consent to undertake evangelistic work under obedience to him' (Bickersteth, letter to Westcott, 11/8/1879 (USPGCMD # 92). Unfortunately Winter never appears to have had time to publish any writings, for the problem seems to have been that he was too liberal for the young Cambridge men! He appears to have held that non-Christian religious teachers should not be considered as a negative influence, and to have believed that converts in the younger churches should still be allowed to attend the festivals of their old religion (see ibid, and LPLBenson, LXV, Bickersteth, 'Memorandum on the Organization of the Missions at Delhi', 3/10/1888, ff. 18–19). It is hard to assess his views accurately, as they must be pieced together mainly from the letters

'the new Alexandrian ethos to little more than a paper apologetic for the Church.'[81] Later on he says:

> Fulfilment theology was impracticable in the circumstances. Indeed[...] one might have expected Bickersteth to have renounced the doctrine altogether[....]
> [....] Yet the Cambridge brotherhood remained steadfast in its admiration for both the doctrine and for Westcott, when one might have expected them to lapse into disillusionment or a scholarly *hauteur*.[82]

The point that Maw fails to appreciate is that, while there may have been difficulties translating fulfilment into an educational environment, at the same time there were many good reasons why fulfilment theology should be adopted, which were seen in the previous chapter, that looks at the missionary situation. The Cambridge Mission to Delhi's fulfilment theology may have all been based upon theory amongst the cloisters of that city's colleges, but nevertheless it had a practical role to play on the ground in India. They were not the only ones with this vision. Previously, Valpy French had invoked the imagery of Alexandria of his college in Agra,[83] and also hoped that one day there may be an indigenous Indian priesthood to translate Christianity into

---

and other writings of Bickersteth, who seems to have taken very much against Winter from early on (Maw, 1990, p. 181), and whose main complaint seems to have been that Winter was too lax with his converts (see further Bickersteth , letter to Westcott, 31/10/1879, and Bickersteth , letter to Carlyon, 18/7/1884. The dispute seems to have been very much personal, neither giving the other the respect they felt was due (Maw, 1990, pp. 183 f.), and so no hasty judgement should be drawn from what Bickersteth said. Besides, if Winter was lax, it should be noted that Winter was overwhelmed by the mass of evangelistic work in Delhi (ibid., p. 181), and so if he let his converts have more freedom than many it may have been due to the fact that he lacked the time and energy to enforce any discipline. However, this is but supposition, and the exact facts appear clouded in the personal animosity of Winter and Bickersteth.

81   Ibid., p. 180.
82   Ibid., pp. 189 and 213.
83   Though his use of the parallel had been more modest, rather than saying that he was founding a new Alexandria, he had more modestly said, 'it might never rival the ancient Christian schools of Alexandria, Edessa, Nisblis, in its *Platonic reasoning, profound and original thinking*, and masterly methods of grappling with Oriental subtleties, still it might become an instrument of extended usefulness, and contribute materially under God to the regeneration of this great people' (French, quoted in Birks, I, p. 44, italics my own).

Eastern terms.[84] This is, surely, the chief saving grace of the Delhi Mission, that whatever the faults of their methodology, and their pleasure of creating an approximation of the English gentleman, they did at least see their role as preparational; it was not their task to translate Christianity into Eastern terms, but to create an atmosphere in which Indians would feel free to form their own Christianity, free from the unnecessary dogmas of Western Christendom.

A good indication of their thought can, perhaps, be gained in more solid form by looking at the architecture of the mission, particularly the new church, Holy Trinity, built in 1907, and designed by one of the mission members, Coore. Whereas the majority of Church buildings in India were built in the Gothic style,[85] the Cambridge Mission to Delhi felt that it should attempt a more indigenous architectural style, in keeping with its principles.[86] Being in Delhi, the mission could not help but feel the Islamic cultural influence,[87] and it was felt that, 'Saracenic architecture is generally considered pre-eminently the Indian style.'[88] The style felt to be most in keeping with this was Byzantine, which, 'while different from any Indian style, it harmonizes generally with what is found in India, being the most oriental of the styles which are associated with church building.'[89] While making a concession to the fact that they were no longer in England, the style was not indigenous, and is hardly alien to Britain.[90] The contrast between this and the policy found

---

84   Ibid., pp. 159 and 232.
85   St. Paul's Cathedral, Calcutta, for example, which Bishop Wilson wanted built 'in the Gothic or rather Christian style of architecture' (quoted in B. F. L. Clarke, p. 10).
86   Coore, pp. 3 ff.
87   In writing the history of the Cambridge Mission to Delhi, Henderson calls Delhi, 'the central shrine in India to the faith of Islam' (Henderson, p. 9).
88   Ibid., p. 6.
89   Ibid., p. 10.
90   Indeed, it may be remarked that Coore's choice may have had more to do with architectural vogues in England, rather than with the desire to blend in with the East, where Byzantine forms were having something of a revival. Two new churches were built in London shortly after this in the Byzantine manner, St. Barnabus, Hackney, and St Jude-on-the-Hill, Hampstead Garden Suburb, the latter built interestingly enough by Lutyens (Leonard, pp. 182–3), who, of course, was to build the magnificent new imperial capital in Delhi. While on a grander scale Bentley's designs for Westminster Cathedral were also in the Byzantine style, (Howell and Sutton, p. 88) and in the architecturtal competition for the new Liverpool Cathedral a Byzantine design had been submitted. The Byzantine style for Liverpool was felt to be unsuitable, Gothic being preferred. The main debate

today should be considered. While the free adoption of the form of the Hindu temple for new Christian chapels is now praised,[91] according to Coore, it could 'no more be adopted for Christian art than can the mythology of Hinduism be accepted for Christian doctrine.'[92] However, we cannot judge them by today's standards, and the innovation which they showed *for their own time* should be appreciated.

---

seems to have been between the architectural profession, who wanted to move away from the Gothic, and the Liverpool Cathedral Committee (who had decreed that 'the style shall be Gothic'), and those outside of the architectural profession (see J. Thomas, 1975), apparently at the time a great deal of controversy attached to this point (see also, Anon., 1902, esp. p. 224). Coore himself referred to the Gothic as the epitome of architectural style (Coore, pp. 16 ff). That Coore then choose Byzantine for a missionary church in India calls to mind the dictates of the Ecclessiological Society, though of many years earlier, that foreign churches should be in, what they regarded as, the baser styles of Romanesque or Early English, rather than the 'perfect' form of Decorated Gothic, as the cruder forms were felt better suited to the tastes and aspirations of the cruder and less civilized nations. A case in point can be seen in reference to New Zealand, where the Romanesque style was recommended '"because, as the work will be chiefly done by native artists, it seems natural to teach them that style which first prevailed in our own country; while its rudeness and massiveness, and the grotesque character of its sculpture, will probably render it easier to be understood and appreciated by them." What was fit for New Zealand, however, was not suitable for the more refined mother country' (White, p. 88, quoting, *Ecclessiologist*, volume I, pp. 4–5). In fact, Coore stated that India's greatest churches should be Gothic in form (Coore, p. 18). Thus, rather than seeing the use of Byzantine as an example of inculturation, its use in this instance is in a sense patronizing, it is used due to the limitations of India, rather than because it is a form that India should aspire to. In fact the mission was even attacked for using these Eastern forms in India (Maw, 1990, p. 226). The later architecture of the mission – the earlier college buildings it may be noted had been in the Moghul style (Maw, 1990, p. 225) – could then be seen as a physical expression of the thought and practice of the Cambridge Mission to Delhi – outwardly trying to be more Indian, and eastern, but done for very Western reasons, that patronizes the East, rather than recognizing what is good in it, and, also, it should be pointed out, not being very Indian at all (an extended version of this argument can be found in my forthcoming article in the *International Review of Mission*).

91   Mackenzie, II, pp. 4–5.
92   Coore, p. 6.

ii) The Fulfilment Theology of the Mission

We turn now to consider fulfilment theology as found amongst the mission members, of whom the two most notable writers are Andrews and Lefroy.[93] Andrews' thought will be considered in a later chapter, leaving Lefroy as the main figure. He was not the only mission member to write on fulfilment theology; others, such as Allnutt, also endorsed the idea.[94] It is interesting that Allnutt quotes Phillips Brooks as his source,[95] as does Lefroy, who quotes two of his sermons as appendices to one of his papers,[96] and also quotes Trench in this regard.[97] The main interest in this is in refutation of Maw's assertion, already noted above, that Westcott was the chief inspiration behind fulfilment theology:[98] that, he notes, Trench indicates that there were many acknowledged sources for these ideas.

Most of Lefroy's work was amongst Muslims,[99] on whom he was considered an expert.[100] It is worth noting that there are certain problems associated with employing fulfilment theology towards Islam, which will be considered in the following chapter.[101] However, as most fulfilment theology is written in relation to Hinduism, we shall concentrate here on what Lefroy

---

93   Maw, 1990, p. 229.
94   See Allnutt, p. 11: 'Christ said He came not to destroy but to fulfil, to complete, to realize.'
95   Ibid., p. 12. Brooks was an American priest, in Boston, well known for his liberal persausion – Dean Stanley was invited to preach in his church on a tour to America (Hammond, p. 212).
96   Lefroy, 1907(a), pp. 23 ff.
97   Ibid., pp. 3 ff.
98   He said the Cambridge Mission to Delhi was largely packed with Westcott's proteges (Maw, 1990, p. 12), and calls him its 'theological mainspring' (ibid., p. 130). Evidently the young missionaries were not infused with Westcott's thought alone, and, as will be seen, Lefroy's thought is not principally Westcottian in form.
99   Lefroy, 1907(a), p. 3. This should not surprise us in view of the Islamic influence at Delhi referred to above, while some considered Islam, after Judaism, to have the greatest claim on Christianity's attentions (Stanton, p. 32). However, the vast majority of the mission's students were Hindus, of whom there were 48, compared to 3 Christians, 4 Muslims, and 1 Parsee (1886 *Cambridge Mission to Delhi Annual Report*, (USPGCMD # 131)).
100   Montgomery, 1920, p. 17.
101   On the Edinburgh Conference.

says of Hinduism, referring to Islam only as it is useful to expand upon certain aspects of Lefroy's thought.

Lefroy believed that Jesus' assertion that he came to fulfil, rather than destroy, applied to all religions, not just Judaism, though Jesus himself only meant it in that way.[102] He sees Christianity not as a 'wholly new truth which attaches itself to and explains and perfects nothing in all the long history of their [i.e. India's] past, but rather as taking up and claiming, interpreting, purifying, perfecting, and fulfilling that past.'[103] In fact, Lefroy notes that all nations have been included in this divine providence, so all will find their fulfilment in Christ.[104] He does make one definite exception to the idea of national characters, noting that Islam tends to create a particular type of person,[105] which he says is one of its great strengths.[106] Also, in language that is reminiscent of Westcott,[107] he speaks of the need for us to recognize both the unity and diversity of man's religious experience, saying, 'only in the recognition of diversity and of the relationship which is thus possible between the various members, can the true unity of the body be attained.'[108]

With reference to what was said above concerning the mission's desire to make Indians in the likeness of English gentlemen, something should be said of Lefroy's opinions about the moral status of non-Christians. This was, according to Lefroy, a great problem:

> [T]here lies as the most serious difficulty of all that we encounter in Mission work an intensely low moral tone, which has permeated and now broods over the whole country, checking really healthy progress in well nigh every direction, and above all blunting the power of conscience and the consciousness of sin to a degree of which you can scarcely conceive.[109]

The main problem, Lefroy believed, was a want of trust in the Indian character.[110] Indeed, he wrote a whole article upon this subject,[111] and often

---

102   Lefroy, 1889 (b), p. cv.
103   Lefroy, 1889 (a), p. 11; see also, Lefroy, 1989 (b), p. cvii.
104   Lefroy, 1907(a), pp. 5–6.
105   Lefroy in Montgomery, 1909, p. 283.
106   Ibid., p. 281.
107   See above.
108   Lefroy, 1989 (a), p. 6.
109   Lefroy, 1887, pp. 3–4; see also, Lefroy, 1903, p. 121.
110   Lefroy, 1887, p. 5.
111   Lefroy, 1903.

referred to it elsewhere.[112] This was a common feeling among many contemporary writers and will be developed further in the next chapter.

Turning to what Lefroy says of Hinduism, he makes the typical comment that the old forms of Hinduism are breaking up.[113] Lefroy notes three particular aspects of Hinduism which he sees 'as anticipations, foreshadowings, feelings after the fulness of truth as it is in Christ Jesus.'[114] First, there is the caste system which he sees as a terrible evil, but which does assert the brotherhood of man.[115] Only in Christ, according to Lefroy, can India keep this ideal and avoid the opposite extreme of rampant

---

112   See, e.g., references above, and Lefroy, 1907(a), pp. 15 ff and18 ff. One interesting case that Lefroy notes may be referred to here, 'An instance which happened some time ago in Delhi will illustrate better than many generalities the kind of tone I refer to. A well-known native judge, addressing his court, begged them not to suppose that he was there to administer justice, or respect truth. 'I have been put here,' he said, 'by the English authorities in this place, and what I intend to do is to keep them content and to give such decisions as may be most agreeable to them.' This incident was told me by a leading member of the bar there, and its accuracy may be entirely relied on' (Lefroy, 1903, p. 124).

     This passage is interesting in two ways. Firstly, it demonstrates the possible misunderstandings between the British and Indians as rulers to subject race, the native judge may well have thought that that was what he was intended to do; besides what faith is a person of a subjugated race meant to have in the justice system that keeps him in that position? Secondly, and stemming from the first, is the related passage in Forster's *A Passage to India* which though based some decades later still brings up the same ideas. In it, the district magistrate, Ronny, has handed over the case, concerning the, alleged, attempted rape of his fiancée, to his Indian assistant, Das:

     '"My old Das is all right," said Ronny, starting a new subject in low tones.

     '"Not one of them's all right," contradicted Major Callendar.

     '"Das is, really."

     '"You mean he's more frightened of acquitting than convicting, because if he acquits he'll lose his job," said Lesley with a clever little laugh.

     'Ronny did mean that, but he cherished "illusions" about his own subordinates (following the finer traditions of his service here), and he liked to maintain that his old Das really did possess moral courage of the public-school brand' (Forster, pp. 218–219). The scene, though almost utterly different materially, is carried off to great effect in the Merchant Ivory film.

113   Lefroy, 1889 (b), p. cvii.

114   Lefroy, 1889 (a), p. 8. Four if sacrifice is included, which he does not discuss on the grounds that it is not particular to Hinduism (ibid.; see also, Lefroy, 1889 (b), pp. cvi f.).

115   Lefroy, 1889 (a), pp. 8–9.

individualism.[116] Then he notes the errors which he feels are typical of transmigration, but which he says do teach, 'that personal immortality for which the soul of man craves.'[117] Thirdly, he considers that the Incarnations of Krishna declare the possibility of intercourse between God and man.[118]

Only one further point of Lefroy's thought need be mentioned, and that is his abhorrence for the Islamic form of prayer, what he calls the 'fearfully mechanical nature of their worship.'[119] In reference to this I merely wish to refer back to Monier-Williams' thoughts on the same subject, that he saw the Mosque and its worship as a place akin to the Christian church and its worship.[120] It provides an excellant example of the subjectivity in what different Western observers see as good and bad in the Orient, with views varying from individual to individual, based as much upon personal taste as anything else. Also, just as these factors change, so does the interpretation of fulfilment theology from individual to individual. As noted above, Lefroy's fulfilment theology has aspects of Westcott's, but it is at the same time his own, and he acknowledges different sources, from England and America. With this point in mind, it is time to look at the consent given to these ideas in Britain at the end of the nineteenth-century, at least within the liberal theological tradition found at Cambridge.

Fulfilment Theology outside of Cambridge

The previous two sections of this chapter have looked at the occurrence of fulfilment theology within the confines of the University of Cambridge, particularly in the liberal Neo-Platonism that dominated its Theology Department in the nineteenth-century. Now it is time to consider how far this thought had spread throughout the rest of the country.

---

116   Ibid., p. 9.
117   Ibid.
118   Ibid., pp. 9–10.
119   Lefroy, 1907(a), p. 17.
120   See above.

Oxford Liberalism: A. P. Stanley

Arthur Penrhyn Stanley, Dean of Westminster Abbey, was an Oxford educated liberal. An intimate friend of Müller,[121] he regarded Maurice's and Rowland Williams' views to be parallel to his own.[122] Stanley never actively expounded a theory of fulfilment theology in an explicit way, yet he does provide references and pointers to the theory; without himself saying any more than that he felt that not all 'heathen' were doomed to hell, and that there was good in their religions.[123] Part of the reason might be that he himself never wrote about the non-Christian religions at any length,[124] and his sermons, when they refer to the subject, are more concerned with missionary practice than the benefits of the non-Christian religions.[125] Nevertheless, there are some revealing passages in Stanley's works.

Stanley suggests that the worship of the non-Christian religions is acceptable to God,[126] and reads the Book of Esther, to imply that it is not necessary to be a Christian to do God's will, and to give testimony to Him in words and actions.[127] The significance he sees in Esther is that of all the books of both Old and New Testaments, it is the only one to omit any mention to the name of God; its reason being, according to Stanley, that even without acknowledging God by name or speaking of Him, a man can be a missionary for God by his actions even if he does not preach,[128] or show that he is already a follower of God even if not a professed believer in Christianity.[129]

The closest he actually comes to propounding a form of fulfilment theology himself is when he says:

---

121   Trompf, p. 214.
122   Parsons, 1988 (b), p. 289.
123   See Stanley, in Müller, 1873 (b), p. 1.
124   With the exception of Judaism (see A. Stanley, 1883)
125   See ibid., and A. Stanley, 1875.
126   See, A. Stanley, 1883, pp. 150 ff.
127   Ibid., pp. 153 ff.
128   It is especially interesting in that he relates the Book of Esther to the Gentile world, as he had previously used the same passage in a sermon to refer to the missionary work of all Englishmen, who should, he said, show God in their actions when abroad, so that, even if engaged in secular work, they would still be testifying for Christianity (A. Stanley, 1875).
129   See both A. Stanley, 1875, pp. 6 ff., and A. Stanley, 1883, pp. 153 ff.

Still, it is difficult for those who believe in the permanent elements of the Jewish and Christian religions to be universal and Divine not to hail these corresponding forms of truth or goodness elsewhere, or to recognize that the mere appearance of such saintlike or godlike characters in other parts of the earth, *if not directly preparing the way for a greater manifestation*, illustrates that manifestation by showing how mighty has been the witness borne to its value even under the most adverse discouragement and with strangely inadequate effects.[130]

Whether the idea that the 'forms of truth and goodness' were a preparation was Stanley's own belief, as might be indicated by this passage, is unclear. The reference can, however, be taken to suggest that he expected his audience to be familiar with the idea, and it is partly by what he fails to say that he endorses the idea. When, for instance, he asked Müller to speak in the Abbey,[131] whilst he did not expand upon fulfilment theology himself, he must have known Müller's views upon the subject. Müller said of him, that he would let the Buddha into the Abbey if he knew what he taught.[132] Evidently, Stanley knew of the idea, and was not adverse to it. His relations with Müller show that, however, he did not perhaps feel it essential to hold to this view. This is to do with conceptions of world-view. The importance of Logos theology has already been dwelt upon at length. Concomitent with this is a sense of the underlying unity or wholeness of creation, as seen in Westcott. Stanley is not a part of this very Platonic Cambridge tradition, and so it is not so important for him; it is not part of the general theological background which informed his thinking. Even if not endorsing fulfilment theology, Stanley shows an awareness of it, and does not have any objections to the idea. It should also be noted that Stanley was writing in the 1870s, and 1880s, when, it has been suggested, fulfilment theology was just coming to popular attention, at least in missionary circles. A decade later, and things may have been different.

130   A. Stanley, 1883, p. 169 (italics my own).
131   Müller, 1873 (b).
132   Hammond, p. 204 – no reference given.

214

Another important party at Oxford was the High Church movement, examples of whom have already been seen in Morris and Banerjea.[133] In relation to Morris, the differences between the Oxford Aristotelian and Cambridge Platonic traditions were discussed.[134] We have seen, however, in relation to Banerjea, that not all thought in the Tractarian tradition was limited to such a model, which according to Maw was very narrow: '[The] Oxford Movement had no recourse to the Greek patristic writings at all, but looked to Latin sources for its energies and justification. Sin and redemption were its prime concern.'[135]

With regard to the Oxford Mission to Calcutta, Maw observes that despite Gore's role in helping to found it, it was nevertheless a place where more traditional Tractarian ideas lingered,[136] and where Müller was regarded with suspicion.[137] Certainly, its journal, the *Epiphany* was felt to be too sectarian.[138] As late as 1902, an article on the Bhagavad Gītā appeared therein whose attitude was wholly hostile, attacking the work continually, rather than seeing any good in it.[139] Goreh's example, however, demonstrates that even this mission was not wholly adverse to fulfilment theology, and at a time

---

133   See above, chapters 2 and 4 respectively.

134   See chapter 2, especially on Maurice.

135   Maw, 1990, p. 258. With regard to this we should note that Maw's statement is perhaps inaccurate. The famous series of works in the 'Library of the Fathers' series which were largely the vision of Pusey and Newman, contained the Fathers of both East and West (Liddon, p. 281). What, I suspect, Maw is driving at in this statement is the idea that there is generally seen to be a difference between a Western, Latin, tradition which focuses upon the sinfulness of creation, of which Tertullian is seen as representative, and an Eastern, Greek, tradition which sees the good in creation as central, where the Logos is stressed. Maw would appear to think that most Tractarians fall into the former camp. It is not the writer's present intention to suggest how far such a view is valid, however the reader may wish to refer back to the second chapter where the difference between Pusey and Maurice on the same theme may be seen as representative of this dichotomy. In any case if any validity should be given to Maw's view it should also be remembered that it would mainly apply to the early Tractarians, the successors of the tradition such as Gore and the Lux Mundi group, were heavily influenced by the 'Greek' tradition.

136   Ibid., p. 261.

137   Ibid., p. 263.

138   Fulfil, p. 90.

139   'The Gita and the Gospel', *Epiphany*, 14/6/1902, in Lacey, pp. 219–226.

when such an idea was still not widely disseminated. That what we may call 'traditional Tractarianism' was not wholly opposed to such ideas, will now be suggested, with reference to the most famous of all the men of the Oxford Movement, John Henry Newman.[140]

Newman's thought was undeniably cast in the same mould as that of Westcott and the Cambridge school in terms of his appreciation of the Alexandrine/ Logos theology that was so popular with the latter. Referring to the Alexandrine tradition, Newman speaks with admiration of 'Origen, Dionysius, and others who were the glory of its see, or of its school.' He continued: 'The broad philosophy of Clement and Origen carried me away[....]'[141] Worth noting in this is that Edwards suggests that in these words Newman 'might have been summing up Westcott's own theology.'[142] Such was the thought of Newman evidently at odds with his fellow convert to Rome, Morris.[143] Turning now to his attitude towards the non-Christian religions, and speaking of the similarities of the Christian and Buddhist ethical systems, Newman wrote: 'There is little in the ethics of Christianity, which the human mind may not reach by its natural powers, and which, here and there, in the instance of individuals, great poets, and great philosophers, has not in fact been anticipated.'[144] In this Newman places himself alongside those who are ready to admit that there is a truth to be found in natural religion,[145] the Logos was continually working throughout history and was intimately involved in it, to such a degree that: 'The religious mind conceives of the natural, not as opposed to the supernatural, but as an outlying province

---

140   This section explores Newman's use and development of fulfilment theology. A recent volume, *John Henry Newman: Universal Revelation*, by Francis McGrath explores a number of themes especially Newman's idea of revelation and the background to his thinking in terms of revelation and his attitude towards the non-Christian religions in greater detail than is possible here.

141   Newman, 1972, p. 115. See Rowell, p. 50.

142   Edwards, p. 223.

143   See above.

144   Newman, letter to W. S. Lilly, 12/6/1882, in Dessain and Gornall (hereafter Dessain), XXX, p. 96.

145   Though it may be noted that Newman had his doubts about the historicity of accounts of the Buddha's life, and felt they may well have been influenced by Christianity (ibid., pp. 96 ff), and he felt there were grave doubts about how trustworthy the transmission of many of the non-Christian religions were, in terms of how far they were true to the original teachings of their founders (Newman, letter to W. S. Lilly, 17/8/1884, in ibid., pp. 391 f).

216

of it; of the economy of the physical world as the compliment of the economy of Grace.'[146]

With the above points in mind, it is now possible to turn to Newman's opinions of Müller and his thought. Newman had met Müller,[147] and from their letters it is possible to see that the two men evidently had a great deal of respect for one another.[148] Müller had sent Newman a copy of his *Introduction to the Science of Religion*,[149] some of the central themes of which have already been examined above. Speaking about this work, Newman says of Müller's speculations[150] that he sees no reason why: 'They will not be found to bear witness to the dogmas of Revelation.'[151] He thus affirms an accord with the tenor of Müller's thought, that there is no religion 'which is entirely false'[152] and that the ancient religions of the world demonstrate 'the *Divine education of the human race*,'[153] to which Christianity has come 'in the fulness of time, and as the fulfilment of the hopes and desires of the whole world.'[154] These ideas were, for Newman (as for Müller) given credence by the Christian philosophers of Alexandria, who stated that:

> I understood them to mean that the exterior world, physical and historical, was but the outward manifestation of realities greater than itself. Nature was a parable: Scripture was an allegory: pagan literature, philosophy, and mythology, properly understood, were but a preparation for the Gospel. The Greek poets and sages were in a certain sense prophets[....] There had been a divine dispensation granted to the Jews; there had been in some sense a dispensation carried on in favour of the Gentiles.[155]

---

146   Lilly, p. 118 – while the words are not his, Newman stated that he gave his 'entire assent' to what Lilly had written here (Newman, letter to W. S. Lilly, 7/12/1882, in Dessain, XXX, p. 159.

147   Dessain, XXVI, p. 291.

148   Ibid., pp. 354–5.

149   Newman, letter to Max Müller, 24/8/1873, in ibid., p. 354.

150   For he notes that they have not yet been fully proved (Newman, letter to Max Müller, 24/8/1873, in Dessain, XXVI, p. 355.)

151   Ibid.

152   Müller, 1873, p. 261.

153   Ibid., , p. 226.

154   Ibid., p. 222.

155   Newman, 1972, p. 115.

That Newman uses the terms 'pagan', and 'Gentile', as distinct from 'Greek', should be read in the light of his approval for Müller's work, to mean more than that only Greek philosophy was a preparation for the Gospel. Newman evidently held the great teachers of the non-Christian religions in high regard. He spoke, for instance of 'the singular greatness of Buddha.'[156] It does not seem unreasonable, then, to suggest that Newman did regard the teachings of the Buddha and of Hinduism to be preparations for the Gospel. Certainly, in his correspondence with Müller, there is nothing to suggest that he rejected this further extension of the thought of the Alexandrian philosophers by whom he set such store. Müller's use of Newman as an authority for his own views has been mentioned previously.

Newman's thought represents, then, almost the antithesis of the type of thought which characterized much of the Tractarian movement,[157] meaning that a more positive attitude to the non-Christian religions could be adopted than that which characterized Morris.[158] Reference should be made back to Goreh's thought, who, as a member of the Oxford Mission to Calcutta, was able to propagate a form of fulfilment theology. This, taken in conjunction with Newman's example, shows that this theory was certainly known, and even accepted, within parts, at least, of the Oxford Movement.

The examples discussed above can be seen to be carried further by later developments in this tradition. Indeed, if we may quote Webb's views on the thought that was felt by him to dominate much High Church thinking at Oxford:

> It was an essential feature of the Oxford Movement that it made the Incarnation rather than the Atonement the central dogma of Christianity. This is a feature in which the later stages of the Anglo-Catholic movement have remained true to type[....]
> This[...] view[...] as it refused to isolate the Atonement from the general process of the Incarnation, so it refused to isolate the Incarnation itself from the general moral education of the human race.[159]

---

156   Newman, letter to W. S. Lilly, 12/6/1882, in Dessain, XXX, p. 98.
157   Particularly note may be made of the differences observed between Pusey and Maurice (see above).
158   See above.
159   Webb, pp. 59 and 60.

The hostility to the non-Christian religions, which can be taken as characteristic of much high Church thought at Oxford, was not a universal truth, as seen above in Newman's case. In the latter part of the nineteenth-century, the so-called Holy Party at Oxford developed the High Church tradition to produce a theology similar to Westcott's.[160] In particular, we shall look at Gore, who was influenced by Westcott as a young man.[161] Gore may be taken as representative of later High Church thought at Oxford where, particularly from the 1860s, more 'liberal' thinking achieved greater acceptance in such circles.[162]

Gore's theology was based upon the Logos,[163] and his attitudes towards the non-Christian religions show many similarities to previous writer. The basics of his fulfilment theology can be seen in a sermon preached for the Oxford Mission in 1887:

> Christianity does not depreciate the elements of good in other religions. It does not depreciate the good in Judaism, but supersedes it; and in like manner it supersedes other religions. Granted that Mohammedanism preaches a living God, granted that Buddhism preaches a holy God; but Christianity preaches a God who is both holy and living, and declares that without holiness no man shall see the Lord. It supersedes other religions by including in it a vaster and more complete whole the broken elements of truth which they possess.[164]

This is a very clear statement of the evolutionary idea of fulfilment theology, where 'lower' religions, are replaced by 'higher' religions. For him the 'truths' found in the non-Christian religions were guaranteed by the Logos:

---

160   Maw, 1990, p. 257.
161   Prestige, pp. 9–10. In particular Carpenter suggests he probably greatly influenced him regarding, 'the spiritual glories of simple living' and in 'love of the poor' (Carpenter, p. 26). It may also be mentioned here that Gore was a great influence upon William Temple (ibid., p. 9), who was mentioned in relation to Maurice, as a follower of the tradition of Logos theology, as well being involved in the Christian Socialist movement, as was Gore (Prestige, pp. 91 ff). In fact on Westcott's death, Gore took over the leadership of the Christian Socialist Union (ibid., p. 241).
162   See Hylson-Smith, pp. 172–3.
163   Maw, 1990, p. 256.
164   Quoted in Prestige, p. 65.

The same divine 'wisdom' or 'word' that was incarnate in Christ had 'everywhere been finding some utterance or echo.' The divine word heard in the Bible was also heard – 'only in different tones and with less certain direction' – in the Iranian seer Zarathustra, and in the poets and moralists of Greece, Rome and the Far East.[165]

While in the above quotation Carpenter uses a late work of Gore's, *Christ and Society*, published in 1928, these ideas are found in his earlier works, being, he believed, in accord with the early Greek fathers: 'But the idea of Christianity as superseding all other religions, not by excluding but by including the elements of truth which each contains, would be an idea thoroughly in accordance with the deeper thoughts of Greek Christian teachers in the first age.'[166]

In the two previous quotations Gore can be seen to be a representative of fulfilment theology throughout its heyday, from the late nineteenth-century through to the 1920s and even beyond.[167]

Another aspect of Gore's theology is his belief in the role of each nation to expand Christianity's understanding of itself:

Each new race which is introduced into the Church not only itself receives the blessings of our religion, but reacts upon it to bring out new and unsuspected aspects and beauties of its truth and influence. It has been so when Greeks, and Latins, and Teutons, and Kelts, and Slavs have each in turn been brought into the growing circle of believers[....] And can we doubt that now again not only would Indians, and Japanese, and Africans, and Chinamen be the better for Christianity, but that Christianity would be unspeakably also the richer for their adhesion – for the gifts which the subtlety of India, and the grace of Japan, and the silent patience of China are capable of bringing into the city of God.[168]

---

165   Carpenter, p. 47, quoting Gore, 1928, p. 24.
166   Gore, 1891, p. 43.
167   Gore's Gifford Lectures of 1929–30, talk about the non-Christian religions at length (Gore, 1930). It must be felt to be a great loss to Christian theology that Gore felt it necessary to decline the offer of the Bishopric of Bombay, and to stay in Birmingham (Prestige, pp. 308–11), for while he wrote upon the relation of Christianity to the non-Christian religions to a limited degree as an English bishop, he would, no doubt, have written much more as an Indian bishop, and as a theologian of his stature would have contributed a great deal to both Iinterfaith Dialogue and the development of Indian Christian theology. Though he may not have been in tune with all the developments of Indian Christianity, for on his final visit to India he said: 'Meanwhile, in spite of Nationalism, Christianity is making constant progress, but very often a queer kind of Christianity' (ibid., p. 525).
168   Gore, 1902, pp. 138–9.

This idea echoes Westcott's own thought, but we cannot, therefore, say that Gore's fulfilment theology was copied from this source, for, as has been seen, this notion is a commonplace of nineteenth-century thought, though Maw suggests that Gore took his fulfilment theology from him.[169] Maw's suggestion that Westcott was the founder and propagator of fulfilment theology in England has already been subjected to a thorough critique.[170] There are other ways in which Gore is similar to Westcott, for just as Westcott had been involved in the foundation of the Cambridge Mission to Delhi, so Gore was deeply involved in the setting up of the Oxford Mission to Calcutta. The idea of mission was of central importance to Gore, who held that: 'A Christian who is not really in heart and will a missionary is not a Christian at all.'[171] In fact, Gore's association with the Oxford mission was far stronger than that of Westcott's with the Cambridge mission, in so far as Gore actually went to India to work in the mission for a while.[172] Thus, as far as Gore is concerned, one of the major charges that Maw lays at the feet of both Müller and Westcott, that they never visited India,[173] is not applicable, yet he, too, adopted fulfilment theology and cannot be accused of merely having some idealized Western vision of India without ever having been there. One further point of Gore's thought should be mentioned, which is that as a result of his time in India he felt that to win over the people of India to Christianity, a monastic form of living would be needed.[174] Much has already been said on this subject above, and so need not be expanded upon here.

Gore was not alone in his Logos-based Incarnational theology, which became widespread in Oxford at the end of the nineteenth-century.[175] That fulfilment theology was also spreading can be observed from a couple of examples. Firstly, Jowett, though not writing about the non-Christian religions in this instance, saw Plato as someone who prefigured Jesus and his teachings.[176] More notably, 'J. Macmillan Brown, an undergraduate in the

---

169   See Maw, 1990, pp. 255 ff.
170   See above.
171   Gore, 1902, p. 138.
172   Prestige, p. 56. In fact Gore visited India several times, apart from his first visit in 1893, he went out briefly in 1899, and again in 1929 (ibid., pp. 56, 111, and 523).
173   See relevant chapters.
174   Prestige, p. 524.
175   Newsome, 1974, p. 83, also, see Maw, 1990, p. 255.
176   Maw, 1990, p. 257.

1870s[...] could remember every one of his contemporaries poring over the latest studies in comparative religion, trying to make sense of the myths and rites of far-flung civilizations that apparently prefigured the Gospel.'[177] Evidently Müller's works were generally read and accepted in this regard; with this in mind, we may refer back to Stanley and Church, both of whom owed a great deal to Müller. They do not specifically say that the non-Christian religions are prophecies of the Gospel, though in giving approval to his work, and therefore that of the Science of Comparative Religion, they were at least tacitly endorsing this point of view, with which this discipline was associated.

Mainstream Anglicanism: E. W. Benson

Finally, it will be useful to give a brief mention of the contribution of Edward White Benson, Archbishop of Canterbury from 1883, to this debate. To place him in context it should be noted that not only was he at school with Westcott,[178] though several years his junior, but later was also at Trinity with him,[179] becoming, in 1849, a private pupil of his.[180] This should assure us of the character of Benson's theological inclinations. While not writing any treatise on the subject of the non-Christian religions, Benson's speeches as President of the Society for the Propagation of the Gospel – a post held by virtue of being the Archbishop of Canterbury – give us a notable insight into the contemporary approach of the mainstream of Anglican missionary thought. I wish here particularly to focus on Benson's Presidential Address of 1892, and the response to it.

Reading the speech, there is nothing that should cause any surprises. He speaks first of the mistakes of the past,[181] some of which he says are still continuing, but it is now generally recognized that there are faults,[182] and his particular concern is with education. He repeats the oft-stated maxim, that it is better not to destroy the religious tone of a nation, or people, and leave

---

177 Maw, 1990, p. 256, see J. M. Brown, pp. 36 ff.
178 A. C. Benson, I, p. 26.
179 Ibid., p. 76.
180 Ibid., p. 82.
181 E. W. Benson, p. 281.
182 Ibid., ff.

them as believers in their own faith rather than introduce irreligion.[183] The non-Christian religions, he says, 'do embody the best thoughts, the best feelings, the best aspirations of men through many ages.'[184] Benson acknowledges that there is much good in the non-Christian religions, and sees them as divinely inspired and ordained:

> When we find Mahomedanism so hard to break, so irresistible, so impregnable a citadel, so impenetrable a rock, it is not because it is a religion which ministers to pride, to lust, and cruelty. I deprecate very much our setting to work – I do not believe we shall ever succeed if we set to work – believing that the religion of any nation which God has allowed to grow up in it, and to be its teacher up to this point, until Christianity is ready to approach it – I do not believe we should succeed if we held that the religion itself ministered to pride, to lust, and cruelty.[185]

Benson, elsewhere, acknowledges Bishop Thomas Valpy French as an inspiration for his seeing, 'the Philosophies of the East and of Greece... as a Preparation for the Gospel.'[186] Returning to his 1892 speech, Benson was fully prepared to acknowledge what was good in the non-Christian religions. Speaking specifically of Islam, he stated that, 'God has brought them a long way on the road to Him.'[187] Benson moves on to make an interesting point, that he believes that, finally, the peoples who are now Muslims will only be converted by oriental Christians,[188] and he ends by saying that all that can be known of the religion and customs of the non-Christian peoples should be studied before any attempt is made to convert them.[189] These last two points reflect a couple of important aspects of Benson's thought:

> He urged the careful study of comparative religion: he was anxious to see the rise of native Churches, not merely as branches of the Church of England working in foreign

---

183   E. W. Benson, p. 283.
184   Ibid.
185   Ibid., pp. 283–4.
186   E. W. Benson, *Speech*, 17/6/1884, delivered at the Annual Meeting of the Society for the Propogation of the Gospel, quoted in A. C. Benson, II, p. 455. He acknowledges his source as T. V. French's *Manual of Moral Philosophy*.
187   E. W. Benson, p. 284.
188   Ibid., p. 285. He believed, like many other,s that there would be a new and distinctive type of Christianity for the East (see also, A. C. Benson, II, p. 447).
189   E. W. Benson, p. 286.

lands, accommodating themselves as far as was consistent with Christian principles to the native habits of thought and devotion.[190]

There is nothing surprising in Benson's speech in the light of what has already been said, and there is no evidence of any concern at what he expressed at the conference. Perhaps the only noteworthy point is that he suggests that it will be the role of the oriental Christians to convert Islam. There appears, however, to have been a reaction from other quarters. Reports of the speech seem to have dwelt on how highly praised Islam was by Benson, so that one correspondent, a certain Edwin Bennett, wrote to him saying: 'The enclosed was given to me by an Agnostic,[191] as a proof that your Grace was in agreement with him in saying that Christianity was only as true as other religions, and equally false[....]'[192]

This correspondent went on to say that while there is much good in Islam,[193] yet it also contains certain erroneous views, that is that it does not, he says, 'teach first and foremost thankfulness to God for salvation through Christ,' and must therefore be called wicked.[194] It is hard to gather from this one letter how far Benson and Bennett really disagree. The dispute may

---

190   A. C. Benson, II, p. 456.

191   'The enclosed' being a report in *The Times* newspaper, of June 16th 1892, entitled 'The Archbishop of Canterbury on Mahommedanism', the contents of which I shall quote below, 'The Archbishop contended that the religions with which Christian missionaries had to encounter were not trivial. They were great, embodying the best aspirations and thought of many men. It was not true that they were wicked. Wickedness might be associated with them, but the same charge might be brought against Christianity. We undervalued the importance to mankind of Mahommedanism, for example. Noble characters were formed under its influence, men of piety, justice, and truth. It was not ministering to pride and luxury that made Mahommedanism so irresistible a faith, so impenetrable a citadel, so impregnable a rock. Then it was startling to find out that on the East coast of Africa the Hindoos were building temples in all directions and that their religion had a stronger hold on them in European spheres of influence than in their own country. Therefore let not Christians believe that any great religion which God had permitted to grow up ministered in itself to pride and lust and cruelty. It would be just as reasonable to attribute to Christianity the sins of London; and the mission which proceeded on such a belief would not succeed' (LPLBenson, 111, ff 18).

192   E. Bennett, letter to E. W. Benson, 7/1892, LPLBenson, 111, ff 13.

193   The reason being, he suggests, is that it is largely based upon the Bible.

194   E. Bennett, letter to E. W. Benson, 7/1892, LPLBenson, 111, ff 14f.

merely be over whether the word 'wicked' is justified or not.[195] Certainly Bennett does not deny that Islam could form a noble character, and does not suggest that it is of the devil.[196] The Agnostic mentioned was totally misguided in his interpretation of the speech, but he was not alone in this interpretation. Lefroy remarked how a Muslim he knew believed that the Archbishop of Canterbury had accepted 'Mahomed as the Seal of the Prophets' and he says that this idea was not particular to this person.[197] Further, there appears to have been a backlash in the form of a pamphlet published in the Punjab, vehemently attacking Mahommed.[198] Lefroy suggests that a balance is needed, and that we should not just offer praise for what is good, but also point out the errors in the non-Christian religions as well.[199] Indeed, in Benson's Presidential address of the following year, he did point out some flaws, as he saw them, in Islam.[200] Nevertheless, in Benson's speech of 1892, further evidence can be seen, if it is needed, of how widely fulfilment theology was accepted, that it can be freely referred to by the Archbishop of Canterbury to the representatives of the Anglican Church's main missionary body without apparent concern expressed. Notwithstanding the pamphlet published in the Punjab, the main reactions seem to be misunderstandings on the part of certain non-Christians, and an apparent quibble over language rather than content. Thus it seems that by the end of the nineteenth-century fulfilment theology was firmly established in Anglican thought in Britain, not just in academic or overtly liberal circles, but also within the very centre of its missionary effort.

---

195   Attention may be drawn to the differences of Maurice and Rowland Williams, on the one hand hand, and Müller, on the other in this matter. See above.

196   Following this in the collection of Benson's letters are two more suggesting that he was wrong in what he said, but they offer no clear views on the author's opinions (see LPLBenson, 111, ff 19 f).

197   Lefroy, 1907(a), p. 13, fn 1.

198   Montgomery, 1920, pp. 92 f.

199   Lefroy, 1907(a), p. 13, fn 1.

200   See A. C. Benson, II, pp. 456–7.

Conclusion to Part III

Throughout the last two chapters the prevalence of the paradigm of fulfilment theology in British thought, both at home and in the missionary field in India, has been stressed. The argument has been advanced that, far from being a little known idea employed by a few isolated figures, fulfilment theology actually enjoyed a considerable following and, contrary to previous suggestions, was widely accepted, particularly by missionaries. Also, as can be seen, the theory of fulfilment theology had received a full and careful study by a number of writers, and very little objection was made to these ideas.

Within the ecclesiastical world, fulfilment theology received its most significant support from the ranks of theologians at Cambridge, but also outside of this school of thought there was more widespread use. The High Church party at Oxford also held many people who held to its principles, and outside the fold of Anglicanism, the many missionaries who were Non-Conformists were also happy to accept the idea. By the 1890s it is probably fair to say that fulfilment theology was the most widely accepted paradigm for approaching the non-Christian religions within British theological thought, and it is from this context that we turn to the next part of this study where the historical survey is concluded.

Part IV: Fruition

Introduction to Part IV

Having seen in Part III the widespread knowledge and dissemination of the ideas of fulfilment theology within British thought, the next two chapters deal with the culmination of this process. Firstly, in chapter 6, the Edinburgh Missionary Conference of 1910 is discussed. Its work and contribution to fulfilment theology as a whole is discussed, along with its reputation as a significant landmark in the history of developing attitudes towards the non-Christian religions.

Chapter 7 marks the end of the historical survey, with a look at fulfilment theology's most famous exponent, John Nicol Farquhar (1861-1929). Having laid the background of fulfilment theology that existed before his time, the question of how far his generally recognized position as a founding figure in fulfilment theology is subjected to severe scrutiny. The main part of the chapter is devoted to analysis of his work, *The Crown of Hinduism*, and the theological position which is revealed therein is discussed.

6 'Edinburgh 1910': The World Missionary Conference

Introduction

The significance of the World Missionary Conference held at Edinburgh in 1910 in establishing the ecumenical movement is universally acknowledged,[1] while in terms of the changing attitudes towards the non-Christian religions, the report of the Fourth Commission is a landmark, still seen as significant today.[2] For the first time a missionary conference – and the fact that it was the most representative Protestant conference ever to have been held added to its significance – devoted a whole commission to an in-depth study of the other religious traditions of the world. In the report of the last major Ecumenical Missionary Conference before Edinburgh, New York 1900, the non-Christian religions are dealt with in a chapter entitled 'Wider Relations of Missions,' which discusses social progress and the peace of the world, non-Christian religions and apologetic problems, with only twenty pages given over to examining the last two items. Before considering the work of this commission, it would be useful to discuss some of the themes which form the background to the Conference. While many of these have been raised before, in relation to the individuals discussed already, the widespread acceptance of many of these ideas can be seen in the context of the thought expressed at Edinburgh.

---

1   See, for example, Neill, 1971, p. 393; Iremonger, p. 388; Tissington Tatlow, in
     Rouse and Neill, p. 405 f; Hogg, p. 98; and Latourette, in Rouse and Neill, p. 355,
     who declares that 'Edinburgh 1910 was one of the great landmarks in the history
     of the Church.'
2   *The Mystery of Salvation*, pp. 152–153.

The World-View of the West at the Time of the Conference

We know with hindsight that a few years after this conference, war was going to ravage Europe and many other parts of the world, leaving behind a dreadful legacy of grief. The words of William Hogg aptly summarize its effects: 'From optimistic belief in progress, the mood of western people turned increasingly to skepticism, cynicism, and pessimism.'[3]

The triumphal tone of nineteenth-century colonialism and its belief in the inherent superiority of western civilization was to be undermined. The First World War was a crucial factor in this, but there were also other changes, such as the growing realization that science could not solve all of mankind's problems,[4] and social changes, such as the rise of Communism, which occurred in the following years. However, the change in attitude were not caused by the war, but had been waiting to occur for a long time, and were indeed already manifesting themselves before then, but it took this event to act as a catalyst for them to become widespread. The context of Edinburgh was thus of a world about to change, but not yet changed.[5] As the historian Asa Briggs says of the Edwardian era, 'if there was much that was "new" before 1901, more that was old survived the queen.'[6]

Firstly, we should note the equation of Christianity with civilization, and more particularly for us here, of British Christianity and British civilization being seen as synonymous.

The three following quotations show how the attitudes of the Victorian era persisted until the time of the Edinburgh conference. The first quotation, from the young Frederick Temple, before he became Archbishop of Canterbury, sums up the spirit of the early Victorian age, '[Great Britain has] the sublimest position ever occupied by a nation hitherto, that of the

---

3   W. R. Hogg, p. 100.

4   Ibid.

5   We are reminded here of Neill's words that most historians regard the nineteenth-century as running from 1789–1914 (see chapter 1), and in this context, Edinburgh may be said to share in the same ethos of Victorian thought which was characteristic of British thinking many decades previously; some demonstration of this postulate will be provided below.

6   Briggs, in Nowell-Smith, p. 48.

authoritative propagator of the Gospel over the world.'[7] This quotation dates from some time before the Edinburgh Conference but the same idea is found in Oldham, whose comparatively liberal views have just been noted:

> it could not have been for nothing that God placed it [India] in the hands of England[... not] merely to have their roads improved, their canals constructed upon more scientific principles, their letters carried by a penny post[...] there must have been in India some far greater want than even these, which England was needed to supply and for which Portugal and France were not found worthy; and that the greatest and oldest and saddest of India's wants is religious truth.[8]

That such a belief, of religious superiority based upon nationality, is still alive at the time of the conference is seen in the words of the following correspondent to the Fourth Commission, 'I have learnt that no one nation or race (not even the Anglo-Saxon) has a monopoly of Christian faith or grace.'[9] Such a statement today would be assumed á priori, but at this time the western world was only just starting to break away from centuries of insular dogmatism. That previous fulfilment theologians held similar ideas has already been observed.[10] They were certainly widespread, for while many have made the point that for those in the Tory Anglican camp the purposes of empire and the spread of English Christianity and culture were seen as combined,[11] it should not be forgotten that many non-Conformists shared these views.[12] Imperialism, it has been said, was essential to the missionary cause.[13] The world was seen as divided between a civilized Christian West, and the non-Christian and uncivilized areas of Africa, Asia, and the Pacific Islands.[14] It should be remembered that here the aim is to give an overall impression of the thought of the times, and that there would be those with more liberal attitudes, as will be seen.

Another factor that bears very much on the whole scene is the political and colonial situation, which is very important to understanding why the West

---

7   Quoted by Hastings in Hamnett, p. 228, from E.G. Sandford (editor) *Memoirs of Archbishop Temple*, p. 54 (Macmillan, London, 1896).
8   Oldham, 1916, pp. 89–90.
9   Rev. Arthur Lloyd, in Ed. IV, p. 108.
10   Even the very liberal minded Westcott held these views.
11   McLeod, p. 99.
12   Clements, 1972, p. 355.
13   Thorne, p. 14, see also, p. 169.
14   Baez-Camargo, pp. 266–7.

felt assured of its own supremacy, not just political but also religious. Simply put, this was the unquestioned dominance of the West as a political, economic, and political power at the time, 'Asia and Africa had been conquered by the Western powers economically and militarily, the Christian mission was to carry out the religious conquest. This was the underlying assumption.'[15] The missionaries held that the successes that they were experiencing at this time could not be related to the human advantages they had, but rather that their success was a result of divine grace.[16] They were most certainly aware of the fact that Western dominance of the Islamic countries was a great humiliation to these nations and their own sense of divine mission,[17] but they did not equate their own superiority with a temporary act of chance or fate: 'The decay of the political power of Islam is one of the striking facts of modern history, and if we believe in a divine purpose at work in human life we cannot be indifferent to its meaning for the Christian Church.'[18] Raising of the question of politics and political power opens up many new questions concerning imperialism, inculturation, and Western orientalist discourse as an exercise in power and knowledge.[19] While these are of importance, they do not, as such, lie within the province of this study, and so I do not propose to discuss them here. However, it is necessary that these questions be raised again later, where further consideration is given to them.

Indicative of the times is the representation of members of the native churches at the World Missionary Conference. The numbers of delegates of the younger churches at Edinburgh was not high, only seventeen out of two hundred and fifty, but this was a great advance from previous conferences of the missionary bodies.[20] Despite the small numbers of delegates they gave six

---

15   Baajo, p. 325.
16   Ed. I, pp. 351–352.
17   Ed. IV, p. 132.
18   Oldham, 1916, pp. 109–110.
19   Particular mention should be made of Edward Said's thought with respect to this (see Said 1985 and 1993). A thorough and well balanced assessment of the strengths and weaknesses of which may be found in J. J. Clarke, pp. 22 ff.
20   Latourette, in Rouse and Neill, p. 359. At the previous conferences there had been: one Indian at Liverpool in 1860; at least six foreign delegates at New York in 1900; none at the Centenary Conference of the Protestant Missions of the World at London 1888; six or seven Chinese at the Chinese Centenary Missionary Conference, Shanghai 1907, and they were only visitors; and fourteen of the

out of forty-seven addresses. Signs of change can also be seen in the numerous calls for the native churches to become self-governing,[21] and there were many speeches in support of this idea.[22] Indeed, the need for the younger churches to become self-governing was summed up as the general consensus of the conference by the Bishop of Birmingham, Charles Gore.[23] Speer also stresses that the majority of the work of the Christian Churches in these lands should not be done by missionaries, 'but through the great Christian Churches which are to grow up indigenously in these nations.'[24] Here, then, is a case of the loosening of the bonds of colonial mastery, showing the development of the trends that were mentioned above regarding the move away from assured superiority by the western nations. Hogg notes that Edinburgh marks the 'metamorphosis from "ecclesiastical colonialism" to global fellowship.'[25] As a final note to this point, it is worth recalling that at Jerusalem in 1928 fifty per cent of the delegates were from the younger churches,[26] but we should not think that this change occurred overnight. The members of the Continuation Committee consisted of ten each from America, Great Britain and Europe, with only five from the whole of Africa, Asia, and Australia.[27]

Despite the faith expressed in the ability of the native Christians to run their own churches, a less favourable attitude is expressed towards those who are not Christians. A few extracts from the report of Commission Two will suffice to give an idea of the general attitude towards these peoples. The report noted that a state of sin is 'characteristic of pagan life.'[28] It was also asserted that the peoples to whom the missions go suffer from hereditary falsehood.[29] Moreover, the report stated that while some of the improvements seen in converts might not be considered very great, that Christian converts

---

delegates at the Bangalore Conference of 1879 were Indians.

21   Gairdner, pp. 104 ff.
22   Ed. II, see for example, pp. 346, 351, and 354.
23   Ed. II, p. 354.
24   Speer, p. 58. It is worth noting that Speer appears to take it for granted that this will happen, emphasizing the belief found throughout the conference that the non-Christian religions will pass away, and that Christianity will naturally take their place. This idea will be explored later in this chapter.
25   W. R. Hogg, p. 101.
26   Ibid., p. 240.
27   Mott, 1912, p. 63.
28   Ed. II, p. 63.
29   Ibid., p. 214.

refrain from bad language for instance,[30] it then went on to say that, considering how bad pagan life actually was, these were great improvements.[31] These few instances give a general idea of the attitudes prevalent towards members of the non-Christian religions. The overwhelming attitude of the conference may be described as paternal condescension towards the East.[32]

Not all the attitudes were so negative. It was recognized, for example, that each of the new churches would bear the characteristics of its native land, so that, for instance, the spirituality of the Indian Church would take on a more contemplative and less worldly form than that of the (Protestant) West;[33] that this was not always done was recognized, whatever the intentions of the missionaries.[34] This, again, raised the question found fifty or more years earlier in Maurice and Rowland Williams, as to what in other cultures is wholly bad, and what is merely neutral. Also, writing shortly after the conference Oldham raised the question again:

> Among less advanced peoples he [the missionary] must be able to distinguish those ideas which are fundamentally anti-Christian from those which, though clothed in unfamiliar forms, represent a movement in the direction of Christian truth[....]
> Which traditional practices must be condemned as fundamentally at variance with the Christian life? Which may be safely tolerated during a transitional stage? Which in spite of their strangeness to western eyes ought to be retained as elements in a civilization that should be at once Christian and indigenous?[35]

Even though elements of value were seen in other cultures, the general consensus of the times still maintained that, 'Indian culture and religion, it

---

30   Ibid., pp. 213–4.
31   Ibid., p. 209.
32   As the following quotation from the Report of the Continuation Committee shows: 'The responsibility of the West towards the East was further urged by Mr. Oldham as a reason for the imperative duty of maintaining peace. At this critical time in the Far East and in the whole Moslem world the Church of Christ is bound to try to give to the people of the West some vision of the responsibilities of the civilized nations of the West towards the less civilized East' (Creighton, p. 123. See also, Speer, p. 57).
33   Ed. II, p. 210.
34   Speer, pp. 66 ff.
35   Oldham, 1916, pp. 171 and 173.

was officially agreed, were good enough for Indians, but they were not something open to an Englishman.'[36]

The sense of cultural superiority also, therefore, corresponds to a sense of religious superiority. As already noted, the attitude of the times was one of optimism, and the Edinburgh conference spoke of 'The Evangelization of the World in this Generation,'[37] though there were those at this time who saw this motto as outdated.[38] The previous century had brought about such changes in the world that the West was assured of its own authority.[39]

One example of this can be seen in the following passage concerning the travels of a Dr Kumm: 'Coming fresh from an adventurous journey right across the a belt of Africa never previously traversed (that between lat. 10° and 5° N., – the 'Moslem fringe'), he spoke of what he had seen in that borderland between Islam and heathendom.'[40] While we today fully understand that what he means was that he was the first white man to traverse that area, this phrasing carries the implication that the native peoples, their history and exploits are not worth considering, the focus being, solely, white western society. This example may be extreme, but was not unusual. Neill's summation is probably representative of the conference's attitude as a whole:

> The delegates differed somewhat in their attitude towards the non-Christian religions; but all were agreed that, as the lordship of Christ came to be recognized, these other religions would disappear in their present form – the time would come when Siva and Vishnu

---

36   Hastings in Hamnett, p. 227.

37   See Gairdner, p. 70. This phrase is associated especially with the conference chairman, John R. Mott, and received some criticism, mainly due to misunderstandings for it only meant that all men should have a chance to hear the Gospel, not that all men should be converted (Neill, 1971, pp. 393–395. In this context see Robert). Mott himself defined the phrase as meaning, 'to give all men an adequate opportunity to know Jesus Christ as their Saviour and to become his real disciples' (Mott, 1900, pp. 4–5). However, the self-belief engendered by the increasing knowledge and power of the Western world led them to believe that this aim was within their sights, in the words of Speer, 'we can[...] make Christ known to all the world in this generation' (Speer, p. 76).

38   Knox, 1907, p. 570, but see also Montgomery, 1908, p. 28, who believed that India would be evangelized within a century.

39   See, for example, Hastings in Hamnett, p. 227: 'The Victorian model coupled a world-wide empire and commerce with the most emphatic commitment, explicit or implicit, to the mental, moral and religious primacy of western man, conceived in a unitary and rather missionary way.'

40   Gairdner, pp. 72–73.

would have no more worshippers than Zeus and Apollo have today. Expressions of these views might differ a little in detail; it cannot be questioned that in 1910 there was a practical unanimity with regard to the substance of them.[41]

This can be said to be one of the assumptions of fulfilment theology, that Christian supremacy could not be doubted, even in, for example, Müller. While the greatest respect might be expressed for the non-Christian religions it was always Christianity, or, at the least, Christ, that provided the only absolute authority, and which, it was thought, must eventually win through.[42] A trawl through the literature of the day would produce many examples of the same idea.[43] It was not always the form of Christianity as then known which was seen by everyone as being the supreme and definitive expression of religion. We can, thus, read in the works of the vice-chairman, Speer:

> in the contention that perhaps, after all, our religion is not final, that we have been misled regarding it, as millions of people have been misled regarding other religions; that our historic Christianity after all, is only a stage in the religious evolution of humanity, some of us can only assure ourselves, and some of us who are undisturbed by such contentions can only convince others, through the actual study and comparison of all the religious thought and life of man.[44]

This represents a counter both to the assumption that Western civilization is supreme, and that it is the West's role to bring its own civilization to the rest

---

41   Neill, 1971, p. 454.
42   See chapter 3, also mention may be made of Miller, who, though rejecting direct evangelism, nevertheless saw Christian influence as leavening Hindu society (chapter 4).
43   Thus we can read: 'The investigator as well as the believer willingly acknowledges a surpassing greatness to Christianity among the religions of the world' (Eucken, p. 10. See also Dods, pp. 197 and 215; Jevons, p. 2; MacCulloch, p. 3; Speer, in the March 1910, World Missionary Conference News Sheet, in *Occasional Bulletin*, 1960); etc. Further, at an evening address during the Edinburgh conference, the Rev. Professor Paterson gave a talk comparing Christianity with the non-Christian religions starting from the assumptions of what religion should be based upon the norms of Western Christendom, and proceeding to 'prove' that Christianity was the ultimate religion as it fulfilled the criteria it had itself provided! (Ed. IX, pp. 156–63).
44   Speer, p. 240. While the idea that people can live their lives 'undisturbed by such contentions' is not restricted to the early part of this century, the very fact that someone as well informed and as highly regarded as Speer can say this is a disturbing insight into the mind of the times.

of the world. But to return to the question of the relation of civilization and religion, two further quotations are worth giving. First, on the relations of language, religion, and civilization :

> a negro who has grown up speaking his own barbarous tongue, will, if educated, prefer and need arabic or English. But the negro dialect does not develop into the higher language, neither does the lower religion develop into the higher. The one must be laid aside that the other may be assumed, as the Red Indian must doff his feathers and buffalo robe before he puts on the dress of a higher civilization.[45]

And, second, 'Dr Paul Rohrbach, a leading German writer on public affairs, asserts that it was right to dispossess the Hereros of their pasture lands in German South-West Africa, since the interests of an inferior race must always give way to those of a superior.'[46]

While we are discussing general attitudes at the time, we should also consider the view that, because of their experience of closeness to the non-Christian peoples, many missionaries would be less liable to develop strong antagonisms towards other cultures.[47] The experience of other cultures, and the tendency to start to take them seriously, allowed many of the old presuppositions to fall away. One notable instance is the change of attitude to the old confessional differences amongst missionaries that had seemed so vital back in Europe, but had lost their meaning outside of that particular social-political context.[48] This change of thought would be particularly characteristic of the period following the Edinburgh Conference.[49] It should be pointed out that it was felt that as the Oriental nations developed they would need Christianity, as the native religions were incapable of meeting the

---

45   Dods, pp. 218–219.

46   From *Deutsche Kolonialwirtschaft*, pp. 17–21, quoted in Oldham, 1916, p. 124. Also, he quotes the words of the Belgian Prime Minister that, 'the natives are not entitled to anything; what is given to them is a pure gratuity' (ibid., p. 125).

47   Knox, 1907, p. 573. This theme has already been discussed in relation to the missionary experience in India (chapter 4).

48   See Latourette, in Rouse and Neill, p. 354.

49   Writing fifty years after the conference, Oldham is very much aware of a changed world. He emphasized the need to re-express Christianity in the light of the new world situation, 'Any excess of dogmatism in intellectual matters cannot fail to alienate those who are increasingly aware of the inadequacy of human thought and speech to express the deepest realities of man's existence' (Oldham, 1960, p. 270).

needs of people as they progressed in their education and industrialization.[50] This was in the minds of those present at Edinburgh, confirmed by what they saw as the disintegration of the other religions, which were believed to be passing away.[51] An idea of the extent to which Christianity and civilization were seen to go hand in hand with each other can be gained from the following quotation: 'Conditions in Christian lands are not what they should be, but they are infinitely superior to the conditions in other lands, and in proportion as they are Christian, famine and disease and want are overcome. Are these blessings to be ours alone?'[52]

At the Edinburgh conference the claim was made that the reason many felt that it was justifiable to compare Christianity to the other religions was because there was now a stronger faith in the Christian community.[53]

Attention should be drawn here to some of the intellectual reasons for the self-doubt in the western world at this time. The effects of developments in the fields of the natural sciences and Biblical criticism had left deep scars across many presumed truths in the course of the nineteenth-century,[54] though by 1910 the various views had, to some degree, been reconciled.[55] We may note again the impact of the theory of evolution, especially after Darwin did much to popularize the notion, giving rise to speculation that, not just the human race, but the world's philosophies and religions could also be part of a continual cycle of evolution and development;[56] this idea is, of course,

---

50   See Ed. IV, p. 232. This idea was continually put forward by a great many people.
51   In the first report it was asserted that the non-Christian religions were losing their hold over the educated classes (ibid., p. 11). This idea was widely held at the time, Farquhar asserted that Hinduism was disintegrating (Crown, p. 34), while, writing several years after Edinburgh, Oldham suggested that the same was true of Islam (Oldham, 1916, p. 112).
52   Speer, p. 25.
53   See Ed. IV, p. 268 and Jevons, p. 18.
54   Baumer, p. 260.
55   An article in the first edition of the *International Review of Mission* speaks of the difficulties being over. Darwinism is no longer seen as an attack but as compatible with Christianity, while the views of Biblical criticism are accepted as valid and are held not to be a threat to the essential elements of faith (Garvie, pp. 661–662). The same view is expressed by H. C. King (pp. 426 f).
56   Smart, pp. 13–14. This view had been brought very much to the fore in England with the publication of *Lux Mundi* where it was seen as very daring. However, in the years following, the view became normative, and the fact that the person seen as the chief propagator of this idea, Gore, became Bishop of Birmingham, showed

essentially Hegelian. Seeds of doubt concerning the religious world-view of the West had been raised, which would not go away. Most important for this study are the effects of the comparative study of religion, which have already been seen in the ideas of early pioneers,[57] the nineteenth-century saw knowledge of the non-Christian religions spreading to a large popular audience.[58] At the conference it was clearly acknowledged that it was necessary for missionaries to study comparative religion,[59] but not, as was often practised, to promote scepticism or a 'sterile religious universalism' but to help to develop Christianity and the mission process.[60] Indeed, it is even called 'the evangelical science of comparative religion.'[61] It should not be supposed that the Edinburgh Conference stood alone in using the methodology of comparative religion to prove the superiority of Christianity.[62] The following may be taken as typical: 'The object of the applied science of religion is to enable the missionary himself to compare forms of religion, incidentally in order that he may know what by faith he feels, and without faith he could not feel, viz. that Christianity is the highest form.'[63] Linked to the development of comparative religion and the application of the historical critical method as applied to the non-Christian religions, is what was called the higher criticism, the use of the same methods of enquiry applied to Christianity itself, especially the Biblical texts. We have seen Rowland Williams' influence in this.[64] The influence of this was very much in the minds of those at Edinburgh. In the Fourth Report each chapter includes a section on the higher criticism, and how it relates and effects the task of evangelization in relation to each religion. At Edinburgh its findings were broadly welcomed and seen as helpful in clearing away much that was merely secondary, and culturally based in Christianity.[65] For those at the

---

how the theological scene had changed.

57	See chapters 2 and 3.
58	J. J. Clarke, p. 71.
59	Gairdner, p. 228.
60	Ibid., p. 149.
61	Ibid., p. 179.
62	See, for instance, the works of Dods, Jevons, Eucken, and MacCulloch, who all seek to use comparative religion to prove the supremacy of Christianity.
63	Jevons, p. 18.
64	See chapter 2.
65	Ed. IV, pp. 200 ff., etc.

Conference the following quotation from the first volume of the International Missionary review is probably a fair assessment of their views:

> The 'higher criticism' is still widely suspected in the Christian Churches; but the new standpoint towards the bible is slowly securing acceptance. Questions of date and authorship, literary character, and even historical value (with some exceptions...), are now seen to be matters of indifference to the Christian faith, so long as the historical reality of a progressive divine revelation culminating in the incarnation of the Son of God, and of a final human redemption in the crucifixion and resurrection of Christ are recognized.[66]

It is not possible for the methods of historical criticism to be rejected out of hand, so they are taken on board in a mild form.

Despite the plethora of agnostic and pluralistic material that had emerged in the previous years, there still seems to be an unshakeable assurance that this criticism will prove Christianity to be true, and help in the inevitable conquest of the other faiths of the world. While there were those who no longer held to this out dated world-view, most of those in the West were still sure enough of their own supremacy to hold to it, though changes were starting to occur. As already mentioned, it was admitted by those at the conference that, as it stood, Christianity was conditioned by society and culture, and could adapt, indeed, it needed to adapt.[67] That the old order was starting to change is shown by the fact that the report can note that, 'there are many European Buddhists in Ceylon.'[68] In a book published by the conference's chairman, he states (no doubt in some shock), that:

> It is reported also that among the adherents of Buddhism in Ceylon and Burma are several Europeans. A general Buddhist society in Rangoon is raising funds for the translation of the Pali Buddhist scriptures into English, for spreading Buddhism in London, and for bringing out from England a number of Englishmen to enter the Buddhist priesthood.[69]

As an indication of change we may note Ernst Troeltsch, who, in his book *Christian Thought*, published in 1923, totally altered his position from that in a previous work of 1902, in which he had stated that Christianity was the supreme religion, but held in his later work that each religion was the one

---

66   Garvie, pp. 661–662.
67   Gairdner, p. 102 fn. 1. Other Christian thinkers at the time also held this view, for instance Eucken, p. 539.
68   Ed. IV, p. 284.
69   Mott, 1911, p. 59.

suited for its own part of the world.[70] It seems that Troeltsch's thoughts upon this matter had changed considerably before 1923, however, for in 1915 he transferred to a chair in Religious, Social, and Historical Philosophy and the History of Christian Religion, also switching departments from theology to philosophy.[71] The conference belonged to the world view of Troeltsch's first book. It was no longer possible for the non-Christian religions to be ignored or dismissed out of hand, but within a few years further great changes would take place as more people questioned aspects of the old dogmas and assumptions.

The Report of Commission Four

In this section the main focus of interest will be the Report of Commission Four, as it was this report that would be read, and can, therefore, be taken as the basis of the authoritative statement that people turn to when considering the attitude of the commission. It should be remembered that the report was compiled from hundreds of answers sent in from missionaries in answer to a questionnaire,[72] and that these formed the main primary material for

---

70   Op. cit., pp. 20 ff.
71   Graf in Eliade, XV, 1987.
72   It would be worth giving a full record of the questions asked:
       1. Kindly give your name, station, and the Church or Society in connection with which you are working. Name the non-Christian religion or religions with which you have to deal in your missionary work, and say with what class of the population you yourself come into contact.
       2. Can you distinguish among the doctrines and forms of religious observances current among these classes any which are mainly traditional and formal from others which are taken in earnest and are genuinely prized as a religious help and consolation?
       3. What you consider to be the chief moral, intellectual and social hinderances in the way of a full acceptance of Christianity?
       4. Have you found in individuals any dissatisfaction with their own faith on specific points? If so, give details.
       5. What attitude should the Christian preacher take towards the religion of the people among whom he labours?
       6. What are the elements in the said religion or religions which present points of

considering the current thought that went into the writing of the report. Following this section attention will be given to the ideas contained within these papers, though we may state now that the report provided a fair and accurate summation of their contents but, as it is important to know what theological position was represented at the Edinburgh Conference, the report itself must be our focus.

In looking at the report of the Fourth Commission at Edinburgh, that dealing with the attitude to be taken towards the non-Christian religions, we shall first make some general points before going on to look at particular comments made about the specific faith groupings considered by the conference.

The report saw itself as seeking to emphasize the positive side of the non-Christian faiths.[73] Throughout the report, the attitude to be taken towards other religions was consistently stated as one of sympathy,[74] and generally the

---

contact with Christianity and may be regarded as a preparation for it?

7. Which elemnets in the Christian Gospel and the Christian life have you found to possess the greatest power of appeal and which have awakened the greatest opposition?

8. Have the people among whom you work a practical belief in a personal immortality and in the existence of a Supreme God?

9. To what extent do questions of 'higher criticism' and other developments of modern Western thought exert an influence in your part of the mission field, and what effect do they have on your missionary work?

10. (This question was addressed to foreign missionaries.) Has your experience in missionary labour altered in either form or substance your impression as to what constitute the most important and vital elements in the Christian Gospel?

11. (This question was addressed to converts to Christianity.) What was it in Christianity that made special appeal to you? Did the Western form in which Christianity was presented to you perplex you? What are the distinctively Western elements, as you see them, in the missionary message as now presented? Was it the sense of sin which enabled you to go behind the Western forms? If not, what was it? (Ed. IV, p. 2).

Each correspondent answered these questions more or less fully, some leaving out certain questions. For the purpose of this study questions 5 and 6 are the most relevant, and attention may be drawn to the wording of the latter of these which seems to presume á priori that there are 'points of contact' between Christianity and the non-Christian religions.

73   Ed. IV, pp. 278–279.
74   Ibid., pp. 20, 52, 267, 268–269, 308, etc.

correspondents to the report saw the beneficial aspects of the other religions, though there were a few who dissented from this generally positive attitude.[75]

The report held to the view that Christianity was the fulfilment of these other religions, though they were not seen as preparations for Christianity in the same way that the Old Testament was, rather, they were on a par with Hellenism.[76] That is to say, it was recognized that at their highest manifestations these religions contained seeds of truth that were in accordance with, and allowed comparison to be made with, aspects of Christian thought, but at the same time there is much that is undeniably wrong and even evil in these religions that must be disposed of before Christianity can fulfil their higher aspects.

Having observed that the conference was very ready to acknowledge the good in other religions, it went a stage further and asked what effect these religions can have for developing Christianity, or rather, 'for the bringing to light of latent elements in the Christian Gospel?'[77] To use the words of W. H. T. Gairdner:

> while of course theories as to the origin and significance of the non-Christian religions vary, there is a general consensus that, representing as they do so many attempted solutions of life's problem[...] the conviction has grown that their 'confused cloud-world' will be found to be 'shot through with broken lights of a hidden sun.' And, these things being true, another conviction has dawned: – Christianity, the religion of the light of the World, can ignore no lights however 'broken' – it must take them all into account, absorb them all into its central glow. Nay, since the Church of Christ itself is partially involved in mists of unbelief, failing aspiration, imperfect realization, this quest of hers among the

---

75   See, for instance, ibid., pp. 24 and 276. Throughout this study, when speaking of the 'attitude of the conference', it should be remembered that while this is the broad consensus there were those at odds with this view. Generally those less favourably inclined to the non-Christian religions, though there are those who have a more positive attitude than that of the majority.

76   Ibid., pp. 20, 22, 53, 58, 94, and 276. One of the precepts of the conference was that it was not to discuss theological questions (see Neill, 1971, p. 454). It is probably for this reason that we get no clear account as to whether the non-Christian religions are purely products of the human mind, or whether they are divinely inspired. The view that seems to be found in the statements of the report is that they are human products though with some dim undefined divine spark behind them. Doubtless the correspondents, and delegates, held varying views, and no attempt was made to reconcile the conflicting opinions, using instead general phrases that could include all and offend none.

77   Cairns in Ed. IV, p. 292.

non-Christian religions, this discovery of their 'broken lights' may be to her the discovery of facets of her own truth, forgotten or half-forgotten – perhaps even never perceived at all save by the most prophetic of her sons. Thus 'by going into all the world' Christ's Church may discover all the light that is in Christ, and become, like her Head, as it is His will she should become, – Lux Mundi.[78]

Whilst ready to speak of Christianity having things to learn from other religions, as we can see from the above, it is not that there is anything of value in them that is not in Christianity, only that certain aspects of Christian truth are less emphasized than they might be. The report also makes constant reference to its belief that it can afford to be so generous to the other religions only because it is assured that Christianity is the final, perfect and complete revelation.[79]

In contrast to this positive attitude expressed towards the non-Christian religions, it should be recalled that the report is also very willing to dwell upon the down side of these religions in contradiction of its expressed intent. Continually, the failure of the other religions to have any effect upon the moral lives of their devotees is stated,[80] though the accounts do seem in places to conflict. For instance, the two following statements are taken from the account of one missionary:

> As to moral results, it is impossible to deny that Buddhism has had a real effect. The absence of the love of money is a characteristic of the Burman. He prizes kindliness above money. He is often really generous. There is also a genuine capacity for devotion[....]
> In spite of the high teaching of Buddhism, the moral standard is very low. thieving, bribery, and lying seem to be indigenous to the soil. It is very hard to find a man of principle.[81]

In relation to this, it may be noted that the low moral standard of the Western world is also observed but no similar criticism of the failure or inability of Christianity to reform people's lives is alluded to. It is seen rather as a lapse

---

78   Gairdner, pp. 137–138. See also Ed. IV, p. 325.
79   Ed. IV, pp. 20, 178, 187, 232, 268, and 324.
80   Ed. IV, pp. 81, 90 ff., 137, 278–279, etc.
81   Ibid., pp. 282 and 283. A possible reason as to why there is such a conflicting testimony over Buddhism's moral grip upon its adherents shall be posited further on.

in individuals, and in no way reflects upon Christianity's truth claims.[82] Whereas in the non-Christian religions the generally conceived failure of these faiths to have had an uplifting moral effect is seen as evidence of their lack of spiritual power, they remain human ideas, very lofty ideas certainly, and, in some small way, reflections of divine inspiration, but nevertheless still, basically, human endeavours: 'Their [the Hindu's] redemption is only an idea, an abstract conception of their philosophy; and ours is a reality that can be tasted by experience.'[83] Again:

> Christianity is more than a school of competitive thought, in the sense that the ethnic faiths are such – something which people are called upon to believe, merely intellectually to believe[....] Christ is the essential reality – the Eternal Word, or Reason – at the heart of the universe. He can be experienced and known in every personal soul, irrespective of race distinction.[84]

This is, perhaps, the main failure of those at the Edinburgh conference, and the writers of the report; an inability to appreciate the good in other religions except in an abstract way. They are very ready to praise the ideals and concepts of other faiths, but there seems an almost total aversion to seeing this in the living faith of the non-Christian religions. Other religions are seen as being destined to pass away, as did the pagan religions of the Roman Empire in the days of the early Church.[85] Despite the no doubt good intentions of the conference, there was little understanding of the other religions, and the constant expression that 'sympathy' was needed in relation to them revealed the patronizing attitude that was still prevalent towards those of other nations and cultures. Here, again, we may quote the words of Mabie, this time echoing, though in distorted fashion, the words of St. Paul,[86] saying of those of the non-Christians faiths that, 'they would have been saved in some infantine [sic] degree.'[87] There were also those present, however, who realized that this attitude existed and should be dealt with:

---

82   See, for instance, the speech by the Archbishop of York reported in Ed. IX, pp. 272–277.
83   W. Dilger in Ed. IV, p. 318.
84   Mabie, pp. 8–9.
85   Ed. IV, pp. 214–218 and 232. This point shall be discussed further later on.
86   Romans II: 12–16.
87   Mabie, p. 4.

the missionaries, except a very few of the very best, seem to me to fail very largely in getting rid of an air of patronage and condescension and in establishing a genuinely brotherly and happy relation – as between equals – with their Indian flocks, though amongst these there are gentlemen in every truest and best sense of the word, with whom relations of perfect equality ought easily to be established.[88]

We may note that this only refers to Indian Christians, for in the same passage the noble bishop says, 'I accept unreservedly the modern position which insists on sympathy as the greatest of all requisites in a Christian apologist approaching those of another faith.'[89]

The report split the world's non-Christian religions into five main categories: Animism, Chinese religions, Japanese religions, Islam, and Hinduism,[90] which we will now examine in turn.

Animism

The correspondents to the report are 'practically unanimous'[91] in their attitudes, noting a number of main points, which are: a) the need to study and know the native religion;[92] b) to be sympathetic and to see and rejoice in the good points of these religions[93] (and one missionary makes the point that: 'He [the missionary] should understand that he has to do with men groping in the dark after light, who are waiting in the dim light of stars for the rising of the sun, who are struggling to get out of the mire and to set their feet on rock.'[94], and, c) the difference between correspondents are noted to be 'apparent rather

---

88   The Bishop of Lahore, George Alfred Lefroy, in Ed. IV., p. 175.
89   Ibid.
90   The schools of Theravada (or 'Southern' as the report calls them) Buddhism are thus not given the consideration of a chapter, a weakness which the report acknowledges not as a deliberate policy but owing to a lack of correspondence from the missionaries working in these fields. While not fully considered then, there is, nevertheless, an appendix given over to the replies from this mission field.
91   Ed. IV, p. 19.
92   Ibid.
93   Ibid., pp. 20–21.
94   Hahn in ibid., p. 20.

than real,'[95] that while some dwell upon the darker aspects and others upon the good points of Animism, the general opinion is felt to be that most feel that there is a 'modicum of truth' to be found therein.[96] Despite this, most of the missionaries deny that there is any 'genuine religious consolation' in animism, though it can help to ease the mind by creating 'an impression that the angry spirit has been appeased.'[97]

There are very few who are prepared to see animism as a 'preparation' for Christianity, though nearly all see points of contact, even if only via analogies.[98] The main points of contact were seen as, firstly, belief in a 'Supreme Being', though it is recognized that this idea of a creator is a long way from Christian conceptions of God, but it does mean that the idea of an omnipotent being is already embedded.[99] Secondly, there is a widespread belief in an afterlife, though again this is seen as very far from the Christian conception, being but a 'vague and shadowy' existence in, what is termed, Hades, the obvious connection between this and the concept of Sheol[100] is, surprisingly, not made in the report.[101] Thirdly, a number of the replies note the possibility of using the idea of sacrifice as a way of explaining doctrines of the atonement.[102] Fourthly, it is noted that 'in some cases a rudimentary moral sense and a dim consciousness of sin' is to be found amongst native tribes.[103] Fifthly, there is sometimes a use of prayer to the highest Spirit, which has obvious analogies to Christian teachings.[104]

Other points worth noting are that not all animism is seen as being of one type. The religion of the Oraon or Kurukh of central India, for instance, is seen as being of a 'higher type.'[105] The majority of replies, about sixty per cent, relate to the Bantu tribes of Africa.[106] While we have referred to animism as a religion, there are a number of correspondents to the report who

---

95   Ibid., p. 22.
96   Ibid.
97   Ibid., p. 10.
98   Ibid., p. 24.
99   Ibid., p. 25.
100   See Cross, pp. 1250–1.
101   Ed. IV, p. 26.
102   Ibid., p. 27.
103   Ibid., pp. 27–28.
104   Ibid., p. 28.
105   Ibid., p. 11.
106   Ibid., p. 7.

'hesitate to apply the name "religion" to this belief and its accompanying rites. "There is no religion in our district," writes one, "simply heathenism."'[107] Indeed, that there is a great deal that the missionaries see as only dark and false, is characteristic of all those who deal with animism; however, the majority, as we have seen, still see vestiges of light amongst the 'dark night of heathen sin.'

Chinese Religions

The three great religions of China, Confucianism, Buddhism, and Taoism, are dealt with in one section, though they are not all seen as being on a par with each other. Generally speaking, it is fair to say that the first two are seen as possessing of a higher calibre than Taoism, which is seen primarily as a mass of superstition. As with animism, these religions are held to provide little in the way of religious consolation, though some see a glimmer of it, especially amongst the devotees of Amitabha and Kwannon.[108] The most devout are held to be found amongst the smaller sects of Buddhism.[109] Also, surprisingly, it is observed that ancestor worship has a genuine value: 'Ancestor worship, too, is a real thing. There can be little doubts that the rites connected with this worship, whether in the home or at family shrines[...] are highly prized and afford real consolation to all classes.'[110]

   The prevailing attitude that sympathy should be the missionaries' attitude is universally expressed, and a need for a thorough knowledge of the religions is asserted.[111] A number of missionaries make the point that, 'Christianity should not be presented as a sword that must sever the people from their historic past but as the flower and fulfilment of it.'[112] Interestingly enough, a number of the missionaries expressing this view believe that the missionary should 'gather up the fragments of original revelation in the old religions and

---

107   Ibid., p. 6.
108   Ibid., p. 40.
109   Ibid., p. 41.
110   Douglas in ibid., pp. 41–42.
111   Ibid., pp. 52 and 53.
112   Bergson in ibid., p. 52, there are also a number of other examples of this attitude (ibid., pp. 52 ff).

use them as stepping stones,'[113] showing a continuation of the belief in a primal revelation.[114] Whatever the rationale, the missionaries believed that Christianity should preserve the best from what had been good in the older Chinese religions.[115] Over and against this view, there are those who doubt this intimately close connection, seeing a greater gulf between the two religions:

> To claim for either religion (Confucianism and Buddhism)[116] that it is a preparation for Christianity, if we mean a preparation divinely designed, is questionable. As it appears to me Christianity goes behind both of them and appeals to the higher nature of man rather than builds upon any foundations that they have prepared.[117]

Thus, there is a divergence of opinion as to the source of this religion which affects the attitude towards it. Whether or not the points of contact are to be seen as preparations for Christianity, quite a number are recognized. There are a great many seen between Christianity and Confucianism, thirteen in all, which overlap to some degree and can be summed up as: belief in Divine providence; belief in a spiritual world and the supernatural; the efficacy of

---

113   Ibid., p. 53.
114   That this idea should find a following in China is interesting. Were the missionaries in China more conservative than elsewhere? Was this perhaps due to the influence of the Jesuit figurists who had employed this thought in China? An interesting line of further research into this could be followed.
115   This was the attitude taken by Timothy Richard, but for which he faced much criticism (Cracknell, 1995, p. 124). Though it is a point worth bearing in mind that we should be careful in reading criticism, for, as has been seen above in relation to Cobban, and will be seen again in the 'Indian Witness Debate', criticism may be misjudged or misread. In this regard, I will recount the following tale concerning a fellow missionary, Herbert Dixon, who was very critical of Richard, 'He described with horror Richard's use of chanted litanies and his hanging of a large white satin cross, flanked by yellow streamers "exactly like those used in Buddhist temples" in the Taiyuan [where they were both stationed] chapel. Dixon's final complaint was that Richard had distributed a Chinese guide to enquirers, whose provisions for a pyramidical structure of ecclesiastical offices amounted to "most barefaced popery"' (ibid.) From this account it sounds as though Dixon may have been more affronted by Richard's use of Roman Catholic style adornments to church and service than his attempts at inculturation (particularly we may bear in mind what was said earlier in relation to Monier-Williams regarding such matters).
116   That only these two faiths are mentioned here can be linked to what was said at the beginning of this section.
117   Bishop Graves in Ed. IV, p. 58.

prayer; notions of sacrifice; and a comprehensive moral code.[118] There are some teachings of Mencius which are spoken of as being a 'preparation', which include the heaven given nature of man, the discipline of sorrow and adversity, and the reverence for conscience.[119] There is, then, a great deal in Confucianism that is held to prefigure, or be consistent with, Christianity. A number of 'negative preparations' are, however, also recognized, amongst which are the failure to acknowledge divine love, lack of sympathy for the poor, and the failure to recognize the frailty of man's will and his own moral fortitude.[120] This is a point brought up in relation to all the non-Christian religions that, while looking for the good, the aspects alien to Christianity should not be ignored or forgotten.

There are also a number of connections seen between Chinese Buddhism and Christianity.[121] First amongst these is the idea of God, and secondly, there is the widespread use of prayer and invocation. Thirdly, the fact that Buddhism tells people that they are in need of salvation is seen as commendable, in making the idea known in China, and the same is said of the Buddhist idea of retribution, though mention is made of the difference of this concept from the Christian view. In the belief in the Western Paradise, Chinese Buddhism is seen to have introduced a view of the afterlife more in tune with the Christian. Also noted as connections are notions of divine incarnation, trinity in unity, and the value of Buddhism's belief in self-repression, self-examination, and moral code. A point that is very much self evident is clearly seen here, that what the missionaries declare to be preparations, are quite simply those aspects of a faith that provide a seminal idea in the minds of the faithful, that will make it easier for someone to accept Christianity by making the basis of its tenets already familiar, though in a different form. Though the fact that they are different is really an advantage for the missionary, a point that shall be made again later, particularly in relation to Islam where the difficulty of converting someone who has already accepted this religion is seen as much greater than that of converting someone who has, what would be deemed at this time, a more primitive faith.[122] In this context, it may be noted that in relating the moral code, the following is

---

118   Ibid., pp. 54–55.
119   Ibid., p. 56.
120   Arnold in ibid., p. 56.
121   Ibid., pp. 56–57.
122   Ibid., p. 147.

252

noted, 'all these prove insufficient to give strength for moral living.'[123] Here, the fact that the Buddhist moral code has been acknowledged to be similar to the Christian,[124] may lead to the need to denigrate the moral power of this religion.[125]

As for Taoism, whilst allowing for the fact that its classical teachings are very noble, the general attitude is that, 'Taoism has reached a great depth of degradation in China to-day.'[126] As regards being a preparation, the virtues it upholds are noted, and the conception of Tao is seen to correspond to 'the wisdom of the Hebrew Scriptures.'[127]

The general attitude towards the religions of China is more positive than that towards animism. While there are a few who don't regard these religions as a preparation for Christianity, the majority see them as providing very many points of contact, if not actual preparations for Christianity, and that their best aspects lead on to Christianity.

Japanese Religion

Again there is 'perfect agreement' on the need for sympathy and understanding towards the native religions.[128] The attitude towards the religions of Japan is even more positive than to those of China: 'Many add their own conviction that the elements of good in all these religions are both extensive and valuable, and many may be regarded as preparatory to

---

123   Kranz in ibid., p. 57.
124   See Dods, p. 211 and Carus, p. 17..
125   The failure of all the non-Christian religions to have any moral force is actually maintained, with rare exceptions, throughout the report, but the point does seem to be made more often in reference to Buddhism. Perhaps the missionaries don't want to give the impression that, having commending the Buddhist moral code, they are implying that there is no need for Buddhists to convert, as they already have equality with Christianity. It is noted in the report, that there are those who say that as the Buddhist and Hindu moral codes are so similar to the Christian then there is no need for anyone to convert (Ed. IV, p. 167). This attitude, it should be noted, is not something peculiar to the report, we may note Dods (Dods, p. 211) and Robinson (Robinson, pp. 72–73) as examples.
126   Ed. IV, p. 57.
127   Ibid., pp. 57–58.
128   Ibid., p. 94.

Christianity. Some go so far as to say that here, as with Judaism, Christ came not to destroy but to fulfil.'[129]

Those who are religious are held to obtain consolation from their faith, particularly noted are the 'simple honest people' who place their faith in the teachings of the Shinshu sect.[130]

Once again 'the want of spiritual power' is noted,[131] and it is observed that Buddhism lacks any grip upon the conscience of the people.[132]

One missionary makes the point that: 'The Christian preacher should constantly take the ground that every good teaching in the native faith is a gift of God, the Father of all men, and is a preparation for the coming of His fuller revelation in Jesus Christ.'[133] While this attitude is prevalent, it is not universal, and the next passage, according to the report, 'is important, as it stands in very striking contrast to the opinions of the Rev. Arthur Lloyd[134] and others.'[135] So:

> If there are those who hope to discover in Shintoism or Buddhism much that is comparable with what is found in Judaism as points of contact with or preparation for, Christianity, they will be disappointed; and if there are any who think to find in the non-Christian religions of the world great truths that will complement Christianity they will not find them in Japan.[136]

Despite the words of the report I do not think that the difference in positions is all that great. For despite noting points of contact, the other correspondents always emphasize the differences, and in looking for things to 'complement' Christianity, the search is not for new truths to supplement the old religion, but for a change in emphasis, and an inspiration to bring out neglected parts of Christian teaching.[137] The point made in the previous section concerning why things were seen as preparations is also pertinent here. Having said this, a number of points of contact are seen here by most.

---

129   Ibid.
130   Ibid., p. 81.
131   Ibid., p. 90.
132   Ibid., p. 81.
133   Gulick in ibid., p. 95.
134   A fascinating character whose thought is dealt with by Cracknell (Cracknell, 1995, pp. 151 ff), he regarded himself as 'a ronin for Christ' (see ibid., p. 154).
135   Ed. IV, p. 99.
136   Imbrie and Ibuka in ibid.
137   See, for instance, Gairdner, pp. 137–138.

Firstly, it is noted that there is almost everywhere 'a dim perception of some Supreme Being or authority.'[138] Peculiar to Buddhism are belief in a future life, belief in causality, and the idea of salvation. Regarding the Shinshu, the Rev. Arthur Lloyd, referred to above, has the following to say:

> Amida has a spiritual son Avalokitesvara, incarnate again and again, on errands of mercy from his Father[....] He has an attendant, Seishi, in whom resides his wisdom, and the three form a Trinity whom the Amidaist will recognize as claiming his worship.
> Be its origins what it will, here is a faith so wonderfully like Christianity that it is difficult to resist the inference that it was, in the Divine Providence, intended as a *praeparatio evangelica* for the Gospel in Japan[....][139]

Lloyd, no doubt, goes further than many others who recognize similarities, but there is, nevertheless, a general tendency to such thoughts amongst the missionaries of Japan. As regards Shintoism, it is observed by one missionary that it provides a more perfect conception of a personal deity than any other oriental religion.[140] Their conception of purification is also seen as a possible preparation for Christian ideas of cleansing and atonement, and the moral teachings contained in Shintoism are likewise seen as being useful.[141]

With a few exceptions, the correspondents express the belief that God 'has not left himself without witness.'[142] While not all those who hold this positive view will see these ideas as divinely inspired, there are certainly those who do, and there are even those who talk of a Japanese Christianity, expressing their view that there is much here compatible with Christianity and capable of providing an adequate interpretation of it.[143]

---

138   Ed. IV, pp. 97–98.
139   Lloyd in ibid., pp. 98–99.
140   Kawai in ibid., p. 98.
141   Ibid., pp. 99–100.
142   Ibid., p. 119.
143   Ibid., p. 121. The Rev. Arthur Lloyd goes furthest in this regard, and speaks of his belief that he can present Christianity to Japan in the theology of Shinran and the Shinshu sect (ibid., p. 118).

The following statement is representative of attitudes towards Islam:

> On the general question, whether Islam can be regarded as a preparation for Christianity, Herr Simon of Sumatra probably expresses the general opinion in the words, 'Islam is not a preparation for Christianity, and it is easier to build on a strange soil than first of all tear down old buildings, which are so firmly set together that they offer an insurmountable obstacle to demolition.'[144]

Having seen the positive attitude to Chinese religions, and the even more positive attitude to the religions of Japan recorded in the report, it might seem strange that a religion that, in many respects, is much closer and similar to Christianity is not treated with the same warmth and affection. The report offers its own explanation for this:

> Islam is unlike the other religions dealt with in that it is later in date than Christianity, and Mohammed, while honouring, claimed to hold a higher place than Christ[....] In the lands of the Near East it has partly supplanted, and partly reduced to subjection, Christian Churches[....] It is probably this circumstance which accounts for the fact that Islam offers the most bitter opposition to, and provokes the most severe condemnation of, Christian missionaries.[145]

These two factors are certainly important. The fact that Islam cannot be seen as many other religions as prior to, and therefore leading to, Christianity, but rather rejects it,[146] and, secondly, the historical antagonism between the two faiths, explains why Islam is seen in a more derogatory light than many other non-Christian religions. Having said this, the point should be made at the outset that, just as there was not universal agreement on the positive value of the other non-Christian religions, so there are those who have a higher regard for Islam than the majority. Before going on to look at what the report says concerning Islam, it will be useful to consider some other factors affecting the attitude taken towards the Islamic faith.

Firstly, one factor that seems dominant in the minds of many of those missionaries dealing with Islam is the difficulty of converting people away

---

144   Ibid., p. 147.
145   Ibid., p. 122.
146   See ibid., p. 138.

from Islam, as compared to converting those who are not.[147] This problem is seen particularly in relation to Africa where: 'The threatening advance of Islam in Equatorial Africa presents to the Church of Christ the decisive question whether the Dark Continent shall become Mohammedan or Christian.'[148] Indeed, it was felt that Islam was the only hindrance standing in the way of the complete Christianization of the world![149] Not only does Islam stand in a different position as regards its historical relationship to Christianity than the other non-Christian religions, but it is also held that: 'It is a great and formidable force in the world in a sense in which other religions are not.'[150] While, at this time, no longer seen as a political or military threat, [151] it was, nevertheless, it was seen as an opponent in that it was a force that was not perceived to be decaying as rapidly as the other faiths. One correspondent noting that any dissatisfaction felt by Muslims does not lead to their converting to Christianity, but causes reform within Islam itself.[152] There is thus a doubt as to the assured position of supremacy felt by the missionaries in regard to Islam as opposed to the other religions, where, slow as progress may have been, the Church saw itself as fighting a winning battle. So, while there is the feeling that towards Buddhism, Confucianism, etc., a generous stance can be taken, perhaps even a sense of patronage comes intoplay, with Islam there is a definite sense of conflict and antagonism, not just because it rejects Christ, or in the past has destroyed many churches, but because it refuses to yield to the determined thrusts aimed at its destruction. The sense of absolute superiority is given as a reason why the missionaries can be generous in their assessments of other religions:

---

147   Ibid., p. 147.
148   Ed. I, p. 364. This is mentioned as a case of 'special urgency' 'on which *the Church as a whole* should concentrate attention and effort.' Worth quoting here are the words of Robinson, who, though admitting that conversion to Islam creates an impasse in terms of any subsequent conversion to Christianity, does, nevertheless, generously concede that, 'nevertheless the failure on the part of the Christians of Europe to preach their faith to the heathen who were not moslems, prevents us from being otherwise than grateful that the hundreds of millions who have died in the faith of Islam during the last thirteen centuries have not lived and died as pagans' (Robinson, pp. 110–111).
149   Gairdner, p. 75.
150   Ed. IV, p. 241.
151   Ibid., p. 132.
152   Ibid.

it is precisely because of the strength of their conviction as to the absoluteness of Christianity that our correspondents find it possible to take this more generous view of the non-Christian religions. They know that in Christ they have what meets the whole range of human needs, and therefore they value all that reveals that need, however imperfect that revelation may be.[153]

In refusing to submit, Islam challenges the notion that only Christianity can satisfy the whole of a man's needs. This relates to a point raised earlier, that preparations for Christianity must be similar in type, but they should not be too similar. Jjust as Buddhist or Hindu morals could be a reason not to convert, so could Islamic monotheism be seen in this way, as could the fact that Islam already has a place for Jesus, and accepts many of the miraculous stories relating to him. Relating to this is the fact that while there is discussion of a possible Japanese, and also an Indian, form of Christianity, when answering the question as to whether exposure to Islam has influenced their faith, the resounding answer is negative, and if any change is noted, it is only in emphasis.[154]

This thinking provided a further motive, beyond those noted in the report, for Islam to be seen at times in a less than favourable light. The authors of the report, however, seemed inclined to a more favourable view noting the difficulties and antagonism felt by many, but always emphasizing that there are those who feel more positively inclined.[155] Having dealt with these points the correspondence to the report can now be considered.

Opinion varies as to whether any religious consolation is derived from Islam, but the general consensus is that it is found by the devout.[156] As with the other religions, the need for a thorough knowledge and a sympathetic approach are emphasized.[157]

---

153   Ibid., p. 268. This view is a constant theme of the report, see pp. 20, 178, 187, 232, and 324.

154   Ibid., p. 153.

155   While this does not mean that the negative reports were ignored, far from it, a more positive stance was emphasized. Thu, in his report of the conference, Gairdner feels able to say that Islam and Hinduism were seen as being on a par with each other (Gairdner, pp. 148–149). This should be seen as reflecting his own personal bias towards Islam, because, as will be shown in the next section, Hinduism was seen very much as the pinnacle of the non-Christian religions, as the report itself notes (Ed. IV, p. 247).

156   Ibid., pp. 126 ff.

157   Ibid., pp. 138 and 139.

Regarding Islam's position, one correspondent sees it as a lesser revelation, while another sees all the non-Christian religions as false.[158] As already noted, most deny that it is a preparation for Christianity, and dwell upon Christianity's uniqueness.[159] It is, nevertheless, noted that: 'Even when this conviction is held as regards Islam it has to be admitted that it has taken over several truths of Christianity, even in a defective form.'[160] It should then come as no surprise that a number of connections are to be found, and the point is made that:

> Owing to the historical dependence on Christianity of Islam, *the points of contact...* are not nearly so significant as they would be in a religion which has no historical connection with Christianity; for in that case any resemblance would show that in the religious thought and life of mankind there is an underlying need at least of thought and unity.[161]

Also, relating to the point made earlier about points of contact, it is observed that some of them 'are in many cases a hindrance to, rather than a preparation for, the acceptance of Christianity.'[162]

As to the similarities, the unity of God is noted, though that the conception of God is very alien is emphasized;[163] also the belief amongst the Shiahs of the idea of incarnation, though again, the conception is different.[164] The fact that both acknowledge the importance of Jesus is considered, and the similarities and differences noted.[165] Any sense of connection over morality is discounted due to the emphasis upon law in Islam.[166] Some also see a point of contact in that the Shiah sect has a notion of forgiveness of sins through sacrifice, but this is seen as a hindrance as it has a rather different emphasis.[167]

---

158 Ibid., p. 140.
159 Ibid.
160 Simon in ibid.
161 Ibid., p. 142. It should be remembered that this statement was made in terms of contemporary knowledge. Scholarship today has moved on, and is more aware of the wider dissemination of Christian beliefs across the globe, the influence on Pure Land Buddhism, perhaps, being a case in point.
162 Ibid.
163 Ibid., pp. 142–143.
164 Ibid., p. 143.
165 Ibid.
166 Ibid., p. 145.
167 Ibid., pp. 145–146.

Again, seen as a point of contact, though the conception of the belief is different, is the mutual acceptance of the existence of heaven and hell.[168] Finally, what is seen as one of the closest points of contact is the Islamic aversion to idolatry.[169]

Hinduism

In contrast to the negative view of Islam generally expressed, the correspondents to the report held, almost unanimously, to a more positive approach to Hinduism, 'no other non-Christian religion approaches this in the gravity or in the depth of its endeavours after God .'[170]

As with all the non-Christian religions, the need for sympathy and a prolonged study are felt to be essential.[171] The influence of bhakti is seen as exercising the greatest influence over people's lives, and is perceived as a source of genuine religious feeling.[172] Indeed, as to the religious value of the religion, one correspondent goes so far as to say that: 'Under favourable conditions of general culture I have met among Hindus and Brahmins as deep, genuine, and spiritual a religious life as is found amongst most Christians; their faith is sincere, though wrongly directed.'[173]

Those elements of Hinduism that are preparations for Christianity are generally agreed amongst the correspondents, though differences of value are applied to them.[174] Amongst those mentioned are the idea of a divine trinity, [175] belief in avatars, sacrifice, ritual,[176] the daily confession of sin required of a Brahmin,[177] and, a point that is seen as important, an acceptance of the

---

168	Ibid., p. 146.
169	Ibid., pp. 146–147.
170	Ibid., p. 247.
171	Ibid., pp. 171 and 175.
172	Ibid., pp. 158 ff.
173	Steinhal in ibid., p. 172.
174	Ibid., p. 177.
175	Ibid., pp. 177 and 182–183.
176	Ibid., p. 177.
177	Ibid., p. 183.

supernatural.[178] Amongst the others, two aspects of Hindu thought stand out as the primary preparations for Christianity, and these are the doctrines of bhakti and moksha.[179] There is a difference of opinion as to which of these two elements, one theistic, the other pantheistic,[180] offers the most important preparation.[181] There are many references made to bhakti as the best preparation for Christianity,[182] and the reasons for this should be straightforward. What might seem more unusual is the prominence given to an idea that salvation is to be gained by renunciation of the world, and absorption back into the oneness of being with the loss of any personal continuation. The rationale behind this is that the importance of the idea of moksha (or mukti) is that it shows the soul's yearning for union with the Supreme Being, though this is interpreted in an erroneous way according to Christian dogma.[183] It is also seen as being concerned with conventional human (and therefore sinful) ideas about selfhood, towards an escape from the wants of the ego, and to draw closer to God.[184] Even amongst those who see the closest connection being bhakti, there is still a recognition of the value of Vedanta philosophy:

> It may[...] correct crude western (a) transcendent ideas of God, (b) individualistic ideas of human personality, (c) creationist theories of the universe, and lead to a more balanced and complete Christian philosophy. In this way it also may be a true preparation for Christianity as a corrective of the West.[185]

---

178   Ibid., p. 186. That this point is mentioned as being of particular importance perhaps forewarns of the danger to be acknowledged at Jerusalem eighteen years later, of the creeping spread of secularism and materialistic belief as the greatest threat to religiosity.

179   Ibid., p. 178.

180   The term 'pantheism' is that used about Vedanta throughout the report as it is the most common expression of its day, though acknowledgement is made of the fact that there are those who object to the term being applied to Indian thought (ibid., p. 245 fn.). Its usage here merely reflects the fact that in discussing the report it is easiest to make use of its terminology for the sake of clarity.

181   Ibid., p. 178.

182   Ibid., pp. 178 ff and 183–184.

183   Ibid., pp. 180 and 187.

184   Ibid., p. 182.

185   Andrews in ibid., p. 178.

The two tendencies of Indian thought, towards theism and pantheism, were both seen inadequate in terms of Christian thought. The report quotes Farquhar, as typical of those who see Christianity fulfilling Hinduism, by saying that the Christian conception of God is a synthesis of the two Indian views, both of which are considered to be partial aspects of a picture of which the Christian idea is a whole, uniting both personal and impersonal aspects in a harmonious balance.[186]

The general opinion was that Hinduism is a preparation for Christianity, and can correct certain western biases in its religious life. A tiny minority, however, dissented from this view, and did not see Hinduism as a form of preparation.[187] One final point, however, that should be made, taken from the conclusions of the report, is that:

> Hinduism cannot be spoken of as a preparation for Christianity in anything like the way as the Old Testament is such a preparation[....] The analogy suggested in the report is not with the Old Testament, but with Hellenism, which assuredly had the baser elements in it side by side with nobler things[....] Yet the presence of this base and cruel side of Hellenism did not prevent St. John nor the author of the Epistle to the Hebrews from using its highest categories of thought, and transforming them through the vital power of the Spirit. Whether the higher Hindu thought and religion, the ideas of redemption from the world, devotion and union with the Supreme Being, are capable of such a use must of course be a matter of individual opinion and of common experience.[188]

---

186   Ibid., pp. 181–182. Farquhar was to become the most famous proponent of the fulfilment notion of religion a few years later with his book, *The Crown of Hinduism*.

187   Only two out of sixty-five correspondents fail to see Hinduism as offering a potential for fulfilment in Christianity (ibid., p. 276). Having said this, I will explore below some of the problems in deciding just who thought what based solely upon the evidence of the Edinburgh papers.

188   Ed. IV, p. 276.

Having considered the report of Commission Four the correspondence it was based on should be considered. I do not intend to examine individual papers here as the most important are discussed in context elsewhere.[189] The report, as stated already, provides a good synopsis of the material. Some general points should, however, be made. First, is the sheer problem of interpreting some correspondent's attitudes, for while a number of papers, such as those of Hogg, Farquhar, Slater[190] and Andrews are quite expansive, some correspondents provide but a few pages in total. It is often hard to tell if an individual really advocates fulfilment theology, and if so, in what form. For this reason I shall not attempt to provide a synopsis, as Maw has done,[191] of the numbers who can be put in camps 'for', 'partially for', or 'against' fulfilment theology. Apart from which, some of Maw's classifications are highly suspect. He, for instance, sees Hogg, the arch critic of fulfilment theology,[192] as being 'partially in favour' of fulfilment theology, while George H. Westcott[193] is seen as opposed.[194] To quote from his paper, however, we see him saying: 'It is seen, then, that even where Indian thought has seemed most antagonistic to prayer it has been preparing men for the more perfect practice of it[....]'[195] While George Westcott certainly is critical of much Hindu thought, this has been seen to be part and parcel of fulfilment theology, and should not be read otherwise.[196] These two examples do not mark the

---

189   Hogg's paper, for instance, detailing his criticisms of fulfilment theology is discussed in the final chapter, while the papers of Farquhar, Slater, and others are referred to as part of the discussion of these individuals in the relevant chapters. Suffice it to say that if all the correspondence of every individual were considered the examination would require a thesis of its own.

190   Whose submission runs to over a hundred pages.

191   Maw, 1990, pp. 391–3.

192   See chapter 8.

193   B. F. Westcott's son.

194   See also, Maw, 1990, pp. 320 ff., esp. P. 323.

195   EDMS, Westcott # 250, p. 5, see also p. 23.

196   As suggested before, Maw often seems unsure in the area of theological thought, and provides only a limited history of fulfilment theology, perhap, not being aware of the full history and range of thought which it encompasses. This history might well not lead him to dismiss George Westcott's thought as somehow not being fulfilment theology. Cracknell, it may be noted, also sees George Westcott as being inclined to see the good in the non-Christian religions (Cracknell, 1995, p. 217).

only disparities to be found between Maw's readings of the Edinburgh manuscripts and my own. To note one more, Maw suggests that the Reverend J. Ruthquist is opposed to fulfilment theology, yet all he says on the subject is, 'I have found that occasionally it has been a real help to connect the gospel message to the good points in their religion and experience[....]'[197] This paper, in fact, provides a good example of the problem I mentioned in reading support or rejection of fulfilment theology into some of the papers. I do not see how Maw reaches his conclusion. There is very little to go on in assessing quite how Ruthquist viewed the non-Christian religions. With this caveat I pass on from discussing the papers sent in to the Edinburgh Conference.

The Collaboration of Cairns and Hogg, and the Writing of Report Four

The important influence of Hogg's thought, especially as reflected in the theology of the Fourth Commission, needs to be considered here. As already mentioned, Hogg was a critic of fulfilment theology, and so his influence on David Cairns, chairman of Commission Four, deserves consideration.[198] The commission's conclusions were drafted solely by Cairns, though Speer approved of them totally.[199] The close collaboration and sympathy of these two thinkers has been seen as important to the theology of Edinburgh by a number of commentators;[200] however, the relation of this to fulfilment theology must be seen as minimal. While Cairns had circulated a copy of Hogg's articles on 'Karma and Redemption' and 'Christianity as Emancipation from this World' to the members of Commission Four,[201] the main theme of their collaboration was the idea of the possibility of miracles occurring today,[202] for which they believed a stronger faith was needed. [203]The main summation of their thought on this matter can be seen on pages 246–267 of the 'General Conclusions' of the report, yet while the conference approved

---

197   EDMS, Ruthquist # 221, p. 2.
198   Cairns was the Professor of Systematic Theology at Christ's College, Aberdeen (Cracknell, 1995, p. 216).
199   Fulfil, p. 276.
200   Sharpe, 1971, pp. 53 ff, Fulfil, pp. 282 ff, and Cox, 1977, pp. 108–119.
201   Cox, 1977, p. 115.
202   Ibid., p. 119.
203   The details of their thought in this matter lie outside the scope of this study, though the best discussion of it may be found in Cox (op. cit.).

Cairns' report, his aims and thinking in this matter seem to have not been noticed:

> It would be inaccurate, however, to describe the discussion of the missionary message at Edinburgh as fundamentally supporting Cairns' position. On the contrary, most speakers made no reference at all to the supernatural message of Christianity, and where any mention was made, it always stopped short of advocating the radical interpretation Cairns had given to it. Most missionaries at Edinburgh thus failed either to take Cairns' challenge seriously or to understand clearly the full intention behind it.[204]

I would suggest that the latter is most likely, as I will argue below that the endorsement of fulfilment theology was the message most people have found in this report, and the particular agenda of Cairns and Hogg was overlooked.[205] In his assessment of the conclusions to the report in *Justice, Courtesy and Love* Cracknell does not mention Hogg's and Cairns' collaboration, nor this aspect of Cairns' own thinking.[206]

Another point that needs raising in relation to considering the background to the writing of the report, is that fact that its correspondents were selected from the leaders of missionary organizations, and from major missionary thinkers.[207] This group would, Sharpe suggests, give rise to the report reflecting mainly the views of an educated and liberal elite, against which something of a popular backlash can be seen from amongst the ranks of ordinary missionaries.[208] I think that Sharpe overstates the case, and that the conservative reaction was not as antagonistic as he suggests,[209] but it does

---

204 Ibid., pp. 121–2.
205 This should not be seen as surprising, Cairns admitted that he toned down the radical implications of the message so it could gain universal approval (see letter Cairns to Hogg, 19/3/1910, from the Hogg Collection, in ibid., p. 116), and unless one were aware of the full implications and context of what Cairns really wanted to say I find it hard to imagine that most readers would guess at what was being implied.
206 Cracknell, 1995, pp. 253 ff.
207 Fulfil, p. 309.
208 Ibid., pp. 309–323.
209 See chapter 8 where I discuss the criticism fulfilment theology came under from the conservative wing of missionary thought, and note that the two sides are not that far apart. Though we may note, writing four years after the conference, Farquhar's suggested that there is a party strongly opposed to the findings of the report of the Fourth Commission at Edinburgh, equally there is another group who maintain that there is no need for missions, feeling it not necessary to convert people from

raise an important issue. Quite simply, in terms of support, and even with regard to its critics, all that may be gathered in regard to forming the conclusions of a study such as this is the opinions of those who wrote or otherwise left some record of their thought. This naturally means that the great mass of ordinary missionaries, and indeed, of Christians in Britain at this time, leave no record of their opinion. In saying that fulfilment theology had popular support, or was widely acknowledged, certain assumptions, which are always necessary in the study of the history of thought, must be made. From the mass of evidence that has been gathered in speeches to missionary conferences, and in terms of the very limited criticism from the ranks of ordinary missionaries, which has been seen already in relation to Cobban,[210] and will be seen again in conservative criticisms of fulfilment theology, the differences were often only misunderstandings or objections to language that was thought to be just too radical. While such matters must be taken seriously, it is one of the contentions of this study that fulfilment theology had a greater popular acceptance and following than has previously been assumed.

The Attitude of the Conference

Before assessing Edinburgh's importance, it would be useful to consider the way the Conference conceived of the missionary endeavour. It has been suggested that the relationship of the missionary enterprise to the colonial conquests can be seen by the strongly militaristic language used by missionaries at this time. For instance, Baago notes that Mott, chairman of the Edinburgh conference, 'tried to inflame students to "conquer nations for Christ."'[211] While to note another case, a certain missionary, W. H. Findley, is quoted as saying: 'We are face to face with the mighty array of heathendom, we are in the forefront – in the very "fire-zone" – of the Church's battle, and surely in no age or land was a sterner crusade adventured

---

another faith (Crown, pp. 16 and 17).
210   Chapter 4.
211   Baago, 1966, pp. 324-325.

than when the missionary band was sent to claim India for Christ!'[212] The continuation committee of the Edinburgh conference also spoke of, 'concentrated aggressive attacks by evangelists on selected towns and villages.'[213] Addison tells us that in the years leading up to Edinburgh: 'The tone of militant hostility became less and less familiar and the need for persuasive sympathy was ever more strongly emphasized.'[214] The assumption of the times was that the role of the West was one of conquest and domination, and while there was talk of indigenous churches and the value of the native cultures, there were few willing to give much time to these ideas. Writing in 1916, Oldham said that the war would be a divide between two epochs,[215] and there is no doubt that he was right, though he could not have known then the full effect that it would have. It brought into the light much that was previously hidden in shadow, breaking open wide fissures in the cliffs of Western dominance where before there had only been the smallest cracks.

At the same time, a growing need for sympathy was seen as essential, which suggests a certain dialectical tension, where the old and new attitudes were in fusion at Edinburgh. So we read: 'He [the missionary] will lose nothing, and he has everything to gain, by recognizing the good in the religion of the region, in order to take advantage of any points of contact with Christianity, and preparations for it.'[216]

The old polemical approach was no longer considered appropriate by many,[217] and there were numerous calls to study the non-Christian religions. [218] It has been observed by Addison that from the 1800s onwards, the general question asked of the non-Christian religions was whether they came from God or Satan.[219] By the time of Edinburgh the latter answer, except amongst

---

212   Ibid., p. 325.
213   *The Continuation Committee in Asia 1912–13* (New York, 1913), p. 32, quoted in ibid.
214   Addison, p. 118.
215   Oldham, 1916, p. 1.
216   Dodd in Ed. IV, p.20.
217   Ibid., p. 53.
218   Ibid., pp. 267 and 268–269; see also Gairdner, pp. 137 and 228.
219   Addison, p. 110.

a few extreme fundamentalists,[220] had been ruled out.[221] Rather, at Edinburgh, the question was whether these religions were of God or man?[222]

Again, in contrast to many of the imperialistic attitudes prevalent at the time, noted in the first section, the comparatively liberal attitude of many of those at Edinburgh has been mentioned. One area this extended to was nationalism, of which it may be noted: 'The greatest fact in modern politics has been the growth of nationalism. The history of the past century has been the history of the arrangement of national boundaries.'[223] In support of this wave of opinion, there were many at Edinburgh who were sympathetic to the wishes of the colonized nations' wishes to be free. However, as stated above, they were 'comparatively liberal' in relation to today's attitudes, expressing the view that, 'it is our duty to govern India that she may be able to govern herself.'[224]

---

220 As is still the case today.
221 It is impossible to precisely date this change in attitudes, as it is something that occurred gradually, and there always had been, and, indeed, still are those who have opinions varying, sometimes widely, from the general consensus. Even to say when this view changed from a minority to a majority view would be impossible, as there is no way of judging the many whose views are not known. However, from the ideas expressed at the missionary conferences at New York in 1900, and at the Anglican Missionary conference in 1894, it is possible to estimate, to some extent. As noted already, the only negative views expressed at New York still recognized the good in the non-Christian religions, yet while there were positive attitudes at the Anglican conference in 1894, there were also very negative ones. I would say that the last decade of the nineteenth-century might be said to mark the turning point. Various factors, such as the growth of comparative religion would have helped to familiarize people with the good in the non-Christian religions, and the occurrence of the World Parliament of Religions show that there was a growing knowledge and appreciation of the other world faiths. That, by 1910, the vast majority of correspondents to the Fourth Commission at Edinburgh had a 'positive' attitude to the non-Christian faiths suggests that there had been a considerable development of this opinion for some time.
222 Though, it should be noted that, even when the answer is given that these religions put men into contact with God, and are in some sense from God, there is still an essential negativity behind this attitude. This will be discussed in the conclusion.
223 Speer, p. 113.
224 Speer, p. 116. The same view is expressed by Oldham, 1916, p. 90.

268

Conclusion

Firstly, in relation to the question of how significant Edinburgh was, it would be useful to consider briefly some of the missionary conferences previous decades. Much that it said can be seen in previous conferences. The following quotation from Bishop Westcott at the Anglican Missionary Conference of 1894 is not untypical:

> Each people has its own peculiar gift, which will, we believe, be brought in due time to Christ through the Church[....] There are great nations – China and India – inheritors of ancient and fruitful civilizations, endowed with intellectual and moral powers widely different from our own, which have some characteristic offering to render for the fuller interpretation of the Faith.[225]

Examples also abound from the ecumenical missionary conference at New York, ten years prior to Edinburgh. The following words, opening the debate on the non-Christian religions, could equally well have prefaced what was said at Edinburgh:

> In time they will become like the religions of Egypt and ancient Greece, and the only serious enquiry which should concern us is our proper attitude towards these doomed systems. What is the temper becoming the Christian mind, and what are the best methods, resulting from this temper, of approach to the non-Christian world.[226]

The same sense that the non-Christian systems were crumbling was, as already observed, present also at Edinburgh. That greater emphasis was given over to discussion of these religions does not demonstrate a new sense of their worth or endurance; that they had religious value, and needed study, was a theme of New York, as the opening speech mentions:

---

225 From the opening sermon of Bishop Westcott, Anglican Missionary Conference, 1894 (Spotiswoode, pp. 4–5). Despite this positive attitude we still find many at this date with quite contrary views, 'Hinduism is one of the most gigantic systems of grovelling idolatry that the world has seen; it is an irrational philosophy; it is a degrading sacerdotalism; and the most thought-stifling and progress-paralysing system of caste that ever existed' (a missionary from Agra at the same conference in ibid., p. 125).

226 Barrows in New York, I, p. 357.

Missionaries are keenly alive to the fact that some of the non-Christian faiths are keeping their place in the world because they minister in a measure to some of the needs of the human heart. They are preserved from utter condemnation by the great truths which, amid all errors and perversions, they undoubtedly contain. There is much beauty in Confucian morals. There are Christian elements, if not a Christian spirit, in the Buddhist ethics[....][227]

Then, further on: 'Knowledge of them is obligatory. We must know them to know man, to know ourselves, and to know God in all his revelations.'[228]

The speeches also suggest that Christianity may rediscover some of its own hidden truths by looking at the non-Christian religions, and that Christianity has in 'perfect form whatever they have in imperfect form.'[229] Even in the couple of speeches which dwell primarily upon the negative sides of the non-Christian religions, some elements of good are admitted in them.[230] There was thus little new to be said. The opinion that Christians now have the confidence to discuss the non-Christian religions fairly had been aired twenty-two years earlier.[231] Others had spoken of the need to study the non-Christian religions,[232] on adopting a positive attitude,[233] and of the need for native Christian Churches,[234] while the principles of fulfilment theology had already been discussed, such as the idea that non-Christian religions answer to the need of the human heart.[235] At the Pan-Anglican Congress, held but two years before Edinburgh, not a single speaker suggested that anything but a positive view be taken towards the non-Christian religions, and many supported fulfilment theology.[236]

One significant point about the report is that no single attitude towards the non-Christian religions prevails. The Fourth Commission's report, in

---

227   Ibid., p. 358.
228   Ibid., p. 360. This theme is often repeated (see, for instance, ibid., p. 363).
229   Jackson in ibid., p. 363. Other such positive attitudes can be seen of the non-Christian religions in various speeches, pp. 357 ff.
230   See Wynkoop and Purves in New York, I, pp. 363 f. and 374.
231   London, 1888, p. 61.
232   Spottiswoode, p. 75.
233   Ibid., pp. 323 f.
234   Ibid., pp. 455 ff.
235   New York, 1900, p. 358.
236   The full account of the meeting at which the non-Christian religions were discussed, 'Christian Revelation and the Similar Claims of Other Religions' can be found in *Pan-Anglican Congress, 1908*, volume III, Section B, pp. 2 ff.; see the appendix for the papers S. B. 1, S. B. 2, and S. B. 3.

summing up the general consensus, uses, as already observed, language designed to be all inclusive of the various points of view. There were, of course, those who thought the report was too liberal or too conservative. There is, nevertheless, a broadly identifiable consensus that allows us to speak of 'the attitude of the conference.' This careful assessment between the opposing schools of thought is seen as a strength of the report, the Church of England report *The Mystery of Salvation* noting that it 'had shown great wisdom in its balance.'[237]

In relation to the question of the further and deepening study of the non-Christian religions, it is worth noting the opinions at Edinburgh that can be seen as more progressive than those of the general consensus of the time. Thus, in terms of the praise given to the non-Christian religions, there were a few individuals who were more generous in their praises than any previously speaking at a missionary conference, but in terms of what people had been saying previously, the thoughts themselves were not new or original. As to what these individuals said, one correspondent to the Fourth Commission's report suggested that the Japanese religions were akin to Judaism, and Christianity was their fulfilment,[238] while the same view was expressed by another of Hinduism.[239] The Bishop of Ossory, who collated all the information on Japanese religions noted that the correspondents as a whole felt that there were definitely 'spiritual aspects' to the Japanese religions.[240] We may note that these positive notes were in a minority, so the suggestion by Sharpe that: 'The World Missionary Conference at Edinburgh in 1910 had given the 'fulfilment doctrine' an official *imprimatur,*'[241] might seem to go beyond the evidence. In particular we might dismiss the idea of any 'official *imprimatur*' in that the report stated, explicitly, that it was up to the individual to decide what he thought of the idea that the non-Christian religions represented a preparation for Christianity.[242] Sharpe, however, probably accurately represents the way the message of the Conference was interpreted. Even amongst those who took this message, we should remember that they did not necessarilly see the non-Christian religions as entirely good:

---

237   Op. cit., p. 152.
238   Ed. IV, p. 94.
239   Ibid., p. 187.
240   Ibid., p. 308.
241   Sharpe, p. 163.
242   Ed. IV, pp. 278–279.

Repeatedly one finds in non-Christian religions adumbrations of the great realities in Christianity, but they are only adumbrations. they are ideals and hopes expressing man's upward reach towards god, but the answer that comes back to this longing echo of the soul is usually vague and too much like a mere echo.[243]

There were also those who were ready to see something truly spiritual in these religions. This understanding would be enhanced by the growth of interest in mysticism, and how the mystical aspects of the non-Christian religions related to the mystical aspects of the Christian faith. Six years after the conference, writing in the *International Review of Mission*, Macnicol stated that the recent works of Underhill and Tagore, 'emphasized the kinship of this type of thought in East and West and the preciousness of much that is the common experience and confession of all devout men for whom, whatever the religion they profess, there have been unsealed the hidden functions.'[244]

The growing interest in things mystical was a feature of Western thought at this time, no doubt a reaction against the overt rationalism of the previous centuries, with the development of a scientific world-view. The study of mysticism in England must also be attributed, at least in part, to the prevalence of idealism as the key intellectual idea of the times, and the stress therefore laid upon the immanence of God.[245] Thus, by the extolling of experience over dogma, not only was the extent of Oriental mystical thought uncovered and appreciated, but the fact that mutual experience rather than conflicting metaphysics was stressed. The prevalence of interest in all things mystical thereby allowed a closer kinship to be seen between the world's religions. This also helps to shed light on the reasons why both Hindu theism and pantheism were seen as preparations to such an extent, at least from the point of view of the English missionaries, one stressing the close personal devotion to a particular deity, the latter stressing the very immanence of the divine and the unreality of things material as opposed to things spiritual, and speaking the very language of the idealists back in England. Amongst the influential proponents of mysticism in England, mention may be made of

---

243   Reischauer, 1928, p. 125.
244   Macnicol, p. 210.
245   Amongst the most famous proponents of this view were T. H. Green, Edward Caird, and F. H. Bradley at Oxford, the former having been the tutor of, amongst others, Charles Gore at Oxford (Quinton, in Nowell-Smith, p. 279). Though the ideology of idealism, so dominant in shaping the thought of these years, was now collapsing (ibid., p. 253).

272

Oliver Quick, Evelyn Underhill, and, of course, Dean Inge. In stressing this point, we might also note that such ideas would be antithetical to many evangelicals, who would still make up the bulk of missionaries, but who were also, nevertheless, led to embrace fulfilment theology.[246] While we may speak of a consensus of opinion at Edinburgh, there was also a diversity of opinion on other matters. While many supported fulfilment theology, there was no agreement on what it meant.

Before concluding this chapter it would be useful to note what is, perhaps, the most significant change that occurred in missionary thought after Edinburgh. This point, which dominated thought at the next great missionary conference in Jerusalem, 1928, was the recognition that it was not the Orient that was the threat to Christianity, but the changes that were taking place in the West. Writing on the twenty-fifth anniversary of Edinburgh, Oldham makes reference to the Jerusalem conference of 1928, noting that its most significant realization was that secularism was the real enemy.[247] There were no longer Western Christian nations and Eastern heathen nations; the old categories had collapsed.[248] However, although the West was now plagued by self doubt, some notions of superiority persisted. In an article written by Reischauer eighteen years after the conference, he sets out to demonstrate how the comparative study of religion shows Christianity to be superior, and ends up saying that it is very difficult to prove, and that what is important is that the missionary needs an absolute faith that he is right, and after all, Christianity is superior.[249]

Edinburgh can be seen as standing at the beginning of an era, previous to which there had been no question of looking at other cultures. After it, a world emerged in which it was difficult for the West to stay assured of its

---

246   That there is such a tension is something mentioned in the first chapter on the types of fulfilment theology, and will also be seen again in the next chapter where Farquhar's fulfilment theology is examined.

247   Oldham, 1935, p. 303.

248   Twenty five years after the Edinburgh conference Oldham observed that: 'The dividing line between Christian and non-Christian countries is tending to disappear' (Oldham, 1935, p. 301).

249   Reischauer, 1928, see especially pp. 132 f.

own position. While many individuals had asked such questions before, the arena of debate would be enlarged.[250]

Those at Edinburgh certainly saw themselves as more liberal than their predecessors. As it was put on the day, the difference between the old and new views was that, before, the non-Christian religions were seen as: "'Perfect specimens of absolute error and masterful pieces of hell's inventions which Christianity was simply called upon to oppose, uproot and destroy,'"[251] whereas, today, 'we seek dialogue with them, because we have a different view of what religion is.'[252] This dialogue is not what we might mean by the term today. The 'dialogue' in fulfilment theology is always one sided. However, Edinburgh must be seen as significant, and largely a sign of a major advance in the development of the thought of missionaries, and by extension of the entire church's attitude to the non-Christian religions. Yet in assessing its significance we should note that it was not radical, nor innovative, in what it said. In terms of the advancement of a positive attitude to the non-Christian religions in British thought, the Pan-Anglican Congress may be seen as giving a far more resounding endorsement to such views. Also, we should note, it did not, as has been generally understood, fully endorse fulfilment theology. The report of Commission Four only really endorsed the concept in relation to Hinduism and Pure Land Buddhism, and it was very cautious as to what meaning should be given to the idea of 'fulfilment'. Its main significance in this regard is not, I would suggest, in what it said, but rather in how it has been interpreted.

With regard to Farquhar's contribution to fulfilment theology, even taking on board our caveat about the not necessarily representative nature of

---

250   As an example of how far those at Edinburgh still held to many aspects of their own sectarian assumptions we may note the following. Particular mention is made of the fact that there are those, 'who come to church sit quietly and often reverently, but do not kneel down in prayer,' as if this fact were of importance, whereas today in the prayer book of the Church of North India the rubrics state that, 'in regard to standing, kneeling and sitting, local custom should be followed, leaving room for agreed experiments[....]
'Presbyters are encouraged to have a truly indigenous setting for worship as regards the arrangements of the place, the postures and clothes, the use of music, flowers, lamps, incense, bells, dance etc' (Rubric 1, in *The Lord's Supper*, of the Church of North India (New Delhi, International Society for the Propagation of Christian Knowledge, 1995)).

251   Sawyer, p. 271, quotation from Gairdner, p. 137.

252   Sawyer, p. 271.

Edinburgh's missionary correspondents, it still undermines concepts of him as a populariser of the idea. That acceptance of it, even if not in any fully formulated way, was widespread, is what the correspondence to the Edinburgh conference indicates.

7 J. N. Farquhar and the Crown of Hinduism

Farquhar's Thought Before 1913

Introduction

The previous chapters have shown the growth and spread of fulfilment theology in a number of different areas of British thought. We may categorize two main areas, one being the academic study of Comparative Religion, and the other being ecclesiastical thought, which finds practical expression in the missionary enterprise. Generally, they may be said to be, if not opposed, then not united. Most theologians and missionaries were not leading scholars of the non-Christian religions, while those whose field of expertise was in the non-Christian religions were not actively involved in missionary work.[1] These two strands of thought, missionary endeavour and academic thought, were to meet in John Nicol Farquhar. While earlier missionaries, such as Slater, had read Müller and Monier-Williams, they were not in themselves leading figures in the academic study of the non-Christian religions, and, conversely, academics such as Monier-Williams, while supporters of missions, were not themselves actively involved in the field.[2] With the advent of Farquhar's

---

1   The main exception to this rule is, of course, Rowland Williams, who combined a thorough knowledge of the non-Christian religions, at least Hinduism, with a thorough grounding in theology, though he, of course, was not involved in missionary work. Westcott and the members of the Cambridge Mission to Delhi may also be posited, but, while often capable or leading figures in their own fields, neither Westcott, nor the missions members can be cited as leading figures in the field of Comparative Religion.

2   Although, we may note that Monier-Williams had an apologetic view in mind, the introduction to his Sanskrit dictionary, for instance, states that it was written with the hope of it assisting in the attempt 'to communicate scriptural and scientific truth to the learned natives, through the medium of their classical language.' (Monier-Williams, 1976, p. ii. The phrase 'and scientific truth' is worth noting, for as we saw in the last chapter there was a definite correlation in the minds of many between 'western religion', i.e. Christianity, and western civilization, i.e. science and technology, and we will see in Farquhar's mind as well a link between the form western society and religion as being, in part at least, one whole package – though

contribution, fulfilment theology was to combine these two elements, and to become even more prevalent. While fulfilment theology had become well known to missionaries in India, and had received some sort of 'official' sanction at Edinburgh, it still awaited a definitive and widely known statement, which it found in Farquhar's *The Crown of Hinduism*. However, as has been seen, the ground-work had been laid long before Farquhar even went to India, and in his early years as a missionary he, too, supported the old antagonistic approach to Hinduism.[3]

Like Slater, Farquhar's work was predominantly amongst the educated higher caste Hindus,[4] and he too came to the realization that the old antagonistic attitude would not win the minds of these people.[5] This raises a question as to whether the more liberal, i.e. non-antagonistic, attitude that he came to adopt was due to a new found sympathy with Hinduism or whether the stance was purely for evangelistic purposes. This question, already raised in relation to Slater, can be gone into further when we have discussed Farquhar's fulfilment theology.

Another aspect of Farquhar's work is his fundamental belief in the necessity of using the methods of the science of comparative religion. This is a constant theme throughout his writings.[6] This in itself is not original.

---

this idea is, it would seem, partially, subconscious, but also partially conscious. Western society, in as far as it is seen to be based upon Christian principles is held to be superior, but at the same time there is a belief that Christianity can be detached from its unnecessary cultural baggage; Farquhar's views upon this will be seen below).

3   Farquhar himself admits to having made many harsh attacks upon Hinduism in his early days, of which he says he is now very much ashamed (Crown, p. 57).

4   Fulfil, pp. 142 and see section on Slater. In his early days in India (1891–1902) Farquhar was a professor, and for three years principal of the London Missionary Society College, Bhowanipur, Calcutta (EDMS, Farquhar # 154, p. 1).

5   For much the same reasons as had Slater, i.e., because, 'Hindus will not read such material[....]' (Crown, p. 35. See Fulfil, pp. 191 ff. and 209 ff., on the Hindu Revival).

6   He says of the work of earlier missionaries: 'Most missionaries have attempted a criticism of the religion they have antagonized; and have often thereby done signal service. Yet such criticism, though practically healthy, and in its main conclusions sound, has seldom been scientific enough to be of permanent value' (Farquhar, 1901, p. 369). Farquhar himself was a brilliant academic, his method was primarily concerned with the historical aspects of how thought developed, Sharpe says of him: 'As a historical scholar Dr. Farquhar was mainly interested in tracing the historical development of this doctrine [moksha], and had little or no use for any attempt to understand all its ramifications as held at present' (Sharpe, 1963, p. ix).

Fulfilment theology sprang from the nineteenth-century's greatest scholars, and, as we have observed, Slater was conversant with both Monier-Williams and Müller. Farquhar was a more thorough scholar than was Slater, and, unlike Monier-Williams and Müller, actually attempted to expound fulfilment theology at length, rather than as just a divergence to his main work.[7] Worthy of note is the fact that, whilst a missionary, Farquhar was also one of the great scholars of Hinduism of his day, making his work not just significant as missionary apologetics, but as a part of the growing knowledge and openness to the non-Christian religions that was a feature of Western thought.[8] Thus the development of dialogue, and respect for the non-Christian faiths, was no longer confined to academics and the intelligentsia back in England, but the actual missionaries took the lead and initiative in these matters, something that is not often remembered to day.[9]

Farquhar was brought up and served his missionary time in India as a Non-Conformist, but converted to Anglicanism in 1923[10].

	He became the first professor of comparative religion at Manchester, and was awarded a D.Litt. from Oxford for his book *Modern Religious Movements in India*, (Sharpe, 1963, p. 65) which, although published in 1915, is still a standard work of reference on the Hindu renaissance today. It is worth noting that Farquhar had never been formally trained in theology, and felt this as a great lack (Fulfil, p. 125, reference to A. J. Appasamy, 'Dr J. N. Farquhar', *Young Men of India*, XLI: 9, September 1929, p. 685).
7	Of course, it could be said that Maurice expanded the fulfilment theology at length, but as already noted his knowledge of the non-Christian faiths was not great. (See section on Maurice).
8	Farquhar considered the intelligent study of Hinduism to be essential to the Indian Missionary (See Farquhar, 1905).
9	Other missionaries, most notably, S. Stokes, C. F. Andrews and Bernard Lucas – who were really in the generation following Farquhar, though partially active in India at the same time – went further in their appreciation and admiration of Hindu religion and culture. They adopted the dress of the Hindu sannyāsi and lived amongst the people, following the Indian way of life (see Chaturvedi and Sykes, pp. 71 ff.). This theme will be developed in the next chapter.
10	Sharpe, 1963, p. 11.

Mention has been made above to the fact that in his early years in India Farquhar was a harsh critic of Hinduism. Indeed, the relationship of Christianity to Hinduism had probably not been of great concern to him before he became a missionary. He was not a theology student,[11] Sharpe noting that it seems that he had little interest in theological controversy,[12] and Fairbairn, his tutor at Oxford, described him as, 'a simple-minded active Christian worker.'[13] According to Farquhar's own testimony, 'Under the influence of modern ideas, I lost my childish belief in Christianity, while I was still young, and it was only to faith in deeper things that I fought my way during undergraduate days.'[14] This might, though, mean only that he had come to accept the findings of the so-called higher criticisms, as he does say that he was still working out his own beliefs when he came to India.[15] It appears from his candidature papers for the London Missionary Society, that he had read at least some of Monier-Williams' work,[16] but there is no reason to suppose that he had read Müller or Maurice, or had picked up on a more liberal approach to the non-Christian religions. This would correspond with Fairbairn's assessment of him, and Sharpe says of his missionary candidature papers that, 'they are brief, and from the evangelical point of view perfectly orthodox, making use of conventional evangelical vocabulary of religious experience. They are not the work of a man who had learned to think either philosophically or theologically on matters of religion, and accord well with Fairbairn's estimate of him.'[17]

If we then ask when Farquhar adopted the principles of fulfilment theology, it is certainly while he was in India. Sharpe suggests he was

---

11   He did, however, take firsts in both Classical Moderations (1887) and Literal Humanities (1889) at Oxford (Fulfil, p. 123).

12   Fulfil, p. 122.

13   Fairbairn, letter to Thompson, 27/10/1890, from the London Missionary Society archives, quoted in Fulfil, p. 127.

14   EDMS, Farquhar # 154, p. 39.

15   Ibid.

16   Fulfil, p. 123. It would seem fair to assume that his adoption of fulfilment theology did not spring from this source, as it was not until ten years after he arrived in India that he seemed to pick up on these ideas.

17   Ibid., p. 131.

introduced to these ideas between 1891 and 1902,[18] and he sees Farquhar's first approaches to fulfilment theology in a series of articles written in 1903 for the *Inquirer*.[19] In the fourth article, in the September edition, we see 'for the first time in Farquhar's written work, the concept of 'fulfilment.''[20] The idea is only briefly mentioned. It is, however, worthwhile to quote from it at length:

> Now Christianity is the only faith in all the world which is purely spiritual and essentially ethical on the one hand, and on the other offers us historical facts of the largest significance and the mightiest emotional power, which fully satisfy the demands of the human heart for sacrifice and an object of worship more imaginable and more comprehensible than the God of the Vedānta. The life of the Son of God on earth satisfies at once the instinct that has produced the avatars of Hinduism and the idols of all the earth; for the story of the life in the Gospels appeals to the feelings and imagination more completely than any mythical incarnation or any idol of stone or wood. And his death on the Cross gives us a sacrifice which satisfies the human desire to make atonement for sin, and thereby explains in a satisfactory manner all the animal and human sacrifices that have ever taken place on this earth of ours.
>
> Thus the belief, that Jesus Christ, the Son of God, died for our sins on Calvary, produces a religion which satisfies the modern mind, and which also proves to be the fulfilment and goal of all the religions of the world, the crudest as well as the loftiest.[21]

A number of common themes of fulfilment theology are to be found here, i.e., of seeing Christianity as spiritual and ethical, and that it possesses the 'mightiest emotional power.'[22] Also, as Sharpe says, it 'is essentially an evolutionist position,'[23] and there is the concept of Christianity satisfying the deepest needs of the human heart.[24] Farquhar's main concern here is showing how Hinduism as an existing entity responds to the innate needs of the human heart. The same emphasis is found in another article of Farquhar's of the next

---

18   Sharpe, 1963, p. 113. Sharpe says Farquhar adopted the fulfilment hypothesis between 1902 and 1913 (Fulfil, p. 23). Certainly there is no trace of the idea in his writings of 1901, and by 1910 he had written a number of articles expounding the idea, and although he does not publish his fully worked out account till 1913, it contains nothing new in essence from his earlier works, and is essentially on much the same lines as Slater's works of years earlier.

19   Fulfil, pp. 187 ff.

20   Ibid., p. 189.

21   Farquhar in *The Inquirer*, V: i., September 1903, p.6, quoted in Fulfil, pp. 189–190.

22   The significance of which points we shall see below.

23   Fulfil, p. 190.

24   See e.g., Boyle, p. 67, and Slater, 1903, p. 214.

year, *The Age and Origin of the Gita*,[25] in which he says in conclusion, and again I shall quote at some length:

> The book [the Gītā] is, then, to be read as the spiritual autobiography of Hinduism. It expresses, as no other book does, what the Hindu feels and thinks. Now the chief feeling that finds expression in the *Gita* is the desire for an incarnate Saviour: that is the chief thing to be learnt from the poem. The Hindu mind calls for a Saviour, a Saviour incarnate for the good of man, incarnate to give a clear revelation of the will of God. The definiteness of the idea and passion with which it is urged stand out in extraordinary contrast with the baselessness of the Krishna story. How startling it is to find that there is not a fragment of foundation for it, yet the belief grew up, and was not only expressed by a few thinkers, but was passionately welcomed by the myriads of people of this land? Clearly, this brings us into the heart of a very large problem. How are we to explain the rise of such a faith? What conclusion shall we draw from it? Shall we conclude that the Hindu people were driven by some insane desire to imagine a baseless phantom? Or shall we regard the picture of the man-god in the *Gita* as an objectification of the deepest needs of the Hindu religious spirit, and, therefore, of untold significance? Shall we regard the desire for the man-god as an empty longing with nothing corresponding thereto in the realities of the universe, or shall we conclude that the Hindu mind has here expressed what it requires, and that He who made the Hindu mind will supply the need? If we take the former alternative, we lose ourselves in absolute hopelessness and scepticism. If we are to make religion in any sense real, then the creation of the Hindu mind must correspond in one way or another with reality. What is the reality which is adumbrated by the Krishna of the *Gita*?[26]

The main thesis of Farquhar's later work is found here, that Christ fulfils the innate needs of the human heart. Hinduism is, for Farquhar, explained by these needs as will be seen below

From the few clues we have here, it seems that Farquhar had accepted at least the basic ideas of fulfilment theology by late 1903. By 1910, in respect of his contribution to the Edinburgh conference, and in his articles published that year, he had already formulated a well developed form of fulfilment theology. Indeed, one of these articles, anticipating his later work, was itself entitled 'The Crown of Hinduism'.[27] There is little of interest in terms of the development of the theory of fulfilment theology in these items, and as this chapter does not intend to give an historical account of Farquhar's

---

25   In fact Farquhar has been described as one of the most important and sympathetic missionary interpreters of the Gītā (see Sharpe, 1985, pp. 96 ff.).

26   Op. cit., p. 925.

27   See also his 'The Greatness of Hinduism', his two articles entitled 'Christianity in India', and especially his 'Christ and the Religions of the World', in the *Student Movement*, XII, 1910, pp. 195 ff.

theological development no useful purpose will be served by analysing these works.

One further important question remains as to Farquhar's adoption of fulfilment theology, and that is his source or sources for these ideas. Sharpe suggests Slater as a possible influence, but admits that we do not, and can never, know his influences.[28] Certainly Farquhar knew of Slater's work,[29] as well of that of Kellett, Banerjea, Monier-Williams and Müller.[30] Also, as we saw in the first chapter, such ideas were becoming commonplace, certainly in Indian missionary circles, by the end of the nineteenth-century, so it would probably be naïve to assume that Farquhar's fulfilment theology can be traced to any one person. Farquhar says that both Kellett and Slater are 'on the right lines,'[31] though, as we noted earlier, he does criticize earlier missionary critiques of Hinduism for lacking sufficient academic vigour.[32]

Having briefly considered the development of Farquhar's theory of fulfilment theology, it would now be useful to turn to examine in detail his classic treatment of the subject, *The Crown of Hinduism*. Mention will also be made to the details he supplied to Commission Four of the Edinburgh conference.

---

28   Fulfil, p. 190.
29   Sharpe tells us that a copy of Farquhar's own copy of his paper 'Missionary Study of Hinduism' contains a reference to Slater, Kellett, and Banerjea (Fulfil, p. 208, fn 8. Sharpe tells us that in the reference to Banerjea the name of the book Farquhar mentions by him is lost, however, I would suggest that it is most likely to be *The Arian Witness*).
30   He refers to Müller's works in reference to his study of the science of comparative religion (Farquhar, 1904, p. 372 ff).
31   Farquhar, 1905, p. 177, fn.
32   See Farquhar, 1901, p. 369.

The Crown of Hinduism

Background and Methodology

i) Introduction

According to Farquhar:

> Down to some ten or twelve years ago a considerable number of Christian books published in India contained harsh judgements, denunciatory language, and, here and there, statements that were seriously inaccurate. But that is now almost altogether a thing of the past[....] Hindus simply will not read such material, and they mark the man who is guilty and will have nothing to do with him.[33]

If Farquhar's estimation is correct, then Slater's major work on fulfilment theology, *The Higher Hinduism*, stands at the beginning of this period of change, and in many ways this is probably a fair estimation. At around that time, the general consensus of missionary thought in India had swung in favour of this approach, so that, in the early years of this century, missionaries were either recognizing the good, or at least realizing that they could not condemn out of hand the bad, as they saw it, in Hinduism.[34] Farquhar's *The Crown of Hinduism* thus came onto the scene at a time when the attitude that he represented, of understanding towards the non-Christian religions, had already been steadily gaining strength for some time, and had become, certainly in Indian missionary circles at least, the dominant view, and what was therefore needed was some solidification of this view. We could, perhaps, style his book the 'crown' of Protestant liberal missionary thought.[35]

---

33   Crown, p. 35.
34   The thought as expressed in the missionary conferences of the late nineteenth and early twentieth-centuries that has been considered in the previous chapters also point to this conclusion, where I have suggested the crucial axial period for the change of thought occurs around the mid to late 1890s.
35   That Slater provided the foundations for Farquhar's popularity is something that we have already discussed in an earlier section, and that all Farquhar did was to come along at the right time after others had made fulfilment theology acceptable and generally known. *The Crown of Hinduism* being the first work to set out these ideas systematically once they had gained general assent, and so rather than propounding anything new, the book's popularity was due to the fact that it set out ideas that people already knew and accepted, but did not yet have a widely disseminated

Mention has already been made to the influence of neo-Hinduism on the development of fulfilment theology, and it should be mentioned that Farquhar is careful to show that he is not setting out to attack Hinduism.[36] Indeed, in his Introduction, he quotes a number of Hindus who attack the old institution of Hinduism,[37] a method he uses throughout the book to show that he is in accord with the thought of Indian Nationalism. He presents the choice quite starkly, saying that: 'The time has come when the Indian patriot must choose between tradition and the health of his country.'[38]

This theme, that much of Hindu society and culture is holding her back from the progress she needs is, as shall be seen, one of the main themes to which Farquhar returns again and again in his analysis of Hinduism and his case for Christianity. These ideas are already familiar to us from the works of previous fulfilment theologians.[39]

One final point worth noting in this introduction is that one of the most familiar images of fulfilment theology, that runs through the works of Indian writers from Banerjea to Slater, sacrifice, is barely mentioned by Farquhar. He notes its importance but says that not enough research has been done in the area for it to be properly dealt with.[40] This shows the basic difference between himself and previous fulfilment theologians, for while they immediately pounce upon this area, which, it must be admitted, provides one of the best examples available of what fulfilment theology needs for its argument, Farquhar stays his hand as all the background research of an historical nature, which takes up a good deal of the book, is not available to him. He does give it a brief mention at the end of the book as one of many ideas within Hinduism that are examples of man's innate religious need finding an expression in the Hindu system.

---

manifesto.

36   See, for instance, Crown, pp. 33 ff.
37   Ibid., pp. 36 ff.
38   Ibid., p. 457.
39   See, e.g., Miller, 1878, pp. 21 ff. Who heavily emphasizes that only Christianity could equip a nation to deal with the modern world.
40   Ibid., p. 3.

ii) Biblical and Patristic Sources

Farquhar uses a number of Biblical verses to build his case upon, which he strings together to form an argument for his case:

> we hold Him [Jesus] to be
> 'the light which lighteth every man;'[41]
> and we believe that even in savage minds God
> left himself not without witness;'[42]
> and that the very lowest men
> 'show the pith of the law written in their hearts.'[43]
> Thus through the grossest religion there is a path to God.
> Christianity frankly acknowledges that a man may be acceptable to God in any religion.
> This is stated in the clearest possible language by Peter:
> 'Of a truth I perceive that God is no respecter of persons: but in every nation he that feareth him, and worketh righteousness, is acceptable to him.[44] [45]

Worth noting is that Farquhar does not use fulfilment theology's most famous quotation[46] here, but he does refer to it later on,[47] when he draws an analogy between the Law of Israel, Greek philosophy, and Hindu thought, suggesting that as the former have both been seen as 'preparations' for Christianity, so it will be with Hinduism. So he quotes Clement of Alexandria saying: 'Philosophy tutored the Greeks for Christ as the Law did the Hebrews.'[48] Going on to say: 'Thus it will be with India.'[49] He seems to see a general comparison between the three traditions, and remarks 'the Hindu Law and Jewish Law stand on a par.'[50] This is only in their general form. In other ways: 'The Law of Moses differs very seriously in many ways from The Law

---

41   John I: 9.

42   Acts XIV: 17.

43   Romans II: 15.

44   'Acts 10: 34, 35. Cf. also Paul's words, Rom. 10, 12' (Crown, p. 27, fn. 4).

45   Ibid., p. 27.

46   Mt. V: 17.

47   Crown., p. 53. Though we may note that in his Edinburgh conference correspondence he made the point: 'Christ's own attitude to Judaism ought to be our own attitude to other faiths, even if the gap be far greater and the historical connections absent' (EDMS, Farquhar # 154, p. 17).

48   Ibid., quoting Stromateis, i. 28.

49   Ibid.

50   Ibid., p. 59.

of Manu.'[51] The comparison is both that each is a set of rules, compared to Christ's precepts,[52] and also that each can provide a preparation for Christianity; but Hinduism and the religions of Greece and Rome differ from Judaism in that they 'could not be the starting-point for the religion of the world.'[53] The major flaw, as Farquhar sees it, in Hinduism, is that its ethical system is not very strong, and this point will be a main theme in Farquhar's argument for why Christianity fulfills Hinduism, as will be seen.

iii) Farquhar's Method in The Crown of Hinduism

Farquhar believed in the need for a systematic and thoroughly academic approach, which, being based in his own day, meant an historical approach. Reference has already been made to an early article of Farquhar's criticizing previous attempts at fulfilment theology for not being sufficiently grounded in the historical critical method. Of the application of this to the comparative study of religion Farquhar says, 'the science has reached great proportions, and the results already attained are of inestimable value for thought.'[54] To Farquhar's these results include:

> The scientific consciousness which recognizes the unity of the religious life of man, the evolution hypothesis through which the most varied and seemingly most contradictory phenomena are ranged in intelligible order within the bounds of that unity, and the eager passion to know how the early tribes of men thought about God and sought to approach Him, provided the conditions required; while the necessary material, viz. information about the religions of the world, became available through the unveiling of the ancient languages of India, Persia, Babylonia, Assyria, and Egypt, and through the opening of communications with all the inhabited lands.[55]

The tremendous self-belief of the Victorian and early Edwardian world-view shines through clearly in this passage; western knowledge, scientific method, and progress are opening up all the world and bringing everything with which they come in contact under the sway of their own overarching paradigm. This is important to remember when looking at Farquhar's work, that he still lives in the world of Maurice and Monier-Williams where there has yet been

---

51   Ibid., p. 58.
52   This point will be discussed elsewhere.
53   Crown, p. 53.
54   Crown, p. 13.
55   Ibid., p. 12.

nothing to shatter the confidence of the western nations concerning their own unrivalled dominance of world affairs, and, by extension thereby, of their own patterns of thought. This will be seen in Farquhar's work where all the structures of the Hindu system are 'wrong', and need to be replaced by the 'correct' Christian (i.e. western) forms. Yet these ideas are not matters of pure a priori assertion but are based in Farquhar's case upon a careful study of the most advanced academic thought of his day.[56]

The importance of the evolutionary principle for fulfilment theology has already been stressed, and for Farquhar it was essential that this principle should be backed up by academic research. So, too, with the unity of man's religious life, where the nineteenth-century study of religion 'has shown us how frequently parallel beliefs and practices have been developed in different nations quite independently.'[57] The importance of this point for fulfilment theology should be immediately apparent as it was a central concern from Maurice onwards,[58] that the prevalence of certain practices across the world will support the hypothesis that they are really responses to an innate human need.

Having noted some of the essential features for fulfilment theology that Farquhar takes from the comparative study of religion, it should be noted that he observes that many writers in the field are wary about rating the religions in relation to one another,[59] suggesting that many feel that this falls outside the limits of the science, and is a matter for personal opinion. Certainly, the field had moved to a more neutral standpoint by Farquhar's day, where the religions would be looked at purely as technical data rather than as spiritual phenomena.[60] While some scholars, such as Frazer, were not Christian, many more, such as Rhys Davids, were, and while their books on Comparative Religion might not contain any comparative ratings of Christianity and the

---

56   The attitude of the Western world to the countries of the Orient is one that has already been dealt with at greater length in the last chapter, and so need not detain us here.

57   Crown, p. 14.

58   See Boyle, e.g., pp. 172 f.

59   Crown, p. 15.

60   In his *Comparative Religion: A History* Sharpe refers to the tension between the 'scientific' and 'religious' approaches, the former 'was concerned to apply a particular method to a body of data – data taken as a rule to refer only to the workings of the human mind' (Sharpe, 1991, p. 144), the latter 'had as its essential point of departure a stance of faith in the actual existence of a transcendent order of being' (ibid.). The changes are perhaps most clearly seen in chapters 4–7.

non-Christian faiths, this does not mean that they did not see Christianity as a superior religion.[61] That Farquhar was more sectarian and did attempt to use Comparative Religion to show Christianity's supremacy was still no bar to his later holding the Chair of Comparative Religion at Manchester.

iv) Farquhar's Standpoint

Having noted Farquhar's beliefs about what the science of religion had proved, it would be useful now to mention some general principles which he took from this as practical guides for his examination of Hinduism and Christianity. These concepts will all be familiar from the works of previous fulfilment theologians.

First, there is the principle of evolution which means that people need to 'upgrade' from 'lower' to 'higher' religions:[62]

> Take the case of a savage who has been living a faithful life, in accordance with his light, in a course cannibalistic religion. He hears Muhammadanism preached, feels the reasonableness of monotheism, the pressure of the doctrine of judgement on his conscience, the high moral value of the ethics of Islam. But, for various reasons, he continues his old life and the practice of cannibalism. What is the inevitable result? The religion through which he formerly received help is no longer of any use to him. He has seen truth and has refused to obey it. He is no longer a religious man.[63]

Along with this goes the necessary belief, already revealed in Farquhar's use of Biblical passages, that all religions are at heart good, 'The condition under which a man reaches God is utter sincerity, the turning of his whole soul towards the light, the frank acceptance of truth into his heart, straightforward obedience to *the very highest he knows.*'[64] Despite these germs of good the non-Christian religions are inherently flawed: 'In the philosophy and theistic theology of Hinduism there are many precious truths enshrined; but, as we shall see, the ancient Hindu system, within which they appeared, effectually prevents them from leavening the people.'[65] These imperfect religions have

---

61   Frazer declined the chair of Comparative Religion at Manchester because his views 'would make it difficult for him to teach men preparing for the Christian ministry' (Sharpe, 1991, p. 133). Rhys-Davids, however, subsequently took the post.

62   See especially Monier-Williams, e.g., 1875, pp. 2 ff.

63   Crown, pp. 27–8.

64   Crown, p. 27. Italics my own.

65   Ibid., pp. 50–1.

a place, for in God's scheme, nations need a preparation, or training, before they are ready for the full and final revelation,[66] 'God's method of revelation is not the presentation, once and for all, of a complete system of truth expressed in a book from all eternity, but a gradual and historical process.'[67] We may note, however, that Farquhar in the Edinburgh papers, where he discusses this, says that he believes that the non-Christian religions are human products.[68] The ideas he is propounding here, however, suggest, along the lines of Rowland Williams' or Müller's thought, that God is actively involved in the non-Christian religions, guiding and inspiring them upwards in an activity of continuing revelation.[69]

To Farquhar, remembering the passage quoted above in which he says that the science of religion has shown the truths of evolution and the unity of man's religious experience, this is the natural process of development, and so he contrasts Buddhism and Christianity by pointing out that while the latter accepted and incorporated the Jewish scriptures, thus building upon what had gone before, the former, by way of contrast, does not incorporate the Ṛig Veda or Upanishads.[70] Here Farquhar is guilty of a certain amount of inconsistency, as, for him, the Hindu scriptures will not be incorporated into a canon of Indian Christian writings.[71]

While the old religions can be built upon they have, nevertheless, done as much as they can on their own, and therefore they need a new input from

---

66   This presents a movement from the position of K. M. Banerjea, who ended his book noting the 'preparations' for Christianity as he saw them, 'These are facts. We do not prescribe any deduction from these facts. We only chronicle the facts. We leave the deduction in the hand's [sic] of the reader' (K. M. Banerjea, 1875, p. 236).

67   Crown, p. 51. Farquhar continues this passage by using the gradual revelation to Israel as an example of this process, 'The simple beginnings of the faith of Israel are laid before us in the book of Genesis; they grow before our eyes in the narratives of the other books of Moses; and they find still richer development in the Prophets and Psalms. But even in them God's will is not completely revealed. Hence, to Jesus, the religion of Israel was given by God, but not given in permanency. It was God's instrument for the training of Israel. He came to crown it by transforming it into the religion for all men, and to crown its knowledge of God by revealing Him as the Father of men' (ibid.). Following on from this passage, Farquhar goes on to show first how the philosophy of Greece and Rome was claimed as a preparation for the Gospel, and then to suggest that the same is true of Hinduism.

68   EDMS, Farquhar # 154, pp. 13–14.

69   More will be said on this problem below.

70   Ibid., pp. 51–2.

71   Fulfil, p. 326. This matter will be discussed below.

outside, i.e. of Christ. To make this point Farquhar uses the symbol of death and resurrection. He says of Hinduism:

> This hard unyielding system must fall into the ground and die, before the aspirations and the dreams of Hindu thinkers and ascetics can be set free to grow in health and strength so as to bear fruit in the lives of Hindu villagers. Hinduism must die in order to live. It must die into Christianity.[72]

A related point, not taken per se directly from comparative religion but showing the same regard for impartiality, is the desire always to judge by the best examples of another religion: 'Like Hinduism, Christianity must be judged by its principles, not by the vicious lives of those who refuse to obey it.'[73] Going side by side with this is the familiar plea from previous writers that it is ideal, not actual, Christianity that must be understood as the fulfilling principle:

> When we say that Christianity is the Crown of Hinduism, we do not mean Christianity as it is lived in any nation, nor Christianity as it is defined and elaborated in detail in the creed, preaching, ritual, liturgy, and discipline of any single church, but Christianity as it springs living and creative from Christ Himself. Christ is the head of the whole Church, not of any one denomination. Christ is human, not Western. Far less is He English, Scottish, American, or German.[74]

The need for such a statement is something that has been dwelt upon previously and need not be reiterated.

Farquhar believed that humanity was heading towards a world culture, wherein 'human life has entered upon a new stage.... We are rapidly approaching the moment when every piece of new knowledge will be absorbed by every nation as soon as it is acquired, and when the experience of any one nation, whether in industry, in art, in morality, or in religion, will be at once appreciated, caught up, used the world over.'[75] This view echoes

---

72   Crown, p. 51.
73   Ibid., p. 119. We may note as an aside here, that in many ways this is very often the attitude of comparative religion which mostly deals only with texts, the ideals, as it were, of a religion, rather than with the actual working out of these ideals – a topic broached in the first chapter.
74   Ibid., p. 59.
75   Ibid., p. 12. Needless to say Farquhar's vision has not yet transpired, and the events of the following year would throw such thoughts out of the window for many years. Of course, in many ways, we are closer to such a situation to-day though personally

the belief of Müller and Miller that a new world religion harmonizing all of man's old religions will be created.[76] This carries the assumption that it will be a modern, that is to say, Westernized, culture that will be created, and, together with Slater,[77] Farquhar believed that the demands of this new world order 'can only be met by Christianity.'[78] Farquhar's book can be seen as attempting to prove that only Christianity is capable of providing the moral and spiritual fibre needed by a society to face the demands of the world.

Farquhar argues that the Hindu system is inherently flawed,[79] and that while there are 'gleams of light' these do not justify keeping the Hindu system as it is.[80] This is not, Farquhar claims, destruction, but purification:

> True, Christ passes everything through His refiners fire, in order that the dross, which Hindus know so well, may pass away; but the gold will then shine brighter.... Hindus, like His own people, imagine Him a destroyer; but, when the period of pain and strife has passed, they too will see that He is not the Destroyer but the Restorer of the national heritage, and all the gleams of light that make Hindu faith and worship so fascinating to the student find in Him their explanation and consummation.[81]

Reading Farquhar one wonders, though, exactly what will be left? Certainly he praises the intention of every Hindu custom, but the actuality and practice is always to him so wholly perverted that it must pass away. In previous chapters we have noted the connection of these ideas to the growth of Indian Christian theology, but in this work Farquhar seems to be sweeping away anything distinctively Indian. More will be said on this below.

Finally, we may quote Farquhar on the principle of fulfilment itself:

> Every true motive which in Hinduism has found expression in unclean, debasing, or unworthy practices finds in Him fullest exercise in work for the downtrodden, the

---

I find it doubtful if such innovations as mass media and the Internet are likely to bring such a world order into being despite the stupendous claims made for them – although editing this text for publication three years later I must say that I have become more convinced of the way technology is making the world a much smaller place, though there are still many places and peoples, the underprivileged in the world, who are increasingly being marginalized in our technology led society.

76   See sections on Müller and Miller.
77   Slater, 1882, pp. 10 f.
78   Crown, p. 33.
79   Ibid., p. 446.
80   Ibid., p. 456.
81   Ibid., pp. 54–5.

ignorant, the sick, and the sinful. In Him is focused every ray of light that shines in Hinduism. He is the Crown of the faith of India.[82]

v) Farquhar's Attitude to Hinduism

Farquhar's beliefs about the inevitable decline of Hinduism are similar to those expressed by Miller, Slater, and the various views of those at the Edinburgh Conference. According to Farquhar, 'Hinduism is being disintegrated. This is the great fact which has to be realized. The ancient religion of India is breaking up.'[83]

The reasons he cites are the same as those found in the earlier writers referred to above, being both the influence of Christianity and the whole range of social, educational, and political ideas and reforms of the Western world:

> Christian teaching by itself introduces new ideas into the Hindu mind; and, in so far as these are wider, deeper, more ethical, more spiritual than the ideas of Hinduism, they do undoubtedly weaken Hindu faith[....]
> The forces that are in the main destructive of Hinduism stand out quite clear. Everything Western brings with it an atmosphere which is most inimical to the old faith. Modern education tells with incalculable force on every student's mind. English literature, modern science, modern inventions, European business methods and the principles of Government action in India, are all disintegrating agents of great efficiency.[84]

Also, while the nature of the Hindu revival had decisively changed course by Farquhar's day,[85] he is still keen to point out that many Hindus are also ready to criticize the faith of their fathers, and, indeed, he says, 'no one delivers such direct or such deadly attacks on Hinduism as the educated Hindu does.'[86]

---

82   Ibid., p. 458.
83   Ibid., p. 42.
84   Ibid., p. 35–6.
85   Reference has been made in the first chapter to the Christ-centred, anti-caste, anti-idolatry stance of many of the reformers of the middle of the nineteenth-century, and how, by the turn of the twentieth-century, the influence of Rāmakrishna and his disciple Vivekānanda, as well as of Annie Besant and the theosophists, had turned to a defence of all aspects of traditional Hinduism. Also there was the rise of a more militant Hindu Nationalism which sought to defend all things Hindu/Indian – terms which they felt to be virtually synonymous.
86   Crown, p. 36.

To substantiate this claim Farquhar goes on to quote from a number of Hindu authors at length,[87] noting their attacks upon various aspects of the traditional Hindu religious schema. That these views will not find universal acceptance amongst educated Hindus he concedes, saying of these writings that many will look 'upon them as treachery, a playing into the hands of the enemy.'[88] The reason for this defence, Farquhar believes, is because Hinduism 'has proved itself through many centuries a really living religion. Men have believed in it and lived by it. It has controlled their thinking and their social and family life, and has produced a characteristic morality.'[89] Emphaszing what he believed to be its positive aspects, he believed that it has 'gleams of light' and that these could be said to represent certain innate qualities:

> It is the dim consciousness of the presence of this basis of spirituality and truth in the worst parts of the religion that makes the educated Hindu burn with righteous indignation against the Christian condemnation of Hinduism. He has felt the power of these things in his own life; and therefore, although he is as conscious as the Christian is of the folly and immorality of many of the practices, he feels it is most seriously unjust to condemn all without qualification.[90]

As noted above, Farquhar did not believe that what he saw as these 'gleams of light' justify leaving Hinduism as it is,[91] and speaking of Vivekānanda he says:

> These apologists of Hinduism point to the gleams of spiritual light visible in customary Hinduism[....] They explain that these truths are the real source and Origin of the religion, and that the immoralities and superstitions, the existence of which everyone acknowledges, are later accretions and corruptions. The religion itself is altogether holy and pure.[92] Therefore, they argue, nothing must be lost[....]

---

87   Ibid., pp. 36–42.

88   Ibid., p. 452.

89   Ibid., p. 446.

90   Ibid., p. 451. In fact Farquhar continues this quote to attack indiscriminate missionary assaults upon Hinduism by saying: '[....] Nor can there be any doubt that the Hindu is right. The missionary who fails to acknowledge the presence of these right ideas amidst all the vice, cruelty, and superstition does not deserve to get the ear of the educated classes.'

91   Ibid., p. 456.

92   This defence of Hinduism which Farquhar is criticizing may to many ears sound like his own defence of Christianity, saying that it must only be judged by Jesus' principle,s not by its actual manifestation in any specific culture or tradition.

Our analysis of the family, karma, caste, and idolatry[93] has conclusively shown that this reasoning is altogether mistaken. It is the very character of the Hindu system itself that is at fault. It is the character of the Hindu system that is at fault. It is the very laws of the Hindu family that require to be laid aside[....][94]

Farquhar's argument is against Hinduism, and in favour of what he sees as the needs of India.[95] He sees the politicians and reformers of India as recognizing the need for this reform,[96] in contrast, as he sees it, to reactionary religious traditionalists such as Vivekānanda. In relation to this we may note in passing,

---

93   Farquhar's analysis of these conceptions will be looked at below

94   Crown, pp. 455–6. It is worth noting the passage from Vivekānanda that Farquhar was explicitly referring to here, 'To the reformers [that is to say Hindu reformers] I will point out, I am a greater reformer than any of them. They want to reform only little bits. I want root and branch reform. Where we differ is exactly in the method. Theirs is the method of destruction, mine is that of construction.* I do not believe in reform. I believe in growth[....] I cannot join any one of these condemning societies. Why condemn? There are evils in every society; everybody knows it; he can stand upon a platform and give us a harangue on the evils of Hindu society. Every educated foreigner who comes in globe-trotting takes a vanishing railway view of India, and lectures most learnedly on the awful evils in India. We admit it. Everybody can show what evil is, but he is a friend of mankind who finds a way out of the difficulty.

'[....] Most of the reforms that have been agitated for during the last century have been ornamental. Every one of these reforms only touches the first two castes, and no other. The question of widow marriage would not touch seventy per cent of the Indian women, and all such questions only reach the higher classes of Indian people who are educated, mark you, at the expense of the masses. Every effort of these classes has been spent in cleaning their own houses, making themselves nice and looking pretty before foreigners. That is no reformation. You must go down to the basis of the thing, to the very roots. That is what I call radical reformation. Put the fire there and let it burn upwards and make an Indian nation' (Vivekānanda, *Speeches and Writings of Swāmi Vivekānanda*, pp. 540, 542, and 543, in Crown, pp. 455–6).

*It is a point worth noting that Vivekānanda sees himself as conducting his reforms in the same way that Farquhar does, not destructing, but constructing. However, as I noted above, it does not seem clear how far Farquhar is building upon Hinduism as he seems to want to destroy everything Hindu, leaving only the desire for God which he sees as lying behind the Hindu system; it does not seem to be the 'fulfilment' that Jesus sought to bring to Judaism where not 'one jot or one tittle shall in no wise pass from the law' (Mt. V: 18).

95   See Crown, e.g., pp. 35 ff., 105 ff., and 457. This point is made over and over again in Farquhar.

96   Ibid., p. 446. See also references in previous footnote.

for this is one of Farquhar's central themes which will be looked at later on, that he believes 'the whole monastic movement of modern India is already in full decay,'[97] because, says Farquhar: 'He [the Sadhu] is altogether out of touch and sympathy with the large questions and mighty activities which are agitating India to-day: Education, Social Reform, Religious Reform, Politics, Economic Progress.'[98]The contemplative life appears to Farquhar's mind to be of no value; his sole interest is with social and political matters.[99] This point is one that affects his whole approach to Hinduism, which is, or at least was perceived, to be more passive compared to 'active' Christianity.[100] Farquhar's mind was always focused on the practical, and he apparently admitted that he had a 'temperamental inability to appreciate what one may call the mystical elements in the religions of India.'[101] And, according to Sharpe, 'Dr Farquhar seemed to feel that, on account of his inability to enter into the real meaning of Mysticism, there were certain places of Hindu thought whose force and value he could not sufficiently realize.'[102] I have

---

97   Ibid., p. 273.

98   Ibid., p. 274.

99   I will argue this point when analysing Farquhar's work below, however I will let it stand here as it is necessary to understand his approach to Hinduism.

100   In the previous chapters testimony to this point of view is given by the constant reference to the fact that Indian Christianity will have a much more contemplative character than 'Western' Christianity.

101   Sharpe, 1963, p. vii.

102   Ibid. The term 'mysticism' is, of course, a notoriously difficult one to define, and one that I do not intend to give a definition of here, though, 'scholarship has progressed to where we now only recognize a plurality of mysticisms without scholarly relevant common qualities[....]

'[....] In fact, it [a definition of 'mysticism'] may look a lot more like a Zen kōan or some Neoplatonic riddle. Even now, the question looks suspiciously like a variation on the riddle of the Sphinx: a life-death challenge to identify the being (who is surely ourselves) that walks on one leg, multiple legs, and no legs all at the same time' (Brainard, pp. 359 and 387). However, I hope that there is enough general understanding of the concept for my intention to be understood here, if I contrast the contemplative/mystical life, and the life of service in the world; of course, I would not suggest that the two are incompatible, and may certainly be complementary. Farquhar, though, seems only interested in religion as an active principle operating in the world, and to quote Sharpe's words again: 'Though he [Farquhar] spoke of fellowship with God, it may be doubted whether his experience in this direction was as vital and profound as with some mystically-minded writers and thinkers of the present day' (Sharpe, 1963, p. vii). Whether this is a fair assessment is not something that I will dwell upon here, but as will be seen below Farquhar has no time for the contemplative, a point of view that may well have been

raised this point here as it relates to the next issue concerning Farquhar's attitude to Hinduism, which is the position and value of Vedānta philosophy.

Like those before him in the tradition of fulfilment theology, Farquhar identifies the Vedānta as the pinnacle of Hindu thought,[103] the essence of which he states as being that which:

> All scholars recognize at once the great insight revealed and the essential truth attained in the conceptions of Brahman as the spiritual Self of the universe and of the identity of Brahman and the individual self. These ideas form the fountain-head of all the greatest thinking that has been done in India.[104]

As we shall see below, it is this conception that he sees as being at the heart of all that is wrong with Hinduism. While, like Slater, he believed that Vedānta is the height of India's thought, the people, he said, have longed for theism, as, he contested, the popular religion demonstrated.[105] Farquhar, however, goes further in his criticism, for lacking an appreciation of the mystical,[106] he has no time for what it may add to contemplation, and

---

different had he been a Roman Catholic or even an Anglican, rather than a Scottish Non-Conformist, where no such tradition of the professional religionist withdrawing from the world to devote himself to God exists. Further, I would suggest that Farquhar has little sympathy with what may be styled 'mystical philosophy' – that is to say, thought contemplating the nature of God and man's relationship to the divine, a point I will develop above with reference to his attitude to Vedānta.

103   Crown, chapter VI.
104   Ibid., p. 226.
105   Ibid., pp. 390–1 and 420. He forgets to mention the alternative, that I mooted when discussing Slater, as to whether the presence of non-theistic and non-dualistic (Advaitic) systems does not rather show the failings of theism, just as Christianity and Islam found room for language that bordered on the Vedānta in apophatic theology, and in the mystical (remembering the caveat with which we used this term earlier, however I would tentatively like to suggest that the language of apophatic theology is something that Farquhar would not feel at home with) philosophy of such figures as Meister Eckhart and Al-Ghazali, who speaks of a virtual union of the individual soul with Allah (see Happold, pp. 238 f.). Eckhart being a particular case in point, as someone who has specifically parallelled to Śankara, the greatest proponent of Advaita-Vedānta by no less a scholar than Rudolf Otto, and, of course, also claimed as a pseudo-Buddhist by Suzuki.
106   In contrast to Slater for whom, 'Indian Christianity should contribute something very beautiful and true, on the side of meditative worship, to the overactive, bustling life of the West.
       'Vedāntic thought is so thoroughly Indian that the *Indian Christianity* of the future

criticizes it by asking: 'How are Hindus to be inspired to unselfish action? Clearly, it cannot be by any form of Hindu philosophy; for that leads to inaction.'[107] So likewise he criticizes Vivekānanda's concept of 'Practical Vedānta,' saying 'that one might as well attempt to warm the house with ice' as to expect 'Vedāntists to be stimulated by their faith to practical service for India.'[108] The real strength of Hinduism, he suggests, lies with the sects and the ordinary religious life of the people, for he says:

> religion is always found in a community, in an organized historical form[....] This is what distinguishes a religion from a mere theory, whether philosophical or religious. Bare theories may have very great interest for thought, and they may even influence the action of the individual to some extent; but their work in the world is not at all comparable to the action of a religion.[109]

Farquhar distinguishes between the philosophy of Hinduism, and its manifestation, the Hindu system, which, he says, 'has proved itself throughout many centuries a real living religion.'[110] That is to say, it has organized and controlled a society, which is what he sees as essential, while all of the system is but a material shell. Sacrifice and idols do not provide spiritual worship. Indeed, they have cramped the spiritual longings of the philosopher,[111] whose desire for a spiritual communion with God not dependent upon external forms, he sees as the flower of Vedānta. For various reasons, which we will consider below, he sees this as being doomed to failure in its goal of reaching towards God.

---

will of necessity take a Vedāntic colouring' (Slater, 1903, pp. 262 and 290).

107   Crown, p. 277. We may note that this attitude had been prevalent up until then, that Indian thought is directed towards quietism, but a new appreciation and understanding of it was growing, 'Speaking of the beginnings of a reformed Hinduism, Brother (later Bishop) F. J. Western drew attention to 'the widespread use of the Bhagavad-Gita as a book of theology and devotion. The book has been, one might almost say, re-discovered by English educated Hindus, and many are learning from it not only quietism, but, to borrow words of Professor [A. G.] Hogg, quoted in the Report – "the strenuous mood, and the consecration of life to service"' (Sharpe, 1985, p. 102, quoting World Missionary Conference, 1910, *Report of Commission IV*, p. 313 f. We may note that the Gītā was even used by certain radicals in the Indian nationalist movement to justify their acts of violence (see Fulfil, pp. 197 f.)).

108   Crown, p. 281.

109   Ibid., p. 445.

110   Ibid., p. 446.

111   Ibid.

Farquhar's attitude towards Vedānta is, then, ambivalent. On the one hand he regards it as groping towards spiritual worship, devoid of images, and in accord with the immanentist thought that was so prevalent in Non-Conformist circles in Farquhar's day.[112] However, as we have noted, he does not believe that it is capable of emerging from its quietude to inspire people to social and political reform, which was, to Farquhar, the judgement of true spirituality.[113]

This antagonism to Vedānta is carried further in Farquhar, for while fulfilment theology is moving towards an Indian Christian theology by adopting an Indian attitude, Farquhar was vehemently opposed to any influence of Indian thought on Christianity. While Farquhar thought some usage of Indian devotional practice might be of use:

> Thus the mode of worship which arose in the *bhakti* sects, and is still used in the Brāhma Samāj in prayer meetings – when people squat on the ground, and by means of prayer and singing stir each other to great spiritual exaltation – may be required to make Indian worship truly indigenous and really effective to the Indian heart.[114]

Nevertheless he still says that:

> Strength and life depend on complete faithfulness to Christ. This is particularly clear in the case of Hinduism; for the genius of the religion is so different from the essential character of Christianity that *to introduce any Hindu doctrine into the Church of Christ would be to pour poison into it.*[115]

---

112   Reference has already been made to this idea in the previously. The following passage from the Rev. R. J. Campbell, gives a good idea as to how far such expression had gone: 'Where, then, some one will say is the dividing line between our being and God's? There is no dividing line except from our side. The ocean of consciousness knows that the bay has never been separate from itself, although the bay is only conscious of the ocean on the outer side of its own being[....]' (R. J. Campbell, pp. 34–5).

113   I would suggest that the subsequent history of India has gone some way to proving Farquhar wrong on this point. Gandhi has been an example to the world in terms of his criticism of social ills, and the practical implementation of reform. He was a great believer in karma-yoga, and is described thus by Zaehner, 'Gandhi the ascetic *sannyāsin* who yet drew no hard and fast line between the life of prayer and the life of action, between religion and politics' (Zaehner, 1990, p. 187).

114   Farquhar, 'Syncretism or Eclecticism?' (a lecture delivered before Continuation Committee Conference, Bengal, in YMCA Hist. Lib.), quoted from Fulfil, p. 302, fn. 5.

115   Ibid., in ibid.

Whilst examining *The Crown of Hinduism*, it shall be seen that virtually anything distinctly Hindu, or Indian in character, particularly as regards thought, is rejected by Farquhar in his analysis as being part of what he sees as the faults of Hinduism. This provides a contrast with the attitude of some of his contemporaries which will be seen when we consider the criticisms of Farquhar's system. There is a major dichotomy in Farquhar; on the one hand there is a recognition of the need for sympathy and appreciation,[116] whilst on the other hand he is hostile to the whole Hindu system.[117]

What I suggest will be seen in *The Crown of Hinduism*, is a criticism of Hinduism based upon Farquhar's perception that it cannot meet the demands and values placed upon it by Western civilization, and a willingness to acknowledge the good intentions and desire for God of the Indian people, but an unwillingness to see value in the way it is expressed.

There is one further point about Farquhar's views that we should note. He, like the neo-Hindus, is very fond of referring back to the Ṛig Veda as the fount of the Indian religious tradition. In so doing, he seeks to show that Hinduism as it now stands is very far from that early faith, and one of his claims is that: 'The religion of Christ is the spiritual crown of the religion of the Ṛigveda.'[118] There is an obvious apologetic purpose to this, in showing that Christianity is the true heir of what Hindus acknowledge to be the religion of their ancestors, the religion from which Hinduism has grown. This is another theme often repeated in Farquhar's book, and is no doubt part of the reason for his methodology of tracing the historical growth of each idea, based upon a desire to show how far modern Hinduism has strayed from its roots.

We should also observe that Farquhar does not see Hinduism to be divinely inspired. The question is passed over in the Crown, and most of his other works, but in his Edinburgh papers, he says:

> But if all religions are human, and yet men can in the long run hold only Christianity, clearly it must be in some sense, the climax of the religious development of the world, the end and culmination of all religions. If all the great religious instincts, *which have created*

---

116   See ibid., pp. 170 f.
117   This matter will be explored further below.
118   Crown, p. 77. The aim, of course, of India's first indigenous fulfilment theologian, K. M. Banerjea.

the other faiths, find ultimate satisfaction in Christianity, then Christianity stands in a very definite relation to every other religion.[119]

Here Farquhar spells out very clearly his belief that the non-Christian religions are only human creations. He sees no notion of a divine element underlying them. Thus, unlike the Cambridge schools usage of the logos spermatikos idea, Farquhar's conception of St John's use of the Logos is significant, but only in as far as 'he was clearly very conscious of the hold which the thought had on the cultivated Greek mind, and saw that it could be used to good purpose as a mediating idea.'[120] In the first chapter, the essential gulf that existed between evangelical modes of thought and those more liberal[121] who were prepared to see revelation, or inspiration, in the non-Christian religions has already been mentioned. As I have suggested, this creates a tension, for Farquhar wishes to argue that 'all religions are in a sense valid, as being genuine products of man's religious nature,'[122] yet they stem not from God but from the corrupt and degenerate human nature. Quite how, drawing this division and denying divine inspiration in the non-Christian religions, Farquhar can argue for the evolution of religions, is a matter unresolved in his thought.

Hinduism and Christianity Compared

i) Caste

The effect of Western reform is something we have already referred to above.[123] Specifically, Farquhar refers to 'the long-continued agitation on the part of the Social Reform leaders in favour of the abolition of caste distinctions.'[124] For Farquhar believes that caste cannot stand up to the

---

119   EDMS, Farquhar # 154, pp. 13–14. Italics my own.
120   EDMS, Farquhar # 154, p. 19.
121   Though 'liberal' may not be the best word to use of all those who employ this idea, Newman, for instance, would no doubt prefer to see his use of the logos spermatikos as 'patristic' rather than 'liberal'.
122   EDMS, Farquhar # 154, p. 13.
123   See Crown, p. 118.
124   Ibid., p. 149. See also p. 170, on Farquhar's observation that the caste regulated principles of whom one may eat with are no longer rigidly followed, and p. 191, on his belief that the religious basis of caste is no longer believed by educated Hindus.

inevitable forces of Westernization, which will be a major blow to Hinduism: 'Caste is the Hindu form of social organization. No man can be a Hindu who is not in caste; and if a group of outsiders is admitted into the community, they must organize themselves as a caste.'[125] Farquhar notes, however, that often movements are found within Hinduism that seek a broader outlook.[126] He refers the Bhagavad-Gītā which goes beyond the usual Hindu outlook that only males of the top three castes are capable of spiritual release, by being open to Śudras and women.[127] Further, many bhakti sects said that outcastes were capable of reaching moksha as well.[128] Farquhar notes that, despite allowing these groups the chance of spiritual release, nothing has been done to aid their social position.[129] This, to him, shows that the presuppositions of the caste system are false, and that the Hindu spirit has always rebelled against it. To his mind, then, caste is failing and something must step in to provide a religious basis for society.[130] Having made these introductory

---

125   Ibid., p. 214.

126   He also observes that although the Vīra Śaiva sect, the Sikhs, and the Ārya Samāj, were, when founded, all opposed to caste, yet all three sects were now bound by its codes (ibid., p. 203).

127   According to ancient Hindu tradition only males of the Brāhman, Kshatriya, and Vaishya castes (the so-called 'twice-born') are allowed to hear Śruti, that is revealed scripture, the Vedas including the Upanishads, as opposed to Smṛti, other scriptures, which are open to all. While the Gītā is technically Smṛti it is regarded as equal to Śruti by most of the Vedāntic schools, and so gives access to the teachings of Vedānta, and therefore moksha, to those who would otherwise be left untutored in Vedāntic philosophy – it should be borne in mind that there are two models of the afterlife in operation in Hinduism, one, that of reincarnation, and the endless round of birth, death, and rebirth of samsāra, and another, involving a heavenly afterlife, which finds expression in the śraddha rites, where rice balls, piṇḍa, are offered to the deceased relative to construct a body for the next realm (Flood, 1996, pp. 207 f.). These ceremonies go back to the time of the Vedas before the doctrine of reincarnation, and still hold considerable weight in Hinduism, 'While the official ideology of Brahmanical Hinduism is reincarnation, and this is the model generally assumed by renouncer traditions[.... M]any non-Brahmans do not claim to believe in reincarnation' (ibid., p. 208).

128   Ibid., p. 203.

129   Ibid., pp. 399–400.

130   See Fulfil, p. 251. Farquhar saw religion as an essential element in man's life. Sharpe suggests that apart from the general assumption that a missionary would have such a view, Farquhar's beliefs about this could be traced to his reading of B. J. Kidd's *Social Evolution* (1894) and his *Principles of Western Civilization* (1902),

points, we turn next to look at a problem of Farquhar's criticism of caste before going on to look at how he saw it being fulfilled.

Historically speaking, Farquhar regarded caste as being a great improvement upon the existing social order when it was introduced, and by providing a solid basis for society, allowed for the growth of civilization.[131] Indeed, he says it only became bad when it became rigid,[132] which did not occur, he believed, until after the time of Gautama, the Buddha.[133] However, in endorsing the need for a social order for the good of 'civilization' it is hard not to draw a parallel to the social situation of the United Kingdom of that time, 'Victorian Christianity – and in particular the Church of England – was indeed addicted to the presentation of Christian doctrine and morality as a means of supporting and justifying the existing social order and controlling the lower social classes.'[134] Certainly Farquhar has to answer the charge of Hindus that England is as caste ridden as India, but his response is that this is done against the spirit of Christianity while caste is inherent in Hinduism.[135]

While Farquhar spends some time looking at what he sees as the religious foundations of caste,[136] this need not concern us beyond noting that he holds that these ideas are not tenable to educated men.[137] What is important for us is what Farquhar sees as the innate yearnings in man that give rise to

---

'His thesis was that religion, providing a "super-rational sanction" for areas of conduct which cannot have a "rational sanction", will always have an important role in the evolution of society, and that without a religious foundation, true progress in society is impossible' (Fulfil, p. 41, fn. 9).

131   Crown, p. 167
132   Ibid.
133   Ibid., p. 169.
134   Parsons, 1988 (b), pp. 40–41. In fact Parsons speaking of the Tractarian outlook, says, 'That outlook was austere. Poverty was morally tolerable because it was the inevitable product of immutable economic laws which were themselves the product of a divinely ordained and designed world' (ibid., p. 43). In thinking of the social situation in England at that time one cannot but recall that verse of All Things Bright and Beautiful which is normally omitted today:
'The rich man in his castle,
'The poor man at his gate,
'God made them high and lowly,
'And ordered their estate.'
135   Crown, p. 192. In the first chapter dealing with Maurice, reference was made to his connections with Christian Socialism which was scandalous to the religious authorities of his day.
136   Ibid., pp. 177 ff.
137   Ibid., pp. 179 ff.

caste, which are, according to Farquhar, a desire for purity, 'the strength of the Hindu desire for purity can be explained only by recognizing that it arises from the inner spiritual consciousness of the need of true purity.'[138] The traditional regulations of purity are an anachronism, Farquhar suggests,[139] and in Christ he believes all men may rise up to, and above, the purity of the Brāhmans.[140] Also, he suggests, there is the question of duty and privilege given by birth, for while in Hinduism only Brāhmans may sacrifice, and the twice-born hear revelation, Christ, Farquhar asserts, makes everyone partake in the duties of priesthood, the offering of spiritual sacrifices.[141] This becomes 'in Christ Jesus every man's birthright.'[142] Christ will also free people from their traditional role in caste, so that all are free men to pursue any occupation, unrestricted by fear of pollution.[143]

As well as making all men Brāhmans, Christ also makes everyone a Śudra, says Farquhar, for he, like them, is the servant of all.[144] Furthermore, he says that in Christianity there is the recognition of the sacred nature of the social order.[145] Farquhar suggests that this is inherent in Christianity, for social duty should be seen in the 'light of His [God the Father's] love for man. The sacramental note is everywhere; for in doing the humblest duty to my brother I touch my Father's hand.'[146] More than this, he suggests that society is more sacred to the Christian, for while the Hindu holy man leaves society when he becomes a sannyāsī, the more religious the Christian, the more he will strive for equality within that existing social order.[147]

Farquhar also uses a theme that appeared in Maurice,[148] which is the notion of the twice-born. Instead of the empty ceremony that these writers believe it to be in Hinduism, it becomes, in Christ, a 'conversion, a revolution within the soul, a spiritual transformation of the man[....] That which in Hinduism has become a formal ceremony is in Christ a spiritual reality.'[149]

---

138   Ibid., p. 450.
139   Ibid., p. 183.
140   Ibid., p. 209.
141   Ibid., pp. 203–5.
142   Ibid., p. 209.
143   Ibid., p. 199.
144   Ibid.
145   Ibid., p. 205.
146   Ibid., p. 206.
147   Ibid., pp. 206–7.
148   Boyle, pp. 166 ff.
149   Crown, pp. 209–10.

In making God responsible for the moral order, Farquhar sees this as improving the Hindu vision.[150] For Farquhar, however, society needs a religious basis,[151] and so he asks:

> Where[...] shall we find a religion whose governing conceptions, when they take organized form in society, will incarnate the great principles of the essential equality of all men, the rectitude and high value of complete social freedom, and the obligation of moralizing all social relations[...]?[152]

And answers by saying: 'It is a very remarkable fact that these three social principles spring directly from the central doctrine of Christianity.'[153]

We can thus see that in a number of ways, Farquhar sees Christianity as giving a new slant to the impetus that led to caste in Hinduism.

ii) Karma and Reincarnation[154]

Farquhar deals with these two ideas together as he sees them to be intimately inter-linked. These two conceptions are closely allied to that of caste,[155] and Farquhar suggests that because of the political agitation for reform of caste the idea of karma is being eroded,[156] while he calls reincarnation a 'fairy tale idea.'[157]

---

150   Ibid., see pp. 409 ff.

151   Ibid., p. 191. See below.

152   Ibid., p. 192.

153   Ibid.

154   It is worth noting that in his Edinburgh papers, when he lists various areas of fulfilment, (EDMS, Farquhar # 154, pp. 31–35) he directs the reader to Hogg's work (suitably entitled *Karma and Redemption*) when mentioning the notions of karma and redemption. However, in the Crown, no reference to Hogg is given. Perhaps Farquhar came to know of Hogg's separate agenda, and something of his criticisms of fulfilment theology (see the next chapter on Hogg and fulfilment theology).

155   See ibid., p. 141.

156   Ibid., pp. 148 ff.

157   Ibid., p. 135. While the idea is fanciful to Farquhar, the idea was being adopted by a number of Western thinkers. We may note the theosophists (see Besant, pp. 23 ff, also Blavatsky, p. 281, who seems to see this idea in St Paul) and Steiner (see Steiner, pp. 84 ff.) as Farquhar's contemporaries, and I would suggest that the idea is now so familiar in the West that it passes these days without question as a reasonable religious belief.

I will deal first with some general points on karma. Farquhar sees it as the reason for India's (alleged) pessimism,[158] regarding it as involving an immutable moral law from which there is no escape, which, being part of an impersonal universal order, does not allow for compassion.[159] He also links it to the notion of saṃsāra, which means, he says, that there is never any progress, there is merely the eternal and unbreakable cycle which inevitably leads 'to hopeless depravity,'[160] which is his interpretation of the cycle of four ages, or yugas, from the kṛita-yuga through to the kali-yuga.[161] The fact that he sees karma as unrelated to God is what he sees as its major weakness.[162]

On the good side, Farquhar says that the concept of karma does not belittle morality, or suggest that it is not hard to overcome the world, but takes full account of man's weakness, and the importance of leading a good life.[163] Further, he identifies three essential beliefs that gave rise to this doctrine, which are: first, that the world is just; second, that our lives are subject to a moral law; and, third, that both good and evil will have their recompense in a future life.[164] Of course, for the Hindu system, reincarnation is the means by which these ends can be achieved.

Reincarnation, while allowing for the theoretical working out of the central ideas noted above, is, however, to Farquhar's mind, a bad thing. Farquhar sees it as being in sharp contradistinction to the 'happy immortality spent in heaven'[165] which marked the Ṛig Vedic religion.

How, then, are these ideas fulfilled? First, God is linked to the moral order in Christianity.[166] This, however, raises other problems which we will deal with below. This is what Farquhar sees as the main difference. He notes that certain sects sought to bring God into the equation, seeing devotion as a

---

158   Crown, p. 139.
159   Ibid., p. 141–3.
160   Ibid., p. 140.
161   The age, according to Hindu cosmology, which we are now in, which we may note is also the shortest, being but 432,000 years, while the Dvāpara-yuga is 864,000 years, the Treta-Yuga 1,296,000 years, and the golden age, the kṛita-, or Satya-Yuga is 1,728,000 years in length. Thus while each cycle always goes from the best to the worst age, the ages of goodness last longer than the darker ages (Schuhmacher and Woerner, p. 435).
162   Crown, p. 152.
163   Ibid., p. 138.
164   Ibid., pp. 135–6.
165   Ibid., p. 144.
166   Ibid., pp. 411 ff.

means of gaining emancipation from the rounds of saṃsāra.[167] Thus there was an attempt to link the idea of karma, and therefore also the conception of moksha, to a theistic system in both the Vaisnavite and Śaivite sects, to escape from the crushing burden of karma, 'the efforts of the Hindu spirit to escape from the sway of karma shows how hard it has been for Hindus throughout the centuries to accept the doctrine in its entirety.'[168]

Beyond saying this, Farquhar does not spell out the method of fulfilment. Having noted what he sees as its practical fruits, caste, crumbling, then, he suggests that the new social order is its fulfilment.

iii) Morality and God

Farquhar's thought here follows on from what we have seen expressed concerning karma, and the moral order in connection with that concept. To recap, Farquhar saw Hindu morals as being apart from God,[169] that is to say Brahman, the pure spirit of the Vedānta. He noted also that particular Gods are thought to be above morality.[170] For these reasons, herefore, Farquhar says the rule of morality is weakened in Hinduism:

> The greatest saints are guilty of the most immoral acts in the service of their gods, and are held to be quite justified. Māṇikka Vāchakar, one of the greatest of Þaivite saints... was originally Prime Minister to the king of Madura. The king entrusted him with a large sum of money to go to a seaport and buy Arab horses. On his way he sees Þiva in the form of a guru surrounded by ninety-nine disciples, is converted and becomes a Þaivite ascetic. He then hands over the whole of the king's money to be distributed to the devotees of Śiva and the poor.[171]

While Vāchakar's behaviour is, perhaps, not entirely correct I think that to call him 'most immoral' because of this would be stretching moral prudery somewhat.[172] Not only does Farquhar see a problem with morality being

---

167   Ibid., p. 147.
168   Ibid., p. 148.
169   Ibid., p. 152.
170   Ibid., pp. 395–6.
171   Ibid, p. 398, reference to Pope, *The Tiruvāçagam*, pp. xxi–xxiii.
172   Maybe the West has a greater consideration for fulfilling one's secular duties before embarking upon the religious life (however it is hard not to feel that a Christian saint would be praised for such an action, being a type (typos) of Robin Hood). To highlight the sense of an alternative ethic, wherein one fulfils existing secular duties

before turning to the religious life, I will give a modern day example, stressing the difference between the tale above, an 'Eastern' type (using the term with considerable reservations), and a 'Western' type (again using the term with major reservations), in this case from one of the great moral stories of our own time, Quentin Tarantino's film *Pulp Fiction*. To quote from the original screenplay:
'[Two gangsters are sitting in a coffee shop when they start discussing a strange incident that had occurred to them that day]
Jules: I just been sittin' here thinkin'.
Vincent: (mouthful of food) About what?
J: The miracle we witnessed.
V: The miracle *you* witnessed. *I* witnessed a freak occurrence.
J: Do you know what a miracle is?
V: An act of God.
J: What's an act of God?
V: I guess it's when God makes the impossible possible. And I'm sorry, Jules, but I don't think what happened this morning qualifies.
J: Don't you see, Vince, that s[***] don't matter. You're judging this thing the wrong way. It's not about *what*. It could be God stopped the bullets, he changed Coke into Pepsi, he found my f[*****]' car keys. You don't judge s*** like this based on merit. Whether or not what we experienced was an according-to-Hoyle miracle is insignificant. What is significant is I felt God's touch. God got involved.
V: But why?
J: That's what's f[*****]' wit' me! I don't know why. But I can't go back to sleep.
V: So you're serious, you're really going to quit?
J: The life, most definitely.
[...........]
V: So if you're quitting the life, what'll you do?
J: That's what I've been sitting here contemplating. First, I'm gonna deliver this case to Marsellus. Then, basically, I'm gonna walk the earth.
[........ After this two small time crooks hold up the coffee shop, and seek to take the case, referred to above, which the 'converted' Jules is returning to his boss Marsellus which is full of (possibly) gold, or some other valuable substance – I have heard, but do not have a reliable reference for the information that, according to Tarantino, the case contains Marsellus' soul – but rather than giving it to the 'poor' as he could the following ensues].
J:[....] Now this is the situation. Normally both of your asses would be dead as f[*****]' fried chicken. But you happened to pull this s[***] while I'm in a transitional period. I don't want to kill ya, I want to help ya. But I'm afraid I can't give you the case. It don't belong to me. Besides, I went through too much s[***] this morning on account of this case to just hand it over to your ass.
[......Jules does, however, give them fifteen hundred dollars of his own money]' (Tarantino, pp. 172–3 and 183 (edited for language)). Thus, in this example of modern 'Western' morality, secular obligations must be fulfilled regardless of the possible religious duty; loyalty is, of course, one of the themes in the film (ibid., pp. 68 f.). One could say that 'Render therefore unto Cæsar the things which are

separate from God, as noted above, but he also sees a problem with the conception of God as ultimately conceived, that is to say, Brahman. Related to this question, Farquhar says that he can only regret that the Varuna, who was the source of Ṛita in the Ṛig Veda, finds no equivalent in later Hinduism, to provide a divine personage to oversee the moral order.[173] Rather he looks at the concept of Brahman, which he feels to be seriously flawed. Speaking of Brahman he says:

> He[174] [Brahman] is constantly spoken of as unborn and as free[....] Hence, since all actions, whether good or bad, necessarily create karma, he is conceived of as altogether inactive[....] So he is said to be without any desire or purpose that could stir him to action[....] He is altogether at peace, altogether indifferent, altogether passionless. This great thought, that Brahman is actionless, has produced very deep results upon Hindu theology. It cut Brahman away from morality and from every form of worship; it made it impossible to conceive him as a purposeful Creator; and it strengthened the tendency to *think of him[175] as impersonal*.[176]

To the Christian, God is moral,[177] 'the supreme personality,'[178] and the Creator,[179] therefore he says: 'Instead of *indifference* Christ's law is *love*.'[180] This, he believes, leads to service, but we shall deal with this point next as it

---

Cæsar's' (Mt. XXII: 21), has won the day over the conceptions of 'let the dead bury their dead' (Mt. VIII: 22) and 'sell that thou hast, and give to the poor' (Mt. XIX: 21). Also, we may observe that Farquhar notes Maṅgai-Āḷvār, who 'breaks into a Buddhist shrine and steals a golden image of Buddha' (Crown, p. 398, reference to Govindāchārya, *The Holy Lives of the Āzhvārs*, pp. 173–9). While we may look upon this story as immoral today we must remember that in medieval Europe the practice of stealing relics was common, and this was held to be justified on the grounds that if the saint had not wanted their bones to be stolen they would not have allowed this 'crime' to take place. Thus in condemning Hinduism Farquhar seems to be forgetting the fact that ideas of morality have changed with time within Christianity.

173   Crown, p. 152.

174   The term 'he' in relation to Brahman is one that would raise serious queries today, but problems with the use of the masculine genitive, even for an impersonal divinity, would be perfectly acceptable in Farquhar's day.

175   See previous footnote.

176   Crown, p. 144. Italics my own.

177   Ibid., pp. 409 ff.

178   Ibid., p. 414.

179   Ibid., pp. 417 ff.

180   Ibid., p. 294.

relates to the ideal holy life, which will be examined separately. Hence Farquhar feels that while the manifestation and activity of God within the world is believed by Indians to be lila, the Christian doctrine sees creation as purposeful, and God's activity therein as purposeful.[181] The difference, as seen by Farquhar, is that in India God is ultimately seen as being amoral, while in Christianity God is the supreme moral being.[182] Thus Farquhar sees Christianity fulfilling Hindu morality by linking it to God, which is also a return to a Ṛig Vedic ideal, of Varuna as the source of Ṛita, and by giving a moral and personal God, Christianity fulfills the impersonal Brahman. Here we may note the dictum Farquhar advances in his Edinburgh papers, that: 'A continuous unfulfilled search for a satisfying monotheism is thus one of the most marked features of Hindu history.'[183] This is what he felt the religious consciousness craved: 'The whole course of the religious history of India exhibits a sustained effort on the part of thinking Hindus to get away from the impersonal God and to reach a God of love and grace.'[184]

iv) The Religious Life and the Sadhu

Continuing from our last point, having established the nature of Brahman as impassible, this implies that, 'emancipation is not conceived as being dependent on morality in any way. It arises altogether from knowledge. Realization of one's unity with Brahman is itself release from rebirth and from the world.'[185] Therefore if the holy man, or sadhu, is to pass on to union with Brahman then they must become, says Farquhar, indifferent as well.[186] It is for this reason that we earlier saw Farquhar say that there could be no

---

181   Ibid., p. 419.
182   Again, this goes back to Farquhar's own knowledge of Christianity, based in Protestant Non-Conformity, which, with his lack of a theological education, seems to have meant his lack of knowledge of the via negativa, and the usage of negative imagery in relation to God (see especially, Sells, *Mystical Languages of Unsaying*, who explores the use of language in Eriugena, Marguerite Porete, and Eckhart; see also Copleston pp. 131 ff., and McGinn pp. 173 ff.). As to what this means for the individual's relationship with God I will deal with below.
183   EDMS, Farquhar # 154, p. 22.
184   Crown, p. 447.
185   Ibid., p. 230.
186   Ibid., p. 231. Yet in adopting the law of ahiṃsā, as well as chastity, truthfulness, and honesty, Farquhar does concede that, 'the moral side of monastic life produced a beautiful ideal of the passive virtues' (ibid.).

such thing as 'Practical Vedānta' for, to his mind, it is Vedānta that results in passivity, and is the cause of Hinduism's essential weakness.This is why Farquhar believed that he must draw a contrast between Christian love and Hindu indifference,[187] and which he feels have different results: 'Instead of the *inaction* which comes fromindifference, Christ commands the service which springs from love.'[188] The practical results of this are, he says:

---

187   Ibid., p. 294.

188   Ibid. Yet even Farquhar has to admit the following, 'But the two are by no means so hopelessly opposed as one might suppose from a quick glance at the words, or from contrasting the sannyāsī in the depths of meditation with the busy missionary. Christ does not command action in general, but service. How much restraint and inaction are implied in that large word as well as active work! Further, the Indian monk has never been able to be truly inactive: the *Gītā* tells us frankly that complete inaction is impossible;(Gītā III: 5) and all the best men have unconsciously found their way past the rule of inaction and into acts of service. The followers of Gautama had many pleasant memories of their master, but none sweeter than his loving attendances on the sick. All the greatest sannyāsīs were teachers, writers, and preachers. Their own hearts and the needs of men were too strong for the rule under which they lived' (Crown, pp. 294–5). I would suggest that Farquhar has misunderstood the rule of 'indifference' which also finds a place, correctly understood, within the Christian mystical tradition. I would like to quote the following definition of the Greek virtue apatheia (ἀπάθεια), generally translated 'dispassion', '[....] St Isaiah the solitary [amongst others...] regard the passions as fundamentally good, and for them dispassion signifies a state in which the passions are exercised in accordance with their original purity and so without committing sin in act or thought. Dispassion is a state of reintegration and spiritual freedom; when translating the term into Latin, Cassian rendered it 'purity of heart'. Such a state may imply impartiality and detachment, but not indifference, for if a dispassionate man does not suffer on his own account, he suffers for his fellow creatures' (Nikodimos and Makarios, p. 359). Similar language is found with reference to the sannyāsī ideal: 'By curbing the senses, by destroying affection (rāga) and hatred, by doing no harm to any living thing (ahiṃsā), he will conform himself to deathlessness[....] Thus by gradually giving up all attachments, liberated from all pairs of opposites, he will abide in Brahman' (*Laws of Manu*, VI: 45–81, in Zaehner, 1990, pp. 113–4). While I would not suggest that the spirituality of the early fathers and the sadhu is the same, it is a point that terms such as 'dispassion' or 'indifference' may mean something else in translation, and that the language of the contemplative life might suggest an indifference to the world while it merely speaks of a break from attachment to the world. Thus Eckhart notes that, 'When I preach it is my wont to speak about detachment, and of how man should rid himself of self and all things' (Walshe, Sermon XXII, p. 177). Such a phrase could be seen as advocating utter nihilism, but clearly this was not Eckhart's intent.* I do not think it is possible for me to comment here on the correct interpretation of the

Hinduism has produced for quite two thousand five hundred years an unending procession of men and women ready to devote themselves to the highest; but, when they are produced, they are comparatively useless; for the mighty religion which inspires them to enter the ascetic life sets before them as their ideal the life of the actionless Brahman.[189]

He says: 'The sadhu, the living modern outcome of the philosophic-ascetic movement is pronounced useless by the modern man.'[190]For, as we noted earlier, all that is of importance to Farquhar is service, and activity in the world, the life of contemplation is a life wasted. True to the principle of fulfilment, however, Farquhar says that because, unlike Hindus, Christians

---

sannyāsī ideal as Hindu ideas are varied even today, and much change has accorded over the course of the three millennia or so of its history. I would like to point out that Farquhar has very little sympathy for the monastic ideal, and that, perhaps, his interpretation of this is less than generous. I have, therefore, made reference above to the Christian contemplative tradition as a counter balance, suggesting that both Hinduism and Christianity have this ideal and that at least in the Christian tradition it is not a life of complete withdrawal and indifference to the world, though some of the language, if not understood, may sound like that.
*Woods, pp. 144 ff. Once the soul has reached the height of contemplation it has to return to action, and Woods notes that: 'The necessary turn to action is recognized both in Eastern and Western forms of mysticism, as William Johnston has shown specially with regard to Zen Buddhism' (ibid., p. 146). Assuming this to be the case for Zen, we cannot generalize more broadly to say all forms of 'Eastern mysticism', even Buddhism, endorse this view, just as we could not say it of Christianity, especially many of its early Gnostic forms.

189   Crown, p. 276. At the risk of repeating myself I will point out that he ignores Christianity's own monastic tradition in this criticism, and the fact that the great majority of Christendom's teachers and saints were within this tradition, and that the great exodus to the desert of the fourth and fifth centuries is seen as one of the great events within the Church's life (McGinn, pp. 131 ff.). In contrast to Farquhar's negativity towards the contemplative, we noted in the last chapter how Slater believed India would 'contribute something to Christendom of the science of the soul' (Slater, 1903, p. 291). Since Farquhar's day the question of a Christian form of the sannyāsī has become a significant theme, as noted by the 1938 'Rethinking Christianity' group, and the relatively important influence of Abhishiktananda (Henri le Saux), and his successor Dom Bede Griffiths in Western perceptions of Indian Christianity (Devasahayam, pp. 215 ff, and see also Wiseman, and Ropers in Griffiths, 1994, pp 555 ff.). Several years after Farquhar was writing an Indian Christian mystic, Sadhu Sundar Singh, achieved a popular appeal both in Indian, and the Western world(see Streeter, pp. 38 ff, and Sharpe, 1976 and next chapter).

190   Crown, p. 447.

serve,[191] then the sannyāsi, the ideal of the man who has given his life to God, is the man who has taken up the life of action, therefore, 'Christ Jesus makes His followers servants of humanity, and in so doing He completes and consummates the ideal of the Hindu monk.'[192]

Farquhar also suggests that Christ fulfills the other aspects of the sannyāsī's life, so that instead of world-surrender, Christianity demands self-surrender,[193] and in place of self-torture, Christ asks for self-sacrifice.[194] These ideas are similar to those previously seen in Slater's analysis;[195] however, whereas Slater saw the whole of the sannyāsī ideal being fulfilled by Christian self-sacrifice, Farquhar makes a further split into self-sacrifice and self-surrender.

v) Idols and Avataras

Farquhar's approach to these two subjects follows on from that of his predecessors when he asks:

> What are we to say about the Hindu use of images in worship? Is it a valuable help to a monotheistic and spiritual faith, as the Neo-Hindu declares, or a coarse and degrading idolatry, as the missionary says, or does the truth lie somewhere between them?[196]

The answer is one that can no doubt be deduced from what Slater and others have said previously, for Farquhar is not very innovative in this area, though he examines the question in greater detail.

Hindu villagers, Farquhar says, see the idol as being the god it represents,[197] which he says is significantly different from the Buddhist and Jain practice as using them as symbols, which is similar to the Roman Catholic usage.[198] Modern educated Hindus have adopted the same attitude, he notes,[199] but this, he says, is not real Hindu idolatry, nor is it what the

---

191   Ibid., p. 277.
192   Ibid., p. 296.
193   Ibid., p. 293.
194   Ibid., p. 295.
195   Slater, pp. 170–1.
196   Crown, p. 297.
197   Ibid., p. 317
198   Ibid., p. 323.
199   Ibid., pp. 334 f.

villager believes.[200] Farquhar also asks, if this were so, then what is the meaning of the ceremony of prāṇapratishthā,[201] the ceremony to bring the god into the idol?[202] He has further noted that many of the great saints and the whole of the Hindu tradition have centred upon treating idols as living manifestations of the gods.[203] He also mentions the theosophical defence of idols by Annie Besant, that they are imbued with 'magnetism', but concludes that this is absurd.[204] Another Hindu defence, Farquhar tells us, is that, because God is everywhere then one can worship God in an image. Farquhar objects, however, that this would deny what is traditionally believed to happen in those ceremonies that bring the god into the idol.[205] None of these answers, Farquhar believes, account for the traditional beliefs regarding idols, which he sees as outmoded, and says that, despite its defence by Neo-Hinduism and theosophy, belief in the Hindu idol is dying.[206] The above

---

200   Ibid., p. 336.

201   Ibid., p. 335.

202   'The image or 'icon'[...] of the deity worshipped must be formally installed. This is called prāṇa-pratiṣṭhā, namely, animating the icon. The ceremony is elaborate, but once it is concluded the deity[...] is believed to take up residence in the image[....] The icon is taken over by the deity and becomes its temporary body' (Lipner, p. 280). According to Flood, the ceremony of giving life to the statue is analogous to the process whereby a guru 'energizes' or gives life to a mantra (Flood, 1996, p. 222).

203   Crown, pp. 317 ff. According to Farquhar, 'Hinduism has never got beyond the superstition that holiness and divine power reside in things' (ibid., p. 392). Perhaps he should consider the importance given to relics throughout Christian history, and their alleged miraculous powers (MacCulloch in Hastings vol. X, 'Relics (Primitive and Western)', see especially, section on 'relics and miracles', pp. 657 f.). Also, if we look at Western Christianity to-day, there is a growth of interest in icons, 'In recent years there has been a sort of 'rediscovery' of icons by Western Christians. There is an increasing awareness that the icon is not merely a work of art, but is also an aspect of divine revelation and of our communing with God in the Church' (Quenot, back cover). Belief in the miracleis alive and well in the church today, 'An icon of Jesus in Bethlehem's Church of the Nativity has been winking and weeping red tears, according to worshippers[....]
'The inexplicable events began about six weeks ago and have been officially declared a miracle by the Greek Orthodox Church' (The Daily Telegraph, Friday, November 29, 1996, p. 22).

204   Crown, p. 336. Not being an expert on the pseudo-scientific method of theosophy I will not presume to comment on this matter.

205   Ibid., pp. 336 f. See above for details on the ceremony.

206   Ibid., p. 334.

arguments show this, he believes, for Hindus now reject the traditional beliefs. Yet although every educated Hindu has lost faith in idols, he says they are defended because 'they are dimly conscious of something noble and good in the practice.'[207] There is thus a religious basis to this practice, which has resulted, Farquhar believes, from man's innate religious needs not having been met in a spiritual form.[208]

Farquhar sees three main reasons lying behind the belief in idols. First, temples are places of theophany. Farquhar believes that people are impressed by a god who cares for us, and comes to us.[209] It is not the god residing apart from mankind in heaven but his localization that the Hindu worships, Farquhar claims.[210] The saints of Hinduism, he notes, have their devotions turned to a specific idol, and further: 'A saint now and then gets the malady known as 'sunset and sunrise,' i.e. he falls ill because he cannot see his favourite god, the doors of the shrine being closed by night to allow the god to sleep.'[211] Moreover, the temple is valued precisely because it is the home of 'a living god.'[212] Secondly, he says they are a response to a desire to know God's nature.[213] The idol is held to be an exact representation of the god by virtue of the fact that the god has been seen on earth and that therefore, by the continuity of tradition, it is possible to make an image in his or her likeness.[214]

---

207   Ibid., p. 338.

208   Ibid., p. 342.

209   Ibid., p. 340.

210   Ibid., p. 324.

211   Ibid., fn. 3.

212   Ibid., p. 327.

213   Ibid., p. 340.

214   Ibid, p. 321. Farquhar notes that, 'Śankara confesses that the gods were never seen in his day, but says: 'What is not accessible to our perception may have been within the sphere of perception of people in ancient times. Smṛiti also declares that Vyāsa and others conversed with the gods face to face' (Crown, p. 321, fn. 6). The portrayal is thus in a form in which the god has manifested himself, so: 'The liṅga is not an image of Śiva, but it is believed that he himself took the form of a liṅga of light in heaven, in order to manifest his greatness, and that he created the earliest liṅgas on earth. Consequently, it is easy to cut a stone in accordance with his will' (ibid., pp. 321–2). It is important that the image should portray something of the god's character, for the worshipper to feel that he is in the god's presence, and has a direct link to him. Farquhar draws a comparison with certain statues in Greek art: 'The ineffaceable impression produced on the Greek mind by the image of Zeus at Olympia may help us to understand how idols lay hold of the common heart of man. Under this spell many a man, who ordinarily is far enough removed from reverence,

feels he can adore and pray. His god is now no mere thought or imagination to him, but a definite person whose character he is in touch with' (ibid., p. 340). The following passage from the guide to the great Vaishnavite temple at Srirangam should express something of the importance of the shrine and its idol to the ordinary Hindu worshipper: 'The worshippers of Vishnu believe that he exists in five different forms. As a transcendental deity, he is known as Paravasudeva or Paramapadanatha and dwells in heaven, Vaikuntha, attended by the goddesses Sri Devi (Lakshmi) and Bhu Devi (The Earth) and votaries who have become immortal (*nityasuri*). In his emanation (*vyuha*), he is Mahavishnu and rests on the Serpent of Eternity, Adisesha, attended by the same gods and votaries. But he is invisible. He comes near to man in his incarnations (*avatara*), but these are now part of the past; the faithful can only worship him and await hopefully his future incarnation as Kalki. (Kalki, the tenth avatara of Vishnu, of whom it is said: 'He will vanquish Yama, or Death, and will resolve all opposites as well as overcome darkness. He will be the divine man, at one with infinite divinity' (Schumacher and Woerner, p. 171). Given this description I am surprised that none of the fulfilment theologians have claimed him as a type of Christ, and say that what Hindus look and hope for is already found in Christ, the divine man, who has overcome Yama). In the form of Antaryani, he dwells in each individual 'like water in the depths of the earth'. His presence can only be vaguely felt by the individual, and fully realized by only a chosen few. Lastly, in the material aspect shown by the images (*murti*), he appears and dwells in his sanctuaries, which traditionally number 108. His Tamil worshippers consider that his chief sanctuary is that of Srirangam, thus bearing out its name: Koil, 'the temple par excellence'. As is said of it: 'One cannot attain to the god; one cannot see him; one can only hope for his future manifestation; with certain exceptions, one cannot have full knowledge of him; but it is possible to venerate him in his shrine. This is the deep significance of a pilgrimage to Srirangam' (Auboyer, p. 8). The idol is thus the way most Hindus approach the gods, and thus the importance of the image being a correct portrayal of the deity, capable of speaking to their religious needs is vital.* A parallel of the importance of the correct portrayal of religious images can be seen in the Christian iconographic tradition (Quenot, pp. 70 ff.), where, 'The art of the icon is imbued with theology' (Quenot, p. 15). To the Orthodox Christian 'the icon is a true sacramental of a *personal presence*' (ibid., p. 79). The importance of them is that they represent the transfigured creation, and are thus 'sacred' rather than merely religious art (ibid., p. 74, see also Burckhardt, pp. 7 ff.): that the icon is a true form of sacred art is guaranteed by the way it accords with tradition (although in some instances innovation is allowed; an example would be the icon of the Transfiguration, a form which is not traditional, and so when the first such icon was created by Brother Aidan, England's leading icon painter, he could create a whole new form – the icon of the Transfiguration was, until early 1997, located in the Christian Community chapel in Lampeter, but is now in private ownership). Also, we may note that a part of the New Testament apocrypha purports to describe Jesus' appearance (Ballou, p. 1280–1, 'A Letter of Lentulus. The note to this work reads, 'A description of Jesus. A fragment which Montague James believes to be an

Third, the idol has a place in people's lives to fulfil their need for daily contact with the god.[215] He believed that the numerous temples and shrines meet people's needs to have God at hand for all eventualities:

> The ordinary Hindu wants a temple near his home, that he may be able to see his god at any moment, to make him an offering of food, to ask for his help in distress or in danger, to pour out his heart in prayer or in praise. It is the living, present god that the human heart adores with rapture and gratitude. This is the reason for the limitless multiplication of temples, for the idols of the home and the little shrines by the roadside. The Hindu must have a living god to turn to wherever he is.[216]

Farquhar can sympathise with this far more than he can with the sannyāsī and his contemplation of the highest essence, so he says:

> Idolatry brought to the Hindu people something which their philosophy never gave them, and never could give them, present and accessible gods. Brahman, being 'beyond thought and speech', can never be to any man what an idol is. It is the god to whom a man can

---

invention contained in a letter, probably of the thirteenth century, supposed to have been written by 'a certain Lentulus to the Roman Senate.' This follows, James writes, 'the traditional portraits closely, and no doubt was written in the presence of one' ibid., p. 1378)) and the fact that this rather late work describes the typical portrait of Jesus in the icon, perhaps indicates the importance given to the idea that pictures of Jesus truly recorded his likeness. Similar concerns can, then, be seen both within Hinduism and Christianity.

*I would like to venture here the tentative suggestion that as it has been observed that certain forms of Indian dance, and the indigenous martial art, kalaripayit, show similarities to postures of the gods seen upon statues, that these arts may originally have had a role as ways of internalizing the god by imitating his outer forms (Reid, pp. 36 and 55). This would make them similar to the classical yogic āsanas of Patañjali, whose primary purpose is to help still the body (Eliade, 1969, pp. 48 and 54 f.), but they do, nevertheless, have another role, especially in other yogic traditions, '[the āsanas] imitate a divine archetype; the yogic position has a religious value in itself. It is true that the yogin does not imitate the 'gestures' and 'sufferings' of the ivinity – and not without reason! For the God of the *Yoga-sūtras*, Īśvara, is a pure spirit[....] Hence[...] what the yogin imitates is at least the mode of being belonging to the pure spirit[....] In other varieties of Yoga, āsana and ekāgratā can obviously acquire religious valences by the mere fact that, through them, the yogin becomes a living statue, thus imitating the iconographic model' (ibid., p. 68).

215   Crown, pp. 340–1.
216   Ibid.

317

turn in prayer at any moment and receive the help or the answer he wants that will finally hold the human heart.[217]

All of these wants and needs are, for Farquhar, met in the person of Jesus, who has been sent 'to crown all former revelation.'[218] Farquhar does not expressly answer the first point above in dealing with idols, and I would suggest that he probably saw this point as being an á priori assumption for his Christian audience, who *knew* that, in Jesus, God had come down to earth, and thus was the *real* theophany of a caring God who comes to us, which Hindus saw in their idols. In relation to the other points Farquhar makes two claims. Firstly, Jesus's character is believed to be the revelation of the nature of God.[219] In his life, God's moral perfection and His love for man is seen.[220] Secondly, Jesus has revealed the Father who Farquhar says was not known directly to anyone in Jesus' day.[221] So, having made Him known, the Father, it is claimed, is now approachable directly. Farquhar says of the early Christians:

---

217   Ibid. Of course, the ineffable Brahman is the spiritual nourishment of the Vedāntin. Yet while the god who is personal and of whom one can ask favours is Farquhar's ideal, there are those who would seek God within Christianity along more mystical lines. The following passage from Bede Griffiths speaks of the Christian use of yoga in contemplation: 'The transformation of body and soul by the Spirit is the work of Yoga[....] Wisdom consists of the knowledge of being in pure consciousness without any modification, and this brings lasting bliss – *saccidananda* – the bliss of the pure consciousness of being. There is certainly profound truth in this doctrine. There is an experience of being in pure consciousness which gives lasting peace to the soul. It is an experience of the Ground or Depth of being in the Centre of the soul, an awareness of the mystery of being beyond sense and thought, which gives a sense of fulfilment, of finality, of absolute truth[....]
'This is the goal of a Christian yoga. Body and soul are to be transfigured by the divine life and to participate in the divine consciousness' (Griffiths, 1987, pp. 136–7 and 137–8). One is, of course, also reminded here of the words of the Blessed Heinrich Suso in his *The Life of the Servant*, in which, tending a disconsolate woman, he says that although the teachings of his master, Eckhart, are very fine they are, no doubt, too abstruse for most people's needs (Knox, 1913, (op. cit.), p. 124 f.).
218   Crown, p. 344.
219   Ibid., pp. 345 ff.
220   Ibid., pp. 346–7. In saying that Jesus shows God's love for man, this indirectly answers the first point above, that in revealing God's nature his care for man in his theophany is shown.
221   Ibid., pp. 348–9.

They no longer needed temple, priest, and sacrifice; they needed no ritual, no forms of prayer. Like children, they turned to their heavenly Father with their every want, in joy or sorrow, in prayer or praise, as readily as Jesus used to do.[222]

This meant, to Farquhar, that Jesus enabled us to worship God in a way that is both purely spiritual and also full of emotion.[223] Thus he says:

It is one of the marvels of Christ that He is able to make such an appeal and to make it effectively; so that the man who has been used to the accessibility of idols and the joy and passion of their worship finds in Him, in purest spiritual form, more than all the emotion and stimulus to reverent adoration which their vividness used to bring him.[224]

In fact, Farquhar goes as far as to say that Jesus takes 'the place which is held by idols in idolatrous systems,'[225] by being the image of God and being the direct and accessible root of access to Him.

We will turn now to avataras, which Farquhar deals with separately, but which fulfil, in part at least, the same role. The similarity is that avataras are seen as revelations of God's character.[226] One point worth noting is that to the Hindu they are not held up as an example of life to be followed.[227] Another main feature is that they show God as having been born, and living and dying, amongst men.[228] Farquhar, however, notes that their humanity is unreal, being but a disguise of the divinity, and their human limitations are only a pretence.[229] Avataras are, also, held to be great teachers.[230] The avatara also comes as a saviour,[231] and in certain of the Tamil poets is seen as a suffering saviour.[232] These points are all met and transcended in Jesus, says Farquhar.

First, as to revealing God's character, and living amongst men, Farquhar says he was perfectly moral and also genuinely human,[233] and unlike the baby

---

222   Ibid., p. 349.
223   Ibid., pp. 347–8. The importance of the direct emotional response to the idol is a topic we touched upon briefly earlier.
224   Ibid., p. 343.
225   Ibid., p. 350.
226   Ibid., pp. 433 ff.
227   Ibid., p. 434.
228   Ibid., p. 429.
229   Ibid., p. 430.
230   Ibid., p. 438.
231   Ibid., p. 441.
232   Ibid., p. 442.
233   Ibid., p. 436.

Krishna, revealed no supernatural powers as a baby.[234] He thus can be an example, as he was truly human, whereas Farquhar notes Hinduism said it was impossible for an avatara to be an example for us.[235] Jesus was also a teacher, Farquhar notes, and, indeed, he says that unlike the semi-mythical Krishna, we know that we have Jesus' teachings in the Bible.[236] Further he claims that these teachings are also inherently superior.[237] As to the avatara as saviour, this, says Farquhar, was Jesus' whole life's work.[238] Interestingly, the main stress laid upon this work by Farquhar is Jesus as the saviour of human society generally. This is part of his emphasis, to stress Christianity's role in forging what he sees as a Westernized society, so he says:

> He [Jesus] was the first religious teacher to take up a healthy attitude to the human body.[239] He knew full well the value of the soul:

---

234   Ibid., p. 431.

235   Ibid., p. 437.

236   Ibid., pp. 438–9. We must not forget that Farquhar's early years had seen the confident Victorian quest for the historical Jesus, and in 1893, only a few years after Farquhar left for India, his tutor at Oxford, A. M. Fairbairn, had written of Jesus that He 'is to-day more studied and better known as He was and as He lived than at any period between now and the first age of the Church' (Fairbairn, *Christ in Modern Theology*, p. 3, in Fulfil, p. 43). Of course, more recent scholarship would cast doubt upon this overly optimistic attitude and particularly as to what we know of Jesus' own words. The following raises some of the problems, 'First, even those who accept that the Bible is divinely inspired, are not obliged to hold that all the words attributed to Jesus in the gospels were spoken by him in that form during his earthly life: otherwise, one would have to admit that he taught the disciples two different forms of the Lord's Prayer, and pronounced the words instituting the Eucharist in four different ways[....]'

'Secondly,[...] in the ancient world[...] it was customary for an author[...] to place upon the lips of his characters speeches written by himself, in order to set forth the man's thoughts' (Léon-Dufour, pp. 206–7).

237   Crown, pp. 439–41. One of Farquhar's main contentions is that Jesus's teachings are only spiritual principles, rather than rules which make His teachings applicable to all men everywhere, and therefore universal (ibid., pp. 58–9). Each nation may therefore have their own laws, but guided by Christ's teachings, which are universally applicable.

238   Ibid., pp. 442 ff.

239   We mentioned in relation to Slater that he felt that in Hinduism the world was looked upon as evil (Slater, 1903, p. 115), and have noted that this was an unsympathetic observation. Here, we see Farquhar suggesting that only in Christianity is the world, and in particular the body, properly, meaning 'well', regarded. This point is most often stressed in relation to the sannyāsī and the

320

'What shall it profit a man, if he shall gain the whole world, and lose his soul?'[240]
Yet he recognized the place of the body, as all modern thought does, and he left us His example of loving care for it. He spent a great deal of time and energy in healing the body. All that modern science has got to say as to the importance of attending to our physical well-being is in accordance with the spirit of Jesus. All that we can do to bring medical aid to the sick, to introduce sanitation into Indian villages, to destroy the germs of disease, and to transform unhealthy conditions, and all our plans for healthy physical exercise, for outdoor games, for drill and gymnastics, are completely in accordance with His teaching and practice. India needs to learn to look after the body.[241]

The message here is clear. Christianity is Western civilization and science, and more than this, Christianity and English culture, at least in their expression in the tradition of 'muscular Christianity', are synonymous. This has been something that we have seen over and over again in Farquhar. Although he says that he is judging Hinduism against 'pure' Christianity, not its actual manifestation anywhere, it is nevertheless the tradition and culture in which he has been raised that provide the criteria for judgement as to what 'essential' Christianity is. This point will be developed further later on. He also notes that Jesus fulfilled the need of a suffering saviour, which Hindus were intuitively aware of, 'Māṇikka Vāchakar and Tulsī Dās realized that the

---

tradition of asceticism, which we have noted, in the minds of Farquhar and Slater, is fulfilled by the Christian tradition of self-surrender, as opposed to 'world-surrender'. However, as far as world denial goes, we must not forget within Christianity the extremes of, 'the Puritan ethic of industry, sobriety, thrift and suspicion of ungodly pleasure, both of the cruel sports of the eighteenth century and *of novel reading and the theatre*' (Gilley, in T. Thomas, p. 22). The denial of pleasur, has a long history within Christianity, as does the tradition of self-mortification, especially during the middle ages: 'In connexion with the rigorous movement emanating from Cluny, there were many monasteries in which from the commencement of the 11th cent.,[...] flagellation was practised in a specially severe form, and with all sorts of refinements added to intensify it[....] Loricatus[...] added to the self-inflicted flagellation yet other methods of mortifying the flesh, notably the performance of numerous genuflections (*metanœæ*) during the singing of Psalms in Divine worship[....]' (Zöckler, in Hasting s, II, pp. 77–8). Moving closer to Farquhar's day ascetic endeavour was also to be found amongst a number of tractarians. The example of Morris and some others already observed, is most instructive on this. This returns to the point made at the beginning, that Farquhar compares his vision of ideal Christianity with what he sees as Hindu abuses, but to his way of thinking Christianity contains as many abuses of true religion as Hinduism does. This is a point that we will return to later on.

240   Mt. XVI: 26.
241   Crown, pp. 442–3.

Incarnate One in His compassion and love would suffer for the sake of men: Jesus fulfilled their thought on the Cross of Calvary.'[242] Farquhar thus sees Jesus as crowning all the Hindu beliefs and needs expressed in idols and the avatara ideal.

vi) The Hindu Family

One area that Farquhar gives a considerable amount of consideration to, that we have not yet examined and which is not given much, if any, thought in the writings of previous fulfilment theologians, is the family. This is, perhaps, not surprising. Previous writers had been concerned very much with central religious ideas, while Farquhar wanted to show that the whole Hindu system is unhealthy and that for India to become a modern society, it needs Christ at its heart. Therefore this is a key issue for him.

Farquhar says that all members of the Reform movement and National movement are in favour of reform to the structure of the Hindu family,[243] but, he says, all of their criticisms are Christian criticisms.[244] To his mind, this shows the insufficiency of the Hindu ideal to meet the needs of the modern world.[245] We now turn to Farquhar's assessment of the Hindu family.

For Farquhar, there are fourteen essential characteristics of the Hindu family which will be outlined very briefly: 1) Everyone should marry and beget a son; 2) not to marry a near relative; 3) the authority of the husband in the household; 4) the large family unit; 5) women are in a state of subjugation; 6) exposure of infants; 7) polygamy; 8) a man should not eat with his wife; 9) girls are not educated; 10) child marriage; 11) prohibition of widow remarriage; 12) satī; 13) perpetual mourning for widows who do not commit satī; and, 14) the seclusion of women.[246] Amongst these regulations and rules, he says, there are some healthy points.[247]

---

242   Ibid., p. 444.
243   Ibid., pp. 104 ff.
244   Ibid., p. 106.
245   See ibid., pp. 106 ff.
246   Ibid., pp. 85–101.
247   Ibid., p. 102. For instance, he says the first rule is healthy (ibid., p. 86), the fifth rule, of joint families he feels attacks selfishness, though it retards individual growth (ibid., pp. 89–90).

In relation to what he said of the reforms within Hinduism, he says that faith has been lost in the śrādhha ceremonies,[248] and also, he says, belief in women's inferiority is passing away,[249] as is belief in child marriage,[250] and it is now permissible for widows to re-marry, at least in educated circles.[251] The source of this, he says, is Christ, whom, he believed to be behind the reform movement.[252]

There is one other point worth noting here, and that is Farquhar's defence of the attacks made upon the immorality of the West. He observes that 'Hindus are accustomed to object that the sexual immorality and the divorce of the West are as bad as anything found in India.'[253]

Farquhar responds that immorality is as rife in India, and that even if this were not so, then it would not disprove that Christ offers the ultimate foundation for the family, arguing that:

> The ignorance of multitudes of people in the slums of European cities is no proof that Western education is unnecessary or unhealthy; and the millions of people who in many parts of the world live insanitary lives do not constitute a disproof of the value of hygiene. Like Hinduism, Christianity must be judged by its principles, not by the vicious lives of those who refuse to obey it.[254]

This, however, does provide a problem for Farquhar and his contemporaries, whose contention is that Christianity provides a more powerful moral force in peoples lives.[255] If this is so, then, why, it can be asked, do so many people in western nations not live up to this ideal, which, assuming that Farquhar is

---

248   Ibid., p. 113. When I was in Bodh-Gaya –the towns of Gaya and Bodh-Gaya being the main focus of the Hindu cult of ancestor worship – in 1995, a Buddhist there told me that, although he believed in reincarnation and did not therefore believe in the Hindu rites for the dead and the custom of paying homage to his ancestors, he still found it necessary to perform these rites, because, amongst his Hindu family and friends, he would be regarded as an undutiful son, and a 'bad person' if he didn't carry out these ceremonies.

249   Crown, ibid.

250   Ibid., p. 114.

251   Ibid.

252   Ibid., p. 118. See especially chapter 4 on the reform movement's attitude towards Jesus.

253   Ibid., p. 119.

254   Ibid.

255   This was stressed in the chapter on the Edinburgh Conference. Also, we saw with reference to idols, that Farquhar believed that Christ provided an emotional and spiritual power that is not found in Hinduism.

right and the Christian religion is the best, would make it a point of academic relevance, as no one, or, very few people at any rate, fulfil it?[256] Farquhar's case does, however, go beyond saying that Christ provides a better basis for the family. The whole Hindu system is, he says, at fault: 'It is the very laws of the Hindu family that require it to be laid aside.'[257] His contention is that many of the wrongs of the Hindu family are endorsed by the system itself, while the flaws in 'Christian' countries are a result of disobeyance of the precepts of Jesus. How Farquhar sees these 'flawed' aspects as being improved upon by Jesus' teachings will now be examined.

Farquhar starts off by insisting that the central message of Christianity is the Fatherhood of God,[258] and that we can have a personal relationship with Him and are made in His image,[259] therefore we must all be seen 'to be a child of God of priceless worth.'[260] This is why he says that Jesus taught the equality of both men and women, and that boys and girls are to be treated equally.[261] This is not just a matter of 'fulfilment' for Farquhar, but is for him a matter of importance for Indian nationalism, that without education for women, there is a piteous waste of human resources.[262] Also stemming from this is the belief that God's children should be free,[263] therefore, there should not be the sort of subjugation to the head of the household that exists in Hinduism. Farquhar does not express this as a point of fulfilment, but in saying that: 'The lofty dignity of the Hindu husband and father is confirmed by Christ, but is conferred upon the wife and mother as well,'[264] there is an

---

256   This point returns to one raised earlier, that Farquhar repeatedly says that the Christian ideal is impeccable, and makes assumptions that only Christianity can provide the inner core of spiritual power to back this up. Such a belief is still prevalent in some circles today; recently (Sunday, 20, April, 1997) I heard a sermon preached in the college chapel at Lampeter in which the preacher, an evangelical, said that Christianity is the only spiritual religion, all others only provide an outer veneer, and used the example that 'all other religions put a new suit on the man, only Christianity puts a new man in the suit.' Even in enlightened institutions the most narrow-minded and prejudiced views of earlier centuries are, it seems, alive and well amongst certain factions of the Christian Church.

257   Crown, p. 456.

258   Ibid., p. 119.

259   Ibid., pp. 119–20.

260   Ibid., p. 121.

261   Ibid., pp. 121 ff.

262   Ibid., pp. 105 ff.

263   Ibid., pp. 124–6.

264   Ibid., p. 132.

implication that the ideal of the dignity of mankind, which in Hinduism finds expression in dignity given to the father, is, in Christ, extended universally. It is worth noting here that, in general, Farquhar does not emphasise each aspect as finding its fulfilment in a specific bit of Christian teaching, preferring instead to say that Christianity has certain ideals which, when applied, can be seen to be a universal form of certain instincts behind Hindu ideas. Often, as in this case, he does not spell out the specific instinct behind Hindu ideas, but rather he just identifies them, and explains how the Christian version differs. In respect of satī, he says that it 'rests in its ultimate analysis on a very high ideal of wifely loyalty and purity, and a deep faith in the reality of heaven and the reunion of loved ones there.'[265] In making this point, however, Farquhar does not go on to stress the Christian fulfilment of this, because he does not see each doctrine of Hinduism being fulfilled, but rather the general ethos and beliefs that lie behind these ideas.[266] Having noted this I will examine what Farquhar believes are the most important points of fulfilment:

> The sacred character which invests every aspect of Hindu family life is deepened by Christ[....]
> Monogamy, which has always been the law for Hindu women, is the Christian law for men as well as women.
> The high ideal of loyalty and chastity which is set before the Hindu wife is demanded in Christianity of the husband as well as the wife.
> Christ bids us treasure both sons and daughters as Hindu parents have been accustomed to treasure sons.
> In ancient India, education, religious and general, was the right of every boy of the twice-born castes: in Christianity, it is the right of every boy and every girl of whatever race or social position.
> The chastity which was so wisely demanded of the Hindu adolescent while a student is laid upon all adolescents without exception by Christian principle.[267]

Farquhar's final paragraph in his chapter on the Hindu family neatly sums up the analysis that we have made of his thought in this chapter:

---

265   Ibid., p. 448.
266   I emphasise this point here when running through Farquhar's portrayal of how Hinduism is fulfilled, because it becomes relevant when we look at one of the particular criticisms levelled against him.
267   Crown, pp. 132–3.

Thus the present weakness and unhealthiness of the Hindu family find their one remedy in the principles of Christ. The divine truths concerning man and woman which He revealed are needed to raise its best customs to their height, to universalize its highest laws, and to correct the glaring abuses. Christ will transfigure the Hindu family to glory.[268]

Farquhar insists that 'Christ thus crowns the Hindu family with a structure which is new, yet is in no sense alien, but is the natural consummation of the older and less perfect system.'[269]

Farquhar's theory seems to be that because, or so he believes, the Hindu reformers are moving towards modifications of the Hindu family that are Western, i.e. Christian, then the Christian family is in some way a natural outgrowth of all that is best in the Hindu system.

As a final note here I will mention that many, particularly today, would read Farquhar's words, especially as regards the family, in a political light, as an aspect of post-colonial criticism. However, as this study is looking at fulfilment theology in the context of its theological development, I shall not develop this subject here, fascinating as it would be to analysize Farquhar's thought in this way.[270] Specific aspects of this may be examined at a later time.

vii) Other Areas of Fulfilment

Beyond the main points noted above, Farquhar also mentions some other areas in which he believes his fulfilment principle is applicable. He does not develop these in as great as detail as the main tenets, but still thinks them worth referring to in his work.

First, Farquhar notes the Hindu custom of bathing in the Ganges to wash away sin,[271] of which he says: 'The custom is not only absurd, but seriously

---

268   Ibid., p. 133.
269   Ibid., p. 132.
270   It may be remarked that for those interested in such matters the closest I come to considering the political and post-colonial aspects of fulfilment theology are in considering the 'typical' Western attitude at the time of the Edinburgh Conference (see previous chapter), and also many of the criticisms made of fulfilment theology which could be seen as post-colonial criticism, or as inspired by the same themes (see next chapter).
271   Ibid., p. 447.

immoral.'[272] Farquhar does, however, go on to say, 'Yet there is behind it the true religious instinct, that there must be a way whereby man can get his sin forgiven, that, since God exists, there must be a fountain for sin and uncleanness.'[273] It is, perhaps, surprising at first sight that Farquhar does not at once see this as a type of baptism, but if we consider that his method is not to show how specific Hindu doctrines are fulfilled by their Christian counterparts, but rather to show how the religious instincts of the Indian people are met in Christ, then it is understandable. Considering, however, the closeness of how his perception of this idea to certain Christian understandings of baptism, notably of infant baptism, the administration of this rite washing away original sin, meaning that even children who do not understand the rite and cannot of themselves repent, are saved by this one act,[274] it is surprising that he can call it 'seriously immoral.'

He also briefly notes the ancient custom of religious suicide, found in both Jainism and Hinduism, behind which he says lies 'the noble desire to discard this sensuous frame, to give up this poor life so as to win the real life.'[275]

On the next point, Farquhar delivers the following damning criticism: 'There is no more shallow superstition than the common Hindu belief in the

---

272   Ibid., he quotes a certain Hindu writer, Mr. V. Kunhikannan, on this subject, 'If we can commit sins and wash them away by bathing in the waters of certain river (while the Ganges is the best known of India's sacred rivers there are several more which are also highly revered, notably the Cauvery in Tamil Nadu), how easy things have become! Such ideas are dangerous to man's moral evolution. They encourage the commission of sin by holding out the hope of cleansing through the holy water of the Ganges' (Crown, pp. 447–8, quoting Kunhikinnan, from the *Madras Christian College Magazine*, April, 1912).

273   Ibid., p. 448.

274   Note, for instance, the Council of Trent's 'Decree Concerning Original Sin', 'If anyone asserts that this sin of Adam... is taken away ... by any other remedy than the merit of the one mediator, our Lord Jesus Christ... or if he denies that the said merit of Jesus Christ is applied, both to adults and to infants, by the Sacrament of Baptism rightly administered in the form of the Church; let him be anathema' (*Dogmatic Canons and Decrees*, op. cit., 3, p. 17). Also the canon XIII *On Baptism*: 'If anyone saith that little children, for they have not actual faith, are not, after having received baptism, to be reckoned amongst the faithful[...]; let him be anathema' (ibid., op. cit., p. 65).

275   Crown, p. 448. commenting on it he says: 'It is a pitiful travesty of Christ's great principle:
    "Whoever would save his life shall lose it; and whosoever shall lose his life for my sake and the gospel's shall save it"' (ibid., quoting Mark VIII: 35).

spiritual value of the mere utterance of the name of the god one adores, or the repetition of the sectarian *mantra*.'[276] However, even in this he sees a saving grace:

> Two things have led to the rise of these unreasoning beliefs; first, the fact that the divine name and the sacred mantra, being the expression of the uttermost reverence of the soul, are uttered with the very deepest feeling; and secondly, the belief that the idea contained in the mantra is the sum of all spiritual truth, is, in fact, the spiritual food which has to be assimilated by the soul.[277]

In offering a critique of this, one hardly knows where to begin. In relation to Monier-Williams' quotation from the Rt. Rev. Robert Milman,[278] we made reference to John Main[279], who has done much to introduce a mantric style of prayer to the West, and who first learnt of the technique from a Hindu Swami.[280] The practice has thus been found to be of deep spiritual value. Also, to note a more established Christian tradition, there is the Jesus Prayer of the Orthodox Church, which has gained a wide audience through the success of *The Way of a Pilgrim*. This prayer, like the mantra,[281] is believed to help take people beyond the level of discursive prayer that seems to be familiar to Farquhar.[282] Referring to the definition of a Russian starets, Bishop Kallistos Ware notes:

> In prayer, says Bishop Theophan the Recluse (1815–94), 'the principal thing is to stand before God with the mind in the heart, and to go on standing before Him unceasingly day

---

276   Ibid., p. 449.

277   Ibid.

278   Monier-Williams, 1889, p. 540.

279   Who has been described as, 'the best spiritual guide in the Church today' by no less a figure than Dom Bede Griffiths (Griffiths in Main, p. vii).

280   Ibid. Whether Fr. Main is right to suggest that this technique is to be found in Cassian is, perhaps, unclear, but certainly the Christian tradition does contain a similar tradition in the Jesus Prayer which we will deal with below.

281   To the Hindu mantras are 'a means to take their user to the source of speech, to its primordial level, which is Godhead' (Padoux, p. 372).

282   'Prayer is here envisaged as something expressed in words, and more specifically as an act of asking God to confer some benefit. We are still on the level of external rather than internal prayer' (Ware, p. 7).

and night until the end of life.' Praying, defined in this way, is no longer merely to ask for things, and can indeed exist without the employment of any words at all.[283]

Certainly Farquhar failed to appreciate the spiritual side of the mantra, and was, perhaps, unaware of a long Christian tradition endorsing, what, in the terms of his criticisms, would presumably be equally bad practices.

Next, he turns to the beliefs of the village Hindu about Brāhmans, whom he believes to be possessed of immense magical powers.[284] The root of these ideas is, says Farquhar, the belief that the 'Brāhman is a spiritual being of the highest rank, and that, on account of his spirituality, he has been chosen and appointed by the gods a priest to his people, to stand between them and their gods in sacrifice, in the revelation of the divine will, and in the use of supernatural power.'[285] Farquhar is not more precise here as to the need this belief answers, but presumably he feels there is an innate need for a mediator between God and man.

The homage paid to the guru is for Farquhar explained by 'the instinct that God will provide a teacher for us, and will pour into him such grace and wisdom that spiritual health and strength will flow to others from him.'[286] Next, Farquhar says that the practice of giving one's daughter to a temple stems from 'the idea that nothing is too good to be given as a gift to God.'[287]

We turn lastly to sacrifice, a subject that, although a rich mine for those writing on Hinduism from K. M. Banerjea to Slater,[288] is barely considered

---

283   Ibid., p. 7, quoting from Igumen Chariton of Valamo, *The Art of Prayer: An Orthodox Anthology*, translated by E. Kadloubovsky and E. M. Palmer (London), p. 63.
284   'He can not only sacrifice to the gods and declare their will, but can wield unlimited power over nature and man. He could blot the sun out of the heavens with a word; he could destroy the village and all its inhabitants with a nod' (Crown, p. 449). Belief in magical powers, not just of priests, was rife in India, Dare's book *Indian Underworld*, written some years later in 1938, details many of these ideas, and many in India today still make a living from such means, while in Delhi I saw one man 'levitating' for the tourists to obtain money, and in Mysore a snake charmer was selling small amulets to Indians to protect them from cobra bites.
285   Ibid.
286   Ibid., p. 450.
287   Ibid., p. 451.
288   See chapters on Slater and Banerjea.

by Farquhar; the reasons for this were noted earlier. While deploring the nature of Hindu sacrifice,[289] Farquhar says:

> Yet sacrifice is perhaps the most constant and the most real element in the average Hindu's worship[.... It] ministers to some of the deepest needs of the human heart, giving expression to man's gratitude to God, his desire to be on friendly terms with God, his desire to make atonement for wrong-doing.[290]

Noting the power of these ideas he says, 'But it is necessary to realize that they [sacrificial practices] cannot be removed, until something equally powerful, but spiritual, takes their place.'[291] This idea was also found in Slater, 'material sacrifices[...] offered to manifold deities have continued, in one form or another, down to the present day, and must continue in India and other non-Christian lands till Christ, the great *Fulfiller* of sacrifices is understood and accepted.'[292] A foretaste of this was seen in Maurice.[293]

The above, then, is Farquhar's assessment of the way in which Christianity fulfills Hinduism.

Main Features of Farquhar's Fulfilment Theology

Christianity as a Universal Religion

The point has been made above that Farquhar's notion of fulfilment was based, primarily, not upon seeing individual doctrines being fulfilled, but rather upon, the fulfilment the principle behind particular doctrines.

Another important point is Farquhar's portrayal of Christianity as a universal religion, as opposed to all others, which are merely national. Farquhar thus places an emphasis upon his belief that it is Christ, not Christianity, who fulfills, and also that Christ set forth precepts, while, he

---

289   We must remember that Farquhar was, for most of his time in India, based in Calcutta, where the great Kali-Ghat temple is notorious for its animal sacrifices.
290   Crown, pp. 449 and 450.
291   Ibid., p. 450.
292   Slater, pp. 66–7.
293   Boyle, p. 184.

believes, Hinduism, like all other religions, set forth laws which have to be obeyed.[294] The first point is found in earlier fulfilment theologians, in that they emphasise that it is Christ, not Christianity, that is the central principle of fulfilment.[295] Farquhar is, however, more specific on this point, stressing that Christianity is a different type of religion, which is, as Farquhar sees it, internal rather than external, that only Christ provides the necessary spiritual power to live by:

> Idolatry has proved its power not only by its mastery over nations but by creating architecture and sculpture. One of the clearest proofs that Christ has completely taken the place of idols is this, that in Judaism and Muhammedanism, the other two faiths which condemn idolatry, the consciousness of the danger and fascination of idols is so great that the faithful are forbidden to make statues and other representations of men and animals, lest they should be drawn to worship them, while Christians, by their knowledge of God in Jesus Christ, are set completely free from this terror, and are therefore able to use sculpture and painting with perfect freedom.[296]

This idea, that only Christianity had sufficient spiritual and ethical power to ennoble the lives of its devotees, was, as we have already seen, common in Farquhar's time.[297] Farquhar certainly admits that Hinduism does exert some influence upon the lives of its devotees,[298] but he often makes the point that Christianity replaces an external form of devotion with a 'spiritual' one.[299] In this we can see him as being in accord with Monier-Williams, seeing the non-Christian religions as merely expressive of man's innate spiritual desires, rather than being based upon an inner experience of God, as Müller, for instance, would have stated.[300]

In our first chapter, the importance of a Logos based theology, for informing an understanding of other faiths based upon a universal spiritual experience, was emphasized.[301] Farquhar, as we have seen, was not a trained

---

294   Crown, pp. 58 ff.
295   See, for instance, the section on Miller.
296   Crown, p. 343.
297   See above.
298   Crown, p. 451.
299   Note in particular what Farquhar says of idols.
300   See first chapter, sections on Monier-Williams and Müller.
301   This thought was seen in Maurice, and followed through to fulfilment theologians in this century, such as William Temple, and the importance of this idea for fulfilment theology, or 'preparationism' as he calls it, by Hoehler, pp. 47 ff.

theologian,[302] and had a straightforward faith,[303] describing himself as a
'liberal evangelical.'[304] Certainly Farquhar's faith had much in common
with the conservative evangelicals of his day,[305] but he was liberal in that he
held that those of other faiths could attain to salvation by following the
highest they knew,[306] which would be effective for them unless they had
come into contact with a higher ideal.[307] However, this belief is not based
upon an acceptance of Hinduism as a religion capable of salvific action in
itself, or of the Hindu's own direct knowledge of God; to Farquhar Hinduism
had no such power, and the Hindu no direct knowledge of God. These could
only come about from faith in Jesus, not, we may note, belief in specific
dogmas, and he said:

> Do not imagine that God has a list of doctrines which each man must accept before he
> can find salvation. Faith in Christ, continuous fellowship with Him, and an active Christian
> life of right actions and eager work for the Kingdom are the essentials of salvation; and
> doctrines are but helps which we need to use in forming our active faith and life.[308]

It was not, then, essentially the acceptance of a higher doctrine that Farquhar
saw as important, but the reason he felt people presented with a 'higher'
religious ideal would need to change, was because it presented a better answer
to what he saw as man's innate religious need. Therefore he felt a 'lower'
religion would no longer be able to inspire people to an act of service. This
is not to say that Farquhar disregarded doctrine altogether. He was
'evangelical in the sense of refusing to part with the basic essentials of the
Christian faith: forgiveness, reconciliation, sanctification.'[309] But he did feel,
'the relative unimportance of rival theories of the Atonement to a man on his

---

302 See above.
303 'Simplicity and childlikeness were to characterize Farquhar's faith through his
     whole life' (Sharpe, 1963, pp. 106–7).
304 'He called himself a 'liberal evangelical' – liberal in the sense of being open to
     knowledge derived from the consecrated use of reason, evangelical in the sense of
     refusing to part with the basic essentials of the Christian faith: forgiveness,
     reconciliation, sanctification' (ibid., pp. 106).
305 As we shall see below.
306 See above, section on his Biblical sources.
307 Crown, pp. 27–8, which is quoted above.
308 Farquhar, a letter to 'an inquirer,' 1927, Sharpe, 1963, p. 107. This says Sharpe is
     possibly the best exposition of Farquhar's faith.
309 Ibid., p. 106.

knees.'[310] I have stressed this here because it would be too easy to suggest that Farquhar was a caricature of a certain type of Christian whose faith was based merely upon the acceptance of certain dogma, without any sense of a living faith.[311] Yet while he recognized the reality of the non-Christian's religious yearnings,[312] there is still a Barthian-style radical distinction between true and false religion. Man is made in God's image, and so 'there is that in man which demands a Revelation – there is *not* that in him which makes the Revelation.'[313] Only with Christ do we have spiritual religion,[314] which to Farquhar marks this distinction, for before Jesus came, he says, no one had direct access to the Father. Yet, Farquhar is ready to concede that Hinduism is a 'really living religion'[315] which might seem to blur this dividing line, but his definition of a religion is if, 'Men have believed in it and lived by it.'[316] It is not that it provides a direct communion with the divine.

This point is demonstrated particularly in Farquhar's condemnation of Vedānta, which he sees as the quest for spiritual religion,[317] but which he says is dead, and does not provide the living energy of the religion.[318] Thus, Farquhar sees Hinduism as being a purely external religion, a matter of forms, but, it must be stressed, forms that *really do* minister to people's deepest

---

310   Ibid., p. 107.

311   Such a parody would be grossly untrue of him, see ibid., pp. 106 ff.

312   'Do we condemn Rāmānuja and the other leaders, both Śaiva and Vaishṇava? Nay by no means. Who does not feel deeply the sincerity and nobility of those men, the high motives that inspired them, the heroic toils and sacrifices they endured for the faith they held? What is clear, however, is this, that the faith which they had received had not *ethical* force and warmth sufficient to condemn widow-burning, female infanticide, and the cruel tyranny under which the Outcaste lives' (Crown, p. 400, italics my own).

313   Boyle, p. 55.

314   Hindus, says Farquhar, seek the spiritual, but do not have it: 'A little reflection will show any one that each of the *spiritual beliefs and motives* which we have found underlying the grosser superstitions of Hinduism reappears in Christ, set in healthy institutions and *spiritual practices*. He provides a religious system at once effective and *truly spiritual*' (Crown, p. 452, italics my own).

315   Ibid., p. 446.

316   Ibid.

317   Ibid., p. 452, see also ibid., chapter VI.

318   Ibid., p. 453.

needs and emotions.[319] Enough has already been said of Farquhar's lack of empathy with the mystical side of religion. without stressing the point here, it is very often from the mystical side of religion that the most powerful advocates of religious unity come.[320]

On the one hand, Farquhar acknowledged the reality of the Hindu spiritual quest, but on the other, he seemed to have a dogmatic belief that only faith in Jesus could supply any authentic spiritual experience. This, I feel, stems from Farquhar's own contemporary scene. The following quotation from John Hick should help to shed some light on this:

> There are many general interpretations of religion. These have usually been either naturalistic, treating religion as a purely human phenomenon or, if religious, have been developed within the confines of a particular confessional conviction which construes all other traditions within its own terms. The one type of theory that has seldom been attempted is a religious but not confessional interpretation of religion in its plurality of forms.[321]

Farquhar's interpretation of religion provides, I would suggest, the worst of both worlds, interpreting other religions, while following what is essentially the secular tool of historical-critical method along humanistic lines. He assumes certain innate needs and asking how Hinduism answers them, while over and against this he sets Christianity, which is spiritual, and 'right', while others are, therefore, á priori, 'wrong'.[322] Of course, Farquhar would never, for political reasons, if nothing else, say this, but it is in actuality the cornerstone of his system.

Death and Resurrection

Related to the above is Farquhar's system of religious evolution, which he explains in terms of death and resurrection, so he says, 'Hinduism must die in order to live. It must die into Christianity.[323] As was the case with the

---

319   The case of a sacrifice is a case in point, where he follows both Maurice and Slater in saying that it cannot be abolished until something else has taken its place. See above.
320   See, for instance, Otto and Suzuki, both already referred to above.
321   Hick, p. 1.
322   As Barth believed. More will be said on Barth in relation to Kraemer in chapter 8.
323   Crown, p. 51.

thought of many previous fulfilment theologians, the fulfilment he envisages is not a natural growth from one religion to the next,[324] but a radical displacement. For Farquhar, this happens by means of death and resurrection, which he sees as one of the great spiritual laws, and he speaks of the 'great lesson of life through death,'[325] which he sees exemplified in Jesus' crucifixion:

> This principle received its highest illustration in Christ Himself. He gained His victory through death. His own resurrection and the birth of the Christian Church were both fruits of His death on the cross.[326] It was Calvary that created Christianity. The living principle of the faith was expressed once for all in the self-devotion and death of our Lord. Like the grain of wheat He fell into the earth and died, in order to bear much fruit.[327]

This dying means, for Farquhar, 'that the individual should renounce his old national religion,'[328] but, as noted above, this is, says Farquhar, that it may have life.[329] Yet throughout his book, we noted Farquhar constantly attacked Hinduism, and saw it all decaying. What then does he believe will live through death? Farquhar's answer is that:

> To Him [Jesus] all that is great and good is dear, the noble art of India, the power and spirituality of its best literature, the beauty and simplicity of Hindu village life, the love and tenderness of the Hindu home, the devotion and endurance of the ascetic schools.[330]

What are these things? Despite Farquhar's use of the term 'Hindu', it does not appear to be anything specifically 'Hindu', rather the best features of the Indian spirit, which, essentially, could be seen as the human spirit; the only things that are notably Indian, would be art and literature, and I would suggest that these are not prized for their 'Indianness', but for expressing the yearnings of the human heart; no characteristically Indian thought is left. I am

---

324   Except, presumably, amongst the so-called 'lower' religions, i.e. from Polytheism to Islam, to use one of Farquhar's examples, but Farquhar does not expand upon this point, being interested only in Christianity.

325   Crown, p. 50.

326   It might be noted here, that, unsurprisingly as a Non-Conformist, Farquhar lets slip that he sees Whitsunday as the foundation of the Church, setting himself in the 'low' camp of Churchmanship.

327   Crown, p. 50.

328   Ibid., p. 49.

329   See, ibid., p. 51.

330   Ibid., p. 54.

not accusing Farquhar of being anti-Indian or racist here, merely noting that, as will be seen, in terms of actual thought as opposed to outer trappings or aesthetics, nothing characteristically 'Indian' or 'Hindu' is left. Though we should not ignore the fact that with Farquhar, perhaps more so than any other missionary fulfilment theologian, a sense of cultural chauvinism marks his attitude. I am sure that he loved India, but, we must ask, on what terms? With Slater and other fulfilment theologians, there was always the feeling that Vedānta would contribute something essentially 'Indian' to Western Christianity,[331] but as we have seen, Farquhar has no time for the tradition which it represents. It would be easy to condemn Farquhar for this from modernist 'liberal,' or post-modernist perspectives,[332] but to do so would be to forget that he was a creature of his own time. This 'liberal' tendency to speak of the good of non-Christian cultures, yet in so doing to deride the religion, and only to see good in the yearnings of the human spirit – interpreted as whatever coincided with preconceived Western notions – was a topic explored in the chapter on the Edinburgh Conference. Certainly there were more advanced thinkers, but, as we have seen, Farquhar's thought here was copied from ideas that had their birth in the middle of the nineteenth-century, and this book was published just one year before the beginning of the First World War, which was the major landmark in, and also to a large degree the cause, of the decline of many of the preconceptions from which this idea grew.[333] Certainly, belief in the supremacy of Christianity was not to flounder seriously amongst believers, but the next major school of thought that succeeded fulfilment would not to seek to show how Christianity could be demonstrated, from the principles of Western thought and culture, to be the superior religion, but would assert this supremacy á priori.[334]

To Farquhar his principle of 'life through death' was an expression of evolutionary thought, indeed, it can be seen as Farquhar's 'sanctification' of

---

331   Whether or not contemplative traditions are essentially 'Indian' is not something I wish to discuss here. Previously, the Western Christian contemplative tradition has been noted in passing as a counter to some of the statements Farquhar has made, but, leaving this question aside, the perception that the West is 'active,' the East 'contemplative' was the impression of such people as Farquhar and Slater.

332   As a possible challenge to Farquhar see, for instance, Bourne's paper, 'Does the Concept of the Person Vary Cross-Culturally?'

333   See ibid.

334   Fulfilment would, however, dominate English theological perceptions of the non-Christian religions until the middle of this century, before the Barthian perspective became prevalent.

this secular value. According to Farquhar this principle was known to Jesus: 'He [Jesus] knew that God's method of revelation is[...] a gradual and historical process.'[335]

Thus he contrasts Jesus and Gautama, the Buddha, saying that Christianity was formed 'correctly' upon evolutionary principles, 'Gautama cut himself adrift completely from Hinduism and denounced the Vedic sacrifices, the Vedas, and all the works of the Brāhmans. He made a clean sweep and anew beginning.'[336] Whereas, 'Jesus, on the other hand, acknowledged that the faith of Israel was from God, yet declared that He had been sent to transform it into a new religion[!]'[337]

Leaving aside Farquhar's claims about Jesus,[338] his suggestion that Christianity offers the paramount example of religious development can be seen to be centred very much in the thought of his day: 'Thus the principle of living growth, of progress and development, is set before us in visible form in the Christian scriptures. The Old Testament is the bud; the New Testament is the flower.'[339] Yet Farquhar, while keeping the best of Indian material culture, does not seem, as he claims, to be treating it as Greek culture was treated, where Christianity 'did not destroy the old civilization, philosophy, literature, and art. Everything of value that the old world contained has been preserved and flowered once more in Christianity. Our modern education, thought, science, and art rest on the ancient foundations.'[340] Yet it is precisely this 'modern education, thought, [and] science' that Farquhar believes is destroying the foundations of Hinduism.[341] He does not suggest that anything new will grow out of the best of Indian thought, whereas Christianity

---

335   Crown, p. 51. See also below.
336   Ibid.
337   Ibid.
338   His suggestion that Jesus knew the principles of evolutionary theory seems bizarre today. Even in his own day this may have seemed so; it was, after all twenty-three years earlier that Gore had posited in his essay 'The Holy Spirit and Inspiration', the idea that while on earth the historical Jesus would only have had the knowledge of a Jew of the first-century in Palestine. Also, incidentally, in the same essay, he had put forward the proposition that: 'The Revelation of God was made in a historical process' (Gore, 1890, p. 351). In line with this, recent scholarship has emphasized Jesus' perception of himself as a Jew, and not as the founder of a new religion (see, for example, Sandmel, chapter VIII).
339   Crown, p. 52.
340   Ibid., p. 53.
341   Crown, pp. 42 ff.

preserved the best of Greek philosophy – compared, of course, with Farquhar's words that, 'to introduce any Hindu doctrine into the Church of Christ would be to pour poison into it.'[342] Indeed, not only does he have no Hindu doctrine, but Farquhar also has no place for any inkling of Hindu thought at all to enter the arena of Christian teachings.

Here we can contrast Farquhar with Hogg, his main contemporary critic, who suggested that, 'the idea of Karma, when modified[...] may be used in formulating a Christian viewpoint of redemption and forgiveness.'[343] Further:

> The motive of the whole discussion has been to draw together Hindu and Christian thought on this great topic. Educated India declares that she will never become Christian; and certainly she will never embrace Christianity until Christian doctrines have been recast in a less alien mould.[344]

Thus, Hogg was moving further ahead of Farquhar in terms of the development of an indigenous Indian Christian theology, in that he was seeking to redefine Christianity in Indian terms.[345] It must certainly be said that Farquhar goes along with part of this aim, if not all of it. This aim was indeed fairly common: 'In India, from the beginning of the arrival of Western Christianity, there was an ongoing effort to free the Christian message from its previous cultural and political accretions and to allow it to stand freely for translation into the new situation.'[346] Farquhar, as we have seen, emphasizes Christ rather than any form of Christianity,[347] but an indigenous Indian Christian theology would go further, to develop 'a distinct tradition in India

---

342   Farquhar, lecture delivered before Continuation Committee Conference, Bengal, (in YMCA Hist. Lib.), quoted from Fulfil, p. 302.

343   Hogg, 1970, p. 116. The work was first published as a series of articles, under the same name, in the *Madras Christian College Magazine*, 1904–5.

344   Ibid.

345   However, in other ways Hogg's thought showed the same stamp as Farquhar's, as we will see in the next chapter.

346   Soans, p. 218.

347   Although, of course, this non-dogmatic Christ-centred Christianity was the standard fare of the intellectual non-Conformism of his day. It has been said about the majority of non-Conformists at this time that: 'They did not believe in evangelical orthodoxy or Anglo-Catholic orthodoxy or liberal heterodoxy, but occupied a denominational and theological middle ground, nurtured by the fellowship and liturgy and traditions of their denomination (and increasingly by a cross-denominational tradition of hymns), and *happily unspecific about the detail of their faith*' (Parsons, 1988 (a), p. 112).

of understanding Christ and Christianity in terms of Indian culture.'[348] While Farquhar's thought is very strong upon the death of Hinduism, he has little to say regarding its finding new life in any meaningful sense.

As has already been stressed, it is the supposed instinct behind particular doctrines that are fulfilled, not the doctrines themselves that are fulfilled in Farquhar's scheme. However, this he calls a fulfilment of Hinduism, although as is argued above, this is not fulfilling anything that can really be called 'Hinduism.' Is there, then, any more to Farquhar's death-to-life principle than this, and is there any sense in which Hinduism is growing into Christianity? Certainly, to Farquhar, at least, there is, for he believed that the reformers of India were adopting Christian principles.[349] To his mind, then, there is a sense in which Hinduism is evolving into Christianity, but, to use the example of the Hindu family, we noticed that Farquhar saw everything distinctly Indian dying out, to leave its 'sacred character'; monogamy would replace polygamy, and the principles of loyalty, dignity, respect, education, and chastity would widen out.[350] He looks at what is passing away,[351] and, as we saw, said that the Hindu critics could only offer Christian criticism.[352]

Indeed, what he sees the Hindu family becoming is, quite simply, his ideal of the Christian family. The scheme is replacement by a 'Western' ideal, not a Christianized Indian family. So it becomes clear here that what, to Farquhar, is the new life that has come out of death, is only what he sees as the most essential yearnings of the human heart, stripped of any national characteristics. Although he shies away from saying so explicitly, he obviously believes that the Indian reformers, having met a 'higher' ideal, are replacing their 'lower' ideal with it, so what has new life are their yearnings for loyalty, dignity, etc. In, then, speaking of Christianity as 'crowning' Hinduism, Farquhar is not really being true to his doctrine. There is no sense in which Hinduism itself is 'crowned,' it is the aspirations which, he believes, give birth to Hinduism that are 'crowned' in his system of fulfilment. While this point may seem unnecessarily pedantic, it should nevertheless be born in mind, for, as will be seen below, many of Farquhar's critics seem to base their attacks upon a misunderstanding engendered by this misrepresentation of his scheme brought about by Farquhar's loose use of terminology.

---

348   M. M. Thomas, 1977, p. 4.
349   Crown, pp 105 f.
350   See, ibid., pp. 132 f.
351   Ibid., pp. 113 ff.
352   Ibid., p. 106.

The belief mentioned above, that man's innate desires are fulfilled is, of course, nothing new, as we have seen the belief that man has a religious instinct that leads to him formulating a religious system which will answer these wants in Maurice.[353]

To give Farquhar credit, he does admit that his system is the death of the old religion:

> The Christian idea, that the individual should renounce his old national religion, is not an excrescence, but belong's to the very heart of Christ's system. The truth He teaches is for all men; and we cannot get the benefit of it except by complete submission to Him and faithful obedience to His laws. That His call, 'Follow me,' should lead to the surrender of the old religion on the part of the individual, and in the end to the death of the old religion, is in full accordance with the leading principles of His teaching.[354]

However, in suggesting that this then leads to an invigorated Hinduism is misleading. What it leads to is Christianity, plain and simple. I would suggest that although Farquhar allows that the best of Hindu art will continue, all this would mean is that, for Farquhar, an Indian Christianity would be a non-dogmatic (Scottish) Non-Conformity in a building that looked like a Hindu temple, or a Moghul mosque.

In this section we have picked up on the three main themes running through Farquhar's thought; firstly, that it is not doctrines, but desires that are fulfilled. Secondly, we noted how Farquhar saw Christianity as universal, which for him meant that it was spiritual rather than a matter of external rites. And, thirdly, his principle of 'life through death' and the implications of it in his scheme were examined.

Farquhar's Contribution to Fulfilment Theology

As has already been suggested, Farquhar was far from being an original or exemplary exponent of fulfilment theology. The same conclusion is offered by Cracknell regarding Farquhar's thought, where, speaking specifically of his contribution to the Edinburgh conference, he says: 'For all their

---

353   See chapter 2.
354   Crown, p. 49.

concreteness and precise scholarship, Farquhar's writings formed only one contribution among many others within the ferment of ideas at this time. From the missiological point of view they are not as important or as original as those of other writers[....]' [355] Compared to many, his thought can be seen as reactionary and not in tune with the main stream of fulfilment theology, in that he sees the non-Christian religions as being human, and does not develop a Logos theology. He adds nothing new to the theory of fulfilment theology. His association with the idea may therefore be surprising, except in as far as he can be seen to have been the right man, in the right place, at the right time. Following on from the Edinburgh conference, where fulfilment theology was felt to have received some form of official approval, a definitive work was needed. Slater's works had appeared a little too early to provide this, though, as has been noted, it was he and others who prepared the ground for Farquhar. The world was hungry for what he had to offer, and he had the ability to produce a popularly accessible, yet also academically sound, volume which would answer this need.

Conclusion to Part IV

In view of the previous history of fulfilment theology which has been considered in this study, the Edinburgh Conference, and Farquhar's *Crown of Hinduism*, can be seen, in terms of their importaance in the development of fulfilment theology, as almost negligible. The idea was already well known and neither the Conference nor the book added anything new. However, both were ultimately significant. The Edinburgh Conference was such an important event in the history of ecumenical relations and missionary history that its

---

355   Cracknell, 1995, pp. 172–3. He goes on to say, '"Fulfilment" was so common a concept within this period that we can see people like Slater, Lucas, Jones and Hume using it without Farquhar's scholastic connotations of evolution and supersession' (ibid., p. 173). I would wholly support Cracknell's first contention here, that 'fulfilment' was a common concept, but would not necessarilly endorse what he says about Slater, in particular using it without reference to evolution (see herein chapter 4; also Maw's long discussion of Slater's usage of evolutionary themes, Maw, 1990, pp. 52 ff), and, as we have seen, supersession is one of the cornerstones of the theory in nearly every form it takes.

endorsements have, no doubt, received a greater credit than they perhaps merited. While earlier conferences may have given general support to the idea of fulfilment theology, they had nothing to compare with the comprehensive report of Commission Four, which could be pointed to as a clear statement of what the Protestant Churches believed. As noted, the endorsement of fulfilment theology was not as full as most have suggested. Cairn's wording gave only limited approval, and then only to its usage in relation to Hinduism and Pure Land Buddhism, but this is not how it was understood, and so it became seen as a giving some sort of 'official' approval to fulfilment theology. Farquhar's book, on the other hand, came at a time when a clear and precise definition of fulfilment theology was needed. While many may have endorsed it as a general theory, it might be asked how many really understood the theory behind it. Here the fact that Farquhar's theology was so conservative may also have helped. This matter will be gone into further when considering Farquhar's conservative critics, but the essence of my argument is that as his fulfilment theology was based upon the idea that the non-Christian religions were from man, he nowhere expounded the kind of Logos based theories of inspiration which may have alienated many of his more evangelical colleagues. As the Crown fails to make this clear, the more liberal supporters of fulfilment theology could well have read such an assumption into his work.

Having considered the history of fulfilment theology up until the time of Farquhar, attention turns in the next chapter to looking at fulfilment theology's critics, and assessing its usefulness and future.

Part V: Conclusions

Introduction to Part V

The purpose of this final chapter is threefold. Firstly, we will consider those criticisms levelled against fulfilment theology in the years when it was most dominant, that is, in the years following the publication of Farquhar's *The Crown of Hinduism*. Essentially, this period may be considered as that stretching from the Edinburgh to the Tambaram missionary conferences. Though reference will be made particularly to Kraemer, the later writings of critics of this period will also be considered. Secondly, later criticisms of fulfilment theology will be offered, whether they be criticisms of Farquhar, other fulfilment theologians, or of the basic premises upon which fulfilment theology is based; and, thirdly, the way fulfilment theology developed after Farquhar,[1] and the other lines of approach that could be taken to the non-Christian religions – which appeared both contemporarily and subsequently – will be considered.

The presentation of these criticisms will be more thematic than chronological, which marks a divergence from the rest of this study, but is the most natural way to deal with the subject matter covered here. The first section will deal with Hogg's criticisms. The next section will look at criticisms coming from an evangelical, or conservative Christian standpoint, looking at the so-called 'Indian Witness' debate and other contemporary conservative criticisms, then considering Kraemer's thought, before assessing the differences in world-view between the conservative and liberal approaches. Next, some final problems raised in relation to fulfilment theology will be considered. The final section will then consider the nature of fulfilment theology after Farquhar, and will look at some contemporary thinkers who were pursuing a different agenda, and how these offer an option to fulfilment theology, and how more recent thought has both offered alternatives to, and provided ways of, continuing the theme of fulfilment.

---

1   Though having noted in the first chapter the wide range of thinkers who may be regarded as using fulfilment theology, those mentioned must inevitably represent a limited range, and can be given but scant mention, as the history of fulfilment theology after 1914 would be the work of at least one more book.

8 Criticisms and Assessment

Hogg's Analysis of Farquhar's Thought

Sharpe calls Hogg's criticism the only major theological criticism of Farquhar's day,[2] other analysis being in the nature of straightforward evangelical rebuttal – the ground having been well prepared by Farquhar's predecessors, so that fulfilment theology was accepted by the majority, leaving but few critics. Hogg's criticisms of *The Crown of Hinduism* itself are found in just two reviews, although he had previously attacked the idea of fulfilment theology in his correspondence to the Edinburgh Conference, where his most extensive criticisms are to be found. With reference first to his reviews, Hogg, despite his hostility to fulfilment theology, is not utterly damning, for he says of Farquhar's work: 'The result is a book to be depended upon; its impressive argument rests on a solid base.'[3] However, having been for the first half of his review generally well inclined towards Farquhar's work, Hogg goes on to say: 'If we must criticize, our criticism is this:'[4]

> Mr. Farquhar proves that Chris[t..]. has brought her [India] to the point at which none but He can satisfy her need. On the other hand, we feel that the claim that Christ is the crown of Hinduism is little more than a debating-point. Doubtless Christ fulfils what is good in Hinduism. But then He leaves out so much of what was in Hinduism, and He fulfils so much of what was never in Hinduism, that Mr. Farquhar's tracing out of the aspect of fulfilment sometimes seems far-fetched. What Christ directly fulfils is not Hinduism but the need of which India has begun to be conscious[....][5]

There are two points to Hogg's criticism here; first, that fulfilment is merely a 'debating-point', and therefore not suitable for apologetic purposes, to

---

2   Fulfil, p. 350.
3   Hogg, 1914, p. 171.
4   Ibid., p. 172.
5   Ibid., pp. 172–3.

which we shall return later. Hogg's second point is somewhat more subtle than might at first appear, for an initial reading might be taken to mean that what is fulfilled is not Hinduism per se but the individual Hindu's religious needs. Certainly this is part of Hogg's contention, but so, as he was at pains to make clear, was it also part of Farquhar's. Significant here are Hogg's final words in the above quotation, where he speaks of the need 'of which India *has begun* to be conscious.' His claim is one which today might be spoken of as 'particularity', that is to say, that each religion should be seen as operating within its own terms of reference, which have reference to different concepts of salvation. This theory has associations with certain forms of post-liberal theology, particularly with regard to cultural-linguistic theory. Here, however, Hogg's own particular employment of these ideas will be considered, which, to examine properly, will necessitate a brief consideration of Hogg's own thought.[6]

In contrast to fulfilment theology, Hogg believed in 'the method of contrast.'[7] To understand his criticism of fulfilment theology, it is necessary to gain an idea of what he proposed in its place, and to this end mention should be made of Hogg's beliefs. His theology had been formed in the 1890s in Scotland when Ritschl and his followers were exercising their influence.[8]

The Ritschlean school made a distinction between theoretical knowledge of things in the world, and the subjective perception of the individual observer, religious belief being founded upon the latter.[9] Ritschleanism also suggested, employing the catch phrase 'judgement of value' that, although based upon subjective knowledge, religious belief could acquire certainty through the experience of the individual. Further, it suggested that, being based upon the historical teachings of Jesus, Christianity was not subjective, while the community of believers provided further certainty for religious

---

6   It may be noted that some mention of him has been made of him in relation to the Edinburgh Conference.
7   EDMS, Hogg # 176, p. 11.
8   Cox, 1977, p. 1, and Sharpe, 1971, p. 23.
9   Ritschl and Ritschleanism are best seen as responses to the many developments in nineteenth-century thought, particularly in the sciences, which were seen as questioning religious belief (the above, and the following account of Ritschleanism are based upon Cox, 1977, pp. 1 ff, Cross, p.1189, and Barth, 1972, chapter 29). The distinction between 'worldly' and 'religious' knowledge might be seen as having influenced Barth, whose account of Ritschl (op. cit.) is notable for its admiration of his thought, whom he contrasts with Schleiermacher.

belief. In this system the focus was not doctrinal formulae, but the historical person of Jesus.[10] Hogg went on to create his own synthesis of this thought, which contrasted 'faith' and 'faiths'. 'Faith' he said was a certainty. To quote from Cox: 'Faith is the most critical element in any human experience of religion. It is best described as a perfect confidence that 'God is light and in Him is no darkness at all.'[11] This is contrasted with: 'Faiths, on the other hand, are those varying beliefs through which the religious man comes first to experience faith and then to understand, verbalize, and intelligibly communicate its meaning.'[12] Thus 'faith' remains constant while the form which 'faiths' assume may change. For him, in Christianity, the external aspects of the religion may change, as long as they remain centred upon the person of Jesus.

It should be mentioned that the Hindu would also have both 'faith' and forms of 'faiths' which are themselves genuine, and he suggested that Hinduism should be seen not just as a searching, but also as a finding of religious truth.[13]

To elucidate the matter further, I will turn again to two points that Hogg makes in his critique of Farquhar, where he says, 'if Mr. Farquhar is right in his claim, then India ought always to have been hungry for Christ. But the reason why mission work is so slow of success is that we have first to make India hungry for Christ before we can be used to give Christ to her.'[14]

Christianity as it is currently formulated, Hogg insists, does not speak to the Hindu in his own language and in response to his own desires. The needs of the Hindu and the needs of the Christian are, he suggests, different. Yet it his contention that Christ can nevertheless answer the Hindu's needs, so he asks:

Now what has Christ to offer to this Hindu soul-hunger? It is the writer's deliberate conviction that He has everything to offer. But what have our customary Christian

---

10   Mention has already been made on more than one occasion in this work to the contemporary belief in the so-called 'quest for the historical Jesus'.

11   Cox, 1977, p. 27, quote from Hogg, *Karma and Redemption* (no page number given, but p. xix in 1970 edition).

12   Cox, ibid.

13   M. M. Thomas, 1987, p. 59. But see most particularly, EDMS, Hogg # 176, pp. 12–13.

14   Ibid., p. 173.

doctrines to offer here? Do they present a succinct and coherent message to the Hindu[...]? It is to be feared that no one can claim that such is the case.[15]

There must, he felt, therefore be a need to create a new form of Indian Christianity;[16] the form of the 'faiths' could change around the unchanging source of 'faith' for the Christian, the person of Jesus. It was not, however, the case that Hogg would concur with Farquhar, who believed in paring Christianity down to the essentials, so that it is the Jesus of the New Testament alone who is represented. Hogg would not concur with this theological reductionism, he felt it necessary to give India 'a comprehensive system of Christian theology,'[17] albeit one suited to her needs. We may contrast this with Andrews' words 'that the Christian Faith should be presented by Indians to Indians, *interpreted by Indians to Indians*; that the worship and life of Indian Christians should not be cut off from the ways and habits of the country.'[18] Of this matter more will be said below. For now, we shall consider further Hogg's method of contrast.

Hogg felt it necessary for the missionary to go to the New Testament and find the Christ there who specifically appeals to the needs of the Hindu mind.[19] Only Christianity, he believed, could 'interpret the world in such a way as to make God worthy of man's complete surrender and trust.'[20] However, because of the way he defined 'faith' and 'faiths', 'faith' was something equally open to the Hindu.[21] As noted already, he believed that Western presentations of Jesus were not helpful, and that the Christian message was an answer to the sense of sin, whereas the need felt by the Hindu and expressed in Hinduism was the desire to escape from the bonds of samsara.[22] To quote from Sharpe:

Christianity is *the solution of a religious problem which the typical Hindu does not feel, the answer to questions he has never asked*, but which can be induced in him, under certain conditions. If the Hindu religious mind can be thrown out of equilibrium in some

---

15   Hogg, 1910, p. 270.
16   Hogg, 1917, pp. 66–7.
17   See Fulfil, p. 291.
18   Andrews, 1911, p. 47.
19   Hogg, 1910, p. 274.
20   Cox, 1979, p. 243.
21   Cox, 1977, p. 105.
22   See below.

way, then it may be argued that the Christian message provides the resolution of the difficulties thereby induced.[23]

This leads on his part to dissatisfaction with the concept of fulfilment, and so he asks:

> Outside of the region of vague abstraction what does it mean? Christian doctrines are not the fulfilment of Hindu doctrines, nor Christian rites of Hindu rites. Christian ideals of practice do not uniformly commend themselves to Hindus as better than their own, and if it be alleged that the Christian's experience of Christian religious fruition is a deeper satisfaction than the Hindu finds in his own experience of Hindu religious fruition, the assertion is one incapable of proof or disproof.[24]

The answer, according to Hogg, is the method of 'selective contrast' epitomized in *Karma and Redemption*,[25] wherein he sought to select what he believed to be the two most significant and contrasting aspects of Hinduism and Christianity. These were the doctrines of karma, from Hinduism, and redemption from Christianity. Selective contrast was intended to demonstrate how the former might be found unsatisfactory from within the Hindu's own world-view, while presenting the latter within the framework of Indian philosophical thought.[26] Rather than presenting Christianity as the fulfilment of Hinduism, he felt that the best method was the accentuation of points of contrast.[27] Alongside this the missionary should seek, where possible:

> To upset the equilibrium of the Hindu consciousness, as to cause the attitude which finds through Hindu beliefs the solution of its problems of life and thought to give place to the attitude which can find no satisfaction for its cravings, and solution for its problems, except through beliefs of a Christian type.[28]

What is important in this, is that he offers a critique of Farquhar's, indeed every fulfilment theologian's, assumption that there are certain innate and universal needs lying behind the whole of man's religious experience. Hogg's criticism would, today, be associated with postmodern (or post-liberal)

---

23   Fulfil, pp. 290–1.
24   EDMS, Hogg # 176, pp. 13–14.
25   See Rao.
26   See ibid, p. 33.
27   Cox, 1977, p. 26.
28   EDMS, Hogg # 176, p. 31.

351

criticisms of the modernist agenda upon which fulfilment theology is based.[29]

---

29 More recent criticism has extended the range of his critique to become an attack upon the modernist world-view, on which fulfilment theology is based, from the perspective of postmodernist thought. The problem can be seen, as Lockhead suggests, in terms of Wittgensteinian 'language games' (Lockhead, pp. 68 f.). Following Wittgenstein's axiomatic notion that words do not refer to concrete objects in the world, but have a meaning based upon their usage and activity, (Wittgenstein, 1958, 7. This is the problem with which Wittgenstein begins his *Philosophical Investigations*, 'Every word has a meaning. This meaning is correlated with the word. It is the object for which the word stands' (ibid., 1; see also, Wittgenstein, 1969, 609–617) then, the fact that religions are based upon different world-views is taken to mean that the words they use must be seen as being engaged in separate language games, that is to say, there is no one common religious experience to which all the religions refer, and each uses language that only makes sense in terms of its own framework. According to this theory, the world's religions cannot be seen as using different dialects of one language, so understandings of all religions as talking about one reality in essentially compatible language, are seen as a form of naive misunderstanding (Lockhead, p. 69; see also some critiques of Hick's pluralism, e.g., the references in Hyman). In theology this theory is developed particularly by George Lindbeck in terms of cultural-linguistic theory (see especially Lindbeck, pp. 30 ff.). Lindbeck asserts, of humans, learning language early on in life, that 'once they do learn a language, this shapes their preexperiential physical basis of their conscious experience and activity' (ibid., p. 37). However, neurology tells us, contrary to what Lindbeck asserts, that certain experiences arise in particular areas of the brain. Love, for instance, is an experience from the firing of various chemical and electrical messages in the brain which can, cross-culturally, be identified (see Gregory, pp. 436–8). Certainly there may be minor differences but not enough, it would seem, to claim that the experience of 'love' felt by peoples of different linguistic groupings is a totally different experience (see Lindbeck, pp. 40–42). Some notable recent thinkers have argued against the trend of those who wish to argue that we cannot trace core ideas behind different religious traditions, suggesting that there are common themes.* Therefore the suggestion that the various religions are mutually incompatible systems seems suspect. Particularly we may note that the long interaction between the thought of the East and West is a subject of growing interest, and means that the old notions of Western (i.e., Judaeo-Christian) religion, as being somehow different from Eastern (i.e., Hinduism, Buddhism, etc) religion can no longer be maintained (see J. J. Clarke, pp. 3 ff, etc.). Clarke also points out that the mystery religions associated with Orpheus, and other deitie,s which influenced early Christianity (as has been argued at length, see H. Rahner) are held to have 'shared a common inheritance with the religions of India' (J. J. Clarke, p. 38). Though, he notes, there is much speculation involved in the early influences, there is no doubt that there are later influences. Clarke, for instance, has examined the way Eastern thought has influenced Western thought since the seventeenth century (ibid., see especially, part

II). Another theme of this study also raises the same issue, that of Indian Christian theology, where two supposedly different faith traditions interpenetrate, or to put this on a more historical footing, we may note that the 'Indian form of Islam is moulded by Hindu beliefs and practices' (Radhakrishnan, 1940, p. 339) Is this religion, according to Lindbeck, a form of Islam, or Hinduism, or something new? The whole history of religions is full of examples of their interaction and influence upon one another. None can be viewed in isolation. The ideas must be seen as related in some ways, not just opposed. Lindbeck's system, also, when considered in relation to the above, suffers from an internal ambiguity in that it wishes to suggest that the Buddhist understanding of compassion or enlightenment is based upon an utterly different framework than the Christian understanding of love or salvation. However, first it must be concluded from the theory that there cannot be any one single form of these ideas, as both Buddhism and Christianity are found in so many diverse cultural-linguistic environs. The followers of these religions, in different countries and at different times, do not have the same understandings of the basic concepts of their own religion, as the devotees to be found in other places and at other times. To Lindbeck, this would, of course, mean that the idea of 'God' which he has is not that of Jesus and his disciples. He is therefore not just suggesting that Buddhism is engaged in a different language game from Christianity, but that Christians are also involved with different language games one from the other, as he said, '[m]eaning is constituted by the uses of a specific language rather than being distinguishable from it' (Lindbeck, p. 114). To suggest, using this paradigm, then, that the religious experience of Buddhists is different from that of Christians, is also to say, that the God of Jesus is not the God of Christianity today, and also that the God of Jesus is not the God of Abraham, Isaac, and Jacob. An English Roman Catholic and a French, or Polish, Roman Catholic would have to be seen as speaking a different religious language if the connections between concepts and languages are not acknowledged. Lindbeck, or others, may be happy with this, but it surely leads to further problems. While Lindbeck's theology of difference must be seen as stretching its premises to an extreme, and therefore invalid, conclusion, this does not mean to say that a milder version of the theory does not cast the classical expression of fulfilment theology in a different light. Cultural-linguistic theory does bring to light problems with the modernist (liberal) assumption that there is a form of direct religious experience, unmediated by our modes of understanding. Thus, even liberals such as David Tracy concede that anyone 'who uses a language bears the preunderstandings, partially conscious, more often preconscious, of the traditions of that language' (Tracy, 1987, p. 16). Though mention should be made here of Forman, who argues for what he calls PCEs, (pure consciousness events, see Forman, in Forman, p. 30) suggesting that mystical experience forms a separate category of experience that does not depend upon mediation through the senses.** In regard to what has been said above I would like to reflect upon the suggestion that has been made that modernism and postmodernism represent two mutually exclusive frameworks (Hyman, who uses Wittgenstein's tract *On Certainty* as a paradigm, e.g., Wittgenstein, 1969, 609).

353

The Christian answer does not directly affirm, or fulfill, the question the Hindu seeks an answer to. Each religion can be seen as involved with its own form of a Wittgensteinian language game.[30] To put this in Hogg's own terms, what he says is that what is particularly missing in the Hindu, is a highly developed sense of sin: 'The sense of sin is present, but the Hindu does not feel helpless in the face of it[....] In short, the Hindu does not share the helpless mortal shuddering at sin characteristic of the awakened Western soul.'[31] Such a heavy emphasis upon sin was certainly more characteristic of

---

This would be so if seen only in the extremes to which Lindbeck takes it. However, as I have suggested here, this extreme is unviable. It is worth noting that similar criticisms to those I have made here are brought against Lindbeck by Lipner (Lipner, seminar '*Are Hinduism, Buddhism, and Christianity Compatible?*', Sheikh Kalifa Building, Lampeter, 17/3/1999). If Hogg's example may be used as paradigmatic, then, the post-modern world-view is not necessarily that far from the modernist notion of fulfilment theology.

*See, for instance, Boyer: 'Although anthropology generally assumes that the systems of ideas grouped under the label "religion" are essentially diverse, a number of recurrent themes and concepts can be found in very different cultural environments' (Boyer, p. 4). Boyer argues that some very strong evidence is needed 'postulate that a same idea is not the same' on the basis that the principle of 'same effects, same causes' is an extremely strong one (ibid., pp. 6 f). On the basis that there is a common 'biological history of the species', he argues against the idea 'that "culture" is an autonomous level of reality, which cannot be "reduced" to psychological or biological constraints' (ibid., pp. 295 f). Robert Torrance has also argued that there is a common trait in humanity, which he identifies as the spiritual quest (Torrance, p. xii), and argues that, 'skepticism concerning often dubious and sometimes ethnocentric affirmations of human uniformities[...] need not eventuate in a relativism that rejects the very possibility of meaningful common human denominators (ibid., pp. xi–xii).

**See Bernhardt, in Forman, p. 232. Also, Perovich, in ibid., p. 250. Forman and his fellow thinkers see themselves as being opposed to 'constructionism,' 'the view that mystical experience is significantly shaped and formed by the subject's beliefs, concepts, and expectations' (Forman, in ibid., p. 3). While essentially opposing the same cultural-linguistic theories I have examined here, Forman, in his argument, draws rather different battle lines from those I have, seeing some liberals as constructionists, e.g., Hick and Zaehner (ibid., p. 9), though interestingly not all his colleagues follow this, Bernhardt, for instance, sees Zaehner as a supporter of there being a universal religious experience (Bernhardt, in ibid., p. 220). However, the case presented by Forman and his colleagues does, nevertheless, provide another line of attack upon the theories of Lindbeck and other post-liberal theologians.

30 See previous footnote.
31 Ibid., p. 267.

the Christianity of Hogg's day, whereas to-day there is a definite shift away from such ideas. Bonhoeffer is one of those who rail against notions such as these. Dwelling upon sin is, he says, something that is not typical of the New Testament.[32] That this sense has also developed in popular religious thought is something we may note, as an example, the ideas of Matthew Fox's Creation Spirituality, where he seeks to move from an emphasis upon 'Original Sin' to one of 'Original Blessing'.[33] Other theologians have also moved away from the idea of our relations to God being based upon a sense of our sinfulness, to emphasizing our relationship to God in terms of loving communion:

> As the blessedness of *agape* consists in self-giving, the Heavenly Father desires to create other self-conscious beings to share in the joy of the Divine Life by being ontologically united with his Son, within the love-bond of the Spirit. This she does through an emergent evolutionary and historical process which the Divine Son enters during his human embodiment.[34]

Hogg, therefore, sees two possibilities:

> Either we must set to work to develop in his [the Hindu's] mind a new framework of ideas which will make it possible for him to begin to feel our own type of spiritual hunger, or we must ourselves learn to feel his type of spiritual hunger and at the same time discover for ourselves in Christ the fulfilment of that hunger and learn ourselves to present Christ in that light.[35]

To this, Hogg addss that we must do both, but more particularly the latter.[36] The religious wants, Hogg implies, are the product of the religion in which a man is brought up, or brought into contact with. In a sense, however, this parallels Farquhar's own ideas, for Hogg says that a person, once brought to Christianity and a knowledge of Christ will, of necessity, come to feel the same longings, 'Is it possible that the Hindu[...] should fall short of this

---

32 See Bonhoeffer, letter to a friend 8/7/1944, pp. 191–2.
33 On this see especially Fox's *Original Blessing*.
34 Smart and Konstantine, p. 201.
35 Hogg, 1910, pp. 267–8. This same dilemma of how to present Jesus and Christianity, whether as the Indian can most readily accept the teachings, or to inculcate 'western guilt' was also felt by other missionaries (see, e.g., Hasler, p. 9).
36 Ibid., p. 268.

deepest consciousness of guilt? Must not he too then join in the heart-broken confession, "Against Thee, Thee only, have I sinned"?'[37]

Hogg, then, like Farquhar, seems to believe that Christ will inevitably draw people to feel certain needs, which he admits were already latent, i.e., the sense of sin.

As well as bringing the Hindu to feel this 'Christian' need, Hogg also stated that the missionary should seek to feel the wants of the Hindu, and present Jesus to him in a way that will answer these needs. To this end he identifies two specific needs, which he says dominate the Hindu mind. These are not directly answered by Western Christianity, and need to be met. First, he says: 'The feeling of spiritual need to which the Hindu is already predisposed is the sense of incurable triviality or intrinsic unsatisfyingness of the whole scheme of existence as he understands it – a hunger of his soul for something diviner and more truly infinite.'[38] The other is the transcendence of God,[39] neither of which he argues are, from the Hindu point of view, satisfactorily answered by the usual portrayal of Christianity.[40] Moreover, Hogg can see a certain portrayal of God, from within the established Christian tradition, as answering the Hindu's specific needs: 'Thus the God revealed as *the Intimate* as well as the Inexhaustible, and these are the two characteristics which the Hindu craves to find in the Infinite.'[41]

Having considered Hogg's own suggestion for the missionary method we are now in a better position to understand his critique of fulfilment theology, a number of points concerning which have already been raised. Firstly, Hogg suggested that fulfilment theology offered a false paradigm, in that the Christian must introduce new desires to the Hindu, as he does not fulfill Hindu desires. This leads to his second point, that the concept of 'fulfilment' can be no more than a debating point. The similarities, he says, are but 'incidental assonances' and only superficial,[42] the true method should be contrast, not fulfilment. He also suggests that this idea is of no use in apologetic or missionary work, whilst Hogg agrees with the fulfilment theologian that none but Christ can satisfy India's deepest needs. He says, 'we

---

37   Ibid., p. 287.
38   Ibid., p. 268.
39   Ibid., pp. 272 f.
40   Ibid. pp. 268 ff.
41   Ibid., p. 280.
42   EDMS, Hogg # 176, p. 25.

think that the message, "You need Christ now," is really more telling than "Christ fulfils your old religion."'[43] To which he goes on to add, 'The latter message can hardly be freed from condescension.'[44]

So far Hogg's criticisms alone have been presented, and it is now only fair to consider their justification. We shall begin with the last point, raised by Hogg. Here he seems to have misunderstood Farquhar, for whom the concept of fulfilment stood as a way for missionaries to understand how Christianity related to Hinduism, and was not intended necessarily as a means of direct apologetic.[45] Commenting upon his own means of apologetic, Farquhar had said: 'In order that Christ may be accepted, the Hindu mind has to be recreated.'[46] Further, he says:

> The method I refer to consists in setting forth Christianity as the fulfilment of all that is aimed at in Hinduism, as the satisfaction of the spiritual yearnings of her people, as the crown and climax of the crudest forms of her worship as well as of those lofty spiritual movements which have so often appeared in Hinduism but have always ended in weakness.[47]

Yet this is but one method, for 'the right way is to forget Hinduism altogether and present only Christ.'[48] While presenting Christ as the answer to the Hindu's needs, Farquhar also said that normally Christianity would not be presented in the manner set forth in the Crown; ordinarily only Christianity, not Hinduism, would be used in preaching.[49] Thus, it would seem that here the two opponents probably did not differ that much. Each held that Christ should be presented in a way suited to the hearer, and Farquhar's fulfilment was essentially only a theory, to be used if serious inquirers were to ask questions about it.[50] Whether it was used in the mission field or not,

---

43   Hogg, 1910, p. 173.

44   Ibid.

45   See Crown, pp. 15 ff.

46   Farquhar, 'Lessons from Experience in India', in *Report of the Conference of the World's Student Christian Federation held at Oxford, England (1909)*, p. 70, in Fulfil, p. 255.

47   Farquhar, ibid., p. 72, in ibid., pp. 255–6.

48   Farquhar, ibid., p. 74, in ibid., p. 256.

49   Farquhar, 1905, p. 3, he also made this point again in defence of the Crown, Farquhar, letter 3/6/1915, in the *Harvest Field* (August 1915), p. 315 f., reference in ibid., p. 357.

50   Ibid.

fulfilment was, or at least was becoming, the popular thought of Farquhar's day. According to Boyd, it 'became for a time almost the accepted orthodoxy for large numbers of thoughtful Christians, both Asian and western, and I think it still has to be reckoned with today.'[51]

Regarding the specific charge of condescension, a charge repeated by later critics, this was a concern which Farquhar, strongly aware of the growing tide of Indian nationalism linked to the Hindu revival, would have been well aware of, and the theory was not there for the purpose of open evangelization. I would see it as almost an unavoidable charge for the missionary. If he is to pursue his career and seek to convert others to his religion, then he must, of necessity, proclaim the supremacy of his own religion. Surely to suggest that the non-Christian religion holds some good is better than to see it as wholly bad.[52] Furthermore, I would suggest that Farquhar, and many other fulfilment theologians, were less arrogant than Hogg, who, in *Karma and Redemption*, set out to write an Indian Christian Theology, whereas others saw this as a task exclusively for the Indian Christians themselves. Hogg himself also spoke, at times, in the most patronizing language, 'The task of the Christian missionary is to transform the pathetic Hindu "aspiration toward ultimate Being" into longing to know the Father.'[53]

In answer to Hogg's other criticisms, I will now consider the way in which Hogg was dependent upon the same patterns of thought as the fulfilment theologians. While Hogg's criticisms of fulfilment theology have been taken by many critics as a severe refutation of its principles.[54] I, however, am not convinced. His contention that the Hindu is not seeking the same things as the Christian in his religion, is something that is contradicted by Hogg himself. First, we should note that Hogg admits that the Hindu does feel a sense of sin, 'The sense of sin,' he says, 'is present, but the Hindu does not feel helpless in the face of it[....] In short, the Hindu does not share the helpless shuddering at sin characteristic of the awakened Western soul.'[55]

I see a major problem here for Hogg, in that this characteristic is one he says belongs to the 'awakened [i.e. Christian] Western soul.' If he maintains

---

51   A. J. Boyd, p. 74.
52   On this point see Radhakrishnan below.
53   Hogg, 1907, p. 141.
54   We may note for instance Sharpe and Maw.
55   Hogg, 1910, p. 262.

that the Hindu temperament is different from that of the West, then he has to reconcile the fact that the 'unawakened' Western soul no more shares the helpless shuddering at sin than does the Hindu. The need to awaken a sense of sin in the unbelieving Westerner was as characteristic of missionary work in Britain as it was in India in the nineteenth-century.[56] Secondly, this sense of sin, so typical of Christianity at around this time, would find little favour today; a sense of sin is no more integral to Christianity than it is to Hinduism. Many modern Christians would be appalled at the idea that their basic attitude should be one of shuddering dread in the face of sin. Bonhoeffer, we saw, noted this in his day;[57] the populist theologian Matthew Fox (whatever his faults) might also be listed as a widely read contemporary Christian writer who explicitly renounced this old sense of sin. To give Hogg his due, however, he did also explore an alternative to introducing fear of sin into the Hindu's mind, saying, as we have noted that we must make it possible for the Hindu to have a sense of 'our own type of spiritual hunger,' or else to discover for ourselves 'his type of spiritual hunger and[...] discover[...] in Christ the fulfilment of that hunger'[58] to be able to present Christ to the Hindu. Accepting this view, however, would mean that Hogg's contention of Hinduism and Christianity being closed systems, and the Indian and Western mind being different, collapses; if Westerners can feel the needs of Hinduism, and Christ satisfies, that is to say fulfils, Hindu desires, then how are the two incompatible? It would, of course, not invalidate his initial contention that both are asking different questions, and responding to different needs, but this does not prove a problem for fulfilment theology, in that as it was so often taken in conjunction with the need to develop an Indian Christian theology, it went together with the idea that the Hindu's needs are not exactly those of the Western Christian. I find it difficult to distinguish where the difference, in practical terms, lies between Hogg's contention that Jesus fulfills the Hindu's sense of sin, which must, he felt, be encouraged more strongly, and the fulfilment theologian's belief that Jesus provides the answer to the need felt by the Hindu for a divine saviour to release him from sin, expressed in the doctrines of Vedic sacrifice. Hogg certainly doesn't accept the metaphysics of the system, which could be seen as suggesting that foreknowledge of the Hindu was quite considerable, but both share the same underlying belief in

---

56   See McLeod, pp. 141 ff, also pp. 127 ff.
57   Bonhoeffer, letter to a friend 13/2/1944, p. 132.
58   Hogg, 1910, pp. 267–8, quoted above.

man's innate religious desires, which are fulfilled in the person of Jesus. He saw the additional baggage of fulfilment theology as neither provable nor unprovable, essentially a 'debating point'; however, as has been seen it proved useful to many. I have already mentioned Hogg's affinities to postmodernist thought, and in this, too, he might be seen as a proto-postmodernist, reflecting Jean-François Lyotard's definition of postmodernism as 'incredulity towards meta-narratives.'[59] Also, his use of the idea of Hinduism and Christianity as particularly situated and incompatible paradigms is akin to the beliefs of post-liberal theologians such as Lindbeck. As seen, there are problems with the paradigm as endorsed by both Hogg and Lindbeck. This kind of postmodern criticism represents a distinct world-view which represents, in many ways, a clash of world-views, an idea to be developed below.

Thus even this critic of fulfilment theology uses similar patterns of thought and language to the fulfilment theologians themselves, and moreover, thought established in the world-view of the day, particularly in the idea of man as a religious creature. As will be seen below, even Farquhar's conservative evangelical opponents accepted that man has certain innate cravings as a religious creature, a view which, it seems, Hogg shares.In relation to such ideas we may note that it was in this period, contemporary with Farquhar, that Jung was developing his ideas of the collective unconscious, seeking to map out the principle archetypes that are held to be innate to the psyche. In her book on Jung, Fordham mentions a patient of Jung's whose visions were seen as expressing these universal mythic types in 1910,[60] and Jung's important books appeared from 1916 onwards.[61] Despite his criticisms, he, too, is of the opinion that the religious needs and desires of the Hindu are met in Christianity.

---

59   Lyotard, p. xxiv.
60   Fordham, p. 26.
61   Ibid., p. 138.

Conservative Criticism

The Indian Witness Debate

This debate took place some time before 1913, and 'blunted the force of the conservative Evangelical missionaries' criticism of *The Crown of Hinduism*.'[62] Its cause was an article by Farquhar, published in June 1910, entitled, 'Christ and the Religions of the World'.[63] We need only dwell briefly on this debate, but it is worth noting in order to show the different attitudes within conservative theological thought at the time.

Sharpe deals with the progress of this debate,[64] so we need only mark the salient features. The debate was started when the editor of *The Indian Witness* quoted a few selected passages from the article cited above. This contained some preliminary suggestions about Christianity fulfilling Hinduism, where Farquhar is quoted as saying, 'Take any low, idolatrous, polytheistic faith. Every element in that religion springs from some genuine instinct, deep seated in the history of our common religious nature.'[65] As we have seen, Farquhar's writings did not endorse idolatry, nor did they say that those other aspects of Hinduism, generally looked at condescendingly missionaries, were in themselves good; but, to a careless reader, his language could be seen to come perilously close to saying this.

It is worth noting that many of Farquhar's critics in this debate spoke highly of him personally,[66] and even his defenders[67] were apt to say that he

---

62   Fulfil, p. 347.
63   First published in the *Student Movement*, pp. 195 ff, reprinted in *Progress* from
      where it was quoted in *The Indian Witness*.
64   Fulfil, pp. 309 ff.
65   Farquhar from *Progress*, in Byork and Culshaw, p. 203. The Revs Byork and
      Culshaw were the editors, and it is not stated which of them was responsible for this
      item.
66   See e.g., Taylor, p. 387 and J. R. Banerjea, p. 429.
67   Farquhar himself was out of the country at the time of this controversy (Macnicol,
      1912, p. 388).

had at times overstated his case.[68] In fact, in certain cases very little difference lies between his attackers and defenders.

One of the first two articles to appear was a mild criticism, warning of the danger of 'an exaggeration of the value of non-Christian religions,'[69] and noting that alongside the 'Refiner's fire' there would be, 'many 'idols' which will have to be shattered by the 'hammer that breaketh the rocks.'[70] However, despite warning of the dangers of what was called 'the new attitude', the article by the Rev. A. W. Davies[71] was, on the whole, in agreement with Farquhar's ideas.[72] However, not all the articles were so mild in their criticism, and sitting next to this is an article by the Rev. Arthur Jewson, who calls Farquhar's view an 'enervating, corrosive error.'[73] While the Rev. Jewson accepts man's innate religiosity,[74] he also says:

> On behalf of God who by idolatry has been insulted and dethroned, and of men who by idolatry have been befooled, and robbed and degraded, I raise a whole hearted protest against the teaching that, 'There is a certain legitimacy in every form that religion has taken any where.[75]

---

68 See Macnicol, Macphail, and Saunders, the last of whom says: 'Mr. Farquhar is a reformer and reformers are doomed to exaggerate' (op. Cit., p. 525).

69 Davies, p. 299.

70 Ibid., p. 287.

71 Of St. John's College, Agra. An Anglican educational institute, founded in 1850 by Rev. T. Valpy French, later to be the first bishop of Lahore (Birks I, pp. 42 ff.).

72 Similar ideas were put forward by Edger, who was generally positive, as was Macnicol, Farquhar's main defendant, who sought to clear up what he saw as misunderstandings,saying that, 'I do not think that in reality the difference between Messrs. Davies and Huntly and Mr. Farquhar is as deep and wide as some of the statements made by the controversialists seem to indicate' (Macnicol, 1912, p. 388). We have already mentioned Davies and suggested that he was, indeed, generally in tune with Farquhar's approach, only warning of the need for destruction as well as fulfilment, which accords with what we have seen of Farquhar's views. Other defenders of Farquhar were J. M. Macphail, and K. J. Saunders, whose articles need not concern us as they are generally in accord with his views. We may, however, note Saunders claim that, 'Again to attack the Dhammapada or the Bhagavadgita as works of the Evil One is an almost inconceivable blasphemy' (Saunders, p. 525).

73 Jewson, p. 299. Jewson was from Calcutta, and seems to have known Farquhar, saying of him that his 'personality is so charming and his erudition so extensively recognized that what he writes becomes a matter of great importance' (ibid).

74 Ibid.

75 Ibid.

The reason for this, he says, is that though the instinct is correct, it does not mean that the expression of it is.[76] Yet, as seen already, Farquhar would agree with this point. What he sees as legitimate is the religious instinct, though the expression of it, e.g. as idolatry, is quite wrong in itself; its 'legitimacy' is in being a partial answer to this need.

The matter is really one of emphasis, and partial misunderstanding. Both Jewson and Davies stand on similar ground here, and so are both close to Farquhar. The real difference is that they both object to the extent to which Farquhar is prepared to praise Hindu practice.[77] The difference lies in the approach, one seeking a conciliatory approach to Hinduism, the other openly attacking – a point I shall expand upon below. Another definite difference here is that, whereas Farquhar had extended the principle of fulfilment (Mt. V: 17) to faiths beyond Judaism, Jewson is very clear that only Judaism was referred to.[78]

In spite of the above we should not think of Farquhar's detractors as opposed to all aspects of Hinduism. Another contributor to the debate, Rev. L. Ireland Hasler, says of two of those who attack Farquhar's approach that, 'from what I know of Dr. Huntly and Mr. Jewson few missionaries can rival them in sympathy with Indians and Indian thought, however outspoken and frank they may be in their references to the baser elements of the Indian faiths.'[79] Thus, even with the more conservative missionaries, Farquhar is not faced with iconoclastic opponents of Hinduism, utterly opposed to all things Indian. The main dispute is not about the noble qualities of Vedānta, but is rather to do with what were seen as the ignoble practices of popular Hinduism, such as idolatry. One critic says:

---

76 Ibid.
77 We may note one of Farquhar's 'critics', the Rev. J. P. Jones, says, 'I do not accept Mr. Farquhar's watchword, – "Christ the fulfiller of all religions." Taking again Hinduism as our illustration, I believe that Christ is the fulfiller of every spiritual yearning of the hearts of the people of this land' (Jones, p. 427). We may again remind the reader that the thought of the American missionary J. P. Jones is dealt with by Cracknell, where his fulfilment theology is discussed (Cracknell, 1995, p. 151). Again, we see another person who accepts Farquhar's beliefs, but rejects his expression of it.
78 Jewson, p. 299, see also J. J. Lucas, p. 389, and J. R. Banerjea, p. 429..
79 Hasler, p. 408.

In all our discussion on this subject we must never forget that the Hinduism of the vast majority of the people of India is not the higher Hinduism of the books. Kali, or some similarly disposed being, is the real deity of the people, and when they worship the higher gods it is on their tricks and their immoralities that the mind is concentrated.[80]

With regard to idolatry, Dr. Huntly, already referred to, suggested that in such a case it should rather be felt that man's religious instinct had led him astray.[81] The instinct, he says, has been 'universally corrupted.' His belief is that idolatry is not a correct, but an incorrect usage of this instinct; just because it comes from it, does not make it right.[82] To quote one of Farquhar's defenders: 'With all due respect to Dr. Huntly, both the title of his article[83] and the spirit of some of his remarks seem to us to indicate a serious misunderstanding of

---

80   Maclean, p. 488. Others followed Farquhar in taking a different view, 'Missionaries ought to understand that it is by no means easy to grasp the high ideals that are contained in the various religious teachings of the world, and that it will never do to take any base and vulgar ideas concerning religion from the lower classes of a people and represent these as the teachings of their religion. Let us at once admit that there would be something unfair in that: just as unfair as it would be for any opponent of Christianity to pretend that Christianity was a religion of easy-going morals, because in Italy and Spain there were highway bandits who prayed to the blessed Mother of god that She should forgive them and save their souls through her merciful intercession, just before they went to perform the most daring and wicked act of felony' (Edger, p. 347). Here we find a point worth noting about the parochialism and bigotry of certain missionaries, that was held not just against Hindus, but also other Christians, who were not in their own tradition, particularly Catholics, of whom we may note the following, 'Charles Booth, commentating in 1903 on the London Irish, conveniently summarised several points of the hostile stereotype:
"'The Irish Catholics form a class apart, being as a rule devout and willing to contribute to the upkeep of their church[...] but at the same time they are great beggars as well as heavy drinkers, and there is no sign that the form that practical religion takes in their case helps to make them in these respects either more self-reliant or more self-restrained."
'Catholicism was thus seen as a bogus form of religion which took to excess the externals, but failed to produce the moral fruits in terms of which the true worth of a religion could be judged' (McLeod, p. 44, quotation from, Booth, *Life and Labours of the People in London*, 3rd Series, Vol. VII, p. 401). There is a certain similarity here then between attitudes to Catholicism and Hinduism, which provides an interesting perspective on the Protestant missionary's attitudes.
81   Huntly, p. 307.
82   Ibid.
83   'Farquhar's Fallacies'.

364

Mr. Farquhar's attitude.'[84] Like Jewson, Huntly appeared to believe that Farquhar was giving legitimacy to idolatry, which he never intended. As we have already seen, Farquhar's thought was in many ways very conservative, and a lot of the debate was over this misunderstanding. I would, again, refer to the point that one approach was more conciliatory, and the other more hostile, towards Hinduism. I would like to illustrate this first with a quotation from Farquhar's article, followed by a rejoinder from one of his defenders, and finally, with the words of one of his critics, to give a clear expression of the point to be made:

> No Christian can wander in a non-Christian city without having the idea forced upon his mind again and again, 'Here is a foreglimpse of the Christ,' 'Here is a cry for the cross.'[85]

> We should not like to go so far as to say that '*no Christian*' can fail to have such thoughts, but we find it difficult to believe that they have not entered the mind of many a *missionary*, more especially of those who have lived in touch with the people.[86]

> Who that has visited the temples of Benares and seen the images worshipped there, forms 'more foul than bacchanals, more monstrous than the fancies of nightmare,' shall assert that this detail of the Hindu religion 'has a right of existence' and 'is a foreglimpse of the Christ'?[87]

I would not necessarily like to say that one is more sympathetic to Hinduism than the other. Taylor and Farquhar, and, doubtlessly, Anstey also, would see the idols of Benares as a gross expression of religion, which must be swept away. Farquhar, however, would fit this into his scheme of religious instincts as fulfilling a purpose.

There was a further worry that this attitude would be seen by Hindus as a defence of their faith, suggesting that Christianity was not a definite alternative.[88]

In these criticisms we have seen a certain difference of emphasis between Farquhar and his opponents. They are all essentially in agreement, but there was also some criticism from a more extreme evangelical position.

---

84   Anstey, p. 405.
85   Farquhar in *Progress*, quoted in Byork and Culshaw , p. 203.
86   Anstey, p. 406.
87   Taylor, p. 387.
88   See e.g., J. R. Banerjea, and J. F. Campbell.

Thus far, man's religious instinct, even if badly astray, has been held to be behind the phenomena of Hinduism, but there was another position:

> All will agree that there is in man a divinely implanted something which distinguishes him from the lower creatures[...] and causes him to reach out towards the infinite. but this is a very different thing from assuming that there is a common religious sensibility which has so guided men in matters of faith that 'every detail of every religion has, as it were, a right of existence and is significant.' Of course, it has a *right* of existence in the sense that man is a free being[...] and of course it is *significant*, but only to show how far astray man's thoughts may go when under the tutelage of Satan.[89]

It would appear that Badley had, too, misunderstood Farquhar, believing that man's religious sensibility causes and builds up a religion,[90] whereas, in fact, Farquhar meant no more by this term than Badley did by his 'divinely implanted something,' or that which causes man to 'reach out hands towards the infinite.' Badley's criticisms of Farquhar are in the main a misunderstanding, but he differs from Farquhar's other critics in that he puts Hinduism down to Satan. He thus sharply contrasts with Farquhar's other 'conservative evangelical' critics, who are, in many ways, very close to the 'liberal' position of Farquhar.[91] Thus, while in the Crown Farquhar can refer to those who are opposed to the 'attitude' of the Edinburgh Conference,[92] if his critics in the Indian Witness debate are any guide then, theologically, the two groups of perceived 'liberals' and 'conservatives' were really not that far apart. Whereas Sharpe suggests 'that the *Indian Witness* debate blunted the force of the conservative Evangelical missionaries' criticism of *The Crown of Hinduism*,'[93] I would suggest that this, to some degree, was not because the conservative wing had earlier vented their spleen, but because they were, in fact, surprisingly 'liberal.' Farquhar and Slater, as we have seen, pioneered the new attitude, at least partly out of need, because of the Hindu revival and

---

89   Badley, p. 447–8.
90   Ibid., p. 447.
91   While we may be tempted to see Badley as on the fringe, we may note that he did later become a bishop in the Methodist Episcopal Church, but this is, of course, an American rather than a British church, from none of which such extremism was forthcoming in this debate.
92   Crown, p. 16.
93   Fulfil, p. 347.

Indian nationalism. This, no doubt, had a growing influence which would affect, if not all, then nearly all, missionaries in the field.[94]

'Conservative' Criticism after 1913

i) D. Mackichan

There was some conservative criticism following the publication of *The Crown of Hinduism*, but most of it added little that was new.[95] The most important critic was D. Mackichan.[96] He added little to what had been said in the Indian Witness debate, but, in him, we see expressed a major point of conservative opposition to the fulfilment concept, which was the antagonism to the notion of evolution.[97]

To a large degree Mackichan seems to have, like Farquhar's earlier critics, misunderstood where Farquhar stood, saying that Christianity comes to supplant rather than supplement Hinduism. The latter, he believed, was the fulfilment standpoint.[98] Most of Mackichan's criticism is not specifically targeted at Farquhar,[99] but he is still singled out for special attention: 'The generalization of the words of Jesus[100] has been used in the defence of some very extreme positions. A remarkable example of this is found in a recently published work on Hinduism which appears under the title *The Crown of Hinduism*.'[101]

---

94 To examine this point properly it would be necessary to do a detailed analysis of changing patterns in conservative missionary writings during the first decade and a half of this century, but, as has been indicated in previous chapters, it does appear as though the majority opinion in missionary circles in India was swinging to a more conciliatory approach from at least the 1890s. According to Sharpe, a more sympathetic attitude became widespread in India in the period 1905–1910 (Fulfil, p. 236).

95 See ibid., pp. 348 ff. and 355.

96 Principal of the United Free Church of Scotland's Wilson College, Bombay.

97 See Huntly, p. 307, and Collier.

98 Mackichan, p. 243.

99 Ibid., in fact Mackichan says: 'This article is not concerned with the teachings or writings of any individual.'

100 Mt. V: 17.

101 Mackichan, pp. 248–9.

Mackichan can say that most of the book is sound, 'its analysis of the teachings and practices of Hinduism, and its exposure of the errors of the one and the evils of the other are uncompromising and complete.'[102]

But what he cannot bear is the proposition that Christianity 'crowns' Hinduism; the difference between the two is, he says, too vast.[103] There is no need here to repeat at length the view that Farquhar wanted to see Hinduism itself destroyed, or that he believed only the instinct behind it had been fulfilled, a point with which he was at one with Mackichan.[104] While it deals with ground already covered, I would like to quote the following passage from Principal Mackichan, which, while meant as a criticism of Farquhar, is nothing less than an alternative statement of his ideas:

India has yet to learn that a spirituality which is reached by the path of abstract metaphysical speculation is a very different product from a spirituality which is essentially ethical in its origin and in its manifestation[....] The message of Christ is the revelation of a new spirituality, not merely the consummation of the spirituality on which India has striven to nourish its life. It is the duty of every Christian to recognize the grandeur of India's effort[...] but it is none the less the duty of every missionary who loves India to point out wherein its highest efforts have failed to reach the true goal of the spiritual life as revealed by Jesus Christ. The mission of Christianity is not to complete or consummate something that has been moving onwards to this completion; but to reveal to India a new power.[105]

In the last clause lies what Mackichan sees as the real difference, that Christianity reveals something new; as Sharpe puts it:

the necessity of a sympathetic approach to Hinduism; a conviction of the unconditional superiority[...] of Christianity over Hinduism; the awareness that replacement of Hinduism by Christianity was the goal of missionary work: on all these points Mackichan and Farquhar shared substantially the same position. But the use of the word 'evolution' was a different matter. The evolutionary position was anathema to the conservative Evangelical mind *a priori*: hence Mackichan's attack.[106]

Mackichan's problem was the associations of the word with what we may call the Müllerite school of comparative religion, but, as we have seen, Farquhar's

---

102   Ibid., p. 249.
103   Ibid.
104   Ibid., pp. 247 f.
105   Ibid., pp. 250–1.
106   Fulfil, p. 348.

368

idea of fulfilment in no sense meant the gradual evolution of man's religions to the same goal.[107] Essentially, he used the terminology of the science of comparative religion to support his views of Christianity's supremacy. This rejection of 'evolution' was, we saw previously, the turning point in Monier-Williams' thought on the non-Christian religions.[108] Yet, I would contest that, although Mackichan shares Monier-Williams' repulsion of this term, he is actually in some respects more liberal in his thought than Farquhar.

In the first chapter, the importance of a Logos-centric theology was stressed for the development of fulfilment theology. This idea is lacking from Farquhar, but is to be found in Mackichan, who says, 'We are all willing and glad to recognize the operations of the Divine Logos in every spiritual truth that has been revealed to the seeking heart of India.'[109]

We can, therefore, see that Farquhar's opponents, the conservative evangelicals, had, at least in part,[110] begun to accept many of the general ideas of fulfilment theology. That is to say, they had come to accept many of the findings of the nineteenth-century study of comparative religion, and its associated world-view.

ii) Hendrik Kraemer

As has been indicated above in relation to Hogg, fulfilment theology not just survived his criticisms of it, but continued to thrive. This was the case at the Jerusalem missionary conference of 1928,[111] on which, however, at Tambaram, in 1938, fulfilment theology received its greatest blow at the hands of Hendrik Kraemer, the then professor of missions at Leiden University in Holland.

Kraemer was a follower of the Barthian school of dialectical theology, though he did not follow Barth in all particulars.[112] Nevertheless, Kraemer's emphasis was on what he called 'Biblical realism', which, for him, stressed the adjective 'Biblical',[113] where, in Barthian manner, all else would have to

---

107   Indeed, as we have seen Müller did not mean this either.
108   See section on Monier-Williams.
109   Mackichan, p. 248.
110   We must not forget those such as Badley who saw Satan at work in Hinduism.
111   Macnicol, 1936, p. 170.
112   Kraemer, in *Tambaram Series*, I, pp. 15–16 and 22, also see Robb, p. 94.
113   Jongeneel, p. 22.

be seen as contrasted with what he believed was the only true revelation of God, the Biblical record.[114] Natural theology, Kraemer stated, must be rejected.[115] In a later work Kraemer discussed the notion of 'the *logos spermatikos* doctrine' found in Justin and other early fathers,[116] and concluded, of the theology typical of the Greek fathers he considered, that:

> There is a tendency inherent in this *logos spermatikos* theory to obscure the central point in the Christian revelation, i.e. that it means entering in and through Christ into a new *life*-relationship with God. Instead the emphasis is shifted towards attaining a fuller rational knowledge of God.[117]

With particular regard to fulfilment theology, Kraemer attacked it on the basis that the term 'fulfilment' implies that if the non-Christian religions were left to their own devices, they would, in their own time, reach Christ.[118] All fulfilment theologians had, however, quite clearly gone out of their way to stress that this was not what they meant. Secondly, Kraemer argued that:

> The cross and its real meaning – reconciliation as God's initiative and act – is antagonistic to all human religious aspirations and ends, for the tendency of all human religious striving is to conquer God, to realize our divine nature (theosis). Christ is not the fulfilment of this but the uncovering of its self-assertive nature[....][119]

Any 'fulfilment', Kraemer argued, happened in an 'unexpected way'[120] for although, to 'be sure, in many men and in the religions of mankind there stir deep aspirations, longings and intuitions which find their fulfilment in Christ'[121] the way God fulfills these longings, are in ways man did not expect. However, with this statement there is little, if anything, with which Farquhar would disagree. He would never have suggested that Christ does not bring something new to the position. Kraemer's paradigm is, I would suggest, entirely in accord with Farquhar's. Interestingly, Kraemer suggested that all

---

114   Kraemer, 1947, p. 109.
115   Ibid., pp. 114 ff.
116   Kraemer, 1956, pp. 148 ff.
117   Ibid., p. 153.
118   Kraemer, 1947, p. 123.
119   Ibid.
120   Ibid., p. 124.
121   Ibid., p. 123.

370

missionaries should be concerned with 'points of contact.'[122] Kraemer, however, also has other criticisms; that fulfilment theology is patronizing, saying it is 'benevolent superiority intending to be gracious modesty.'[123] He also follows Hogg's criticism, that:

> The supreme longing of the hindu after escape from *samsara* is not satisfied by Christ. The gift of Rebirth as offered by Christ does not appeal to the Hindu. On the contrary, Jesus kindles new hopes not felt before and kills some of the deepest and most persistent longings of man.[124]

However, the substance of these two criticisms is dealt with elsewhere, and it is the question of continuity or discontinuity that concerns us here. According to Kraemer:

> When we try to define the relation of the Christian message[...] to the spiritual world manifest in the whole range of religious experience and religious striving of mankind, we cannot account for it by an unqualified conception of 'fulfilment' or continuity. We must, out of respect for the proper character of the Christian Faith and other religions, begin by pronouncing emphatically the word 'discontinuity' – *Totaliter aliter* – with emphasis on both words.[125]

Such was the message of Kraemer's words, that he was seen as being radically opposed to the liberal agenda of fulfilment, suggesting instead that there was an utter divide between the Christian and non-Christian world-view.[126] As has been intimated above, Kraemer was not so far removed from Farquhar as some may have supposed. The main difference was linguistic rather than theological. According to another contributor to the Tambaram debate, H. H. Farmer,[127] Kraemer could concur with the term 'fulfilment' in as far as it meant, 'that the religious aspirations and longings of men which come to expression in the non-Christian faiths find their fulfilment, in the sense of satisfaction, in Christ and in Christ alone,'further he said, 'This

---

122   Ibid., p. 130.
123   Ibid., 1956, p. 215.
124   Ibid., pp. 215–216.
125   Ibid., p. 224.
126   See Braybrooke, 1973, pp. 2 f.
127   Who was called by Kraemer 'one of the ablest of the English theologians' (Kraemer, 1956, p. 218).

interpretation of the word is an eminently proper, even unavoidable, one according to ordinary usage, as Dr Kraemer grants[....]'[128]

Thus, for Kraemer, there was good to be seen in men's strivings and aspirations after God, and he was not totally opposed to the world-view of fulfilment theology.[129] Kraemer, however, is seen as representing one extreme at the Tambaram conference, in contrast to the 'Johannine,' i.e. Logos based, fulfilment theology approach.[130] It was believed that the message of discontinuity was felt to be that coming from Tambaram,[131] and with this went a 'new shift of emphasis in evangelism from 'sharing' to 'proclaiming'.'[132] The reasons why Kraemer, and the whole Tambaram conference, were seen as utterly opposed to fulfilment theology, must be linked to Kraemer's association with Barth, whose theology was seen as repudiating the basis of fulfilment theology. This has been seen as marked by a world-view very different from that associated with Logos theology, 'The utter inability of man to do anything for himself, to discover God, promote his own salvation, or be an organ of spiritual values has received new emphasis in the Crisis Theology of Karl Barth and his followers.'[133]

It has been said that, 'Barth's criticisms are primarily directed against those liberals whose interest centres in man's religious experience[....] He is also critical of theologians such as Temple[134] who see a universal revelation of God.'[135] Thus, the Neo-Orthodoxy of Barth and Kraemer was seen as implacably hostile to the concept that any good could be found within the non-Christian religions. They are identified with the exclusivist position,[136] and such was certainly Barth's early position, epitomised in the following

---

128   Farmer, in *Tambaram Series*, I, p. 166. He goes on to quote the passage quoted above from Kraemer's *The Christian Message in a Non-Christian World*, concerning mankind's 'deep aspirations... which find their fulfilment in Christ' (op. Cit., p. 123).

129   Kraemer, 1956, pp. 223–4.

130   See Cox, 1977, pp. 364 f.

131   Braybrooke, 1973, p. 3. It should be noted however that Kraemer's views did not take over at Tambaram (Hallencreutz, 1988, p. 356), and a task of reconciliation between the two sides was undertaken, mainly by Farmer (Cox, 1977, p. 366).

132   Devanandan, P. D., 'After Tambaram – What?', *The Guardian* (Madras), 26/1/1939, p. 42, quoted in, Hallencreutz, 1970, p. 33.

133   Radhakrishnan, 1940, p. 74.

134   The younger William Temple, Archbishop of Canterbury.

135   Braybrooke, 1971, p. 16. See Barth, 1961, pp. 49 ff.

136   Race, pp. 11 ff.

quotation, 'It has been reported that D. T. Niles, a Christian theologian from India, in conversation with Barth, once asked him how he knew that Hinduism was unbelief when he had never met any Hindus himself. Barth's reply was, '*A priori!*'[137]

Lockhead defends Barth from the charge of exclusivism, arguing that this is not a comment on Hinduism but on all human activity.[138] Elsewhere, however, Barth declares that the non-Christian religions must be seen as the 'foes' of Christianity, declaring that the only correct Christian response is to ignore their claims to truth and oppose them directly with the proclamation of Christianity.[139] Though, as Macnicol wrote in 1936, it seems 'that Barth himself is modifying his extreme position.'[140] Nevertheless, the dialectical school has generally been seen as representing a direct opposition to the liberal basis of fulfilment theology. While Kraemer represented the 'soft' side of this, wherein man's religious strivings were 'fulfilled' by Christ, the basic premise of the school was that the revelation of Christ was a unique event and that one was saved in relation to this. The idea of a universal revelation, or of people being saved by the presence of an indwelling Logos which validated their natural theology, was anathema to this school. The difference is essentially a clash of world views, one which asserts that there can be a

---

137   Race, p. 16, referred to Gerald H. Anderson, 'Religion as a Problem for the Christian Mission', in D. Dawe and J. J. Carmen (editors), *Christian Faith in a Religiously Plural World*, Maryknoll, NY, Orbis Books, 1978, p. 114.

138   Lockhead, p. 34 f.

139   See Barth's papers quoted in Macnicol, 1936, pp. 168 ff, the first a paper '[t]ranslated (as a 'Lutterworth Paper') under the title 'Questions to Christendom' (op. Cit., p. 168, fn. 1.) Macnicol claims this was delivered in 1928, though the internal evidence of the paper suggests it was 1931, as it speaks of the Jerusalem missionary conference as being, 'Three years ago' (ibid., p. 168). The second paper is 'from a French publication, *Le monde Non-Chrêtien*, issued in December 1932, by *Foi et Vie*. Dr Barth's article is entitled 'La Theologie et la Mission â l'heurre presente' (ibid., p. 169, fn 1).

140   Ibid., p. 173, see especially, fn 2, where he quotes from Barth's commentary on Romans. I would suggest that Barth's later works manifest an openness to the possibility of a human contribution to theology that differs from his earlier narrowness, 'Church proclamation can suffer at one point from all too excessive many-sidedness and unhealthy overextension; at another point, from equally unhealthy one-sidedness and narrowness in its subject matter. Here it may suffer from liberal softening and distraction; there, from confessionalistic [sic] and, perhaps also, biblicistic [sic] or liturgical ossification and constriction[....]' (Barth, 1963, p. 192).

connection between Christianity and the non-Christian religions, the other which denies this, saying that they are utterly different. As with the difference between liberal and post-liberal thought, no fruitful dialogue can take place as long as those on each side maintain this basic difference of attitude. Of course, both fulfilment theologians and dialectical theologians would agree upon the supremacy of the Christian faith, and Christ's revelation, but in their attitude towards the non-Christian religions there is no common meeting place beyond this. As we have seen, a softening of extreme discontinuity led to the essentially linguistic disparity which we observed standing between Kraemer, and, for instance, Farquhar; both would have agreed that the aspirations of non-Christians are met in Christ, but not on whether this should be called 'fulfilment'.

Further Criticisms of Fulfilment Theology

Some of the criticisms that will be raised here have already been mentioned previously, though they have not always been fully developed.

Firstly, Radhakrishnan should be mentioned as a critic of fulfilment theology. Although cited as such,[141] Radhakrishnan really made only one criticism, for while noting that fulfilment theology was preferable to intolerance, he, nevertheless, felt that 'there is, right through, the imperialistic note that Christianity is the highest manifestation of the religious spirit; that is the moral standard for the human race while every other religion is to be judged by it.'[142] Furthermore, he accuses Farquhar and Macnicol as perceiving other religions as being good as far as they go, but ultimately seeing the non-Christian religions as blockages to spiritual progress.[143] His charge was essentially one of condescension and imperialist dominion. While, to many, these criticisms seem to constitute a serious assault on fulfilment theology, as Radhakrishnan no doubt felt, they do not, in themselves, constitute a serious challenge to the truth claims of the system. To say that

---

141   See, e.g., Fulfil, p. 351 fn 1.
142   Radhakrishnan, 1933, p. 24.
143   Radhakrishnan, 1940, p. 344.

'my system is better than yours' might be arrogant: the fact that it is does not make it incorrect. Certainly, to take such a stance may arouse opposition, but if someone believes that their system can complete another system then the person making the claim must have the right, not just to believe that this is so, but also to say as much. To attack fulfilment theology on these grounds as bearing upon its truth-claims seems a dubious exercise. The attack is a moral, rather than an intellectual, one, though, it may itself be seen as infringing upon the liberty of the person who wishes to assert their own beliefs.

Throughout this work reference has been made to Hoehler's study of fulfilment theology,[144] and the problems he identifies with fulfilment theology should be mentioned. One of his criticisms is something which has already been given some attention, and which is the way fulfilment theology attempts to see all religions as part of one larger inter-connected system.[145] He says that this ignores Tillich's theory of 'polarities' within religions.[146] According to Tillich's theory, all religions have contrasting elements, and these exist in relation to one another, so one cannot posit, for example, a Hegelian idea of evolution. That is to say, the older elements of religious life are not left behind, but are merely contrasting poles, with each religion having different contrasting poles within itself.[147] The problem, Hoehler notes, is mainly found in early forms of fulfilment theology, where, due to limited knowledge, the non-Christian religions were often seen in a mono-thematic way. Yet even where this was so, we have seen the idea presented that each religion has one great idea;[148] but, while so viewed, they are nevertheless perceived as contrasting 'poles'. Fulfilment theology is, though, guilty of reading all these 'poles' into one larger scheme, or of seeing a common religious urge behind every similar doctrine, although, as I have argued above, this is more of a problem if one holds to a different world-view. From the modernist liberal perspective, there may well be a case for seeing a common element underlying all religions, though not from certain conservative, or post-liberal, frameworks.[149] As Whaling has noted, 'all religious traditions are very

---

144   Which forms part of a larger work on the numerous Christian approaches to the non-Christian religions.
145   Hoehler, p. 45.
146   Ibid.
147   Tillich, pp. 54 ff
148   As in Maurice's thought.
149   See above.

complex, and to posit a monolithic fulfilment of one by another, either actively or statically, is usually to do an injustice to the intricacies of both.'[150]

Hoehler's second criticism is of what he calls the 'Darwinian-Hegelian logic of religious development.'[151] Here, he argues that religions cannot simply be read as a progression from lower to higher forms in terms of chronology, and asks whether a very recent sect is superior to an ancient established religion. Certainly no fulfilment theologian is so naive as to suggest this, recognizing that there is a far more complex interplay of ideas at work, whereby religions are not in a simple linear state of progression. He is correct, however, in observing that every religion has its own perspective on what is and what is not 'progression'.[152] As has been seen, fulfilment theology posits the theory that there is some known form of the highest expression of religion, and that religions either move to, or away, from this.[153] Problems are, of course, raised in relation to the fact that no one axiomatic standard can be set, even within one religion, let alone between religions.[154] The implications of this will be considered further later on.

Hoehler also suggests that seeing the non-Christian religions as a form of preparation for Christianity distorts their actual meaning.[155] This relates to the point above, in that it suggests that what good there is to be found in the non-Christian religions, is that which is related to Christianity,[156] and it thus suggests that the non-Christian religions do not have any worth of their own apart from the Christian Gospel.[157] In response to this, we may cite the rejoinder made to Kraemer and Radhakrishnan above, that while this may be patronizing it is no more so than an exclusivism.[158] Hoehler observes, however, that there is a further problem, in that it distorts what the religion

---

150   Whaling, 1986, p. 87.
151   Hoehler, p. 46.
152   Ibid.
153   In the case of Farquhar and Slater for instance, the apex is the religion of Christ (see above).
154   See for instance, Wiggins, chapter 2. As John Hick in his classic work has noted, we cannot 'reasonably claim that our own form of religious experience, together with that of the tradition of which we are a part, is veridical whilst the others are not' (Hick, p. 235).
155   Hoehler, p. 51.
156   Or the form of Christianity the particular fulfilment theologian favours.
157   This argument is essentially that raised by Cobban (see chapter 5).
158   See above.

actually means to its adherents, by highlighting those aspects which are most useful for Christian apologetics.[159] It might be suggested that some fulfilment theologians, such as Westcott,[160] sought to avoid this error by suggesting that, firstly, a full understanding of Hinduism should be gained, so that then an Indian Christianity could be founded upon this knowledge, although it is hard to imagine that any such attempt would not necessarily 'distort' both religions. This begs a yet greater question, as to how different this would be from the 'distortions' that occur from generation to generation within any religious tradition?[161] Hoehler's final point is again that of Hogg, in that he asks, 'what does the doctrine of *praeparatio evangelicae* actually mean.'[162] He says that all 'completion theories' must amount to no more than the effort to make other people's religions fit into our own,[163] though he does note that some have attempted to get round this problem.[164] This is done by entering more deeply into a dialogue with those of other faiths, but while acknowledging that Jesus represents the pinnacle of Christian experience, no universal finality of God's revelation is to be seen in him.[165] The problems raised by this will be dealt with in the next section.

Liberal Perspectives

In the previous discussion, various criticisms of fulfilment theology have been raised. Often these stem from a clash of world-views, and so, as I have argued, do not lead to any constructive criticism of fulfilment theology. Hogg's criticisms, which may be seen as the most damning, are in fact based upon an attack on a false fulfilment theology. Hoehler also fail to account for the reflective subtlety of many fulfilment theologians, and, while other critiques might raise problems, they cannot offer a disproof of fulfilment

---

159   Hoehler, p. 52. This criticism is also made by Allen (see Allen, p. 124).
160   See chapter 4.
161   More will be said on this subject below.
162   Hoehler, p. 52.
163   Ibid.
164   Which he sees as caused by linking the Logos doctrine to fulfilment theology.
165   Hoehler, pp. 52 ff.

theology. If an argument against fulfilment theology is to develop then, it must, I suggest, come from the same starting place as fulfilment theology itself, otherwise it will merely set paradigm against paradigm. To this end, it would be useful to see how fulfilment theology, and other liberal thought, developed in the contemporary and later periods.

Fulfilment Theology after Farquhar

As has been seen already in this study fulfilment theology was pervasive throughout all sections of British theological and missionary thought well before Farquhar's time. In the years following 1914, fulfilment theology became, if anything, more prevalent, Hogg's criticisms evidently making little impact upon those who wished to endorse the theory. To demonstrate this, I would like first to consider the Jerusalem missionary conference of 1928, and some key figures involved there, and then to look briefly at the thought of another fulfilment theologian, Sydney Cave.

After the Edinburgh conference, where, as has been seen, fulfilment theology was generally felt to have received an endorsement, it is not surprising that this doctrine continued. In the next few years the *International Review of Missions*, set up after Edinburgh, published a series of articles on the 'vital forces' of various forms of Buddhism 'in relation to the Gospel.' In these, fulfilment theology was endorsed to a greater or lesser extent. One author spoke of 'point[s] of contact' and 'an anticipation of Christianity,'[166] while another said, 'the ethical teachings of Buddhism should be treated as the silver rule which needs only the fulfilment of the golden rule.'[167] Elsewhere, Buddhism was seen as a 'schoolmaster.'[168] This should be seen as the attitude that foreshadowed Jerusalem. Similar principles were followed at this second conference, where the non-Christian religions 'were dealt with positively[....] Chief attention was given to bringing out their values – values to be appreciated, conserved and where necessary supplemented.'[169] A new element, however, entered into the debate, so that: 'Nothing remains more clearly in the mind, out of all the discussions that went on in those crowded

---

166   Purser, pp. 240 and 238.
167   Reischauer, p. 581.
168   Saunders, 1914, p. 487.
169   Mott, 1938, p. 306.

days, than the emergence of secularism as the great antagonist of Christianity.'[170] The main debate, therefore, shifted away from discussion of Christianity in relation to the non-Christian religions, because now: 'The peril is the substitution of a purely secular culture in which the older faiths will simply wither and die.'[171] Still, the same attitude towards the non-Christian religions continued, where people could speak of 'Christ, the fulfiller not of Hebrew prophecy alone, but also of every human aspiration after that kingdom of god which is the one true fellowship of men. The Christ is the human Saviour whom men have sought and partially found in the persons of Sakyamuni, Muhammad, Confucius and many another sage and saint, prophet and reformer, who has followed and pointed the way towards the one true God.'[172] This, then, was the atmosphere at Jerusalem, and while I do not wish to dwell at length upon this conference, it would be useful to mention two significant figures, first, Macnicol, and second, Temple.

Macnicol prepared the preliminary paper on Hinduism for the Jerusalem conference,[173] and so his views are of evident importance. According to Sharpe, around 1913, his journal the *Indian Interpreter* had 'for some years been following an almost identical line'[174] of thought to Farquhar. At Jerusalem,[175] however, he used the term 'enrichment' rather than 'fulfilment', though they were understood, at least by some, as being synonymous.[176] According to Ariarajah, the methodology of the Jerusalem conference was to see the 'spiritual values' of the non-Christian religions, and to see how Christian faith could 'transcend them'.[177] It seems that only the Germans dissented from this approach to the non-Christian faiths.[178] Examining Macnicol's thought elsewhere, this seems to fit in with his general strategy, for he felt that it was in the 'mystical intuitions' rather than the 'philosophical

---

170 Paton, 1928, p. 439.

171 Cairns, 1929, p. 327.

172 Quick, 1928, p. 454.

173 Ariarajah, p. 34. It may also be noted that he had contributed material for the work of Commission Four at Edinburgh in which he spoke of fulfilment theology (EDMS, Macnicol # 198, p. 14).

174 Fulfil, p. 352.

175 That is to say in his paper, for he himself was not present (Ariarajah, p. 34).

176 Ariarajah, p. 49.

177 Ibid., p. 37.

178 Ibid.

interpretations' of Indian thought that value was to be found,[179] that is to say, he looked for 'spiritual values.' It was from these, then, that Hinduism could be spoken of as having a revelation,[180] which provided 'stepping-stones leading[...] onward to Christ.'[181] He had earlier written an article entitled 'Hindu Devotional Mysticism'.[182] Regarding the philosophy, he felt that Advaita was India's major problem and needed to be 'shattered,'[183] while he had also said of the Vedānta system, that it 'possesses no living springs.'[184] This was the thought of the author of the main report on Hinduism for Jerusalem, a man broadly sympathetic to fulfilment theology, and dissent to his views came mainly from the continent.[185] The other influential figure was Temple, who was chairman of the committee where this report was discussed.[186] He has already been mentioned in connection with fulfilment theology, and reference may be made to his *Readings in St. John's Gospel* where, speaking of the Logos he says: 'By the word of God – that is to say, by Jesus Christ – Isaiah, and Plato, and Zoroaster, and Buddha, and Confucius conceived and uttered such truths as they declared. There is only one divine light; and every man in his measure is enlightened by it.'[187]

Temple was influential in drafting the final statement of the Council which had to reconcile the various views.[188] However, it still affirmed the notion that, 'the "rays of light" that shone in Jesus Christ are to be found "where He is unknown or even rejected."'[189] That this was the message of the conference as a whole cannot be doubted, for speaking of 'Dr Temple's compact and brilliant paper,'[190] Cairns, who had opposed fulfilment theology

---

179   Macnicol, 1930, p. 209.
180   Macnicol, 1943, p. 254.
181   Ibid., p. 257.
182   Macnicol, 1916.
183   Macnicol, 1930, p. 209.
184   Macnicol, 1929, p. 70.
185   Which does not for the purposes of this study concern us.
186   Ariarajah, p. 44.
187   Temple, p. 10.
188   Ariarajah, p. 44. Space has meant that one of the most important themes of the Jerusalem conference, secularism, has not been addressed (see Quick, 1928, p. 448), for which Hocking's work is of vital importance.
189   *Report of the Jerusalem Meeting of the International Missionary Council*, I, p. 490, in Ariarajah, p. 46.
190   Cairns, p. 330.

at Edinburgh, quoted the following passage as the summation of the Conference's message, stating clearing the concept of fulfilment:

> How are we to proceed from the assertion of the uniqueness of Christ to its demonstration, unless there is instituted a comparison between the Gospel and other religions at their best? Moreover, uniqueness is not the only attribute of the gospel; universality is another. And how are we to present Christ as the fulfilment and more than the fulfilment of the highest aspirations of the many races of mankind, unless we know sympathetically what those highest aspirations are?[191]

Clearly, then, fulfilment theology was the message that came from Jerusalem, and so it can be seen as dominating missionary thought since Edinburgh. Thus, the criticisms of Hogg and others made little impact. That fulfilment theology became not just the popular creed, but also received further detailed exposition of a high standard, can be seen in Cave's works, especially his *Redemption Christian and Hindu*.

Caves's first book[192] was part of Farquhar's 'The religious Quest of India' series,[193] the title of which itself is, I would suggest, important in that it is about India's religious 'quest', thus ruling out Hogg's belief that there was also a finding of religious truth in India.[194] In this work, Cave's aim was to show that, 'Christianity is a religion of deliverance and, as such, meets the aspirations of Hinduism.'[195] There is no need to develop Cave's thought at length, as it mirrors much earlier fulfilment theology, though with more finesse than is typical. It is noteworthy that, particularly in a later work, Cave stresses that the religious aims of Christianity and Hinduism are different.[196] This is something which is already present in earlier fulfilment theologians. To demonstrate that they suggest that the differences are not so great, Cave, for instance, had earlier spoken of Hinduism in these words: 'The deepest and most persistent aspiration of higher Hinduism is for redemption, for

---

191   *Report of the Jerusalem Meeting of the International Missionary Council*, I, p. 463, in Ariarajah, p. 46.

192   Op. Cit.

193   Sharpe, 1979, p. 61, which also included a work by Macnicol.

194   See above.

195   Cave, 1919, p. 18.

196   Cave, 1944: 'To us, because we are Christians, communion with a personal God seems the highest form of religion. A Hindu will not so judge, who sees in the extinction of personality life's highest aim.'

deliverance from the seen and temporal.'[197] This form of wording minimises the differences between Hinduism and Christianity, though even in his later work 'he believes that the aspirations expressed in other religions may find in Christ their full satisfaction.'[198]

Evidently, then, fulfilment theology continued unabated after Edinburgh, but there were other perspectives, not hostile to fulfilment theology, but looking for a different way forward.

The Future of Missions and a Theology for India

Hogg can, probably, be seen as the only 'liberal' critic of Farquhar, the fulfilment principle being generally accepted by the likes of Bernard Lucas[199] and C. F. Andrews.[200] Yet these two, and others, had a different agenda to Farquhar, so:

> Those who, like Lucas, were calling for a transformation of missionary methods, found in *The Crown of Hinduism* little real support, since the book was not written to advocate new methods but to stress the need for a new *attitude*; its purpose was rather one of justification of the existing missionary enterprise in face of changed conditions.[201]

---

197   Cave, 1919, p. 223.

198   Cave, 1944, p. 7.

199   He defended Farquhar's position in the debate that followed Mackichan's article (see Lucas, 1914(b)).

200   Who read and 'made many suggestions' to the Crown prior to publication (Crown, p. 4).

201   Fulfil, p. 346.

i) Christian Vedānta

It is worth noting that Lucas had originally supported fulfilment theology,[202] but this was in his first work, *The Empire of Christ*, published in 1907. His thought moved on, however, and Lucas, who had a profound understanding of Hinduism,[203] came to see missions in a new light, where mission 'was about spiritual growth and mutual enrichment.'[204]

For Bernard Lucas, the action of the Logos allowed religious experience to be seen as man's main source of inspiration:

> The modern mind frankly recognizes that the basis of its theology is not the Bible, regarded as an infallible book whose words and thought-forms are the moulds into which its religious thought must be pressed, but the religious experience of the race, and supremely of Jesus, the highest manifestation of the thought and mind of God.[205]

If this is allowed, then the religious experience of the Hindu has a greater validity Lucas' thought is thus closer to that of Müller or Miller rather than Farquhar, 'The eastern mind has yet to give us its interpretation of the Christ, and the Eastern nature has yet to furnish us with its representation of the Christian life, ere the revelation is complete.'[206] Lucas, in fact, looked forward to the day when the Indian Church would produce its first heresy, which he felt would be a sign that it had truly become indigenous![207]

202　See Cracknell, 1995, p. 163, who sees this as Lucas' main paradigm.

203　According to a historian of the London Missionary Society, A. T. S. James, Lucas 'seemed to be able to think Hindu' (A. T. S. James, *Twenty Five Years of LMS Work* (1923), p. 168, quoted in Cracknell, 1995, p. 161.

204　Cracknell, 1995, p. 167

205　Lucas, 1910, pp. 294–5. He was not, however, rejecting the Bible's authority, for he goes on to say, 'It [the modern mind] finds in the Bible the richest religious experience of humanity, but it recognizes that that experience has been expressed in thought-forms which are essentially temporary, representative of the age in which the writers lived, and coloured with views of the Universe which the present age has outgrown' (ibid., p. 295). We have already made reference to Gore and Lux Mundi which did a great deal to make such views acceptable in English theology, and we see here also, in the final clause, a clear pointer towards Bultmann and his de-mythologizing, 'To de-mythologize is to reject not Scripture or the Christian message as a whole, but the world-view of Scripture, which is the world-view of a past epoch[....]' (Bultmann, p. 35).

206　Lucas, 1907, p. 37. See also Cracknell, 1995, pp. 166 f.).

207　Ibid., p. 17.

He also aimed at a way of combining Christianity and Vedānta. To do this, Lucas sought a reinterpretation of the idea of Vedānta away from that normally given by western commentators, by saying that instead of regarding Brahma as impersonal, 'it is quite as legitimate for us to regard Brahma (neuter) as superpersonal.'[208] He, thus, seeks to suggest that the Christian interpretation and the Vedāntin interpretation of 'God' are not wholly disparate.[209] Though Christianity will provide the basis for the new doctrine: 'His [Jesus'] appearance on the horizon of Indian religious thought foreshadows the rise of a New Vedanta in which the old dualism of a noumenal and a phenomenal Brahma is resolved.'[210]

Such language would, of course, be anathema to Farquhar, who rigidly opposed the use of Hindu thought.[211]

Lucas was in sympathy with the New Theology of R. J. Campbell, to whom we have already referred, as was his fellow missionary E. P. Rice.[212] The difference of this immanentist thought to Farquhar's has been mentioned above, as has the close connection, in this respect, to certain forms of Christian mystical thought, so we need not dwell upon this matter here. The growing interest in mysticism in the early part of this century[213] would, however, lead many people to take the view that every religion was based upon a direct experience of 'God'.[214]

---

208   Lucas, 1914(b), p. 453. Lucas uses the term 'Brahma' rather than 'Brahman' when referring to the 'Godhead'. In emphasising Brahman as 'superpersonal' Lucas did not, as did Farquhar, stress Śankara's Advaita-Vedānta as the ideal, but rather Madhva's Dvaita-Vedānta or Rāmānuja's Vishishtādvaita-Vedānta. While for Rāmānuja Brahman was personal, he was not, in the ordinary sense, a 'person': 'Rāmānuja's philosophy was in fact a different version of the *Advaita* doctrine. To put it succinctly, he claimed that the world, the *Ātman* and God (*Īsvara*) are distinct though not separate. The individual souls and the concrete world are like the body of God, and *Īsvara* possessed of the two is the *Brahman*' (Sen, p. 84).

209   See Lucas, 1914(b), p. 453.

210   Lucas, 1910, p. 404. Once again he uses 'Brahma' in the stead of the more normative 'Brahman'.

211   See fulfil, p. 302.

212   See Fulfil, p. 324 f, also Rice. In fact the British and Foreign Bible Society considered Rice a heretic (See, Fulfil, p. 325).

213   Such figures as W. R. Inge and Evelyn Underhill were popularizing the study of mysticism in England.

214   See, for instance, Macnicol who speaking of the bhaktas of India says, 'We see in them men seeking not God's gifts but God Himself. "The seekers" said Cromwell, "are the next best sect to the finders." But dare we say that these are not "finders"?

384

Related to the above is the idea that the Hindu scriptures should replace the Old Testament in India.[215] Indeed, one early advocate of this position called theistic Vedānta 'the Old Testament of India.'[216] Farquhar believed that there was too vast a 'difference between the Christian and Hindu scriptures.'[217] More recent thought has, however, accepted a greater usage of indigenous scripture.[218] This, of course, leads on to questions of the development of an indigenous Indian Christian theology, 'a contextual theology, a theology which has the ability to speak the language of the people.'[219] This would mean more than Farquhar's Jesus as-he-is, an idea found in Lucas, 'India, however, must be left to give her own interpretation of the personality of Jesus, and to relate His religious significance to her own thought.'[220]

Lucas stated the difference between his views and those of others as being 'the proselytising of Hindus, or the evangelisation of India.'[221] In this he sees India as having its own special religious genius to which Christianity must adapt,[222] believing further that 'the true home of religious thinking is the East.'[223]

While Farquhar stated that he thought Christianity should become indigenous, we have seen that this in reality meant very little, while both Lucas and Hogg sought to give Christianity in India a new flavour along the lines of India's own indigenous thought.[224] It should be mentioned that though

---

"'I have tasted sweetness at his feet'" says Tukārām. He claims to have found a peace such that "'the threefold fever has passed utterly away'" (Macnicol, 1916, p. 219).

215 Milburn, pp. 158 ff.
216 Ibid., p. 154.
217 Fulfil, p. 326.
218 See ibid., pp. 325 ff. Also we may note today at the Jesuit Centre for Indian Spirituality at Kalady, Sameeksha, the following arrangement is to be found in the meditation hall, 'At the centre of the hall, which is seven metres square, there is an oil lamp in the form of a lotus. Arranged around this in the cardinal directions are four sacred scriptures: – The Koran, The Upanishads, The Dhammapada and the Bible' (Mackenzie, p. 9).
219 Soans, p. 220.
220 B. Lucas, 1910, p. 404.
221 Lucas, 1914(a), pp. 3–4.
222 Ibid., p. 30.
223 Lucas, 1907, p. 36.
224 See Fulfil, pp. 64 f.

his thought in this area was moving in a different direction from Farquhar's, Lucas was still, nevertheless, an advocate of fulfilment theology as the basis from which to understand the relation of Christianity to Hinduism.[225] While seeing this interpretation as valid, he does not see it as his aim, saying, 'I leave that for those who care to show that Christianity as a system is the fulfilment of Hinduism as a system.'[226]

Lucas was not the only person seeking to unite Christianity and Vedānta in India. Another missionary, R. Gordon Milburn, also had this aim in mind, arguing that Christianity in India needed Vedānta.[227] He saw it as a counter to the one-sided transcendent monotheism of Israelite religion,[228] and argued that only Christianity offered an effective ethical monotheism, only the Vedānta offered a genuine immanentalist monotheism, and that both were needed.[229] Milburn also offered a suggestion for which texts from works such as the Dhammapada and Upanishads could be utilized as a new Old Testament, or at least as an additional apocrypha, in India.[230] It should be mentioned that he, too, endorsed the ideas of fulfilment theology.[231] There was also another stream of thought which emphasized, not doctrine but praxis, and to which consideration will now be given.

The main focus of this in Farquhar's day was the Brotherhood of the Imitation associated with the Cambridge Mission to Delhi.[232] It was intended to be an imitation of the Franciscan ideal,[233] and to approach to the Indian ideal of the holy man, an approach pioneered by one of the Brotherhood's number, Samuel E. Stokes, who tried to live the life of the 'bhagat.'[234] He believed that the Indian would only be won over to Christ when he 'becomes absolutely certain that we love him with a true love.'[235] In this way, Stokes' mission was one of service rather than preaching, and he believed the

---

225   See Lucas, 1914(b), p. 456.
226   Ibid., though whether this is what fulfilment theologians try to do is another matter, as has already been discussed.
227   Milburn, p. 155.
228   Ibid., pp. 155–6.
229   Ibid., p. 158.
230   Ibid., p. 159.
231   Ibid., p. 153.
232   See O'Connor, 1974, p. 26, and Chaturvedi and Sykes, pp. 71 ff.
233   Stokes, p. 123.
234   Ibid., pp. 126 ff.
235   Ibid., p. 130.

Christian faith would be taught and believed in by the way the missionary lived his life. He did not advocate direct evangelization: 'There were no religious meetings, as I had made it a rule never to talk of Christ unless questioned about Him.'[236]

ii) Charles Freer Andrews

Mention should also be made to Charles Freer Andrews, who was also in the Brotherhood,[237] and who also gave up direct evangelization: 'Andrews credo[...] was Johannine – that Christ is "the Eternal Word, the Light and the Life of all mankind," and that there is an "experience of Christ-life outside the Church of the baptized." The phrase "missions to the heathen" he had come to regard as "positively repellent."'[238]

Andrews had been a missionary with the Cambridge Mission to Delhi from 1904–1914,[239] but eventually became disenchanted with the standard missionary approach. He identified three main problems, first, the fact that British missionaries were associated with imperial power, second, that they failed to treat others with sympathy and love, and, third, that they had failed to create an indigenous church.[240] He saw the missionary movement as a failure, and indeed, from the meagre results produced among high caste Hindus, the missionary movement has been judged to be a failure by its own standards.[241] His preference was for dialogue and service rather than direct evangelization, in which the Christian motivation for service would be explained.[242] This was, of course, not a new idea, Miller had advocated the method of Christian presence rather than preaching,[243] and others in the Cambridge Mission to Delhi shared Andrew's vision.[244]

---

236   Stokes, p.132.
237   Andrews, 1938, pp. 87 ff.
238   Fulfil, p. 327, references to Andrews, 'A Missionary's Experience', *Indian Interpreter*, IV, 3, October 1909, p. 102. This is an expression of Logos theology.
239   Cox, in Mews, p. 226
240   Ibid., pp. 233–4.
241   See ibid., p. 240; see also, Kent, pp. 193–4.
242   Cox, in Mews, p. 234.
243   See chapter 5.
244   Andrews, 1938, p. 81.

In some ways Andrews was not then out of line with other missionaries, indeed, he advocated fulfilment theology,[245] but felt that a deeper way must be sought.[246] This for him involved attempting to return to the simplicity of the early church, and to live a life of 'poverty and humiliation and renunciation.'[247] He saw the Indian renouncer ideal as essential to engaging with Indian life.[248] He expressed both his theology and his missionary approach as being Johannine rather than Pauline in this regard.[249] His personal connection with Westcott should also be considered with respect to this,[250] as he saw a unity in the religious literature of all nations.[251] He did not, however, go out to India. Even with Westcott's guidance, he was not as open to Indian culture as may be supposed. In an early article he spoke of the religious history of India as being one of degradation,[252] which contrasted strongly with his rich appreciation of the Indian religious experience a few years later.[253] Seeing the good in Indian religion, he, like many, believed that Christianity should take an indigenous form in India.[254] Going further than many contemporaries, he argued against the prayer book and the Thirty-Nine Articles as having no place in India,[255] suggesting that an Indian Christianity must be built up out of the 'living fabric' of Hinduism.[256] What is most important for us is that Andrews, who must be considered a 'missionary theorist of considerable stature,'[257] felt that only an approach of presence was

---

245   See Andrews, 1911(a), pp. 46 ff., O'Connor, p. 36, and also Andrews later works, e.g., Andrews, 1928, p. 660. Also see his contribution to the Edinburgh correspondence (EDMS, Andrews # 123, pp. 11 ff.).
246   Andrews, 1911(a), p. 47.
247   Ibid. His connection to Stokes and the Brotherhood of the Imitation has been mentioned above.
248   Andrews, 1908(a), pp. 68 and 163–4.
249   Andrews, 1932 and Andrews, 1928, p. 660. By which he means that while Paul's epistles seek to argue the case for conversion, and are thus directly evangelistic, the Johannine tradition, as he saw it, coming through the Alexandrian School, advocated seeing the truths in other traditions, rather than seeking to persuade others to adopt one's own point of view.
250   Andrews, 1938, p. 81, and Chaturvedi and Sykes, pp. 60–1.
251   Andrews, 1933, p. 115.
252   Andrews, 1905, p. 369.
253   See, e.g., Andrews, 1913, pp. 275 and 277.
254   Andrews, 1911(b).
255   Andrews, 1908(a), p. 227, and Andrews, 1938, p. 84.
256   Andrews, 1911(a), p. 49.
257   Cox, in Mews, p. 226.

388

suitable, having been disgusted by the 'racial hauteur' of the English.[258] This also led him towards the aspect of his work and thought for which he is best remembered, his association with the national movement.[259] In this he saw the closest approach to Christian ideals within India.[260] He believed that the Indian reformers of old had been inspired by God,[261] and that the only hope for Indian nationalism was to be found in Christian faith.[262] In fact, he believed that 'Nationalism could be accommodated in terms of the sort of 'fulfilment' theory which Farquhar was making popular in some Christian circles.'[263]

It should be mentioned that in renouncing direct missionary work, Farquhar felt Andrews to be 'grievously mistaken,' but 'Farquhar continued to be supportive of Andrews throughout his most troubled years, continuing to publish articles by him in *Young Men of India.*'[264] As an interesting aside, it is recounted that Andrews demonstrated his attitude towards Kraemer's school of thought when he 'unceremoniously dumped' the copy he had of *The Christian Message in a Non-Christian World* into a waste-paper basket![265]

iii) Sadhu Sundar Singh

Finally, some mention should be made of the third member of the Brotherhood, this time not a white missionary,[266] but an Indian, Sadhu Sundar Singh.[267] Although his influence on the West occured at a later date, the 1920s, when his fame spread across the world,[268] he also deserves a mention here. His thought itself does not concern us directly,[269] but rather the way it was perceived within the British theological tradition. Here he was met with

---

258   Andrews, 1912, p. 172 – this work of Andrews was a 'phenomenal success' as a missionary text (Chaturvedi and Sykes, pp. 77–8).
259   He was a close friend and associate of Gandhi (Cox, in Mews, p. 226).
260   Ibid., p. 231 f.
261   Andrews, 1908(b), p. 2.
262   Ibid., p. 4, and Chaturvedi and Sykes, p. 62.
263   O'Connor, 1990, p. 136.
264   Ibid., p. 300, fn 8.
265   Ibid., p. 4.
266   Stokes was American, and Andrews English.
267   Sharpe, 1990, p. 162.
268   Sharpe, 1976, p. 48.
269   Though later in life he published many devotional works (see Singh, 1996), which were read by hundreds of thousands (Sharpe, 1976, p. 48).

great acclaim, as seen by the book by Streeter and Appasamy,[270] for 'he summed up in his person a great deal of what Christians had long hoped and prayed for from mission and church in India [.... A] convert [... who] appeared to have access to the innermost chambers of Indian spirituality.'[271] This was seen as heralding what many had long wished for, the beginnings of an indigenous Christian church, though some felt him to be too Indian to be Christian.[272] Certainly his theology may well have owed more to the Upanishads than the Bible,[273] but in the English speaking world he met with almost universal approval.[274] The reason, at least in part, for the Sadhu's popularity came from his being seen as a mystic[275] Important in this was his use of St. John's Gospel. As Streeter and Appasamy pointed out in their study of the Sadhu regarding his use of this Gospel, 'it is one little instance of the way in which, as Westcott prophesied, India, if converted, will bring new life to the interpretation of St. John.'[276]

The Sadhu went in and out of Samadhi experiencing many visions,[277] which was seen as the 'most important thing about him.'[278] It was as someone in communion with India's mystical heritage, yet also a Christian, that gave Sundar Singh his importance to the West, and also provides his relevance here.

There was thus, amongst the more adventurous liberal thinkers of Farquhar's day, in India an impetus away from direct evangelization of Hinduism, and towards a deeper understanding of a new Indian Christianity, which can be seen in the works of those such as Lucas, Stokes, Milburn, and Andrews. While they may have been, as Andrews was, in favour of fulfilment theology, their thought nevertheless represented a move away from the world-

---

270   Which was immensely popular. First published in April 1921, it was reprinted five times by the following June (Streeter and Appasamy, p. iv).
271   Sharpe, 1990, p. 161.
272   Ibid., fn. 3, p. 166.
273   Baajo, p. 70. An interesting account of his thought as bhakti theology may be found in Soans.
274   Nevertheless, he had many opponents who branded him a pathological liar (Sharpe, 1990, p. 163), although most of his critics were writing in German or the Scandinavian languages (Sharpe, 1976, p. 49). There was also a large amount of criticism from the Roman Catholic church (ibid., pp. 61 ff).
275   Sharpe, 1990, p. 162.
276   Streeter and Appasamy, p. 159.
277   Sharpe, 1990, p. 162, see also, Singh, 1926.
278   Sharpe, 1990, p. 162.

view that gave support to fulfilment theology, as I will now go on to argue. Because the liberal faction[279] did not attack, but rather supported, fulfilment theology, it is, perhaps, misleading to include this section under Farquhar's critics, but in so far as the thought they represented was an indirect critique of Farquhar, and pointed the way towards further development, it is useful to include their perspectives.

The Development of Liberal Thought

Evidently Farquhar's contemporaries shared his vision to some degree, though from the themes that were developing in their thought it is possible to see how later liberal thought moved away from this perspective. I would suggest that three themes can be found. First, the movement towards the integration of Christian and Hindu thought in an indigenous Indian Christian theology. Second, the movement away from evangelization to presence as a paradigm for Christian expression in relation to non-Christian religions. And, third, interest in the mystical, or spiritual, elements in religion as providing the unifying factor of experience.

In Farquhar's day all of these three points may have been recognized, yet they were all subsumed within a paradigm where Christianity was a priori assumed to be the definitive religion; however, throughout 'the twentieth-century, and especially since World War II, Christian confidence in Christian superiority has eroded.'[280] As Swidler has expressed it, humanity has passed from the 'Age of Monologue' to the 'Age of Dialogue.'[281] In relation to our three points above, there have thus been some changes. Firstly, some, such as Hick and Cobb, have argued that we must change our interpretation of the Christ event, no longer seeing it as decisive, and adopting a more modest Christology.[282] Secondly, the approach to other religions is now seen as one

---

279   The term 'faction' is to some degree misleading as fulfilment was, at least in India, 'warmly welcomed by the majority' (ibid., p. 346–7).

280   Cobb, p. vii.

281   Swidler, et. al., p. vii.

282   Lockhead, pp. 89 ff. Lockhead's argument that Hick and Cobb have adjusted their Christological understanding merely as a way of not wanting to present Christ as an ultimatum to other religions does though appear unsound. Wildman has identified numerous factors why a modest Christology can be found in theologians such as Hick and Cobb, of which religious pluralism is only one (Wildman,

of 'open dialogue'[283] in which for the Christian: 'Theology is not just the explication of our faith in Jesus Christ. It involves also putting that faith alongside other faiths[...] allowing the examination of each, including our faith, in the categories of the others. In this process we, as Christians, risk Christ for Christ's sake.'[284] With regard to this Knitter, has shown how many recent interpretations of the Christian missionary imperative have seen dialogue as being essential to this endeavour in today's world.[285] Such movements, according to David Tracy, 'hold real promise by their Christian entry into a genuine conversation with Hinduism[...] and Buddhism.'[286]

Thirdly, the religious experience of all the world's religions are treated and regarded as not just valid, but of equal value.[287] Each of these three points corresponds with the three aspects noted in the liberal thought of Farquhar's day, suggesting that the thought that then supported the notion that Christianity fulfilled Hinduism, now would not be able to support such a claim. For his part Smart has argued that the pluralist view-point was in the ascendancy and has spoken of an agreement on this point being the consensus of the future.[288] See also Whaling's words: 'Religious parochialism is still the pervading order of the day yet, year by year, global awakenings are conspiring to transcend it.'[289]

Having noted the world-view of liberalism, it is time to consider what assessment can be made of fulfilment theology today.

---

chapters 6 and 7), and there is a whole history of Biblical criticism which provides a background to explaining why theologians today might wish to see the figure of Jesus in a new light (ibid., pp. 1 ff.).

283	Wiles, 1992, p. 20.
284	M. M. Thomas, 1987, p. 7.
285	Knitter, 1996, pp. 136 ff.
286	Tracy, 1987, p. 450. He refers specifically to the thought of Panikkar and Cobb.
287	All being, to use Hick's terminology, apprehensions of the Real (Hick, pp. 292 ff.).
288	Smart, 1993, pp. 128 ff., see especially p. 138: 'I think that in the long run a pluralist victory is likely. Or, at least less unlikely than other outcomes.'
289	Whaling, 1987, p. 40.

Fulfilment Theology: A Contemporary Paradigm?

Fulfilment theology has, thus, been subjected to a number of criticisms from various quarters. As we have seen, however, these have done little to attack the theory from within its own terms; the most extreme challenges of Neo-Orthodoxy and post-liberal theology can only offer alternative world-views. However, if held moderately the same is not true. Thus we saw Kraemer adopting a limited form of fulfilment theology, and the extremes of post-liberal thought being untenable,[290] would have to give way to thought along the lines of Hogg's, which was seen not to be incompatible with fulfilment theology. The liberal school of theology has, however, moved on from the position of fulfilment theology, though that is not to say that it finds no advocates today. It has been argued that Cragg's thought, for instance, gives a contemporary version of Farquhar's thought.[291] Liberal thought as a whole has, however, tended to see a need for our theology to be recast in the light of new knowledge and new ways of looking at the world.[292] Alongside this

---

290   Mentioned in relation to Hogg.

291   Wood, p.78.

292   Kaufman has suggested that what is needed is a theology of 'reconstruction', where our old ideas of the nature of God and theology which are 'implausible, indeed unacceptable or even intolerable' can be recast in a new light (Kaufman, p. 3. For accounts of the way theology has been recast, see Wiles 1974, and more recently Badham 1998. A survey of more radical Anglican thought in recent years can be found in Nichols, pp. 160 ff.). Though we may note that recent postmodern theology has sought to restate a more traditionally orthodox Christianity, and to dismiss liberal theology as being engaged with an essentially un-Christian and non-theological agenda through association with the 'secular' cult of enlightenment rationality and reason (see Milbank, et. al., 1999, pp. 1 ff., and also Milbank in ibid., p. 21). It may be noted that Milbank, Graham Ward and others associated with this thought do not see themselves as engaged in the post-modern agenda with its 'nihilistic drift' (ibid., p. 1). They must, however, be seen in relation to it, and in this it seems to me that they are involving themselves in the current of thought of liberal theology, one of the aims of which has always been to restate and reinterpret theology in the terms of contemporary thought, which leaves perhaps rather a neat paradox, that in rejecting liberal theology for post-liberal theology they are engaging in an act of liberal theology. This should perhaps not surprise us, for as was observed in the methodological introduction to this work, postmodernism can be seen as incipient, and a refinement only of modernism/ liberalism (a view supported by others, see, e.g., Montag in ibid., p. 38). This school of thought,

agenda the belief that Christianity can be presented as the fulfilment of the non-Christian religions has also evaporated, being replaced by the notion of dialogue. Within its own terms, however, the notion of fulfilment remains particularly potent, and for those who wish to advocate Christian superiority yet also acknowledge the good to be found within the non-Christian religions it remains, not just an attractive, but, in one form or another, an extremely compelling option.[293] While fulfilment theology has had its critics, and theological thought may have moved on from its hey-day in the early decades of this century, fulfilment theology is far from being dead. The affinities that the non-Conformist and Anglican notions portrayed in this work have with the thought of Roman Catholic thinkers such as Rahner may also be noted,[294] further showing the strength of the idea.

The prevalence of the concept of fulfilment throughout many centuries, and in so many traditions, probably says more than anything else could about the strength of the idea. In terms of modern, especially contemporary theology, however, fulfilment theology, especially as traditionally expressed is, perhaps, an outdated idea. To-day, the increasing globalization and growth of respect for the non-Christian religious traditions makes it more difficult than ever to speak of one tradition being fulfilled by another, yet the endurance of the concept of fulfilment should make us feel that it can still have a usefulness for contemporary religious discourse. Though if the paradigm of one tradition fulfilling another tradition may seem a reflection of

---

associated with the term 'radical orthodoxy' is, it has been suggested, largely opposed to seeing any unity or harmony between religions (Lipner, *'Are Hinduism, Buddhism and Christianity Compatible?'* – seminar referred to earlier). I would support Lipner's assessment, seeing their thought as having close parallels with that of Lindbeck, and Barthianism, the latter a tag they disown, though admitting some resemblances (Milbank, et. al., p. 2). The similarity has, however, also been remarked upon before (Philip Sheldrake, *'On Becoming a Theological Person'*, seminar, Lampeter, 4/2/1999).

293   See for instance the recent endorsement of it by the Church of England's Doctrine Commission of the General Synod, *The Mystery of Salvation*, especially. pp. 152 ff.

294   The widespread use of 'fulfilment theology' type ideas has already been mentioned, and is often brought up by such writers as Race, D'Costa, etc. Rahner's thought, as a type of fulfilment theology, is also explored by Barnes, who looks at a number of the criticism's raised against him which may be seen as reflecting those raised against fulfilment theology in general (Barnes, pp. 52 ff. The general tenor of criticism against Rahner can be seen in Vorgrimler, pp. 121 ff).

naive liberalism, certain aspects of the world-view of fulfilment theology may be taken as examples of fulfilment. For instance, one of the themes of this study has been the development of an Indian Christian theology, and linked with this, the notion that Hinduism and Eastern religions can provide a supplement to Western Christianity. Examples of this may be seen in the Christian meditation tradition founded by John Main.[295] Yoga has been seen as capable of being adapted to Christian use by a number of writers,[296] and writers such as Bede Griffiths have suggested the need for a fusion of Eastern and Western ideas.[297] It is, perhaps, in such instances that the term may be employed, not speaking of 'fulfilment' in terms of a grand over-arching completion, but in smaller areas where elements of one tradition may be useful, and on a more individual basis, adding depth and meaning to the religious life. In this way each religion may be said to find its fulfilment in every other tradition, in terms of learning through dialogue and adaptation. The above proposal may be objected to on the grounds that each religion represents a closed system, making such an approach, at best, naive; however, to the idea that religions are closed systems, objection has already been made. Considering the examples of where it has occurred, it is, I suggest, merely naming a process which is already a reality, rather than proposing some new paradigm. Again, objection might be made in Hogg's terms, of asking what, in this sense, does fulfilment mean. I would respond that it does not seek to provide an overall framework, but merely to make contemporary use of a very potent idea in religious thought. Of course, many of a more conservative religious standpoint might suggest that their religious tradition has fixed values and can find all it needs with reference to its unchanging past, and does not need any fulfilment or supplement from external traditions.

The objections above reject, however, what Whaling has referred to as the 'interplay' between religious traditions.[298] That is to say, the processes whereby all religions must be seen as developing and changing. The contemporary proponents of Neo-Orthodoxy seem to read Christianity as a

---

295   While John Main claims to have found the method of mantra in John Cassian and the desert fathers, there is a strong influence from the Eastern religious traditions on his thought and those of his followers (see Griffiths, 1992, especially Freeman's introduction, p. ix).
296   See e.g., Frenz, and Déchanet.
297   See most particularly Griffiths 1983 in this regard.
298   Whaling, 1987, pp. 28 ff.

closed entity, incapable of change or alteration from some state of supposed patristic purity. This attitude, especially in view of today's globalization, where every faith tradition cannot be seen as independent from other religious traditions, but as inherently involved with them, is utterly untenable. Moreover, Badham has argued that, from the Christian standpoint, what are now seen as 'traditional' or 'conservative' religious values represent a development, if not a total change, in the religion.[299] We must not become stuck, as Lipner has observed:

> When Christian communities cling to their culturally outmoded, isolated or alien forms of worship, doctrine and religious language, they enclose themselves in a self-contained religious world that has little or no contact with the life of their non-Christian neighbours. They live in a ghetto with a siege mentality – sources of religious curiosity or irritation for others.[300]

They often look for a 'pure Gospel', which, speaking in terms of inculturation, Stockwell has observed cannot exist,[301] and it is to the question of inculturation that we now turn in order to note the dangers inherent in the view I have outlined. It is not easy to free ourselves of Western preconceptions. As has been said, many examples of an Asian Christian theology have only been, 'Karl Barth in Eastern fables!'[302] As Kitagawa has observed, much talk of Asian Christian traditions has been undertaken by Westerners,[303] and we see many Western commentators ready to speak of the benefits (Western) Christianity can gain from religions such as Hinduism.[304] In this we must be careful not to commit the excesses of earlier ages, where it has been noted that there 'has been a tendency for Europeans to idealize India,'[305] but there has also been another tendency for the West to put down the East and seek to control it.[306] Such would be the opinion of many

---

299   Badham 1999; originally 'Christianity as a New Religion', paper delivered at the British Association for the Study of Religion Annual Conference 1998, Lampeter.
300   Lipner, 1985, p. 162.
301   Stockwell, p. 154.
302   Philip, 1993, p. 113.
303   Kitagawa, p. 3.
304   See, e.g., Organ.
305   Drew, p. ix.
306   Inden, pp. 86 ff. Inden's argument dwells too much on those nineteenth-century writers, such as Wilson, Mill, and Colebrooke who attacked India, while only passing mention is given to more positive commentators, however influential,

commentators. However, more recent scholarship has questioned how far such allegations of bias can be justified, showing that the East has frequently not been used by the West to support its own presuppositions, but also as a corrective and critic.[307] However, if Christianity is to take seriously its role in a multi-cultural and pluralist world, it must be self-reflexively aware of the pitfalls that may befall it. We should also ask what is aimed at in this endeavour. The idea might suggest a world culture, but others have questioned whether this is the ideal that should be aimed for. Lipner has employed the phrase 'diversity-in-unity,'[308] in arguing that Christianity must be clothed increasingly 'in the diversified garb of cultural identity.'[309] As has been observed, the growing world culture has led to: 'The "contradictory" rise of both universalistic and particularistic tendencies as the result of globalization.'[310] We should thus be warned that the changing world scene offers no sure answers of the way forward. Rather, as important as questions of methodological integrity and preparedness are, we should remember that it has also been stated that, 'There are no blueprints for a dialogue in the context of inculturation. Praxis must precede theory.'[311] Certainly in a new world situation, Christianity (indeed all religions) must seek for further expression, or fulfilment, of their potential for growth in light of the changing nature of the world today.

This new paradigm of fulfilment is certainly far from the doctrine of fulfilment theology as found in its proponents of the late nineteenth and early twentieth-centuries, but is, perhaps, the best reinterpretation of its principles in accordance with contemporary circumstances. It is an interpretation that I feel is in the spirit of Rowland Williams, F. D. Maurice, and Max Müller, representing a further development in the same tradition of religious belief.

---

among whom we may note Monier-Williams and Müller (each of whom gets but a brief mention, the former on p. 99, the latter on p. 105).

307   See J. J. Clarke, esp. pp. 22–34, and 214–225. For a discussion of many of the themes of post-colonialism in relation to Religious Studies, see King 1999.

308   Or 'discontinuity-in-continuity' to employ the language of Kraemer and his opponents.

309   Lipner, 1985, pp. 165 ff.

310   Bhatt, p. 39 – references are made to D. Harvey, *The Condition of Postmodernity*, Oxford, Basil Blackwell, 1989, pp. 272–4, and, also, A. McGrew, 'A Global Society?' (pp. 61–102) in *Modernity and its Futures*, edited by S. Hall, D. Held, and A. McGrew, Cambridge University Press, 1992, p. 92.

311   Amaldoss, p. 176.

Bibliography

Books and Articles

Addison, James Thayer, 'The Changing Attitude Toward Non-Christian Religions', *International Review of Mission*, volume XXVII, pp. 110–121, 1937.

Aleaz, K. P., *Jesus in Neo-Vedanta: A Meeting of Hinduism and Christianity*, Delhi, Kant Publications, 1995.

Allen, E. L., *Christianity Among the Religions*, London, George, Allen, and Unwin Ltd, (no date given).

Allnutt, S. S., *India's Religious Needs*, Cambridge Mission to Delhi Occasional Papers No. 13, Cambridge, Cambridge University Press, 1888.

Almond, Philip C., *The British Discovery of Buddhism*, Cambridge, Cambridge University Press, 1988.

Amaladoss, Michael, 'Culture and Dialogue', *International Review of Mission*, 169–177, volume LXXIV, # 294, April 1985.

Anderson, J.N.D., *Christianity and Comparative Religion*, Inter-Varsity Press, London, 1973.

Andrews, Charles Freer, 'The Effect of the Japanese Victories Upon India', *The East and the West*, pp. 361–372, October, 1905.

————, *North India*, Handbooks of English Church Expansion Series No. 8, London, A. R. Mowbray and Co. Ltd., 1908(a).

————, 'The First Principles of a National Movement', *The Stephanian*, pp. 1–4 (note the page references do not refer to the original article, but to a typed copy), May 1908.

————, 'The Indian Missionary Ideal', *The East and the West*, pp. 45–51, 1911(a).

————, 'The Indigenous Expression of Christian Truth', *The Young Men of India*, volume XXII, # 3 and 4, pp. 47–51 and 72–75, 1911(b).

————, *The Renaissance in India: its Missionary Aspect*, Church Missionsry Society, London, 1912.

————, 'The Body of Humanity', *The Modern Review*, pp. 272–279 and 379–382, September and October 1913, .

————, 'A Quest for Truth', *The Young Men of India*, volume XI, # 8, 9, 10 and 11, pp. 443–446, 522–526, 581–585, and 660–664, 1928.

————, 'Christian Missions and the Eastern Mind', *The British Weekly*, 18/8/1932.

————, *Christ in the Silence*, London, Hodder and Stoughton, 1933.

————, *What I Owe to Christ*, London, Hodder and Stoughton, 1938 (first published 1932).

Anonymous, 'Christianity and Hinduism', *Eclectic Review*, Vol. 105, originally from the *Christian Remembrancer*, pp. 359–387, 1857(?).

Anonymous, 'Review of the Life and Letters of Rowland Williams, D.D.', *Dublin University Magazine*, volume 85, pp. 761–764, 1875.

399

Anonymous, 'Recent Periodical Literature', *Madras Christian College Magazine*, volume XIII, #1, p(p). 58(ff), July 1895.

Anonymous, 'The Tyranny of Style', *The Building News and Engineering Journal*, volume LXXXII, # 2458, pp. 223–224, 14/2 1902.

Anstey, J. C. Knight, 'Mr. Farquhar's Zeal for the Kingdom', *The Indian Witness*, volume XLIII, # 21, pp. 405–408, 21/5 1912.

Appasamy, A. J., *Christianity as Bhakti Marga*, Madras, Christian Literature Society, 1991 (first published 1926).

Argyle, Michael, and Beit-Hallahmi, Benjamin, *The Social Psychology of Religion*, London, Routledge and Kegan Paul, 1975 (second edition).

Ariarajah, Wesley, *Hindus and Christians: A Century of Protestant Ecumenical Thought*, Currents of Encounter Series, volume V, Grand Rapids (Michigan), William B. Eerdmans Publishing Company, 1991.

Arnold, Edwin, *The Light of the World; Or, the Great Consummation*, London, Longmans, Green and Co., 1893.

——, *The Light of Asia; Or, the Great Renunciation (Mahâbhinishkramana*, London, Kegan Paul, Trench, Trübner and Co. Ltd, 1905.

Ashby, Philip H., *Modern Trends in Hinduism*, New York, Columbia University Press, 1974.

Auboyer, Jeannine, *Srī Ranganāthaswāmi*, Vedaraniam (India), Gurukulam Off Set Printers, 1994.

Baago, Kaj, 'The Post-Colonial Crisis of Missions', *International Review of Mission*, volume LV, pp. 322–332, 1966.

——, *Pioneers of Indigenous Christianity*, Confessing the Faith in India Series No. 4, Madras, Christian Literature Society, 1969.

Badham, Paul (editor), *Religion, State, and Society in Modern Britain*, Lampeter, Edwin Mellen Press, 1989.

——, *John Hick's Global Understanding of Religion*, Tokyo, International Buddhist Study Centre, 1992.

——, 'Rowland Williams', *Bulletin of the British Association for the Study of Religion*, No. 81, pp. 4–9, June 1997.

——, *The Contemporary Challenge of Modernist Theology*, Cardiff, University of Wales Press, 1998.

——, 'Contemporary Christianity as a New Religion', *Modern Believing*, volume XL, #4, pp. 17–29, October 1999.

Badley, Brenton T., 'Does the Hindu Image Point Forward to Christ?', *The Indian Witness*, volume XLIII, # 23, pp. 447–448, 4/6 1912.

Ballou, Robert O. and Spiegelberg, F., *The Bible of the World*, London, Kegan Paul, Trench Trubner and Co., Ltd., 1940.

Banerjea, Krishna Mohan, *Dialogues on the Hindu Philosophy, Comprising the Nyaya, the Sankhya, the Vedant [sic]; To Which is Added a Discussion of the Authority of the Vedas*, London, Williams and Norgate, 1861.

——, *The Arian Witness*, Calcutta, Thacker, Spink and Co., 1875.

Banerjea, J. R., 'Mr. J. N. Farquhar on "Christ and the Religions of the World"', *The Indian Witness*, volume XLIII, # 22, p. 429, 28/5 1912.

Barnes, Michael, *Religions in Conversation: Christian Identity and Religious Pluralism*, London, Society for the Propogation of Christian Knowledge, 1989.

400

Barrows John Henry, *The World's Parliament of Religions*, II volumes), London, The Review of Reviews Office, 1894.

Barth, Karl (editor Helmut Gollwitzer) (translator and editor G. W. Bromiley), *Church Dogmatics: A Selection*, New York, Harper and Row, 1962.

—— (translator B. Cozens, J. Bowden, and Others), *Protestant Theology in the Nineteenth Century*, London, Student Christian Movement Press, 1972 (first published 1946).

—— (translator Grover Foley), *Evangelical Theology: An Introduction*, Grand Rapids (Michigan), William B. Eerdmans Publishing Company, 1979 (first published 1963).

Baumer, Franklin L., *Modern European Thought: Continuity and Change in Ideas, 1600–1950*, London, Collier Macmillan Publishers, 1977.

Beare, Francis Wright, *The Gospel According to Matthew: A Commentary*, Oxford, Basil Blackwell, 1981.

Bebbington, David William, *Evangelicalism in Modern Britain: A History from the 1730s to the 1980s*, London, Routledge, 1995 (first published 1989).

Begbie, Harold, *Other Sheep: A Study of the Peoples of India, with Particular Reference to the Collision Between Christianity and Hinduism*, London, Hodder and Stoughton, (no date given).

Bennett, Clinton, *In Search of the Sacred*, London, Cassells, 1996.

Benson, Arthur Christopher, *the Life of Edward White Benson: Sometime Archbishop of Canterbury*, II volumes, London, Macmillan and Co., 1900.

Berry, Philippa and Wernick, Andrew (editors), *Shadow of Spirit: Postmodernism and Religion*, London, Routledge, 1992.

Besant, Annie, *The Riddle of Life: And How Theosophy Answers It*, London, Theosophical Publishing Society, 1911.

Bhatt, Chetan, *Liberation and Purity: Race, New Religious Movements, and the Ethics of Postmodernity*, London, University College Press, 1997.

Binyon, Gilbert Clive, 'Christianity and Hindu Character', *Constructive Quarterly*, pp. 359–369, June 1917.

Birks, Herbert, *Life and Correspondence of T. Valpy French: Bishop of Lahore*, II volumes, London, John Murray, 1895.

Blake, William (editor Geoffrey Keynes) *The Complete Works of William Blake*, London, Oxford University Press, 1966.

Blavatsky, H. P., *Isis Unveiled*, volume II: *'Theology'*, New York, J. W. Bouton, 1889.

Boase, C. W., *Register of Exeter College, Oxford*, Oxford, Oxford Historical Society Publications, volume XXIX, 1894 (new edition).

Bonhoeffer, Dietrich (editor Eberhard Bethge, translated by Reginald Clarke and revised by Frank Clark and others), *Letters and Papers from Prison*, London, Student Christian Movement Press, 1967 (third edition).

Bose, Pramatha Nath, *A History of Hindu Civilisation During British Rule*, volume I: 'Religious Condition', New Delhi, Asian Publication Services, 1975 (first published 1894).

Bothwick, Meredith, *Keshub Chunder Sen: A Search for Cultural Synthesis*, Calcutta, Minerva Associates, 1977.

Bouquet, Alan Coates, *The Christian Faith and Non-Christian Religions*, London, James Nisbet and Co. Ltd, 1958.

Bourne, Edmund J., 'Does the Concept of the Person Vary Cross-Culturally?', in Richard A. Shweder, *Thinking Through Cultures: Expeditions in Cultural Psychology*, Cambridge (Massachusetts), Harvard University Press, 1991.

Bowie, Fiona, 'Tresspassing on Sacred Domains: A Feminist Anthropological Approach to Theology and Religious Studies', *Feminist Studies in Religion*, volume XIV, #1, pp. 40–62, Spring 1998.

Bowker, John, *The Sense of God: Sociological, Anthropological and Psychological Approaches to the Origin of the Sense of God*, Oxford, Oneworld Publications, 1995 (second edition).

Boyd, A. J., *Christian Encounter*, Edinburgh, The Saint Andrew Press, 1961.

Boyd, Robin H. S., *India and the Latin Captivity of the Church*, Cambridge, Cambridge University Press, 1974.

——, *An Introduction to Indian Christian Theology*, Madras, Christian Literature Society, 1979 (second edition).

Boyer, Pascal, *The Naturalness of Religious Ideas: A Cognitive Theory of Religion*, Berkeley and Los Angeles, University of California Press, 1994.

Brainard, Samuel, 'Defining "Mystical Experience"', *Journal of the American Academy of Religion*, volume LXIV, # 2, pp. 359–393, 1996.

Braybrooke, Marcus, *Together to the Truth: A Comparative Study of Some Developments in Hindu and Christian Thought Since 1800*, Madras, Christian Literature Society, Delhi, Indian Society for Promoting Christian Knowledge, 1971.

——, *The Undiscovered Christ: A Review of Recent Developments in the Christian Approach to the Hindu*, Madras, Christian Literature Society, 1973.

Brockington, John, *Hinduism and Christianity*, London, Macmillan Press Ltd., 1992.

Brookman, David M., 'Bede Griffiths: Prophet of Cultural Transformation,' *Anima*, volume XVI, pp. 61–69, Fall 1989.

Brown, George William, 'The Modern View of Christianity and its Relation to Other Religions', *The Indian Witness*, volume XLIII, # 22, pp. 428–429, 28/5 1912.

Brown, John Macmillan, *The Memoirs of John Macmillan Brown*, University of Canterbury Publication No. 19, Christchurch (New Zealand), Whitcombe and Tombs, 1974.

Buckland, C. E., *Dictionary of Indian Biography*, London, Swan Sonnenschein and Co. Ltd, 1906.

Bultmann, Rudolf, *Jesus Christ and Mythology*, New York, Charles Scribner's Sons, 1958.

Burckhardt, Titus, *Sacred Art in East and West*, Bedfont (Middlesex), Perennial Books, 1986.

Burton, J. W., 'Christian Missions as Affected by Liberal Theology', *The Harvest Field*, volume XX, pp. 66–72, February 1909.

Byork, John and Culshaw, Joseph, 'Editorial: The New Attitude to Religion', *The Indian Witness*, volume XLIII, # 10, p. 203, 12/3 1912.

Cairns, David S., 'Christion Missions and International Peace', *International Review of Mission*, volume 1, pp. 193–201, 1912.

——, 'The Christian Message: A Comparison of Thought in 1910 and in 1928', *International Review of Mission*, volume XVIII, pp. 321–331, 1929.

Campbell, R. J., *The New Theology*, London, Chapman and Hall, Ltd., 1907.

Campbell, J. Fraser, 'The New Attitude', *The Indian Witness*, volume XLIII, # 21, p. 408, 21/5 1912.

Capps, Walter H., *Religious Studies: The Making of a Discipline*, Minneapolis, Fortress Press, 1995.

Carlyle, Thomas, *On Heroes, Hero Worship and the Heroic in History*, London, Macmillan and Co Ltd, 1901 (first published 1841).

Caröe, William Douglas, 'Church Furniture', *Journal of the Royal Institute of British Architects*, volume I, pp. 423–429, 1894.

Carpenter, James, *Gore: A Study in Liberal Catholic Theology*, London, Faith Press, 1960.

Carus, Paul, 'Has Christianity the Moral Right to Supplant the Ethnic Faiths: Missions from the Standpoint of Comparative Religion', *The American Journal of Theology*, volume XI, 1, pp. 13–24, 1907.

Cave, Sydney, *Redemption Christian and Hindu*, London, Humfrey Milford, 1919.

——, *Christianity and Some Living Religions of the East*, London, Duckworth, 1944 (first published 1929).

Chadwick, Henry, *The Vindication of Christianity in Westcott's Thought, 'The Bishop Westcott Memorial Lecture 1960'*, Cambridge, Cambridge University Press, 1961.

Chatterton, Eyre, *A History of the Church of England in India*, London, Society for the Propogation of Christian Knowledge, 1924.

Chaturvedi, Benarsidas, and Sykes, Marjorie, *Charles Freer Andrews*, London, George, Allen and Unwin, 1949.

Chetty, O.K., *William Miller*, Madras, Christian Literature Society, 1924.

Church, Richard William, *The Sacred Poetry of Early Religions*, London, Macmillan and Co., 1874.

——, *The Oxford Movement: Twelve Years 1833–1845*, London, Macmillan and Co., 1891.

Clarke, Basil F. L., *Anglican Cathedrals Outside the British Isles*, London, Society for the Propogation of Christian Knowledge, 1958.

Clarke, James Freeman, 'Buddhism: Or the Protestantism of the East', *The Atlantic Monthly*, volume XXIII, pp. 713–28, 1869.

——, *Ten Great Religions: An Essay in Comparative Theology*, Boston, James R. Osgood and Company, 1876.

Clarke, John James, *Oriental Enlightenment: The Encounter Between Asian and Western Thought*, London, Routledge, 1997.

Clements, Keith W., *Lovers of Discord*, London, Society for the Propogation of Christian Knowledge, 1988.

Cobb, John B., Jr., *Beyond Dialogue*, Philadelphia, Fortress Press, 1982.

Cobban, G. Mackenzie, 'The Latent Religion of India,' *Contemporary Review*, volume LXVII, pp. 853–863, 1894.

Coleridge, Samuel Taylor, *Aids to Reflection and the Confessions of an Inquiring Spirit. to Which are added his Essays on Faith and the Book of Common Prayer, Etc.*, London, George Bell and Sons, 1884 (new revised edition).

Collet, Sophia Dobson, 'The Brahmo Samaj Versus the "New Dispensation"', *Contemporary Review*, volume XI, pp. 726–736, 1881.

Collier, A. E., 'Break down Idols, do not Whitewash them', *The Indian Witness*, volume XLIII, # 22, p. 429, 28/5 1912.

Coore, A., *Some Remarks on Indian Church Architecture: With Special Reference to the New Churches in the Delhi Mission*, Cambridge Mission to Delhi Occasional Paper No. 32, Cambridge, Cambridge University Press, 1907.

Copleston, F. C., *Aquinas*, Harmondsworth, Penguin Books Ltd, 1965 (first published 1955).

Copleston, Reginald Stephen, *Buddhism: Primitive and Present in Magadha and in Ceylon*, London, Longmans, Green, and Co., 1892.

Cornille, Catherine, *The Guru in Indian Catholicism*, Louvain Theological and Pastoral Monographs No. 6, Louvain, Peeters Press (undated – 1993?).

Cousins, Ewart H., *Christ of the 21st Century*, Shaftesbury, Element Books Ltd, 1992.

Coward, Harold G. (editor), *Modern Indian Responses to Religious Pluralism*, Albany, State University of New York Press, 1987.

——, *Hindu-Christian Dialogue: Perspectives and Encounters*, Maryknoll (NY), Orbis Books, 1990.

Cox, James L., *The Development of A. G. Hogg's Theology in Relation to Non-Christian Faith: its Significance for the Tambaram Meeting of the International Missionary Council, 1938*, unpublished PhD Thesis, University of Aberdeen, March 1977.

——, 'Faith and Faiths: The Significance of A. G. Hogg's Missionary Thought for a Theology of Dialogue', *Scottish Journal of Theology*, volume XXXII, pp. 241–256, 1979.

Cracknell, Kenneth, *Towards a New Relationship*, London, Epworth Press, 1986.

——, *Justice, Couresy and Love: Theologians and Missionaries Encountering World Religions, 1846–1914*, London, Epworth Press, 1995.

Cragg, Kenneth, *The Christian and Other Religion*, London, Mowbrays, 1977.

——, *The Call of the Minaret*, London, Collins, 1986 (second edition).

Creighton, Louise, 'Meeting of the Continuation Committee of the World Missionary Council', *International Review of Mission*, volume II, pp.118–125, 1913.

Cross, F. L. (editor), *The Oxford Dictionary of the Christian Church*, London, Oxford University Press, 1958 (first published 1957).

Crossan, John Dominic, *The Historical Jesus: The Life of a Mediterranean Jewish Peasant*, Edinburgh, T and T Clark, 1993.

Dare, M. Paul, *Indian Underworld*, London, Rider, (undated, introduction written 1938).

Davie, Ian, *Jesus Purusha: A Vedanta-Based Doctrine of Jesus*, West Stockbridge, Massachusetts, Inner Traditions/ Lindisfarne Press Book, 1985.

Davies, A. W., 'The "New Thought" and the Missionary Message', *The Indian Witness*, volume XLIII, # 14, pp. 287–289, 9/4 1912.

Davies, Margaret, *Matthew*, Sheffield, JSOT Press, 1993.

D'costa, Gavin, *Theology and Religious Pluralism*, Oxford, Basil Blackwell, 1986.

—— (editor), *Christian Uniqueness Reconsidered*, Faith Meets Faith Series, New York, Orbis Books, 1998.

Déchanet, J.-M., *Christian Yoga*, Tunbridge Wells, Search Press, 1984 (first published 1960).

Dessain, Charles Stephen, and Blehl, Vincent Ferrer (editors), *The Letters and Diaries of John Henry Newman*, volume XIV: 'Papal Aggression July 1850 – December 1851', London, Thomas Nelson and Sons Ltd, 1963.

——, *The Letters and Diaries of John Henry Newman*, volume XVI: 'Founding a University January 1854 – September 1855', London, Thomas Nelson and Sons Ltd, 1965.

——, *The Letters and Diaries of John Henry Newman*, volume XXVI: 'Aftermaths January 1872 – December 1873', London, Thomas Nelson and Sons Ltd, 1974.

——, *The Letters and Diaries of John Henry Newman*, volume XXX: 'A Cardinal's Apostolate October 1881 – December 1884', London, Thomas Nelson and Sons Ltd, 1976.

Devasahayam, D. M. and Sudarisanam, A. N. (editors), *Rethinking Christianity in India*, Madras, A. N. Sudarisanam, 1938.

Devdas, Nalini, 'The Christ of the Ramakrishna Movement', *Religion and Society*, pp. 13–28, September 1964.

Dickinson, G. Lowes, *An Essay on the Civilizations of India, China, and Japan*, London, J. M. Dent and Sons Ltd, 1914.

Dictionary of National Biography, Sidney Lee (editor), volume XXXIX, London, Smith, Elder, and Co., 1894.

Dods, Marcus, *Mohammed, Buddha, and Christ*, Hodder and Stoughton, London, 1893.

Dogmatic Canons and Decrees, Rockford (Illinois), Tan Books and Publishers, Inc., 1977.

Doss, Y. V. Kumara, 'The Swadeshi Movement and the Attitude of the Protestant Elite in Madras,' *Indian Church History Review*, volume XXII, pp. 5–22, (June) 1988.

Douglas, I.H. and Carmon, J.M., 'The Post-Colonial Crisis of Missions: Comments', *International Review of Mission*, volume LV, pp. 483–489, 1966.

Drew, John, *India and the Romantic Imagination*, Delhi, Oxford University Press, 1987.

Duff, Alexander, *India, and Indian Missions*, Edinburgh, John Johnstone, 1839(a).

——, *Missions the Chief End of the Christian Church*, Edinburgh, John Johnstone, 1839(b).

——, 'India and its Evangelization', in *Twelve Lectures Delivered Before the Young Men's Christian Association*, pp. 75–160, London, James Nisbet and Co., 1851.

Edger, P., 'Letter: The New Attitude', *The Indian Witness*, volume XLIII, # 18, pp. 347–348, 30/4 1912.

Edwards, David L., *Leaders of the Church of England 1828–1978*, London, Hodder and Stoughton, 1978.

Eliade, Mircea (translator Willard R. Trask), *Yoga: Immortality and Freedom*, London, Routledge and Kegan Paul, 1969 (first published 1958).

—— (editor), *The Encyclopedia of Religion*, XVI volumes, London, Collier Macmillan, 1986–7.

Elliot-Binns, L. E., *Religion in the Victorian Era*, London, Lutterworth Press, 1946 (first published 1936).

——, *English Thought 1860–1900: The Theological Aspect*, London, Longmans, Green and Co., 1956.

Essays and Reviews, London, Longman, Green, Longman, Roberts and Green, 1865 (12th edition, first published 1861).

Eucken, Rudolf (translator W. Tudor Jones), *The Truth of Religion*, London, Williams and Norgate, 1911.

Faber, Geoffrey, *Oxford Apostles*, London, Faber and Faber, 1993.

Fairbairn, A. M., *The Philosophy of the Christian Religion*, London, Hodder and Stoughton, 1902.

——, *The City of God*, London, Hodder and Stoughton, (no date given).

Farquhar, John Nicol, 'The Science of Religion as an Aid to Apologetics', *The Harvest Field*, volume XII, pp. 369–374, 1901.

——, *The Future of Christianity in India*, Pice Pamphlets # 1, London, Christian Literature Society, 1904(a).

——, 'The Age and Origin of the Gita', *East and West*, volume not known, pp. 905–925, 1904(b).

——, 'Missionary Study of Hinduism', *Harvest Field*, volume XVI, pp. 166–178, 1905.

——, *Gita and Gospel*, London, Christian Literature Society, 1906 (first published 1903).

——, 'Christianity in India', *Contemporary Review*, volume not known, pp. 597–616, 1908 (a).

——, 'Christianity in India', *Indian World*, volume VIII, pp. 61–68, 1908 (b).

——, 'What Apologetic has Proved most Popular among Hindu Students', *The Young Men of India*, volume XX, # 12, pp. 199–202, December 1909.

——, 'The Greatness of Hinduism', *Contemporary Review*, volume XCVII, pp. 647–662, 1910 (a).

——, 'The Crown of Hinduism', *Contemporary Review*, volume XCVIII, pp. 56–68, 1910 (b).

——, 'Glimpses of Hinduism: The Worship of Siva in Tamil Lands', *The Young Men of India*, volume VII, pp. 76–79, July 1911.

——, 'The Relation of Christianity to Hinduism', *International Review of Missions*, volume III, pp. 417–431, 1914.

——, *Modern Religious Movements in India*, London, Macmillan and Co., 1918 (first published 1915).

——, *The Crown of Hinduism*, London, Humphrey Milford: Oxford University Press, 1930 (first published 1913).

Feuerstein, Georg, *Holy Madness*, London, Arkana, 1992.

Findlay, G. G., and Holdsworth W. W., *The History of the Wesleyan Methodist Missionary Society*, volume V, London, Epworth Press, 1924.

Flood, Gavin, *An Introduction to Hinduism*, Cambridge, Cambridge University Press, 1996.

——, *Beyond Phenomenology: Rethinking the Study of Religion*, London, Cassell, 1999.

Ford, David F., *The Modern Theologians*, I volume edition, Oxford, Blackwell Publishers, 1997 (second edition).

Fordham, Frieda, *An Introduction to Jung's Psychology*, Harmondsworth, Penguin, 1982 (third edition).

Forman, Robert K. C., *The Problem of Pure Consciousness: Mysticism and Philosophy*, Oxford, Oxford University Press, 1990.

Forster, Edward Morgan, *A Passage to India*, London, Penguin Books, 1989 (first published 1924).

Fox, Matthew, *Original Blessing*, Santa Fe (Nm), Bear and Co., 1983.

Francis, T. Dayanandan, *The Relevance of Hindu Ethos for Christian Presence*, Madras, Christian Literature Society, 1989.

—— (editor), *The Christian Bhakti of A. J. Appasamy*, Madras, Christian Literature Society, 1992.

Frazer, James G., *The Golden Bough*, New York, Gramercy Books, 1981 (first published 1890).

Fremantle, W. H., 'The Brahmo Samaj and the Religious Future of India', *Contemporary Review*, volume XV, pp. 67–80, 1870.

Frenz, Albrecht, *Yoga in Christianity*, Madras, Christian Literature Society, 1986.

Gairdner, W.H.T., *'Edingburgh 1910': An Account and Interpretation of the World Missionary Conference*, Oliphant, Anderson, and Ferrier, Edingburgh, 1910.

Garland, David E., *Reading Matthew: A Literary and Theological Commentary on the First Gospel*, London, Society for the Propogation of Christian Knowledge, 1993.

Garvie, A. E.., 'The Christian Challenge to the Other Faiths', *International Review of Mission*, volume I, pp. 659–673, 1912.

Gellner, Ernest, *Postmodernism, Reason, and Religion*, London, Routledge, 1992.

Goel, S. R., *Catholic Ashrams*, New Delhi, Voice of India, 1988.

Goodall, Norman, *A History of the London Missionary Society 1895–1945*, London, Oxford University Press, 1954.

Goodenough, E. R., *The Theology of Justin Martyr*, Amsterdam, Philo Press, 1968.

Gore, Charles (editor), *Lux Mundi*, London, John Murray, 1890 (first published 1889).

——, *The Incarnation of the Son of God*, being the Bampton Lectures for 1891, London, John Murray, 1891.

——, *The Epistle to the Ephesians*, London, John Murray, 1902.

——, *Christ and Society*, being the Halley Stewart Lectures for 1927, London, George Allen and Unwin, 1928.

——, *The Philosophy of the Good Life*, being the Gifford Lectures 1929–30, London, John Murray, 1930.

——, *Belief in God*, Harmondsworth, Penguin Books Ltd, 1939 (first published 1921).

Gregory, Richard L. (editor), *The Oxford Companion to the Mind*, Oxford, Oxford University Press, 1987.

Griffiths, Bede, *The Golden String*, London, Collins, 1979 (first published 1954).

——, *The Marriage of East and West*, London, Fount, 1983.

——, *Return to the Centre*, London, Fount, 1987.

——, *The New Creation in Christ*, London, Darton, Longman and Todd, Ltd., 1992.

—— (editor and translator), *Universal Wisdom*, London, Fount, 1994.

Grimes, Cecil John, *Towards an Indian Church*, London, Spck, 1946.

Gupta, Upendra K., 'The Christ-Ideal of the Brahmo Somaj,' *East and West*, volume I, pp. 1434–1444, 1902.

Halbfass, Wilhelm, *India and Europe: An Essay in Understanding*, Albany, State University of New York Press, 1988.

Hallencreutz, Carl F., *New Approaches to Men of Other Faiths*, World Council of Churches Research Pamphlet No. 18, Geneva, World Council of Churches, 1970.

——, 'Tambaram Revisited', *International Review of Mission*, volume LXXVII, pp. 347–359, 1988.

Hammond, Peter, *Dean Stanley of Westminster*, Worthing, Churchman Publishing, 1987.

Hamnett, I. (editor), *Religious Pluralism and Unbelief*, Routledge, London, 1990.

Hampson, Daphne, *After Christianity*, London, Student Christian Movement Press, 1996.

Happold, F. C., *Mysticism: A Study and an Anthology*, Harmondsworth, Penguin, 1964.

Hart, David A., *One Faith? Non-Realism and the World of Faiths*, London, Mowbray, 1995.

Hasler, L. Ireland, 'The "New Thought" and the Missionary Message', *The Indian Witness*, volume XLIII, # 21, pp. 408–409, 21/5 1912.

Hastings, James (editor), *Encyclopaedia of Religion and Ethics*, XII Vols, Edinburgh, T. and T. Clark, 1908–1921.

Healy, Kathleen, *Christ as Common Ground: A Study of Christianity and Hinduism*, Pittsburgh, Duquesne University Press, 1990.

Heelas, Paul, *The New Age Movement*, Oxford, Blackwell Publishers Ltd, 1996.

Hegel, Georg Wilhelm Friedrich (editor Peter C, Hodgson), *G. W. F. Hegel: Theologian of the Spirit*, The Making of Modern Theology Series No. 8, Edinburgh, T. and T. Clark, 1997.

Henderson, Lilian F., *The Cambridge Mission to Delhi*, London, Offices of the Mission, 1931.

Hick, John, *An Interpretation of Religion*, London, Macmillan, 1989.

Higham, Florence, *Frederick Denison Maurice*, London, Student Christian Movement Press, 1947.

Hocking, William Ernest, *Re-Thinking Missions*, London, Harper and Brothers, 1932.

Hoehler, Harry H., *Christian Responses to the World's Faiths, being the Unitarian Universalist Christian* (Summer/Winter 1990, volume XLV, Nos. 2–4), Boston, Unitarian Universalist Christian Fellowship, 1991.

Hogg, Alfred George, 'All Things to All Men', *The Harvest Field*, volume XVIII, pp. 134–141, 1907.

——, 'The Presentation of Christ to the Hindu', *The East and the West*, volume VIII, pp. 264–287, 1910.

——, 'Reviews of Books: 'The Crown of Hinduism,' and Other Volumes', *The InternationalReview of Missions*, volume III, pp. 171–174, 1914.

——, 'The God That Must Needs Be Christ Jesus', *International Review of Mission*, volume VI, pp. 62–73, 221–231, 383–394, and 521–533, 1917.

——, *Karma and Redemption*, Madras, Christian Literature Society, 1970 (first published 1909).

Hogg, William Richley, *Ecumenical Foundations*, Harper and Brothers, New York, 1951.

Holland, Henry Scott, *Brooke Foss Westcott: Bishop of Durham*, London, Wells Gardner, Darton and Co., Ltd., 1910.

Howard, Leslie, *The Expansion of God*, London, Student Christian Movement Press, 1981.

Howell, Peter and Sutton, Ian (editors), *The Faber Guide to Victorian Churches*, London, Faber and Faber, 1989.

Hughes, Edward J., *Wilfred Cantwell Smith: A Theology for the World*, London, Scm Press Ltd, 1986.

Hunt, William Remfry, *Heathenism Under the Searchlight: The Call of the Far East*, London, Morgan and Scott Ltd, 1908.

Huntly, 'Farquhar's Fallacies', *The Indian Witness*, volume XLIII, # 15, pp. 306–307, 16/4 1912.

Hylson-Smith, Kenneth, *High Churchmanship in the Church of England*, Edinburgh, T and T Clark, 1993.

Hyman, Gavin, 'Hick and Loughlin on Disputes and Frameworks', *New Blackfriars*, volume LXXIX, # 931, pp. 391–405, 1998.

Inden, Ronald, *Imagining India*, Oxford, Blackwell Publishers, 1992 (first published 1990).

Illingworth, J. R., *Personality Human and Divine*, being the Bampton Lectures for 1894, London, Macmillan, 1895.

Iremonger, F.A., *William Temple: His Life and Letters*, Oxford University Press, London, 1948.

James, Lawrence, *Raj: The Making and Unmaking of British India*, The Softback Preview, 1998 (first published 1997).

James, William, *The Varieties of Religious Experience*, London, Longmans, Green and Co., 1928 (first published 1902).

Jasper, David (editor), *Postmodernism, Literature, and the Future of Theology*, New York, St Martin's Press, 1993.

Jersey, M. E., 'Buddhism and Christianity', *National Review*, volume IV, pp. 577–91, 1884–5.

Jevons, Frank, Byron, *Introduction to the Study of Comparitive Religion*, Macmillan Co., New York, 1908.

Jewson, Arthur, 'The New Attitude', *The Indian Witness*, volume XLIII, # 14, p. 289, 9/4 1912.

Johnston, James (editor), *Reports of the Centenary Conference on the Protestant Missions of the World, London 1888*, II volumes, London, James Nisbet and Co., 1889.

Jones, J. P., 'The Modern Missionary Attitude', *The Indian Witness*, volume XLIII, # 22, pp. 427–428, 28/5/1912.

Jones, Owain W., *Rowland Williams: Patriot and Critic*, Llandysul, Gomer Press, 1991.

Jongeneel, J. A. B., 'Christianity and the – Isms: A Description, Analysis and Rethinking of Kraemer's Theology of Missions', *Bangalore Theological Forum*, volume XX, pp. 17–41, January – June 1988.

Jordan, Louis Henry, *Comparative Religion: its Genesis and Growth*, Edinburgh, T. and T. Clark, 1905.

Justin Martyr (edited and translated by Alexander Roberts and James Donaldson; revised by A. Cleveland Coxe), *The Ante-Nicene Fathers*, volume I: 'The Apostolic Fathers, Justin Martyr, Irenaeus', Edinburgh, T. and T. Clark, 1996.

Kaufman, Gordon D., *in Face of Mystery: A Constructive Theology*, London, Harvard University Press, 1995 (first published 1993).

Kellogg, Samuel Henry, *The Light of Asia and the Light of the World a Comparison of the Legend, the Doctrine, and the Ethics of the Buddha with the Story, the Doctrine, and the Ethics of Christ*, London, Macmillan, 1885.

Kent, John, *The Unacceptable Face: The Modern Church in the Eyes of the Historian*, London, Student Christian Movement Press, 1987.

Killingley, Dermot, *Rammohun Roy in Hindu and Christian Tradition*, being the Teape Lectures 1990, Newcastle Upon Tyne, Grevatt and Grevatt, 1993.

King, Henry Churchill, 'Christianity the Only Hopeful Basis for Oriental Civilization', *International Review of Mission*, volume II, pp. 417–429, 1913.

King, Richard, *Orientalism and Religion: Postcolonial Theory, India and 'The Mystic East'*, London, Routledge, 1999.

Kitagawa, Joseph Mitsuo, *The Christian Tradition: Beyond its European Captivity*, Philadelphia, Trinity Press International, 1992.

Knight, Francis, *The Nineteenth-Century Church and English Society*, Cambridge, Cambridge University Press, 1998 (first published 1995).

Knitter, Paul F., *No Other Name? A Critical Survey of Christian Attitudes Toward the World Religions*, London, Student Christian Movement Press, 1985.

——, *Jesus and the Other Names: Christian Mission and Global Responsibility*, Oxford, Oneworld Publications, 1996.

Knox, Thomas Francis (translator), *The Life of the Blessed Henry Suso: by Himself*, London, Methuen and Co. Ltd., 1913.

Kopf, David, *The Brahmo Samaj and the Shaping of the Modern Indian Mind*, Princeton, Princeton University Press, 1979.

Kraemer, Hendrik, *The Christian Message in a Non-Christian World*, London, Edinburgh House Press, 1947 (first published 1938).

——, *Religion and the Christian Faith*, London, Lutterworth Press, 1956.

Küng, Hans (translator John Bowden), *Global Responsibility*, London, Student Christian Movement Press, 1991 (first published 1990).

Lacey, Robert Lee, *The Holy Land of the Hindus*, London, Robert Scott, 1913.

Larsen, L. P., 'The Interest of Mystical Christianity to Missionaries', *The Harvest Field*, volume XVI, pp. 3–17 and 46–54, 1905.

Lefever, H.C., 'The Preparation of Missionaries 1910 and 1960', *International Review of Mission*, volume LIX, #3, pp. 281–290, 1960.

Le Goff, Jacques, *The Birth of Purgatory*, London, Scolar Press, 1984.

Lefroy, George Alfred, *Missionary Work in India*, Cambridge Mission to Delhi Occasional Papers No. 12, Cambridge, Cambridge University Press, 1887.

——, *Christ the Goal of India*, Cambridge Mission to Delhi Occasional Papers No. 15, Cambridge, Cambridge University Press, 1889 (a).

——, 'The University Pulpit' being a 'Sermon' 9/6/1889, *Supplement to the Cambridge Review*, volume X, # 257, pp. cv–cvii, 13/6/1889 (b).

——, 'The Moral Tone of India', *The East and the West*, volume I, pp. 121–133, April, 1903.

——, *Mahomedanism: its Strength and Weakness*, Cambridge Mission to Delhi Occasional Papers No. 21, Cambridge, Cambridge University Press, 1907(a) (first published 1894).

——, in John Ellison and G. H. S. Walpole (editors), *Church and Empire*, London, Longmans, Green and Co., 1907(b).

Léon-Dufour (translator and editor John Mchugh), Xavier, *The Gospels and the Jesus of History*, London, Fontana, 1968.

Leonard, John, *London's Parish Churches*, Derby, Breedon Books, 1997.

Liddon, H. P., *The Life of Edward Bouverie Pusey*, volume I, London, Longmans and Co., 1893 (second edition).

Lightfoot, Joseph Barber, *Historical Essays*, London, Macmillan and Co., 1895.

Lilly, W. S., 'The Religious Future of the World' Part I, *Contemporary Review*, pp. 100–121, January 1883.

Lindbeck, George, *The Nature of Doctrine, Religion and Theology in a Postliberal Age*, London, Society for the Propogation of Christian Knowledge, 1984.

Lipner, Julius, '"Being One, Let Me Be Many" Facets of the Relationship Between the Gospel and Culture', *International Review of Missions*, volume LXXIV, pp. 158–168, 1985.

——, 'On "Hindutva" and a "Hindu-Catholic," with a Moral for Our Times, *Hindu-Christian Studies Bulletin*, No. V, pp. 1–8, 1992.

——, *Hindus: Their Religious Beliefs and Practices*, London, Routledge, 1994.

——, Ancient Banyan: An Enquiry Into the Meaning of 'Hinduness'', *Religious Studies*, pp. 109–126, 1996.

——, *Brahmabandhab Upadhyay: The Life and Thought of a Revolutionary*, Delhi, Oxford University Press, 1999.

Livingstone, Elizabeth A. (editor), *The Concise Oxford Dictionary of the Christian Church*, Oxford, Oxford University Press, 1977.

Lockhead, David, *The Dialogical Imperative*, London, Scm Press Ltd, 1988.

Longridge, George, *A History of the Oxford Mission to Calcutta*, London, John Murray, 1900.

Lucas, Bernard, *The Empire of Christ: Being a Study of the Missionary Enterprise in the Light of Modern Religious Thought*, London, Macmillan and Co., Ltd., 1907.

——, *Christ for India*, London, Macmillan and Co., Ltd., 1910.

——, *Our Task in India: Shall we Proselytise Hindus or Evangelise India?*, London, Macmillan and Co., Ltd., 1914(a).

——, 'Not to Destroy, But to Fulfil', *Harvest Field*, volume XXXIV, # 12, pp. 451–464, 1914(b).

Lucas, J. J., 'Our Attitude to Non-Christian Religions', *The Indian Witness*, volume XLIII, # 20, pp. 388–389, 14/5 1912.

Lyotard, Jean-François (translator Geoff Bennington and Brian Massumi), *The Postmodern Condition: A Report on Knowledge*, Theory and History of Literature Series, volume 10, Manchester, Manchester University Press, 1992 (first published 1979).

Mabie, Henry C., 'Has Christianity the Moral Right to Supplant the Ethnic Faiths: The Divine Right of Christian Missions', *American Journal of Theology*, volume XI, #1, pp. 1–13, 1907.

Macculloch, J.A., *Comparitive Theology*, Methuen and Co., London, 1902.

Macdonell. Diane, *Theories on Discourse: An Introduction*, Oxford, Basil Blackwell, 1989 (first published 1986).

Mackenzie, Caroline, 'Indian Christian Ventures' (Ii Parts), *Church Building*, volumes XL and XLI, pp. 8–10, and pp. 4–7, July – August 1996 and September – October 1996.

Mackichan, D., 'A Present-Day Phase of Missionary Theology', *The International Review of Missions*, volume III, pp. 243–254, 1914.

Mackintosh, Hugh Ross, *Types of Modern Theology*, London, Nisbet and Co. Ltd, 1954.

Maclean, J. H., 'The New Attitude', *The Indian Witness*, volume XLIII, # 25, pp. 487–488, 18/6 1912.

Macnicol, Nicol, 'The Missionary Message and the Non-Christian Religion', *The Indian Witness*, volume XLIII, # 20, p. 388, 14/5 1912.

——, 'Hindu Devotional Mysticism', *International Review of Missions*, volume V, pp. 210–222, 1916.

——, 'A Christian Looks At India', *International Review of Mission*, volume XVIII, pp. 59–73, 1929.

——, *India in the Dark Wood*, London, Edinburgh House Press, 1930.

——, *Is Christianity Unique?: A Comparative Study of the Religions*, being the Wilde Lectures for 1935, London, Student Christian Movement Press, 1936.

——, 'Is There a General Revelation? A Study in Indian Religion', *International Review of Mission*, volume XXXII, pp. 241–257, 1943.

Macphail, James M., 'Letter: St Paul at Athens', *The Indian Witness*, volume XLIII, # 20, p. 389, 14/5 1912.

Macquarrie, John, *Twenieth-Century Religious Thought*, London, Student Christian Movement Press, 1967 (first published 1963).

Magnus, Philip, *Gladstone: A Biography*, London, John Murray, 1954.

Main, John, *The Inner Christ (comprising: Word Into Silence, Moment of Christ, and the Present Christ)*, London, Darton, Longman andTodd, 1991.

Marshall, P. J. (editor), *The British Discovery of Hinduism in the 18th Century*, Cambridge, Cambridge University Press, 1970.

411

Martin, W. A. P., 'Is Buddhism a Preparation for Christianity?,' *The Chinese Recorder and Missionary Journal*, volume XX: 5, pp. 193–203, May 1889.

Maurice, Frederick, *The Life and Letters of Frederick Denison Maurice: Chiefly told in his Own Letters*, II volumes, London, Macmillan and Co., 1884.

Maurice, Frederick Denison, *The Religions of the World: and their Relations to Christianity*, London, Macmillan and Co., 1886 (first published 1847).

——, *The Kingdom of Christ: Or Hints on the Principles, Ordinances and Constitution of the Catholic Church in Letters to a Member of the Society of Friends*, II volumes, London, James Clarke and Co., 1959 (first published 1838)

Maw, Martin, *Fulfilment Theology, The Aryan Race Theory, and the Work of British Protestant Missionaries in Victorian India*, PhD Thesis, University of Leicester, 1986.

——, *Visions of India*, Studies in the Intercultural History of Christianity, volume LVII, Bern, Verlag Peter Lang, 1990.

Mcginn, Bernard, *The Foundations of Mysticism*, The Presence of God Series, volume I, London, Scm Press, 1992.

Mcgrath, Francis, *John Henry Newman: Universal Revelation*, Tunbridge Wells, Burns and Oates, 1997.

Mcleod, Hugh, *Religion and Society in England, 1850–1914*, Social History in Perspective Series, Basingstoke, Macmillan, 1996.

Mews, Stuart (editor), *Modern Religious Rebels*, London, Epworth Press, 1993.

Milbank, John, *Theology and Social Theory: Beyond Secular Reason*, Oxford, Blackwell Publishers Ltd., 1998 (first published 1990).

Milbank, John, Catherine Pickstock, and Graham Ward (editors), *Radical Orthodoxy*, London, Routledge, 1999.

Milburn, R. Gordon, 'Christian Vedantism', *The Indian Interpreter*, volume VII, pp. 153–160, 1913.

Miller, William, *Indian Missions and How to View Them*, Edinburgh, James Thin, 1878.

Monier-Williams, Monier, *The Study of Sanskrit in Relation to Missionary Work in India*, London, Williams and Norgate, 1861.

——, *Indian Wisdom*, London, Wm. H. Allen and Co., 1875.

——, 'Progress of Religious Thought in India', *Contemporary Review*, volume XXXIII, pp. 242–271, 1878.

——, 'Progress of Religious Thought in India', *Contemporary Review*, volume XXXIV, pp. 19–44, 1879(a).

——, 'Progress of Religious Thought in India', *Contemporary Review*, volume XXXV, pp. 843–861, 1879(b).

——, *Religious Thought and Life in India*, Part I: 'Vedism, Brāhmanism, and Hindūism', London, John Murray, (first edition:) 1883, (second edition:) 1885 and (third edition:) 1887(a).

——, *Modern India and the Indians*, London, Trübner and Co., 1887(b) (fourth edition).

——, *Buddhism and its Connexion with Brāhmanism and Hindūism and in its Contrast with Christianity*, London, John Murray, 1889.

——, *Hinduism*, London, Society for the Propagation of the Gospel, 1894.

——, *Sanskrit Dictionary*, Delhi, Motilal Banarsidas, 1976 (originally published 1899).

Montgomery, H. H. (editor), *Mankind and the Church: Being an Attempt to Estimate the Contribution of Great Races to the Fulness of the Church of God*, London, Longmans, Green, and Co., 1909.

——, *The Life and Letters of George Alfred Lefroy*, London, Longmans, Green, and Co., 1920.

Morgan, R. W., *St Paul in Britain; Or, the Origin of British as Opposed to Papal Christianity*, London, Covenant Publishing Company, Ltd, 1930 (sixth edition).

Morris, John Brande, *An Essay Towards the Conversion of Learned and Philosophical Hindus*, London, J. G. F. and J. Rivington, 1843.

Moses, D. G., 'Apologetic Literature Since Farquhar', *National Christian Council Review*, pp. 276–286, 1963.

Mott, John R., *The Evangelization of the World in this Generation*, Student Volunteer Missionary Union, London, 1900.

——, *The Decisive Hour of Christian Missions*, Church Missionary Society, London, 1911.

——, 'Continuation Committee', *International Review of Mission*, volume I, pp. 62–78, 1912.

——, 'Present Possibilities of Co-Operation in the Mission Field', *International Review of Mission*, volume III pp. 209–224, 1914.

——, 'At Edinburgh, Jerusalem and Madras', *International Review of Mission*, volume XXVII, pp. 297–320, 1938.

Moule, C. F. D., 'Fulfilment – Words in the New Testament: Use and Abuse', *New Testament Studies*, volume XIV, pp. 293–320, 1967–8.

Müller, Friedrich Max, *Introduction to the Science of Religion*, London, Longmans, Green, and Co., 1873(a).

——, *on Missions: A Lecture Delivered in Westminster Abbey on December 3, 1873, with an Introductory Sermon by Arthur Penrhyn Stanley, D.D.*, London, Longmans, Green, and Co., 1873(b).

——, 'Forgotten Bibles', *The Nineteenth Century*, pp. 1004–1022, June 1884.

——, *Anthropological Religion*, being the Gifford Lectures for 1891, London, Longmans, Green, and Co., 1892.

——, *Natural Religion*, Collected Works volume I, London, Longmans, Green, and Co., 1899.

——, *Chips from a German Workshop* volumes I and IV: 'Recent Essays and Addresses', and 'Essays on Mythology and Folklore', Collected Works volume VIII, London, Longmans, Green and Co., 1900 (first published 1867 and 1875).

——, *The Upanishads*, Sacred Books of the East Series volume I, Delhi, Motilal Banarsidass, 1969 (first published 1879).

Müller, F. (editor), *The Life and Letters of the Honourable Friedrich Max Müller*, volume II, London, Longmans, Green, and Co., 1902.

Neill, Stephen, *Anglicanism*, Penguin, Harmondsworth, 1958.

——, *A History of Christian Missions*, Penguin, Harmondsworth, 1971.

——, *Crises of Belief*, London, Hodder and Stoughton, 1984.

Neufeldt, Ronald, 'Christianity and 'Other Religions': Contributions from the Work of F. Max Müller', *Hindu-Christian Studies Bulletin*, volume V, pp. 9–12, 1992.

Newbigin, Leslie, *The Gospel in a Pluralist Society*, London, London, Society for the Propogation of Christian Knowledge, 1990 (first published 1989).

Newman, John Henry, *Apologia Pro Vita Sua*, London, Fontana Books, 1972 (first published 1864).

——, *An Essay on the Development of Christian Doctrine*, Harmondsworth, Penguin Books, 1973 (first published 1845).

Newsome, David, *Bishop Westcott and the Platonic Tradition*, being the Bishop Westcott Memorial Lectures, 1968, Cambridge, Cambridge University Press, 1969.

——, *Two Classes of Men: Platonism and English Romantic Thought*, London, John Murray, 1974.

——, *The Victorian World Picture*, London, John Murray, 1997.

New York 1900: *Report on the Ecumenical Conference on Foreign Missions*, volume I, London, Religious Tract Society, 1900.

Nichols, Aidan, *The Panther and the Hind: A Theological History of Anglicanism*, Edinburgh, T. and T. Clark, 1994 (first published 1993).

Nikodimos, St., of the Holy Mountain and Makarios, St., of Corinth (editors) (translators and editors by G. E. H. Palmer, Philip Sherrard, and Kallistos Ware), *The Philokalia*, volume I., London, Faber and Faber, 1983.

Norman, Edward, *The Victorian Christian Socialists*, Cambridge, Cambridge University Press, 1987.

Norris, Christopher, *Deconstruction: Theory and Practice*, London, Methuen, 1982.

——, *What's Wrong with Postmodernism: Critical Theory and the End of Philosophy*, Hemel Hempstead, Harvester Wheatsheaf, 1990.

Nowell-Smith, Simon, *Edwardian England 1901–1914*, Oxford University Press, 1964.

Occasional Bulletin, volume XI, #5, New York, Missionary Research Library, 14/6 1960.

O'connor, Daniel, *The Testimony of C. F. Andrews* Confessing the Faith in India Series No. 10, Madras, Christian Literature Society, 1974.

——, *Gospel, Raj and Swaraj: The Missionary Years of C. F. Andrews 1904–14*, Studies in the Intercultural History of Christianity No. 62, Frankfurt, Verlag Peter Lang, 1990.

Oddie, Geoffrey A., 'India and Missionary Motives, C. 1850–1900', *Journal of Ecclessiastical History*, volume XXV, #1, pp. 61–74, January 1974.

——, *Hindu and Christian in South-East Asia*, London Studies on South Asia No. 6, London, Curzon Press, 1991.

Oldham, J.H., *The World and the Gospel*, United Council for Missionary Education, London, 1916.

——, *Christianity and the Race Problem*, Student Christian Movement, London, 1925.

——, 'After Twenty-Five Years', *International Review of Mission*, volume XXIV, pp. 297–313, 1935.

——, 'Fifty Years After', *International Review of Mission*, volume XLIX, #3, pp. 257–272, 1960.

Organ, Troy, 'Some Contributions of Hinduism to Christianity', *Religion in Life*, volume XLVII, pp. 450–59, 1978.

Osborn, Eric Francis, *Justin Martyr*, Tübingen, J. C. B. Mohr, 1973.

Otto, Rudolf, *Mysticism East and West*, London, Theosophical Publishing House, 1987 (first published 1932).

Owen, John, 'The Rev. Dr. Rowland Williams, and His Place in Contemporary Religious Thought', *Contemporary Review*, volume XIV, pp. 58–79, 1870.

Paden, William E., *Religious Worlds*, Boston, Beacon Press, 1988.

Padoux, André (translator Jacques Gontier), *Vāc*, Albany, State University of New York Press, 1990.

Palmer, Bernard, *Reverend Rebels*, London, Darton, Longman andTodd, 1993.

Pan-Anglican Congress, 1908, volume III, Section B, 'Christian Truth and Other Other Intellectual Forces', London, Society for Promoting Christian Knowledge, 1908.

Panikkar, Raimundo, *The Trinity and the Religious Experience of Man*, London, Darton, Longman and Todd, 1973.

——, *The Unknown Christ of Hinduism*, London, Darton, Longman and Todd, 1981 (second edition).

Parrinder, Geoffrey, *Avatar and Incarnation*, London, Faber and Faber, 1970.

Parsons, Gerald (editor), *Religion in Victorian Britain*, volume I: 'Traditions', Manchester, Manchester University Press, 1988 (a).

—— (editor), *Religion in Victorian Britain*, volume II: 'Controversies', Manchester, Manchester University Press, 1988 (b).

—— (editor), *The Growth of Religious Diversity: Britain from 1945*, volume II: 'Issues', London, Routledge, 1994.

Paton, William, 'The Jerusalem Meeting and After', *International Review of Mission*, volume XVII, pp. 435–444, 1928.

Paul, C. Kegan, 'Rowland Williams, D.D. in Memoriam', *Theological Review*, volume VII, pp. 234–248, 1870.

Philip, T. V., *Krishna Mohan Banerjea: Christian Apologist*, Confessing the Faith in India Series No. 15, Bangalore, Christian Literature Society, 1982.

——, 'Relation Between Theology and Culture in the Perspective of Church History', *Voices from the Third World*, volume XVI, #2, pp. 94–116, 1993.

Prestige, G. L., *The Life of Charles Gore*, London, William Heineman Ltd, 1935.

Purser, W. C. B., 'The Vital Forces of Southern Buddhism in Relation to the Gospel: Part Ii in Burma', *International Review of Mission*, volume IV, pp. 232–247, 1915.

Quenot, Michel, *The Icon: Window on the Kingdom*, London, Mowbray, 1992.

Quick, Oliver, Chase, 'The Value of Mysticism in Religious Faith and Practice', *Journal of Theological Studies*, volume XIII, pp. 161–200, 1912.

——, 'The Jerusalem Meeting and the Christian Message', *International Review of Mission*, volume XVII, pp. 445–454, 1928.

Race, Alan, *Christians and Religious Pluralism*, London, Student Christian Movement Press, 1983.

Radhakrishnan, S., *East and West in Religion*, London, George Allen and Unwin Ltd., 1933.

——, *Eastern Religions and Western Thought*, London, Geoffrey Cumberlege, 1940 (second edition).

Rahner, Hugo (translator Brian Battershaw), *Greek Myths and Christian Mystery*, London, Burnes and Oates, 1963 (first published 1957).

Rahner, Karl, *Theological Investigations*, volume V, London, Darton, Longman and Todd, 1966.

Rai, Lala Lajput, 'Christianity and Hinduism', *The Indian World*, 1908, volume VII, pp. 485–493.

Raine, Kathleen, *Blake and Tradition*, volume II, London, Routledge and Kegan Paul, 1969 (first published 1968).

415

Ralston, Helen, *Christian Ashrams: A New Religious Movement in Contemporary India*, Studies in Religion and Society volume XX, Lampeter, Edwin Mellen Press, 1987.

Ramsey, Arthur Michael, *F. D. Maurice and the Conflicts of Modern Theology*, Cambridge, Cambridge University Press, 1951.

Rao, C. G. S. S. Sreenivasa, 'The Doctrine of Karma and Dr A. G. Hogg', *Indian Journal of Theology*, volume XXV, pp. 30–37, January– March 1976.

Reardon, Bernard M. G., *From Coleridge to Gore*, London, Longman Group Ltd, 1971.

Reid, Howard and Croucher, Michael, *The Way of the Warrior*, London, Century Publishing, 1986.

Reischauer, A. K., 'Vital Forces of Japanese Buddhism in Relation to Christianity', *International Review of Mission*, volume IV, pp. 565–583, 1915.

——, 'The Christian Message and the Non-Christian Religions', *International Review of Mission*, volume XVII, pp. 119–133, 1928.

Rhys-Davids, T. W., 'Buddhism and Christianity,' *The InternationalQuarterly*, volume VII, pp. 1–13, March – June 1903.

Rice, E. P., 'The New Theology and Missionary Work', *The Harvest Field*, pp. 363–376, October 1908.

Richards, Glyn, *A Source-Book of Modern Hinduism*, London, Curzon Press, 1985.

Robb, J. Wesley, 'Hendrik Kraemer Versus William Ernest Hocking', *Journal of Bible and Religion*, volume XXIX, pp. 93–101, April 1961.

Robert, Dana L., 'The Origen of the Student Volunteer Watchword: "The Evangelization of the World in this Generation", *International Bulletin of Mission*, volume X, #4, pp. 146–149, 1986.

Robinson, C.H., *An Interpretation of the Character of Christ to Non-Christian Missions*, Longmans, Green, and Co., London, 1910.

Robson, John, *The Science or Religion and Christian Missions*, reprinted from *British and Foreign Evangelical Review* of January 1875, Glasgow, (publisher not known) 1876.

——, 'Differentia of Christianity', *Contemporary Review*, pp. 547–563, April 1898.

——, *Hinduism and Christianity*, Edinburgh, William Oliphant and Co., 1874 (first edition), and London, Oliphant, Anderson, and Ferrier, 1905 (third edition).

Rouse, R. and Neill, S.C., *A History of the Ecumenical Movement 1517–1948*, London, Society for the Propogation of Christian Knowledge, 1954.

Rousseau, R.W. (editor), *Interreligious Dialogue*, Ridge Row Press, Scranton, 1982.

Rowell, Geoffrey, *The Vision Glorious: Themes and Personalities of the Catholic Revival in Anglicanism*, Oxford, Oxford University Press, 1983.

Roy, Rammohun, *The Precepts of Jesus: the Guide to Peace and Happiness. To which are Added, the First, Second, and Final Appeal to the Christian Public*, London, John Mardon, 1834 (second edition, works first published, 1820–1823).

Royle, Trevor, *The Last Days of the Raj*, London, John Murray, 1997 (first published 1989).

Rudra, S. K., 'Christ and Modern India', *Student Movement*, pp. 81–85, January 1910.

Ruskin, John, 'The Nature of Gothic', in *The Stones of Venice*, volume II, chapter VI, pp. 138–212, Everyman's Library Edition, London, J. M. Dent and Co., (no date given).

Said, Edward, *Orientalism: Western Conceptions of the Orient*, London, Penguin, 1985.

——, *Culture and Imperialism*, London, Chatto and Windus, 1993

Sambrook, A. J., 'A Welsh Heretic: Rowland Williams', *Church Quarterly Review*, volume CLXVI, pp. 448–462 , October – December 1965.

Sanders, Charles Richard, *Coleridge and the Broad Church Movement*, New York, Octagon Books, 1972 (first published 1942).

Sandmel, Samuel, *Judaism and Christian Beginnings*, New York, Oxford University Press, 1978.

Saunders, Kenneth J., 'The so called New Attitude: A Few Platitudes for the Laity', *The Indian Witness*, volume XLIII, # 27, pp. 525–526, 2/7 1912.

——, 'The Vital Forces of Southern Buddhism in Relation to the Gospel: Part I in Ceylon', *International Review of Mission*, volume III, pp. 470–87 , July 1914.

——, *The Gospel for Asia: A Study of Three Religious Masterpieces: Gita, Lotus, and Fourth Gospel*, London, London, Society for the Propogation of Christian Knowledge, 1928.

Sawyer, Harry, 'The First World Missionary Conference: Edinburgh 1910', *International Review of Mission*, volume LXVII, pp. 255–272, 1978.

Schumacher, Stephan and Woerner, Gert (editors) (translator Michael H. Kohn, Karen Ready, and Werner Wünsche), *The Rider Encyclopaedia of Eastern Philosophy and Religion*, London, Rider, 1989 (first published 1986).

Scott, Archibold, *Buddhist and Christianity: A Parallel and a Contrast*, being the Croall Lecture for 1889–90, Edinburgh, David Douglas, 1890.

Scott, David L., 'Rowland Williams, 1817–1870', *Modern Churchman*, volume XLV, pp. 118–125, June 1955.

Seager, Richard Hughes (editor), *The Dawn of Religious Pluralism*, La Salle (Illinois), Open Court, 1994.

Selbie, W. B., *The Life of Andrew Martin Fairbairn: First Principal of Mansfield College, Oxford*, London, Hodder and Stoughton, 1914.

Sells, Michael A., *Mystical Languages of Unsaying*, Chicago, Chicago University Press, 1994.

Sen, Kshiti Mohan, *Hinduism*, Harmondsworth, Penguin Books, 1986 (first published 1961).

Sharpe, Eric J., *John Nicol Farquhar: A Memoir*, Calcutta, Young Men's Christian Association Publishing House, 1963.

——, *Not to Destroy But to Fulfil*, Uppsala, Gleerup, 1965.

——, 'Christ the Fulfiller', *Bangalore Theological Forum*, volume III, # 1, pp. 1–12, 1969.

——, *The Theology of A. G. Hogg*, Confessing the Faith in India Series, volume VII, Madras, Christian Literature Society, 1971.

——, 'Sadhu Sundar Singh and His Critics', *Religion*, volume VI, pp. 48–66, 1976.

——, *Faith Meets Faith*, London, Scm Press Ltd, 1977.

——, 'The Legacy of J. N. Farquhar', *Occasional Bulletin of Missionary Research*, April 1979, volume III, pp. 61–64.

——, 'Protestant Missionaries and the Study of the Bhagavad Gītā', *International Bulletin of Missionary Research*, volume VI, pp. 155–59, October 1982.

——, *The Universal Gītā*, La Salle (Illinois), Open Court Publishing, 1985.

——, *Understanding Religion*, London, Duckworth, 1988 (first published 1983).

——, 'The Legacy of Sadhu Sundar Singh', *International Bulletin of Missionary Research*, volume XIV, pp. 161–167, October 1990.

——, *Comparative Religion: A History*, La Salle (Illinois), Open Court, 1991 (second edition).

Singh, (Sadhu) Sundar, *Visions of the Spiritual World*, London, Macmillan and Co., Ltd, 1926.

417

—— (editor T. Dayanandan Francis), *The Christian Witness of Sadhu Sundar Singh: A Collection of His Writings*, Madras, Christian Literature Society, 1996 (first published 1989).

Slade, Herbert E. W., *A Work Begun: The Story of the Cowley Fathers in India 1874–1967*, London, Society for the Propogation of Christian Knowledge, 1970.

Slater, Thomas Ebenezer, *God Revealed: An Outline of Christian Truth*, Madras, Addison and Co., 1876.

——, *The Philosophy of Missions: A Present Day Plea*, London, James Clarke and Co., 1882.

——, *Studies in the Upanishads*, London, Christian Literature Society for India, 1897.

——, *The Higher Hinduism in Relation to Christianity*, London, Elliot Stock, 1903 (first published 1901).

Smart, Ninian, *Worldviews*, Macmillan, New York, 1983.

——, *Buddhism and Christianity: Rivals and Allies*, Basingstoke, Macmillan, 1993.

——, *Dimensions of the Sacred: An Anatomy of the World's Beliefs*, London, Harper Collins Publishers, 1996.

Smart Ninian, Clayton, John, Sherry, Patrick, and Katz, Stephen T. (editors), *Nineteenth Century Religious Thought in the West*, III volumes, Cambridge, Cambridge University Press, 1988 (first published 1985).

Smart, Ninian and Konstantine, Steven, *Christian Systematic Theology in a World Context*, London, Marshall Pickering, 1991.

Smith, Wilfred Cantwell, *The Meaning and End of Religion*, London, Society for the Propogation of Christian Knowledge, 1978.

——, *Towards a World Theology: Faith and the Comparative History of Religion*, London, Macmillan Press, 1981.

——, *What is Scripture?*, London, Student Christian Movement Press, 1993.

Soans, Chandra Shekar, 'The Water of Life in an Indian Cup', *Koinonia*, volume V, pp. 218–239, 1993.

Sontheimer, Günther-Dietz and Kulke, Hermann (editors), *Hinduism Reconsidered*, New Delhi, Manohar, 1997, revised edition (first published 1989).

Speer, Robert E., *Christianity and the Nations*, Fleming H. Revell Co., London, 1910.

Spink, Kathryn, *A Sense of the Sacred: A Biography of Bede Griffiths*, London, Society for the Propogation of Christian Knowledge, 1988.

Spottiswoode, George A., *The Official Report of the Missionary Conference of the Anglican Communion (1894)*, London, Society for the Propogation of Christian Knowledge, 1894.

Stanley, Arthur Penrhyn, 'Theology of the Nineteenth Century', *Fraser's Magazine for Town and Country*, volume LXXI, pp. 252–268, February 1865.

——, *England and India: A Sermon Preached in Westminster Abbey*, London, Macmillan and Co., 1875.

——, *Lectures on the History of the Jewish Church*, volume III: 'The Captivity to the Christian Era', London, John Murray, 1883 (second edition).

Stanley, Brian, *The Bible and the Flag*, Leicester, Apollos, 1990.

Stanton, V. H. (editor), *The Story of the Delhi Mission*, Westminster, Society for the Propogation of the Gospel, 1908.

Steiner, Rudolf, *Reincarnation and Karma*, being 5 Lectures Delivered During January – March 1912, New York, Anthroposophic Press, 1992 (first published 1961).

418

Stock, Eugene, *The History of the Church Missionary Society*, volume III, London, Church Missionary Society, 1899.

Stockwell, E.l., 'Editorial', *International Review of Mission*, volume LXXIV, pp. 153–7, 1985.

Stoffner, Hans, *Jesus Christ and the Hindu Community: is a Synthesis of Hinduism and Christianity Possible?*, Anand, Gujarat Sahitya Prakash, 1987.

Stokes, Samuel E., 'Interpreting Christ to India. A New Departure in Missionary Work.', *The East and the West*, pp. 121–138, April, 1908.

Streeter, Burnet Hillman and Appasamy, A. J., *The Sadhu: A Study in Mysticism and Practical Religion*, London, Macmillan and Co., 1922 (first published 1921).

Supple, Paul Charles, *Christians and Religious Pluralism C. 1830–1914: Changing Attitudes to Other Faiths*, unpublished MLitt Thesis (Theology), University of Oxford, 1991.

Suzuki, Daisetz Teitaro, *Mysticism: Christian and Buddhist*, Westport (Connecticut), Greenwood Press, 1975 (first published 1957).

Swidler, Leonard, Cobb, John B., Jr., Knitter, Paul F., and Hellwig, Monika K., *Death or Dialogue: From the Age of Monologue to the Age of Dialogue*, London, Student Christian Movement Press Ltd, 1990.

Swindells, John (editor), *A Human Search: Bede Griffiths Reflects on His Life*, Tunbridge Wells, Burns and Oates, 1997.

Symonds, Richard, *Oxford and Empire: The Last Lost Cause?*, Oxford, Clarendon Press, 1991 (first published 1986).

Tambaram Series, volume I: 'The Authority of the Faith', London, Oxford University Press, 1939.

——, volume Iii: 'Evangelism', London, Oxford University Press, 1939.

Tarantino, Quentin, *Pulp Fiction*, London, Faber and Faber, 1994.

Taylor, George P., 'Fulfilment or Antithesis: Which?', *The Indian Witness*, volume XLIII, # 20, pp. 387–388, 14/5 1912.

Teasdale, Wayne, 'The Nature of Sannyāsa and its Value for Christian Spirituality,' *Communio: International Catholic Review*, volume XII, pp. 325–334, Fall 1985.

Temple, William, *Readings in Saint John's Gospel* (first and second series), London, Macmillan and Co., 1949.

Tenzin Gyatso (H. H. The Dalai Lama), *The Good Heart: His Holiness the Dalai Lama Explores the Heart of Christianity – and of Humanity*, London, Rider, 1996.

The Mystery of Salvation: A Report by the Doctrine Commission of the General Synod of the Church of England, Church House Publishing, London, 1996.

Thomas, John, 'The Style shall be Gothic', *Architectural Review*, volume CLVIII, # 943, September 1975.

——, *Saint David's College, Lampeter: Tradition and Innovation in the Design of its First Building*, reprint from *Ceredigion, Journal of the Ceredigion Antiquarian Society*, Llandysul, Gomer Press, 1984.

——, 'What is it this Gothic', based on a lecture delivered at St David's University College, Lampeter 1996, *Newsletter of the Society of Architectural Historians*, No. 63, pp. 1–2, Spring 1998.

Thomas, M. M., *The Acknoweldged Christ of the Indian Renaissance*, London, Student Christian Movement Press, 1969.

——, 'Some Trends in Contemporary Indian Christian Theology', *Religion and Society*, volume XXIV, pp. 4–18, 1977.

——, *Risking Christ for Christ's Sake: Towards an Ecumenical Theology of Pluralism*, Geneva, World Council of Churches Publication, 1987.

Thomas, Owen C. (editor), *Attitudes Towards Other Religions: Some Christian Interpretations*, Student Christian Movement Press, London, 1969.

Thomas, Terence (editor), *The British: Their Religious Beliefs and Practices 1800–1986*, London, Routledge, 1988.

Thomson, Harry, 'Karl Ludwig Reichelt and his Place in the Mission of the Future', *International Review of Mission*, volume XLIX, # 2, pp. 215–216, 1960.

Thorne, Susan Elizabeth, *Protestant Ethics and the Spirit of Imperialism: British Congregationalists and the London Missionary Society, 1795–1925*, unpublished PhD Thesis (history), University of Michigan, 1990.

Tillich, Paul, *Christianity and the Encounter of the World's Religions*, being the Bampton Lectures in America for 1961, Number 14, New York, Columbia University Press, 1963.

Tomlinson, W. E., 'An Evangelistic Experiment', *The Harvest Field*, pp. 87–97, 126–136, and 176–181, 1915.

Torrance, Robert M., *The Spiritual Quest: Transcendence in Myth, Religion, and Science*, Berkeley and Los Angeles, University of California Press, 1994.

Tracy, David, *The Analogical Imagination: Christian Theology and the Culture of Pluralism*, London, London, Student Christian Movement Press, 1981.

——, *Plurality and Ambiguity: Hermeneutics, Religion, Hope*, San Francisco, Harper and Row, 1987.

Trapnell, Judson B., Bede Griffiths, Mystical Knowing, and the Unity of Religions', *Philosophy of Theology*, volume VII, pp. 355–379, Summer 1993.

Trench, Richard Chevenix, *Christ the Desire of all Nations, or the Unconscious Prophecies of Heathenism*, being the Hulsean Lectures for the Year 1846, Cambridge, Macmillan, Barclay, and Macmillan, 1846.

Trigg, Roger, *Rationality and Religion*, Oxford, Blackwell Publishers Ltd, 1998.

Troeltsch, Ernst, *Christian Thought: its History and Application*, University of London Press, London, 1923.

Trompf, Garry W., 'Friedrich Max Müller: Some Preliminary Chips from his German Workshop', *Journal of Religious History*, volume V, pp. 200–217, 1968–9.

Underhill, Evelyn, *Mysticism: A Study in the Nature and Development of Man's Spiritual Consciousness*, London, Methuen and Co. Ltd, 1945 (first published 1911).

Urban, Hugh B., 'The Extreme Orient: The Construction of "Tantrism" as a Category in the Orientalist Imagination', *Religion*, volume XIX, pp. 123–146, 1999.

Vidler, Alec R., *Witness to the Light: F. D. Maurice's Message for To-Day*, being the Hale Lectures for 1947, New York, Charles Scribner's Sons, 1948.

——, *F. D. Maurice and Company*, London, Student Christian Movement Press Ltd, 1966.

——, *The Church in an Age of Revolution*, London, Pelican, 1985 (second edition).

Vorgrimler, Herbert (translator John Bowden), *Understanding Karl Rahner: An Introduction to his Life and Thought*, London, Student Christian Movement Press, 1986.

Walshe, Maurice O'connell, *Meister Eckhart: Sermons and Treatises*, III volumes, Shaftesbury, Element, 1991, 1989, and 1990.

420

Wang, C.T., 'The Importance of Making Christianity Indigenous', *International Review of Mission*, volume V, pp. 75–86, 1916.

Ware, Kallistos (Timothy), *The Power of the Name*, London, Marshall Pickering, 1989.

Washington, Peter, *Madame Blavatsky's Baboon: Theosophy and the Emergence of the Western Guru*, London, Secker and Warburg, 1996.

Webb, C. C. J., *Religious Thought in the Oxford Movement*, London, Society for Promoting Christian Knowledge, 1928.

Webster, John C. B., '"Arya Evidences" – a Study of Christian Influence', *Indian Church History Review*, volume XII, pp. 1–19, (June) 1978.

Weightman, Simon, 'Hinduism', in John R. Hinnells (editor), *A Handbook of Living Religions*, Harmondsworth, Penguin, 1984.

Welch, Claude, *Protestant Thought in the Nineteenth Century*, volume I: '1799–1870', London, Yale University Press, 1972.

Westcott, Arthur, *Life and Letters of Brooke Foss Westcott*, II volumes, London, Macmillan and Co., 1903.

Westcott, Brooke Foss, *On some Points in the Religious Office of the Universities*, London, Macmillan and Co., 1873.

——, *The Cambridge Mission and Higher Education at Delhi*, Cambridge Mission to Delhi Occasional Papers No. 3, Cambridge, Cambridge University Press, 1882.

——, *Commentary on the Gospel According to St John*, London, Macmillan, 1887.

——, *Christus Consummator: Some Aspects of the Work and Person of Christ in Relation to Modern Thought*, London, Macmillan and Co., 1890.

——, *Essays in the Religious Thought of the West*, London, Macmillan and Co., 1891.

——, *The Gospel of Life*, London, Macmillan and Co., 1892.

——, *Christian Aspects of Life*, London, Macmillan and Co., 1897.

——, *Lessons from Work*, London, Macmillan and Co., 1901.

——, *The Incarnation and Common Life*, London, Macmillan and Co., 1908.

Whaling, Frank (editor), *Contemporary Approaches to the Study of Religion*, II volumes, New York, Mouton Publishers, 1984 and 1985.

——, *Christian Theology and World Religions*, Basingstoke, Marshall Pickering, 1986.

—— (editor), *Religion in Today's World*, Edinburgh, T and T Clark, 1987.

White, James F., *The Cambridge Movement: The Ecclesiologists and the Gothic Revival*, Cambridge, Cambridge University Press, 1979.

Whitehead, Henry, 'The New Movement in India and the Old Gospel', *The East and the West*, volume IX, # 33, pp. 1–11, January 1911.

Wiggins, James B., *In Praise of Religious Diversity*, London, Routledge, 1996.

Wildman, Wesley J., *Fidelity with Plausibility:Modest Christologies in the Twentieth Century*, Albany, State University of New York Press, 1998.

Wiles, Maurice, *The Remaking of Christian Theology*, London, Student Christian Movement Press, 1974.

——, *What is Theology*, Oxford, Oxford University Press, 1976.

——, *Christian Theology and Inter-Religious Dialogue*, London, Student Christian Movement Press, 1992.

Wilkins, William J., *Modern Hinduism*, Calcutta, Rupa and Co., second edition, 1975 (first published 1887).

Williams, Ellen, *The Life and Letters of Rowland Williams, D.D.*, II volumes, London, Henry S. King and Co., 1874.

Williams, Rowland, *Rational Godliness: After the Mind of Christ and the Written Voices of His Church*, London, Bell and Daldy, 1855.

——, *Paraméswara-Jnyána-Góshtí: A Dialogue on the Knowledge of the Supreme Lord, in which are Compared the Claims of Christianity and Hinduism, and Various Questions of Indian Religion and Literature fairly Discussed*, Cambridge, Deighton, Bell and Co., 1856.

Wilson, W. (translator), *The Writings of Clement of Alexandria* (Ante-Nicene Library, volumes IV and XII), Edinburgh, T. and T. Clark, 1867 and 1869.

Wiseman, James A., '"Enveloped by Mystery": The Spiritual Journey of Henri Le Saux/ Abhishiktananda', *Église et Théologie*, volume XXIII, pp. 241–260, 1992.

Wittgenstein, Ludwig (translator G. E. M. Anscombe), *Philosophical Investigations*, Oxford, Basil Blackwell, 1958 (first edition 1953).

—— (editors G. E. M. Anscombe and G. H. Von Wright) (translators Denis Paul and G. E. M. Anscombe), *On Certainty*, Oxford, Basil Blackwell, 1969.

Wolf, William J. (editor), *The Spirit of Anglicanism*, Edinburgh, T. and T. Clark, 1982.

Wolffe, John (editor), *Religion in Victorian Britain*, volume V: 'Culture and Empire', Manchester, Manchester University Press, 1997.

Wolz-Gottwald, Eckard, 'Mysticism and Ecumenism: On the Question of Religious Identity in the Religious Dialogue', *Journal of Ecumenical Studies*, volume XXXII, # 1, pp. 25–34, Winter 1995.

Wood, H.G., *Frederick Denison Maurice*, Cambridge, Cambridge University Press, 1950.

Wood, Nicholas J., *Confessing Christ in a Plural World: A Missiological Approach to Inter-Faith Relations with Particular Reference to Kenneth Cragg and Leslie Newbigin*, unpublished DPhil Thesis (Faculty of Theology), University of Oxford, 1996.

Woods, Richard, *Eckhart's Way*, London, Darton, Longman andTodd, 1987.

World Missionary Conference, Edingburgh 1910, Report No. I: 'Carrying the Gospel to the Whole Non-Christian World', Oliphant, Anderson, and Ferrier, Edingburgh, 1910.

——, Edingburgh 1910, Report No. II: 'The Church in the Mission Field', Oliphant, Anderson, and Ferrier, Edingburgh, 1910.

——, Edingburgh 1910, Report No. IV: 'The Missionary Message in Relation to Non-Christian Religions', Oliphant, Anderson, and Ferrier, Edingburgh, 1910.

——, Edingburgh 1910, volume No. IX: 'History, Records and Addresses', Oliphant, Anderson, and Ferrier, Edingburgh, 1910.

Zaehner, R. C., *Concordant Discord: The Interdependence of Faiths*, being the Gifford Lectures 1967–1969, Oxford, Oxford University Press, 1970

——, *Hindu Scriptures*, London, Everyman's Library, 1988 (first published 1938).

——, *Hinduism*, Oxford, Oxford University Press, 1990 (first published 1962).

Manuscript Sources

A) Rhodes House Library

Material filed under the United society for the Propogation of the Gospel, sub-heading the Cambridge Mission to Delhi (abbreviated to USPGCMD in references followed by the box number of the material).

No. 87: Miscellaneous letters.
No. 92: Miscellaneous letters.
No. 131: *Cambridge Mission to Delhi Annual Reports* for years 1886–1896. Items published Cambridge, Cambridge University Press, year following the report's date.

B) Lambeth Palace Library

Material filed under Benson (references to LPLBenson, followed by the number of the collection of papers, then the page number, as numbered in the archives as ff numbers).

No. 65, ff. 17–24: Bickersteth, Edward, *Memorandum on the Organization of the Mission at Delhi*, 3/10/1888.
No. 111, ff. 13–17: Bennett, Edwin, Letter to Archbishop Benson, July 1892.
No. 111, ff. 18: 'The Archbishop of Canterbury on Mahommedanism', *The Times*, 16/6/1892.

C) Christ's College Library, Aberdeen (items on permanent loan to the Special Collections Library, University of Aberdeen)

World Missionary Conference, Edinburgh 1910, Manuscripts: Responses to Questionnaire of Commission Four, 5 volumes. Typewritten. (The original copies of D. S. Cairns).

Volume on Islam (including the copy of the Commission's Report on Islam).
Volume on Chinese Religions.
Three volumes on India:

(List of correspondents from India included in the volumes, order as appearing in the volume, giving response number, length of typewritten pages, and affiliation)

India, Volume I:
Rev. C. F. Andrews	123	23	SPG
Rev. T. G. Bailey	126	6	UFCSM

J. R. Banerjea	129	6	UFCSM & YMCA
Rev. Wm. Bonnar	130	24	UFCSM
Rev. J. Ali Bakhsh	121	3	CMS
Bishop of Calcutta	135	10	SPG
Rev. W. B. Boggs	129	10	ABU
Rev. F. Braun	130a	4	BM
Mr. Andrew Campbell	136	5	UFCSFM
Rev. William Howard Campbell	133	18	LMS
Rev. L. B. Chamberlain	134	18 (plus continuation 27)	RCA
Mrs Ferguson-Davie	155	44	SPG
Rev. William Dilger	147	11	BM
Mr G. S. Eddy	153	5	YMCA
Mr. John Nicol Farquhar	154	43 (plus memorandum 34)	YMCA
Rev. MalcolmG. Goldsmith	163	10	CMS
Deaconess Ellen L. Goreh	164	5	SPG
Rev. O. J. Grainger	165	5	FCMS
Rev. Edwin Greaves	166	20	LMS

India, Volume II:

Rev. H. G. Grey	167	6	CMS
Rev. Henry Gulliford	168a	14	WMS
Rev. R. H. A. Haslam	171	11	CMS
Rev. Ch. Herman	174	9	BM
Mr A. G. Hogg	176	66	MCC
Rev. W. E. S. Holland	177	6	CMS
Rev. W. Hooper	178	7	CMS
Rev. George Howells	179	12	BMS
Rev. Dr R. A. Hume	180	16	ABCFM
Rev. W. R. James	183	22 (plus appendix 7)	ABCFM

Rev. J. P. Jones	184	25	CMS
Rev. D. L. Joshi	185	6	AMM
	(plus continuation 7)		
Rev. S. V. Karmarkar	186	7	SIUC
Rev. Francis Kingsbury	187	9	SPG [and CMD]
Bishop of Lahore	190	23	
	(with notes by S. S. Allnutt)		
Rev. John Lazarus	192	9	DM
Rev. D. G. M. Leith	193	23	WMS
Rev. Bernard Lucas	196	16	LMS
Rev. Nicol Macnicol	198	26	UFCSM
Rt. Rev. Bishop of Madras	201	18	

India, Volume III:

Rev. J. Mathers	203	37	LMS
Rev. J. H. Messmore	203a	4	FBM
Rev. John Morrison	206	7	UFCSM
Rev. Prof. N. C. Mukerjee	208	8	NIAPM
Pandita Rambai	212	8	MM
Prof. S. K. Rudra	261	5	CMD
Bishop J. E. Robinson	217	16	MEC
Rev. J. Ruthquist	221	4	ENSS
Rev. A Schosser	223	6	BEM
Miss A. de Selincourt	224	10	ZBMM
Rev. Ahmad Shah	225	17	SPG
Rev. J. A. Sharrock	226	17	SPG
Canon Nihal Singh	211	12	CMS
Rev. T. E. Slater	229	90	In connection with the LMS
	(plus continuation 33)		
Rev. F. W, Steinthal	234	43	IHMS and YMCA
Mr. Joseph Taylor	237	8	FFMA
George P. Taylor	238	13	PCI

Rev. A. P. Veerasawmy	243	7	ABU
Rev. Dr E. M. Wherry	251	7	APC
Rev. Dr H. V. Weitbrecht	249	8	CMS
Canon C. H. Westcott	250 (plus article 10)	27	SPG
Rev. W. A. Wilson	254	19	CPC

Abbreviations used in above table:

ABCFM: American Board of Commissioners for Foreign Missions
ABU: American Baptist Union
AMM: American Marathi Mission
APC: American Presbyterian Church
BM: Basel German Evangelical Mission
BMS: Baptist Missionary Society
CMD: Cambridge Mission to Delhi
CMS: Church Missionary Society
CPC: Canadian Presbyterian Church
DM: Danish Mission
ENSS: Evangelical National Society of Stockholm
FBM: Foreign Board of Missions, Methodist Episcopal Church
FCMS: Foreign Christian Missionary Society
FFMA: Friends Foreign Missionary Association, Ireland
IHMS: Indian Home Mission to the Southals
LMS: London Missionary Society
MCC: Madras Christian College
MEC: Methodist Episcopal Church, South Asia Missions
MM: Mukti Mission
NIAPM: North India American Presbyterian Mission
PCI: Presbyterian Church in Ireland
RCA: Reformed Church in America
SIUC: South Indian United Church
SPG: Society for the Propogation of the Gospel
UFCSM: United Free Church of Scotland Foreign Mission
WMS: Wesleyan Methodist Missionary Society
YMCA: Young Men's Christian Association
ZBBM: Zenana Bible and Medical Mission

Material referenced as Edinburgh Manuscripts (EDMS) followed by volume number, then the name and number of the individual quoted, followed by the relevant page number(s).

STUDIEN ZUR INTERKULTURELLEN GESCHICHTE DES CHRISTENTUMS
ETUDES D'HISTOIRE INTERCULTURELLE DU CHRISTIANISME
STUDIES IN THE INTERCULTURAL HISTORY OF CHRISTIANITY

Begründet von / fondé par / founded by
Walter J. Hollenweger und / et / and Hans Jochen Margull †

Herausgegeben von / edité par / edited by

Richard Friedli	Jan A.B. Jongeneel	Klaus Koschorke
Université de Fribourg	Universiteit Utrecht	Universität München

Theo Sundermeier	Werner Ustorf
Universität Heidelberg	University of Birmingham

Band 105 Thomas G. Dalzell SM: The Dramatic Encounter of Divine and Human Freedom in the Theology of Hans Urs von Balthasar.

Band 106 Jan A. B. Jongeneel: Philosophy, Science, and Theology of Mission in the 19th and 20th Centuries. A Missiological Encyclopedia. Part II: Missionary Theology.

Band 107 Werner Kohler: Unterwegs zum Verstehen der Religionen. Gesammelte Aufsätze. Herausgegeben im Auftrag der Deutschen Ostasien-Mission und der Schweizerischen Ostasien-Mission von Andreas Feldtkeller.

Band 108 Mariasusai Dhavamony: Christian Theology of Religions. A Systematic Reflection on the Christian Understanding of World Religions.

Band 109 Chinonyelu Moses Ugwu: Healing in the Nigerian Church. A Pastoral-Psychological Exploration.

Band 110 Getatchew Haile, Aasulv Lande & Samuel Rubenson (eds.): The Missionary Factor in Ethiopia: Papers from a Symposium on the Impact of European Missions on Ethiopian Society, Lund University, August 1996.

Band 111 Anthony Savari Raj: A New Hermeneutic of Reality. Raimon Panikkar's Cosmotheandric Vision.

Band 112 Jean Pierre Bwalwel: Famille et habitat. Implications éthiques de l'éclatement urbain. *Cas de la ville de Kinshasa.*

Band 113 Michael Bergunder: Die südindische Pfingstbewegung im 20. Jahrhundert. Eine historische und systematische Untersuchung.

Band 114 Alar Laats: Doctrines of the Trinity in Eastern and Western Theologies. A Study with Special Reference to K. Barth and V. Lossky.

Band 115 Afeosemime U. Adogame: Celestial Church of Christ. The Politics of Cultural Identity in a West African Prophetic-Charismatic Movement.

Band 116 Laurent W. Ramambason: Missiology: Its Subject-Matter and Method. A Study of Mission-Doers in Madagascar.

Band 117 Veli-Matti Kärkkäinen: Ad Ultimum Terrae. Evangelization, Proselytism and Common Witness in the Roman Catholic Pentecostal Dialogue (1990–1997).

Band 118 Julie C. Ma: When the Spirit meets the Spirits. Pentecostal Ministry among the Kankanaey Tribe in the Philippines. 2., revised edition.

Band 119 Patrick Chukwudezie Chibuko: Igbo Christian Rite of Marriage. A Proposed Rite for Study and Celebration.

Band 120 Patrick Chukwudezie Chibuko: Paschal Mystery of Christ. Foundation for Liturgical Inculturation in Africa.

Band 121 Werner Ustorf / Toshiko Murayama (eds.): Identity and Marginality. Rethinking Christianity in North East Asia.

Band 122 Ogbu U. Kalu: Power, Poverty and Prayer. The Challenges of Poverty and Pluralism in African Christianity, 1960–1996.

Band 123 Peter Cruchley-Jones: Singing the Lord's Song in a Strange Land? A Missiological Interpretation of the Ely Pastorate Churches, Cardiff.

Band 124 Paul Hedges: Preparation and Fulfilment. A History and Study of Fulfilment Theology in Modern British Thought in the Indian Context.